CW01246300

ALLIED DUNBAR LIBRARY

BUSINESS TAX AND LAW GUIDE

ALLIED DUNBAR LIBRARY

BUSINESS TAX AND LAW GUIDE

by

W I Sinclair, FCA,

A Partner in Kidsons

and

John McMullen, MA (Cantab), MIPM, Solicitor

LONGMAN

© Allied Dunbar Financial Services Ltd 1990

ISBN 0 85121 566-1

Published by
Longman Law, Tax and Finance
Longman Group UK Limited
21-27 Lamb's Conduit Street, London WC1N 3NJ

Associated Offices

Australia, Hong Kong, Malaysia, Singapore, USA

All rights reserved.
No part of this publication may be reproduced, stored in a retrieval system, or transmitted, in any form or by any means, electronic, mechanical, photocopying, recording or otherwise, without either the prior written permission of the publishers, or a licence permitting restricted copying issued by the Copyright Licensing Agency Limited, 33-34 Alfred Place, London WC1E 7DP.

No responsibility for loss occasioned to any person acting or refraining from action as a result of the material in this publication can be accepted by the authors or publishers.

The views and opinions of Allied Dunbar may not necessarily coincide with some of the views and opinions expressed in this book which are solely those of the authors and no endorsement of them by Allied Dunbar should be inferred.

A CIP catalogue record for this book is available from the British Library.

Printed in Great Britain by Biddles Ltd, Guildford, Surrey

Abbreviations

ACAS	Advisory Conciliation and Arbitration Service
CA	Companies Act
CGTA	Capital Gains Tax Act 1979
EPA	Employment Protection Act 1975
EP(C)A	Employment Protection (Consolidation) Act 1978
FA	Financial Act
IHTA	Inheritance Tax Act 1984 (previously Capital Transfer Tax Act 1984)
s	Section
Sch	Schedule
TA	Income and Corporation Taxes Act 1988
VATA	Value Added Tax Act 1983

The authors

WALTER SINCLAIR qualified as a chartered accountant in 1959 and has remained in the profession since, first in general practice and then concentrating on taxation. He is now a taxation partner with Kidsons.

His interest in taxation led to writing on the subject and his authorship of *The Allied Dunbar Tax Guide* dates from its inception, as the *Hambro Tax Guide* 18 years ago.

Walter Sinclair is also the joint author of *The Allied Dunbar Capital Taxes and Estate Planning Guide*, now in its fourth edition. In addition, he contributes to a wide range of publications, including various national newspapers, as well as being general editor of the *International Employment Tax Handbook*.

JOHN McMULLEN is a solicitor in private practice where he advises on Labour Law and Company Law. He is a member of the Institute of Personnel Management and a member of the Law Society's Standing Committee on Employment Law.

He has published articles in a number of legal journals and is a consultant editor of *The Company Lawyer*. He is the author of *Business Transfers and Employee Rights* (Butterworths, 1987) and a contributor to the forthcoming *Butterworths Employment Law Guide*.

He has lectured and talked widely to management groups, personnel managers and others.

Introduction

This book is the second edition of a companion volume to *The Allied Dunbar Tax Guide* and deals particularly with tax and law related to businesses. Thus, the book is designed to be of use to sole proprietors, partnerships and limited companies, covering not only those engaged in trading activities, but also the professions.

Insurance and pensions are of particular interest to businessmen and so two chapters deal with this area. One relates to general insurance and the other to life assurance and pensions.

The book has been designed as a general guide for both the professional and non-professional user. However, since the book concisely covers a very wide field, it has been necessary to omit some of the exceptions and qualifications with which the law abounds.

Obviously, the coverage of legal topics in a book of this size has also had to be selective. The book concentrates on key aspects of business law and no reference has been made, for example, to areas such as land law, employers' liability for accidents under health and safety legislation, and intellectual property law. Thus, if a particular problem is not fully covered by this book, you should look at a more detailed textbook or consult a specialist, such as a solicitor or accountant. Furthermore, if you are looking at a specific legal case or transaction of any complexity, you should seek appropriate professional advice.

For ease of reference, there is a full contents table and index. Also, a glossary explains technical words and should be referred to if necessary. A particular feature is that all indexing and cross-referencing uses chapter and topic numbers. Thus 7.6 means the 6th-numbered topic in chapter 7.

This edition is based on the law as at 30 September 1989 and in particular contains tax law relating to 1989–90. We also draw the reader's attention to two Bills which, at the time of writing, were before Parliament but still some way from receiving the Royal Assent. The Companies Bill and the Employment Bill (referred to as such in the text) are expected to receive the Royal Assent in or about November 1989 (if so they will become the Companies Act 1989 and the Employment

viii Introduction

Act 1989 respectively). It is unlikely that their content as Acts of Parliament will materially differ from the description in the text concerning Bill form, but some change is possible in transition from Bill to Act. If the issue is important, the up-to-date position should be checked. Also, no commencement dates were to hand at the time of writing.

We acknowledge, with thanks, the very valuable assistance given to us in connection with this book by our respective colleagues, including Messrs KGS Stockings, ATII and G Wilson, FCA of Kidsons and VJ Jerrard, LLB and DC Vessey, BSc of Allied Dunbar Assurance plc. Our special thanks are extended to Vince Jerrard for contributing the chapter on Pensions and Life Assurance and to Mrs Gill Clark of Eagle Star Insurance, for writing the chapter on General Insurance.

30 September 1989   WI Sinclair
                                                         John McMullen

Contents

		Page
Abbreviations		v
The authors		vi
Introduction		vii

1 Making a choice between different forms of trading vehicle — 1
  1.1 Introduction — 1
  1.2 Choosing a format — 1
  1.3 Sole traders — 2
  1.4 Partnerships — 2
  1.5 Terms implied in partnerships by the Partnership Act 1890 — 2
  1.6 The importance of an express partnership agreement — 3
  1.7 The liability of partners for a firm's debts — 3
  1.8 Personal insolvency — 4
  1.9 The limited liability company — 6
  1.10 Forming companies — 7
  1.11 Private and public companies — 7
  1.12 Limited liability of shareholders of companies — 7
  1.13 Advantages and disadvantages of incorporation compared with partnership — 8
  1.14 Conclusion — 11

2 Tax on business income — 13
  2.1 Introduction — The taxation of income — 13
  2.2 Table: Classes of income — 13
  2.3 Income tax rates and personal reliefs — 14
  2.4 Table: Income tax rates for 1989–90 — 14
  2.5 Table: Personal reliefs — 1989–90 — 15
  2.6 Deductions from income — 15
  2.7 Trades, professions and vocations — 16
  2.8 Indications of trading — 16
  2.9 Computing the assessable profits for Schedule D Cases I and II — 17
  2.10 Example: Schedule D Case I computation — 18
  2.11 Stock and work in progress — 19

	2.12	Basis of assessment	20
	2.13	Opening years	20
	2.14	Example: Schedule D Cases I and II — Assessments for opening years	21
	2.15	Closing years	21
	2.16	Example: Schedule D Cases I and II — Assessments for closing years	22
	2.17	Capital allowances	22
	2.18	Base period	23
	2.19	Capital allowances on plant and machinery	23
	2.20	First year allowance	24
	2.21	Writing down allowance	24
	2.22	Sales of plant and machinery — Balancing allowances and charges	24
	2.23	Example: Capital allowances on plant and machinery	25
	2.24	Fixtures — Entitlement to capital allowances	26
	2.25	Short-life assets	26
	2.26	Example: Short-life assets — De-pooling	26
	2.27	Motor vehicles	27
	2.28	Hire purchase	27
	2.29	Machinery for leasing	28
	2.30	Industrial buildings	28
	2.31	Enterprise zones	28
	2.32	Agricultural buildings	29
	2.33	Hotel buildings	29
	2.34	Scientific research allowance	29
	2.35	Patent rights (and know-how)	30
	2.36	Mines, oil wells and dredging	30
	2.37	Assured tenancies	30
	2.38	Safety at sports grounds	31
	2.39	Security assets	31
	2.40	Class IV National Insurance contributions	31
	2.41	Earnings basis and cash basis	31
	2.42	Post-cessation receipts	32
	2.43	Losses	32
	2.44	Example: Relief for losses	33
	2.45	Loss in new business	34
	2.46	Terminal losses	34
	2.47	Farming	34
	2.48	Sub-contractors	35
	2.49	Authors' copyright sales and royalties	36
	2.50	The assessment and payment mechanism	36
	2.51	Class 4 National Insurance	37
3	**Partnership taxation**		**39**
	3.1	Introduction	39
	3.2	Partnership defined	39

3.3	The taxation of partnership income	39
3.4	Example: Partnership assessments	40
3.5	Losses	41
3.6	Changes of partners	42
3.7	Continuation election	42
3.8	Overseas partnerships	42
3.9	Partnership capital gains	43
3.10	Husband and wife partnerships	43
3.11	Example: Husband and wife partnership	44

4 The taxation of companies 47

4.1	Introduction	47
4.2	Corporation tax	47
4.3	Small companies rate	47
4.4	Associated companies	48
4.5	Accounting periods and payment dates	48
4.6	Interest and repayment supplement	49
4.7	The imputation system	50
4.8	ACT on dividends etc	50
4.9	Distributions and franked payments	51
4.10	Setting off ACT	51
4.11	Surplus ACT	52
4.12	Computing the assessable profits	52
4.13	Capital allowances	53
4.1.	Example: Corporation tax computation	53
4.15	Losses	55
4.16	Terminal losses	55
4.17	Capital gains and losses	55
4.18	Groups of companies	56
4.19	Group loss relief	56
4.20	Groups — Other reliefs	57
4.21	Close companies	58
4.22	Apportionment of income	58
4.23	Abatement	59
4.24	Close companies — Loans and distributions	60
4.25	Cessations and liquidations	60
4.26	Close investment holding companies (CICs)	61
4.27	Non-resident companies	61
4.28	UK companies with overseas income	62
4.29	Controlled foreign companies	63
4.30	Demergers	63
4.31	Unquoted company purchasing its own shares	64
4.32	Business expansion scheme	64
4.33	Deciding whether to incorporate	66
4.34	Example: Saving tax by incorporating	67

xii Contents

5 Company and partnership law — 71

Part A Company Law

5.1	Introduction	71
5.2	Public companies	71
5.3	Private companies	72
5.4	The de-regulation of private companies	72
5.5	Company law in general	74
5.6	Starting up	74
5.7	Name	74
5.8	Documents to be delivered	74
5.9	Memorandum and articles of association	75
5.10	Statement of first directors and secretary	76
5.11	Subscribers' shares	76
5.12	Accounting reference date	76
5.13	Registered office address	76
5.14	Statutory declaration of compliance with procedures	77
5.15	Certificate of incorporation	77
5.16	Minimum membership requirement	77
5.17	First meeting of directors	77
5.18	Suggested minutes of first directors' meeting	78
5.19	Capital structure, borrowing and other questions	81
5.20	Capital	81
5.21	Limited liability	82
5.22	Raising capital	82
5.23	Floating charges	84
5.24	Registration of company charges	85
5.25	Receivers appointed by debenture holders	86
5.26	Stamp duty	86
5.27	Transfer of shares	87
5.28	The memorandum of association and the doctrine of *ultra vires*	87
5.29	The doctrine of *ultra vires*	87
5.30	Protection of third parties by s 35 of the Companies Act 1985	89
5.31	The Department of Trade consultative document	90
5.32	The position under the Companies Bill	91
5.33	A director's responsibility for *ultra vires* acts	92
5.34	Constructive notice	92
5.35	Alteration of the memorandum	92
5.36	The articles of association	93
5.37	The articles as a contract	93
5.38	Alteration of the articles	94
5.39	Shareholder protection and the articles	94
5.40	Class rights	95
5.41	Company officers, their appointment, tenure and removal	96
5.42	The secretary	96

5.43	The director	96
5.44	Contractual or other liability to company officers for dismissal	97
5.45	Third party protection against internal irregularities and the authority of officers of the company to bind the company	97
5.46	The indoor management rule	98
5.47	Statutory provisions protecting a third party against internal irregularities	99
5.48	Protection under section 35 of the Companies Act 1985 prior to the Companies Bill	100
5.49	The Department of Trade consultative document	100
5.50	Section 35(A) of the Companies Act 1985 as proposed by the Companies Bill	100
5.51	Constructive notice	102
5.52	Agency principles in relation to companies	102
5.53	The actual implied authority attaching to various posts	104
5.54	Meetings and resolutions	104
5.55	The Annual General Meeting	105
5.56	Extraordinary General Meetings	106
5.57	Types of resolution	106
5.58	Procedure at meetings	109
5.59	Relationship between the general meeting and the board of directors	109
5.60	Books, records, accounts and returns	110
5.61	Directors' duties	111
5.62	Duties of skill and care	111
5.63	Fiduciary duties	111
5.64	A director's interest in a contract with the company	111
5.65	Secret profits	112
5.66	Corporate opportunities	112
5.67	Misapplication of the company's property	113
5.68	Acting *bona fide* and for the benefit of the company as a whole	114
5.69	What is 'the company as a whole'?	114
5.70	The duty to apply powers for their proper purposes	114
5.71	Some statutory rules governing directors' duties and fair dealing by directors	114
5.72	Collective abuse of shareholder power against minorities	115
5.73	Statutory protection for minorities	116
5.74	The statutory petition to wind up under the just and equitable ground under section 122(g) of the Insolvency Act 1986	116
5.75	Example: Winding up under the just and equitable ground	116
5.76	The unfair prejudice petition	117

xiv Contents

5.77	Department of Trade investigations	118
5.78	Some rules about maintenance of capital	119
5.79	Corporate insolvency	120
5.80	Receivership	120
5.81	Administration order	121
5.82	Liquidation	122
5.83	Voluntary winding up	122
5.84	Compulsory winding up	122
5.85	Choice of liquidator	122
5.86	An administrator's or liquidator's powers	123
5.87	Wrongful and fraudulent trading	125
5.88	Order of distribution of assets	126

Part B Partnership law

5.89	Introduction	127
5.90	Indicators as to whether a partnership exists	127
5.91	Size of partnerships	128
5.92	Rules implied by the Partnership Act 1890	128
5.93	Partnership agreements	129
5.94	A partner and third parties	130
5.95	Liabilities of new and retiring partners	131
5.96	Partners' duties of fair dealing to one another	131
5.97	Partnership property	132
5.98	Dissolution of partnerships	132
5.99	Order of application of assets on dissolution	133
5.100	Limited partnerships	134

Part C Company and business names

5.101	Company names	134
5.102	Change of name	135
5.103	Directors' names	135
5.104	Use of company name	135
5.105	Business names	137
5.106	Companies and business names	137
5.107	Business names for individuals and partnerships	137
5.108	Passing off and trade marks	138

6 Capital gains tax   139

6.1	Introduction	139
6.2	Capital gains tax and businesses	139
6.3	Liability to capital gains tax	139
6.4	Annual exemptions for individuals	140
6.5	Capital gains tax rates	141
6.6	Liable and exempt assets	141
6.7	Table — Assets exempted from capital gains tax	142
6.8	Disposals for capital gains tax purposes	142
6.9	The computation of chargeable gains	143

6.10	Re-basing to 31 March 1982 values	144
6.11	Indexation allowance	145
6.12	Table: Retail prices index	146
6.13	Example: Capital gains tax — Indexation relief	146
6.14	Capital losses	147
6.15	Loss on unquoted shares in trading companies	147
6.16	Assessment and payment of capital gains tax	147
6.17	Assets owned on 6 April 1965	148
6.18	Valuations	149
6.19	Quoted shares and securities	149
6.20	Company reorganisations and take-overs	150
6.21	Unquoted shares	151
6.22	Part disposals	151
6.23	A series of disposals	151
6.24	Leases and other wasting assets	151
6.25	Relief for gifts	152
6.26	Replacement of business assets — Rollover relief	153
6.27	Transferring a business to a company	154
6.28	Business retirement relief	154

7 Inheritance tax 157

7.1	Introduction	157
7.2	Property chargeable	157
7.3	Potentially exempt transfers	158
7.4	Tapering relief	158
7.5	Deemed domicile	158
7.6	Rate scale	158
7.7	Table: Inheritance tax rates after 5 April 1989	159
7.8	Valuation	159
7.9	Valuation of related property	160
7.10	Exempt transfers	160
7.11	Exempt transfers — Lifetime gifts	161
7.12	Example: Inheritance tax	161
7.13	Administration and collection	162
7.14	Relief for business property	163
7.15	Relief for agricultural property	164
7.16	Woodlands	165
7.17	Close companies	165
7.18	Anti-avoidance	165
7.19	Deeds of family arrangement	166
7.20	Quick succession relief	166
7.21	Settled property	166

8 Value added tax 169

8.1	Introduction	169
8.2	Registration	170

	8.3	Accounts and administration	171
	8.4	Penalties	172
	8.5	Appeals	173
	8.6	Groups of companies and divisions	174
	8.7	Business	174
	8.8	Zero-rated supplies	175
	8.9	Table: Zero-rated supplies	175
	8.10	Exemption	177
	8.11	Table: Exempt supplies	178
	8.12	Land and buildings	179
	8.13	Motor cars	179
	8.14	Business entertainment	180
	8.15	Second-hand goods	181
	8.16	Self-supply and personal use	181
	8.17	Gifts	182
	8.18	Bad debts	182
	8.19	Retailers	182
	8.20	Tour operators	182
	8.21	Charities	183
	8.22	Official literature	183
9	**Tax and National Insurance for employees**		**185**
	9.1	Introduction	185
	9.2	The three cases of Schedule E	185
	9.3	Schedule E income	187
	9.4	The PAYE system	187
	9.5	Your code number	188
	9.6	PAYE records and general operation	189
	9.7	Employer's PAYE returns	190
	9.8	Change of employer	190
	9.9	Fringe benefits	191
	9.10	Table: Fringe benefits — Taxation 1989–90	192
	9.11	Travelling and entertainment allowances	193
	9.12	Motor cars	194
	9.13	Table: Car and fuel benefit scales 1988–89 and 1989–90	195
	9.14	Living accommodation	195
	9.15	Assets provided for employee	196
	9.16	Pension and life assurance arrangements	196
	9.17	Beneficial loan arrangements	197
	9.18	Employee shareholdings	198
	9.19	Profit-sharing schemes	199
	9.20	Unapproved share option schemes	200
	9.21	Savings-related share option schemes	200
	9.22	Approved share option schemes	200
	9.23	Employee share ownership plans (ESOPs)	201
	9.24	Director's PAYE	202

9.25	Form P11D	202
9.26	Deductions from income	203
9.27	Compensation for loss of office	203
9.28	National Insurance contributions	204
9.29	Table: National Insurance contributions for 1989–90	205
9.30	Class I National Insurance contributions	205
9.31	Table: Class I National Insurance contributions for 1989–90	206
9.32	Statutory sick pay	207
9.33	Profit-related pay	207

10 Employment law 209

10.1	Introduction	209
10.2	Recruiting employees	209
10.3	Sex and race discrimination and recruitment	209
10.4	Rehabilitation of offenders and 'spent' convictions	212
10.5	Disabled persons	212
10.6	Future laws on discrimination: new trends	213
10.7	The status of your workforce: employees or self-employed persons?	213
10.8	How does the law distinguish between employment and self-employment?	215
10.9	The contents of the contract of employment	219
10.10	Terms of the contract	219
10.11	The employer's obligations	219
10.12	Duties of the employee	222
10.13	Should a contract of employment be in writing?	227
10.14	The written statement under the EP(C)A	228
10.15	A written contract of employment	229
10.16	Statutory employment rights	230
10.17	Continuity of employment	230
10.18	Unfair dismissal	233
10.19	Dismissal	234
10.20	The test of unfair dismissal	235
10.21	Reasons	235
10.22	Reasonableness	236
10.23	Establishing reasonableness	236
10.24	The test of reasonableness in unfair dismissal	237
10.25	Dismissals relating to trade union membership	243
10.26	Pregnancy and dismissals	243
10.27	Automatically unfair dismissals and the Transfer of Undertakings (Protection of Employment) Regulations 1981	244
10.28	Strikes and industrial action	244
10.29	Written statement of reasons for dismissal	245
10.30	Remedies for unfair dismissal	245
10.31	Compensation levels	246

10.32	Redundancy	246
10.33	Wrongful dismissal and breach of contract claims at common law	251
10.34	Inter-relationship between wrongful and unfair dismissal summarised	254
10.35	Settling dismissal and other claims	254
10.36	The taxation of ex gratia payments	255
10.37	Other significant statutory rights in employment	256
10.38	Maternity rights	256
10.39	Guarantee payments	257
10.40	Written statement of main terms and conditions	257
10.41	Payment during suspension on medical grounds	257
10.42	Protection from action short of dismissal on grounds of trade union membership and activities	257
10.43	Itemised pay statements	257
10.44	Time off for trade union and other reasons	258
10.45	Statutory minimum periods of notice	259
10.46	Payment of wages — cash or cheque? The Wages Act 1986	259
10.47	Deductions from wages and the Wages Act 1986	259
10.48	Sex and race discrimination in employment	262
10.49	Discrimination in the employment field: definition	263
10.50	Direct and indirect discrimination	263
10.51	Genuine occupational qualification	265
10.52	Discrimination by other bodies	265
10.53	Victimisation	265
10.54	Liabilities and remedies	266
10.55	Discriminatory retirement ages	266
10.56	Practical information	267
10.57	Formal investigations and the role of the CRE and EOC	267
10.58	Equal pay	267
10.59	Equal pay for like work and equivalent work	268
10.60	Equal value claims	268
10.61	Establishing an equal pay claim	269
10.62	Equal Opportunities Commission	270
10.63	Statutory maternity pay	270
10.64	Statutory sick pay	271
10.65	Employees' rights on insolvency of the employer	272
10.66	Data protection	273
10.67	Access to medical records	273
10.68	Contracting out of statutory rights	276
10.69	Buying or selling a business: The Transfer of Undertakings (Protection of Employment) Regulations 1981 and Other Rules	276
10.70	Buying and selling limited companies	276
10.71	Buying and selling a business which is not a limited company	277

10.72	The Transfer of Undertakings (Protection of Employment) Regulations 1981	277
10.73	A relevant transfer	278
10.74	Regulation 5 and the transfer of employment liabilities	279
10.75	Pre-transfer dismissals	279
10.76	The *Litster* case	280
10.77	Other applications of Regulation 8	282
10.78	Consultation with unions on business transfers	283
10.79	Statutory continuity on transfers and protection under the EP(C)A	284
10.80	Redundancy liability on business transfers	284
10.81	Getting advice on business transfers	285

11 Life assurance, pensions and permanent health insurance 287
by Vince Jerrard

11.1	Introduction	287
11.2	Life Assurance: Types of policy	288
11.3	Traditional and unit linked policies	289
11.4	Qualifying and non-qualifying policies	290
11.5	The advantages of qualifying policies	290
11.6	Tax treatment of policies	291
11.7	Gain on the happening of a chargeable event	292
11.8	Taxing gains on chargeable events	293
11.9	Pensions: Introduction	293
11.10	The State pension scheme	294
11.11	Contracting-in and contracting-out	295
11.12	Occupational pension schemes	296
11.13	Personal pensions	298
11.14	Moving between different types of pension arrangement	301
11.15	Permanent Health Insurance: Introduction	301
11.16	Sole traders — Life assurance	303
11.17	Pensions	305
11.18	Permanent Health Insurance	307
11.19	Partners: Life assurance	307
11.20	Pensions	308
11.21	Permanent Health Insurance	309
11.22	Companies: Life assurance	309
11.23	Pensions	312
11.24	Permanent Health Insurance	312

12 The business and the outsider 315

Part A Contract law

12.1	Introduction	315
12.2	Components of a contract	315
12.3	Intention to create legal relations	315

12.4		Presumptions about legal enforceability	316
12.5		Offer and acceptance	317
12.6		Offers and invitations to treat distinguished	317
12.7		Termination of offers	318
12.8		Acceptance	318
12.9		Offers, counter offers and acceptances illustrated in business contracts	319
12.10		Consideration	320
12.11		Privity	321
12.12		Form	321
12.13		Terms of the contract	322
12.14		Terms implied by the courts	322
12.15		Excluding terms	322
12.16		Conditions, warranties and other terms	324
12.17		Vitiating elements	325
12.18		Mistake	325
12.19		Misrepresentation	327
12.20		Duress and undue influence	328
12.21		Termination of contracts	329
12.22		Breach of contract	329
12.23		By effluxion of time	330
12.24		By agreement	330
12.25		Frustration	330
12.26		Remedies	331
12.27		Declaration	331
12.28		Damages	332
12.29		The action for an agreed sum	333
12.30		Specific performance	333
12.31		Illegality and unenforceability	335
Part B	**Sale of goods**		
12.32		Introduction	336
12.33		Title and quiet possession	336
12.34		Conformity with description	336
12.35		Merchantable quality and fitness for purpose	337
12.36		Sales by sample	337
12.37		Exclusion of liability in contracts for the sale of goods	338
12.38		Implied terms in contracts other than sale of goods	339
12.39		Other rules in sales of goods	339
12.40		Time	339
12.41		Passing of property	339
12.42		Risk	340
12.43		Delivery	341
12.44		Acceptance	341
12.45		Remedies	341
12.46		Reservation of title clauses	342
12.47		Conditions of trading	344

12.48	Credit sale, conditional sale, and hire purchase agreements	345
12.49	Consumer credit	346
12.50	Other examples of consumer legislation	347
12.51	International sales of goods	348
12.52	EC and domestic competition law	349
Part C	**Product liability**	
12.53	Introduction	350
12.54	Liability in tort	351
12.55	Product liability	352
12.56	The Consumer Protection Act 1987	353
12.57	Practical points arising out of the Consumer Protection Act 1987	355
12.58	Consumer safety	355

13 General insurance
by Gill Clark

13.1	The need for insurance cover	357
13.2	Protection	357
13.3	The main compulsory insurance requirements	357
13.4	The insurance intermediary	358
13.5	Types of cover available	360
13.6	Property insurance	360
13.7	Liability insurances	362
13.8	Motor insurance policies	364
13.9	Business interruption insurance	365
13.10	Other insurances to consider	367
13.11	Type of policies available	368
13.12	Single risk policies	368
13.13	Package/combined policies	368

14 Key rates and allowances — 1989/90   371

15 Glossary   373

Index   381

1 Making a choice between different forms of trading vehicle

1.1 Introduction

Any business ought to consider and review the type of trading structure most appropriate to it and to its proprietor or proprietors. The following is a summary of the main considerations which might influence your choice of trading format. The discussion which follows is based mainly on English Law. In relation to partnerships in particular, and indeed otherwise, Scottish Law has certain rules which might differ slightly from the rules set out here.

1.2 Choosing a format

There are various modes of carrying on business. The choice of which one to adopt should always be carefully considered. Very often, tax considerations will be highly relevant and, in some cases, may be the main reason for the adoption of a particular type of trading vehicle (chapter 4). That aspect in particular should always be carefully reviewed with the help of your accountant or other financial adviser (4.33).

In this chapter, three common vehicles are discussed, namely the sole trader, the partnership and the limited company. There are other forms that can be used, such as a limited partnership, a workers' cooperative, a company limited by guarantee, an unlimited company or, indeed, an unincorporated association (such as a club or society) but these tend to be rarer and some of them include organisations set up otherwise than solely with a view to profit. This of course contrasts with the main aim of the sole trader, a partnership or a limited company, which is usually the making of profit.

1.3 Sole traders

This is possibly the simplest form in which you can trade. It requires little or no formality in itself (although, as in the case of a partnership or company or any trading vehicle, there may be inevitable formalities such as income taxation administration, consumer credit obligations, value added tax administration and employment obligations that affect all businesses). An individual sole trader can freely contract with any other person or, indeed, another company and can employ people. He or she can, of course, also incur liabilities, and the individual is personally liable on all contracts made. Commonly, if overdraft facilities are required from a bank, individual guarantees may be required and the individual's personal assets will often be required to secure such a loan.

Despite the advantages that controlling your own business can give you, sole responsibility without being able to share this with others, and unlimited liability are two major drawbacks to being 'your own boss'. The ultimate consequences of unlimited liability in the event of business failure are described at 1.8.

1.4 Partnerships

A partnership is defined by the Partnership Act 1890 as being the relationship which subsists between persons carrying on a business in common with a view of profit. The definition of partnership is more fully dealt with in chapter 5.

1.5 Terms implied in partnerships by the Partnership Act 1890

The Partnership Act 1890 implies certain rules into a partnership arrangement. For example, every partner is the agent of the firm and can bind the others; every partner is liable jointly with the others for the firm's debts (and jointly and severally liable for torts); unless the contrary is agreed all partners share equally in the profits and capital of the firm (and also its losses); a partnership is determinable at will; and no new partner can be introduced without the others' consent. These rules and others are set out in detail in chapter 5.

1.6 The importance of an express partnership agreement

It can be seen that there are internal rules that will be implied into a partnership relationship in the absence of a provision to the contrary which may prove inconvenient. For example, it is inconvenient for a partner to be able to leave the partnership at will, to cause an automatic dissolution by his death, for the partnership shares of the profits and contribution to capital to be fixed equally by statute, and for the powers of the partners to be fixed by statute. And you might want to determine your own rules as to continuing share of profits throughout illness, provision for holidays, remuneration of the partners, pursuit of private interests apart from the partnership business, and so forth. Much of this problem can be solved by use of an express partnership agreement (chapter 5).

1.7 The liability of partners for a firm's debts

One of the main drawbacks of a partnership is the fact that the partners can be personally liable for the partnership's debts. For this reason, some partnerships convert themselves into limited companies to obtain the benefit of limited liability. Certain partnerships, such as firms of solicitors and accountants, are, to this date, prohibited by their professional associations from so doing (although this may change in the future).

One exception to the rule about personal liability of partners is the case of a limited partnership which may be set up under the Limited Partnerships Act 1907. If a partnership is set up under this Act, it is possible for one or more partners to have limited liability for the partnership's debts. The limit of that liability would be by agreement with the other partners. However, in order for such a partnership to exist, it must still have one or more general partners who are liable for the firm's debts on an unlimited basis.

Further, the status of a limited partner is lost if there is any participation in the management of the partnership firm by the limited partner. A limited partnership (unlike general partnerships) has to be registered with the Registrar of Companies and, if there is failure to register, it is deemed to be a general partnership and every limited partner is deemed to be a general partner. Having regard to the fact that limited liability may be achieved by use of the limited liability company, the limited partnership is comparatively rare. As at 31 March 1988 there were only 871 limited partnerships in England and Wales registered at Companies House.

1.8 Personal insolvency

The most drastic consequence of business failure either as a sole trader (1.3) or as a member of a partnership is personal insolvency as a result of unlimited liability. The continual risk of this possibility cannot be underestimated. The following is a brief discussion of individual bankruptcy. (The rules can be a little more complicated in the case of partnerships).

Personal insolvency, or bankruptcy, arises as a result of an individual's inability to discharge his debts.

Sometimes, formal bankruptcy proceedings can be avoided by making a voluntary arrangement with your creditors with the assistance of a qualified insolvency practitioner. This procedure was introduced by the Insolvency Act 1985 and repeated in the provisions of the Insolvency Act 1986. In such a case, the procedure involves the preparation of a detailed proposal, delivery of a statement of affairs, application to the court, a nominee's report and a creditors' meeting to consider the debtor's proposal and the nominee's report. The proposal for a voluntary arrangement will be binding on creditors if a three-quarters majority of creditors in value present or by proxy voting on the issue agree. The arrangement will apply to all creditors who had notice of the meeting and were entitled to vote at it, even if they did not attend or vote. The arrangement is then implemented by a supervisor approved by the meeting who may or may not be the nominee who handled the proposal and the initial stages of the whole process.

Arrangements can still be made under the Deeds of Arrangement Act 1914, by deed of arrangement with creditors registered with the court. Use of this procedure has not been too popular, because execution of such a deed carried the risk of being an 'act of bankruptcy' under the Bankruptcy Act 1914, which might have allowed a dissentient creditor to petition for bankruptcy nonetheless. The notion of 'an act of bankruptcy' has now been repealed and this argument may therefore no longer apply, although some commentators still think there is a similar, surviving risk, in that such a deed would amount to an admission by a debtor that he is unable to pay his debts and so might entitle a creditor to serve a statutory demand on that ground (see below) and hence commence proceedings. There are arguments, however, that a court might not allow a petition to proceed, if a reasonable composition is being put forward.

It is to be stressed that, due to the complexity of this area, advice from an insolvency practitioner is necessary on what option to take and how to proceed with it.

If, however, bankruptcy proceedings cannot be avoided, they are initiated by petition. A debtor may petition on the ground that he is unable to pay his debts. A creditor may petition on the ground either that the debtor appears to be unable to pay his debts (and this is established when either execution of a debt is returned unsatisfied in whole or in part, or the debtor fails to comply with a statutory demand) or he appears to have no reasonable prospect of paying his debts (which is where a debt is not immediately repayable and a statutory demand requiring the debtor to show reasonable prospects has been served by a creditor but the debtor has not complied with it or obtained leave to set it aside within the relevant time limits).

If a bankruptcy order is made you become an undischarged bankrupt and are deprived of ownership of your property. You lose control over administration of your affairs and purported dispositions of your property are void.

Your trustee in bankruptcy may also be able to apply to the court to avoid or adjust certain transactions that have taken place within a certain period prior to the onset of the insolvency, such as transactions at an undervalue and preferences. A person enters into a transaction with another at an undervalue if:

(1) he makes a gift or otherwise enters into a transaction on terms that he receives no consideration;
(2) he enters into a transaction with another in consideration of marriage;
(3) he enters into a transaction with another for a consideration the value of which, in money or money's worth, is significantly less than the value, in money or money's worth, of the consideration provided by him.

A person gives a preference to another if:

(1) the other person is a creditor or a surety or a guarantor of any of his debts or liabilities; and
(2) he does anything or suffers anything to be done which (in either case) has the effect of putting that person into a position which, in the event of bankruptcy of the giver of the preference, will be better than the position he would have been in if that thing had not been done.

The time limits are:

(1) in the case of transactions at an undervalue: within five years of presentation of a petition of bankruptcy;
(2) in the case of a preference which is not a transaction at an

undervalue but is given to an associate (an associate includes a spouse or other fairly close relation): two years;
(3) if the preference is neither a transaction at an undervalue nor given to an associate: six months.

For a preference to apply, the debtor must have been influenced by a desire to put the creditor into the better position in which he now finds himself. This is presumed unless proved to the contrary where associates are concerned. It must also be shown in the case of both preferences and transactions at an undervalue that the debtor was insolvent at the relevant time (though not in the case of a transaction at an undervalue within 2 years of the petition), and this will be presumed unless disproved in the case of a transaction at an undervalue with an associate.

There are also rules which allow a court to unravel transactions defrauding creditors, ie where the debtor has entered into a transaction at an undervalue and the court is satisfied that it was made for the purpose of putting assets beyond the reach of a creditor or otherwise prejudicing the interests of such a person.

Bankruptcy commences on the day a bankruptcy order is made and continues until the order is discharged. In summary administrations, the time of discharge is two years and, in other cases, three years. In criminal or repeated bankruptcy, the period is five years with the permission of the court.

An undischarged bankrupt cannot be a company director, nor directly or indirectly take part or be concerned in the promotion, formation or management of a company, unless the court consents, and, generally, the consequences of bankruptcy are traumatic.

1.9 The limited liability company

Because of the circumstances set out in 1.8 and for other reasons, the limited company is an extremely popular form of trading vehicle. As at 31 March 1989 there were 1,113,900 companies on the register at Companies House, the vast majority of which were private companies; for example, only 6,600 were public companies (see 1.11).

A company must be registered under CA 1985 or have been registered already under one of the Companies Acts which preceded this Act. Many companies are incorporated under CA 1948 or earlier Companies Acts such as CA 1929 or 1908. Any new company would now be incorporated under CA 1985.

Making a choice between different forms of trading vehicle 7

1.10 Forming companies

More formalities are necessary to incorporate a company than, for example, to form a partnership and these are discussed more fully in chapter 5. This can be one of the drawbacks of companies when compared with partnerships.

1.11 Private and public companies

The basic division between types of limited company is between private companies and public companies. Briefly, a public company is a company which may offer its shares to the public, which uses the suffix 'public limited company' or 'plc' and which has to meet certain minimum capital requirements (such as a minimum issued share capital of £50,000, a quarter of which must be paid up).

A public company is generally also subject to more stringent requirements in CA 1985 and, if a listed company, to detailed Stock Exchange rules. In practice, public limited companies are much more substantial than the minimum figure of capital mentioned above indicates.

A private company is a company which is not a public company. Also, no private company may apply for admission to the Stock Exchange Official List nor (unless falling within an exception in an order issued by the Secretary of State) may a private company issue an advertisement offering securities to be issued by that company. These rules, presently contained in the Financial Services Act 1986, are a restatement of the long-standing principle that a private company should not be allowed to offer its shares to the public.

1.12 Limited liability of shareholders of companies

Being a member of a limited company gives you the advantage of limited liability. The leading case illustrating this is *Salomon v Salomon & Co Ltd* (1897), where a promoter who had carried on the business of a leather merchant and wholesale boot manufacturer transferred his business to a newly formed limited company. The nominal capital of the company was £40,000 and Salomon took £20,000 worth of shares in part payment of the price of the business transferred. A further £10,000 of the purchase price was secured by debentures. The company went into liquidation with many trade creditors unpaid. Salomon took priority over them in respect of the £10,000 secured by debentures (see chapter 5). The trade creditors attempted to say that the company's debts were really Salomon's. Not so. The House of Lords held that the new company was a separate legal entity from Salomon and his liability was limited to the amount that he had agreed to subscribe for his shares, a sum he had, in fact, already paid.

Since then, the principle of separate corporate personality has been reinforced by many decisions, thus leaving the liability of members separate from the liability of the company. Occasionally, the courts 'lift the veil' of incorporation, look inside the company, and treat the company's debts as the members' debts. These instances are very rare indeed, such as in the case of enemy activity, fraud, some revenue cases, some unusual cases involving groups of companies, and certain other exceptional examples.

Example

In *Gilford Motor Co Ltd* v *Horne* (1933) a director of a company was bound by a restrictive convenant which applied after the end of his employment and which prevented him from soliciting his employer's customers. When he left, in order to avoid the covenant, he formed a separate limited company under his control through which he solicited customers, in breach of the covenant. It was held that the former employer was entitled to restrain this activity. The new company was a sham, set up solely to avoid the covenant, and its actions could be attributed to the director.

There are also some instances where, under statute, members or directors or other officers can be personally liable and these are discussed in chapter 5. Again, they are the exception rather than the rule. Limited liability must be one of the primary motives, apart from tax (4.33), for a businessman to incorporate his previously unincorporated business.

1.13 Advantages and disadvantages of incorporation compared with partnership

Having discussed the basic format of sole traders, partnerships and companies, perhaps it is now appropriate to set out a checklist which shows both the advantages and disadvantages of incorporating a previously unincorporated business and also the specific differences between companies and partnerships. This list ignores tax considerations, which, in themselves, may be a primary or even decisive motive for transferring an unincorporated business into a limited company form or indeed for maintaining the status quo (4.33). Some relevant considerations will be as follows:

(1) As a company is a separate legal person from its members the debts and liabilities of a company are those of the company and not the members (contrast a partnership where the partners may be jointly liable in contract, and jointly and severally liable in

tort). Although partners can be sued in the firm name this does not detract from the principle that, at the end of the day, if the partnership firm is unable to meet a claim, the partners are individually liable as above mentioned (see chapter 5). One exception is in the case of a limited partnership under the Limited Partnerships Act 1907 (1.7).

(2) As a company is a separate legal person, it enjoys perpetual succession. Thus, a company is not affected by the death or retirement of any of its proprietors. The company continues notwithstanding these events. Under the Partnership Act 1890, a partnership is dissolved *automatically* by death or retirement of one of the partners. Also, if a shareholder of a company dies, his or her share does not have to be bought out by the other members. It can simply pass to the personal representatives of the deceased member.

(3) Shares in a limited company can be transferred to any other person. This is not the case in a partnership where the partners may resist the introduction of a new partner without their consent.

(4) The property of a company belongs to the company and there is no need to change the deeds of title when the members change (eg by death or sale of shares). This contrasts with a partnership, in which case the property will be vested in the names of the partners. Any change in the composition of the partners may necessitate a change in the deeds of title.

(5) Each partner may take part in the management of a partnership. In a company, unless a member is a director, he may not take part in the management of a company. Membership of a company does not necessarily carry with it management rights.

(6) In principle, a member may mortgage his share in a company. But in a partnership the partners may dissolve a partnership if any partner charges his share.

(7) A company can contract with its members (for example, enter into contracts of employment with its members and directors).

(8) A company may have greater versatility in borrowing powers than a partnership, in the sense that it can issue certain specialised forms of security for loans, such as debentures and floating charges. A floating charge may not be issued either by a partnership or a sole trader since a floating charge involves, in practice, a charge over chattels. Chattels can only be mortgaged by an individual or a partnership through a bill of sale under the Bill of Sale Acts 1878 and 1882. This would require each chattel to be specified, which, in reality, is not practicable. The floating charge is further described at 5.23.

(9) There are fewer formalities to be observed in relation to a partnership than in relation to a company. There are no documents required to be sent to a registry, such as in the case of companies, where, for example, the Memorandum & Articles, statement of first directors and secretary, forms in relation to the issue of shares,

certificate in relation to compliance with formation regulations, and statement of registered office are required to be prepared and filed with the Companies Registry. (Having said this, the Companies Bill provides for a lifting of some of the administrative burdens on private companies by, for example, allowing an election to dispense with the requirement to hold Annual General Meetings and to lay the annual accounts and reports before the general meeting and by allowing certain company decisions to be effected by members' written resolution instead of a resolution passed at a formal meeting; see chapter 5 in more detail.)

(10) There is no limit to the number of members of a company, whereas partnerships are limited to 20 members (although certain (professional) firms are allowed to exceed 20 members (eg solicitors and accountants) (see chapter 5)).

(11) There is less publicity in relation to a partnership in that the partnership deed, if any, is not required to be registered on any public register and the firm's accounts are not made public. By contrast, a company has to register its Memorandum & Articles (see chapter 5) and also many other documents during the life of the company, such as its annual returns and accounts, special and extraordinary resolutions and records of certain transactions and meetings and it has to publish accounts.

(12) There are continuing expenses in the case of companies which are not applicable to partnerships, such as the requirement of an audit and the making of annual returns.

(13) Certain rules in company law do not apply to partnership law, such as the *ultra vires* doctrine (5.28) (the effect of the doctrine of *ultra vires* is partially mitigated in favour of third parties by CA 1985 s 35 (see chapter 5) and the protection of third parties will be improved by the amendments made to s 35 by the Companies Bill, but the doctrine is still relevant in some ways even in the face of those provisions, eg for the purposes of a director's liability to his company (see chapter 5)), and the various special duties imposed on directors by statute. The assumption of the office of director also makes a proprietor a fiduciary who owes quite extensive duties to the company as a separate legal entity under the general law. (see, in detail, chapter 5).

(14) A company is subject to stringent capital requirements if a public company and must still observe certain rules as to capital even if a private company. A partnership may trade more or less as if it were an individual.

Some of these rules can be altered by agreement in the Articles of a company or the partnership deed as the case may be, and the distinction between companies and partnerships blurred. For example, you will often see that in smaller private companies the right freely to transfer shares to outsiders is restricted, thus making the position with regard to transmission of shares more analogous to partnerships in that context.

1.14 Conclusion

There are certainly advantages and disadvantages either way to be considered in choosing between the corporate and non-corporate form. Apart from the taxation considerations involved, a significant advantage of incorporation is limited liability. Choosing the partnership and sole trader form has advantages, by contrast, in lack of formality and expense and, also, freedom from the considerable restrictions and regulations contained in CA 1985 and elsewhere. As always, specialist advice is needed on which trading form is most appropriate, at whatever particular stage of a firm's evolution.

2 Tax on business income

2.1 Introduction — The taxation of income

If you trade as an individual or in partnership, your taxable income will be liable to income tax at a basic rate of 25% and a higher rate of 40% (2.4). These rates apply for the tax year 1989–90 (ending 5 April 1990) and also for 1988–89. In arriving at your taxable income certain deductions are appropriate such as capital allowances (2.17), charges on income (2.6) and personal reliefs (2.5).

The capital gains of individuals and partnerships are considered later (chapter 6). The rate is generally 25% and/or 40% subject to certain reliefs. Both the income and capital gains of companies are subject to corporation tax (chapter 4). The rate is 35%, subject to a small companies rate of 25% which generally applies where profits are sufficiently low (4.3).

The income of companies etc, partnerships and individuals is taxable according to a system of schedules and cases as follows.

2.2 Table: Classes of income

Schedule A
Income from land and buildings. This includes rents and lease premiums.

Schedule B
This applied to woodlands managed on a commercial basis and the 'assessable value' was taxed. This schedule was abolished as from 6 April 1988.

Schedule C
This covers income from government securities payable in the UK; also overseas public revenue dividends paid through a banker, etc here.

Schedule D
This is the main schedule applicable to the income connected with businesses. It is divided into separate categories as follows:

Case I	Trades (2.7).
Case II	Professions and vocations (2.7).
Case III	Interest, annuities and other annual payments received. This is now restricted on account of the 'composite rate' scheme applying to much bank and building society interest.
Cases IV & V	Income from certain investments, possessions and businesses overseas.
Case VI	This is a 'sweeping-up' case applying to miscellaneous profits not covered by any of the other cases of Schedule D.

Schedule E
This schedule applies to directors' remuneration as well as wages and salaries earned by other employees. It comprises:

Case I	The work is done in the UK and the employee is resident here.
Case II	Generally this case applies to a non-resident working in the UK.
Case III	The work is done wholly abroad by a UK resident but the salary is sent here during the course of the overseas employment. However, this case does not apply if the income is already taxed under Case I or Case II of Schedule E.

Schedule F
This schedule covers distributions made by companies including in particular dividends (4.8).

2.3 Income tax rates and personal reliefs

The 1989–90 rates of income tax and personal reliefs are given below. For further details, reference should be made to the *Allied Dunbar Tax Guide*.

2.4 Table: Income tax rates for 1989–90

Taxable Income £	Slice £	Rate %	Tax £
20,700	20,700	25	5,175
Excess over 20,700		40	

2.5 Table: Personal reliefs — 1989-90

Personal allowances	1989-90 £
Single	2,785
Married	4,375
Wife's earnings (maximum)	2,785
Single parent addition	1,590
Age allowance	
Single (age 65-74)	3,400
(age 75 and over)	3,540
Married (age 65-74)	5,385
(age 75 and over)	5,565
Income limit	11,400
Additional personal	
allowance for children	1,590
Widow's bereavement allowance	1,590
Blind person's allowance	
Single	540
Married (both spouses blind)	1,080

2.6 Deductions from income

As well as personal reliefs (2.5) you are able to make various other deductions in arriving at your taxable income. The following are some examples:

(1) One half of your Class IV National Insurance contributions.
(2) Business losses and capital allowances.
(3) Allowable retirement annuity premiums.
(4) Parts of certain transfers to reserve made by Lloyd's Underwriters or other approved underwriters.
(5) Donations to charity under Deeds of Covenant which are capable of exceeding three years. This normally entails four annual payments.
(6) Loan interest payments are allowable in certain circumstances including:
  (a) On the first £30,000 of your mortgage on your main residence
  (b) On property which you let out for at least half of the year (only relievable against your lettings income).
  (c) For buying plant and machinery for use in your partnership. (Relief is given for three years after the tax year when the loan is taken out.)

(d) On money which you borrow for acquiring ordinary shares in a close company or lending money for its business. (Not applicable to a close investment company nor for any shares bought after 13 March 1989 on which BES relief is claimed (4.32). You must either own broadly at least 5% of the shares or own some shares and work for the company for much of your time.)
(e) For buying a partnership share or lending it money for its business if you are a partner.
(f) For paying inheritance tax. (Interest unrelieved in the year of payment can be spread forward or backward.)

(7) Generally, allowable mortgage interest is payable under the deduction of basic rate income tax, as are various other *charges on income*. The following are examples and are deductible from your income:
   (a) Annual payments to retiring partners or their widows in accordance with partnership agreements.
   (b) Certain annual payments made concerning the purchase of a business, such payments being made to the former owner or his widow or dependants.

2.7 Trades, professions and vocations

As mentioned above (2.2), profits from trades are assessed under Schedule D Case I whilst those from professions and vocations are taxed under Case II of Schedule D. The remainder of this chapter deals with the position concerning individuals and most of the general rules apply also to partnerships and companies. However, there are certain special rules which apply to partnerships (chapter 3) and companies (chapter 4).

For tax purposes, trade includes manufacturing, retailing, wholesaling and trading ventures in general. It may also encompass certain isolated transactions according to the rules (2.8).

A profession is an occupation requiring special intellectual skills. This is sometimes coupled with manual skills. Examples of those engaged in professions are doctors and dentists, solicitors, barristers, accountants and architects.

A definition of vocation is the way that a person passes his life; for example an author, actor, singer, composer or dancer.

2.8 Indications of trading

Normally, there will be no doubt that you are carrying on a trade (or profession or vocation) assessable under Schedule D, Case I or

Tax on business income

II. However, other activities might constitute trading and the following are indications:

(1) Dealing in property is likely to be treated as trading.
(2) Possessing expert business knowledge in connection with a transaction which you carry out will make it more likely that you are treated as trading.
(3) Repeating the same transaction is often evidence of trading.
(4) Should you buy an asset, work on it and then sell it, this might be treated as trading, for example buying a ship, converting it and then selling it.
(5) Isolated transactions in assets which produce income are not normally regarded as trading. Capital gains tax would generally apply.
(6) Regular buying and selling normally constitutes trading. However, purchases and sales of shares by an individual are not usually treated as trading, capital gains tax then applying.
(7) Where there are isolated purchases and sales of works of art, this is not normally regarded as trading since the works of art are owned to be admired rather than for commercial purposes.
(8) An isolated transaction might be held to be trading if its very nature is commercial. An example is a single purchase and sale of a quantity of unmatured whisky.

2.9 Computing the assessable profits for Schedule D, Cases I and II

Normally, you will have annual accounts prepared for your business or profession. These will include a profit and loss account or an income and expenditure account. These accounts should generally be drawn up to the same date every year but need not coincide with the tax year (ending on 5 April). The profit shown by your accounts forms the basis of your assessment under Case I or Case II of Schedule D. However, adjustment to your profit (or loss) should be made as follows:

(1) Add any non-deductible expenses (see below) charged in your accounts.
(2) Deduct any profits included in your accounts which are not taxable under Cases I and II of Schedule D because they are non-taxable or liable to tax under other cases or schedules. Examples are: interest receivable taxed under Schedule D Case III, capital profits liable to capital gains tax, rents receivable taxed under Schedule A, interest received net having been taxed at source, and dividends.
(3) Deduct amounts previously put to reserve and now recredited in your accounts (unless the original amounts were allowed against your taxable profits).
(4) Deduct any allowable expenses not already charged.

18 Allied Dunbar Business Tax and Law Guide

(5) Add any trading profits not already included.
(6) Exclude government grants towards specified capital expenditure or compensation for loss of capital assets. Also, generally exclude regional development grants under the Industrial Development Act 1982 and certain grants to assist industry in Northern Ireland. However, often these items can be added to the costs of the assets for capital gains tax purposes.
(7) Add entertaining expenses (unless concerning overseas customers and their agents prior to 16 March 1988 or your own staff).
(8) Add fines for illegalities and connected legal costs.
(9) Add charitable donations unless wholly for business purposes. (Non-close companies are allowed donations up to 3% of their dividends.)
(10) Add political donations.
(11) Add the cost of acquiring capital assets (plant and machinery, buildings, motor vehicles etc). Capital allowances are frequently available.
(12) Add private or domestic expenses of yourself or your family.
(13) Add a proportion of expenses containing some private element. Should a private house be used for business purposes, the proportion deductible is not normally allowed to exceed 2/3rds of the rent and other costs.
(14) Where you own or partly own a business, your drawings are not deductible.
(15) If you are self-employed (for example, a partner) you can deduct security expenditure covering assets and services to meet threats to your personal security arising in the course of your business.

2.10 Example: Schedule D Case I computation

Jack Box trades on his own account in a manufacturing business. His accounts for the year to 30 June 1989 show a net profit of £40,000 including the following:

Expenses	£
Depreciation — Motor car	3,000
— Plant and machinery	6,000
Legal expenses re: debt collection	500
Bad debts provision (5% x sales debtors)	2,000
Entertaining expenses — UK customers	600
— Overseas customers	400
Loss on sale of motor car	1,500
Non-business charitable donations	100
Legal expenses re new lease	400

Income	£
Bank deposit interest	300
General bad debts provision no longer required	500

Tax on business income

Ignoring capital allowances compute Jack Box's adjusted Case I profit.

Jack Box Schedule D Case I computation based on accounts for year ended 30 June 1989:

	£	£
Net profit per accounts		40,000
Less:		
Bank deposit interest	300	
Bad debts provision no longer required	500	800
		39,200
Add: Disallowable expenses:		
Depreciation (£3,000 + £6,000)	9,000	
General bad debts provision	2,000	
Legal expenses re: new lease	400	
Charitable donations	100	
Entertaining (600 + 400)	1,000	
Loss on sale of motor car (capital)	1,500	14,000
Adjusted profit		£53,200

2.11 Stock and work in progress

In preparing business accounts, stock and work in progress is normally valued at each accounting date. The profits are augmented or decreased by the excess or deficit of the closing stock and work in progress compared with the opening position. Thus, if the closing stock is valued on a more generous basis than the opening stock, the profits shown by the accounts will be higher than the true amount.

Your stock and work in progress is the amount of unsold raw materials, finished goods and work in hand that was owned at the end of the accounts period. The Inland Revenue pay special attention to the manner in which businesses value their stock and normally insist that, for tax purposes, the opening and closing stocks are valued on an identical basis. Normally, each item in stock is valued at the lower of its cost or net realizable value. The exact cost for each item may or may not include an addition for expenses, depending on the exact basis adopted. The general rule to ascertain cost is that identical items are identified on the basis that the earliest purchases were sold or used first (FIFO). The method chosen must be used consistently. 'Net realizable value' is the estimated proceeds from disposing of the stock in the ordinary course of business at balance sheet date. This is after allowing for all expenses in connection with the disposal.

For a period of about nine years up to 12 March 1984, generous stock relief was available in arriving at the taxable profits of businesses. This applied to individuals, partnerships and companies. Since the relief does not apply after 12 March 1984, however, no further mention is made here and if details are required, reference should be made to the *Allied Dunbar Tax Guide.*

2.12 Basis of assessment

Having computed your assessable profits from a business or profession, the question remains, for which tax year are they assessable? Assessments under Cases I and II of Schedule D are normally based on the profits of the accounts year ending in the preceding tax year. Thus if a business prepares accounts to 30 September each year, its 1990–91 Schedule D Case I assessment will be based on the profits for the year to 30 September 1989 (ending in the preceding tax year 1989–90).

Obviously, when you first start your business, you will have no previous year on which to be taxed. Therefore, special rules apply to the opening years of assessment. Similarly, there are separate rules for closing years and where you change your accounting date.

2.13 Opening years

(1) For the first tax year of a business, profession or vocation, you will be assessed on the profits from the starting date until the next 5 April. This may involve taking a proportion of your profit for a longer period. Thus if your business started on 6 July 1989 and makes up its accounts to 5 July 1990 showing a profit of £24,000 for that year, the assessment for 1989–90 will be based on the period from 6 July 1989 to 5 April 1990, giving 24,000 × 9/12 = £18,000.

(2) Your assessment for the second tax year would normally be based on the profits for the first complete 12 months. Thus, in the above example, your 1990–91 assessment will be based on the profits for the first complete year, which ends on 5 July 1990, giving £24,000.

(3) The third year's assessment is generally based on the preceding year. Thus in the example above, your 1990–91 assessment would be £24,000 (the profits for the accounts year ending in the preceding tax year).

(4) You will have the option to elect that the assessments for both the second and third tax years (but not only one of these) should be based on the actual profits for those years (see example 2.14). This election must be made to the Inspector of Taxes within seven years of the end of the second year of assessment.

(5) Special rules cover commencements following certain partnership changes (3.6).

2.14 Example: Schedule D Cases I and II — Assessments for opening years

Jack Box started in business on his own account on 1 July 1987 and prepared accounts for an 18 month period to 31 December 1988 producing an adjusted profit of £27,000. He selected 31 December as his regular accounting date and his adjusted profit for the year to 31 December 1989 was £9,000 and for 1990 it was £7,200. What are Jack's Schedule D Case I assessments based on those profits?

Jack Box — Schedule D Case I assessments

Tax year	Basis	Base period	Calculations	Assessment
1987–88	Actual	1.7.87–5.4.88	£27,000×9-1/6/18	£13,750
1988–89	First year	1.7.87–30.6.88	£27,000×12/18	£18,000
1989–90	Preceding year	1.1.88–31.12.88	£27,000×12/18	£18,000
1990–91	Preceding year	1.1.89–31.12.89		£ 9,000
1991–92	Preceding year	1.1.90–31.12.90		£ 7,200

The assessments for Jack's second and third tax years total £36,000 (£18,000 + £18,000). Jack Box can effect a saving by electing that his assessments for those years should be on the actual profits made in 1988–89 and 1989–90 as follows:

1988–89	6.4.88–31.12.88	£27,000×8-5/6/18	£13,250	
	1.1.89–5.4.89	£ 9,000×3-1/6/12	£ 2,375	
				£15,625
1989–90	6.4.89–31.12.89	£ 9,000×8-5/6/12	£ 6,625	
	1.1.90–5.4.90	£ 7,200×3-1/6/12	£ 1,900	£ 8,525

The reduction in the aggregate assessments for 1988–89 and 1989–90 is £11,850 (£36,000 − (£15,625 + £8,525)).

2.15 Closing years

(1) If you permanently cease your trade, profession or vocation, your last year is assessed on an actual basis. That is to say, your assessment under Schedule D Case I or II is based on the actual profits from the previous 6 April until the date when your business ceases.
(2) The Inland Revenue has the right to make additional assessments in respect of the two tax years prior to the year in which cessation takes place. These are known as the two penultimate years.
(3) The Revenue has the option of increasing your assessments for the two penultimate tax years to the actual profits for those years. This is illustrated in the following example.

2.16 Example: Schedule D Cases I and II — Assessments for closing years

Jack Box ceases to trade on 31 July 1990 having made adjusted profits as follows:

Year ended 31 July 1987	£25,000
Year ended 31 July 1988	£18,000
Year ended 31 July 1989	£36,000
Year ended 31 July 1990	£27,000

What are Jack's final assessments on these profits?

Before it was known that Jack was ceasing to trade, his assessments would be as follows:

Tax year	Basis	Base period	Schedule D Case I Assessment
1988–89	Preceding year	Year to 31.7.87	£25,000
1989–90	Preceding year	Year to 31.7.88	£18,000
Total for 1988–89 and 1989–90			£43,000

When cessation on 31.7.90 is notified to the Revenue they will adjust the assessments for 1988–89 and 1989–90 as follows:

			£	£
1988–89				
Actual	6.4.88–31.7.88	£18,000 × 3-5/6/12	5,750	
	1.8.88–5.4.89	£36,000 × 8-1/6/12	24,500	30,250
1989–90				
Actual	6.4.89–31.7.89	£36,000 × 3-5/6/12	11,500	
	1.8.89–5.4.90	£27,000 × 8-1/6/12	18,375	29,875
Revised total for 1988–89 and 1989–90				60,125
Less: Already assessed				43,000
Additional assessments 1988–89 and 1989–90				£17,125
1990–91				
Actual	6.4.90–31.7.90	£27,000 × 3-5/6/12		£ 8,625

2.17 Capital allowances

Although you are not normally allowed to deduct from your taxable profits the cost or depreciation of capital assets, you are generally allowed to deduct capital allowances. These are based on the cost of certain assets which you use in your business or profession including:

(1) Plant and machinery (2.19).
(2) Industrial buildings (2.30).

(3) Agricultural and forestry buildings, etc (2.32).
(4) Hotel buildings, etc (2.33).
(5) Scientific research expenditure (2.34).
(6) Patents and know-how (2.35).
(7) Mines, oil wells etc (2.36) and dredging (2.36).
(8) Assured tenancies (2.37)
(9) Safety expenditure at sports grounds (2.38).
(10) Expenditure on 'security assets' (2.39)

If you have expenditure which qualifies for allowances under more than one of the above codes, you will be able to make an irrevocable choice. This applies to accounting periods ending after 26 July 1989.

2.18 Base period

Capital allowances are computed with reference to the assets purchased and those used in your annual business accounts period. This is known as the base period. You must take the date when the expenditure was incurred, which is generally when the obligation to pay becomes unconditional. An exception is where part of the capital expenditure is payable more than four months later, in which case you take the date when that part is payable.

Having found the total capital allowances for a given tax year, they are deducted from the Schedule D Case I or Case II assessment for that year. For example if your business makes up its accounts to 31 December, then its Schedule D Case I assessment for 1990–91 will be based on its accounts for the year to 31 December 1989. In the same way, its 1990– 91 capital allowances will be based on the year to 31 December 1989.

Base periods of less than one year might arise in the opening or closing years of the business. Also, one base period might apply to two tax years. In that case, the additions during the base period must be allocated to the earlier tax year in order to calculate the allowances. Should there be a gap between base periods, this is added to the second base period unless this marks a cessation of trading. In that case, you must add the gap to the first period.

2.19 Capital allowances on plant and machinery

In general, the main category of business assets attracting capital allowances is plant and machinery. This includes furniture, fittings, office equipment, motor vehicles, the thermal insulation of industrial buildings and making certain buildings comply with fire regulations.

The main allowance available is a 25% writing down allowance each year (2.21). There are special rules relating to motor vehicles (2.27) and plant which you lease out (2.29). When plant is sold balancing charges and allowances might arise (2.22). First year allowances applied to expenditure before 1 April, 1986 but not subsequently (see below).

2.20 First year allowance

For expenditure prior to 1 April 1986, a most important allowance was available, which is noted here for completeness. Known as first year allowance, it applied at a rate of 100% on expenditure prior to 14 March 1984. After 13 March 1984 and before 1 April 1985, the rate was 75% with 50% applying for expenditure after 31 March 1985 and before 1 April 1986. In general, first year allowance did not apply in respect of motor cars.

2.21 Writing down allowance

Each asset is put into a 'pool' at cost price and a writing down allowance of 25% is given on the balance. (If you obtained any first year allowance, this was deducted from the cost in arriving at the 'pool' figure.) You have the option of taking less than 25% in any year, if you so wish.

Before 1 April 1986, writing down allowance was not normally given in respect of the first year. Expenditure after 31 March 1986 in general qualifies for no first year allowance, and writing down allowance runs from the first year.

Where the base period relative to the expenditure is less than a year, the rate of writing down allowance is proportionately reduced. For example, if the base period for your business is only six months for a given year of assessment, then any writing down allowances for that period would be at the rate of $12\frac{1}{2}\%$ (25% × 6/12).

2.22 Sales of plant and machinery — Balancing allowances and charges

When you sell an item of plant from your 'pool', you simply deduct the sale proceeds from the 'pool' balance. However, should the proceeds exceed the original cost of the plant, you only deduct the cost. Where the sale proceeds exceed your 'pool' balance, the excess is a balancing charge which is added to your assessment for the year.

Balancing allowances normally only occur in the event of a cessation. If you permanently cease to trade during a period, you receive a 'balancing allowance' equal to the remainder of your 'pool', consisting of expenditure less allowances already obtained, less its disposal value.

2.23 Example: Capital allowances on plant and machinery

Jack Box has been carrying on a manufacturing business for many years and makes up his accounts to 31 December each year. At 31 December 1985 the capital allowances written down value of his plant, etc was £5,250. He purchased the following new plant:

Date	Description	Cost £
on 1 March 1986	Machinery	6,000
on 30 June 1987	Machinery	7,400
on 30 September 1988	Office furniture	1,500

No other additions were made before 31 December 1988.

During the year to 31 December 1986 Jack Box sold machinery costing £1,000 for £450.

Compute his capital allowances for 1987–88, 1988–89 and 1989–90.

		'Pool' £	Total allowances £
Balance brought forward 1987–88 (base period year to 31 December 1986) Additions:		5,250	
1 March 1986	6,000		
First year allowance 50%	3,000	3,000	3,000
Sale proceeds		(450)	
		7,800	
Writing down allowance 25% × £4,800		(1,200)	1,200
Balance forward		6,600	£4,200
1988–89 (base period year to 31 December 1987) Additions:			
30 June 1987		7,400	
		14,000	
Writing down allowance 25% × £14,000		(3,500)	£3,500
Balance forward 1989–90 (base period year to 31 December 1988) Additions:		10,500	
30 September 1988		1,500	
		12,000	

26 Allied Dunbar Business Tax and Law Guide

Writing down allowance 25% × £12,000	(£3,000)	£3,000
Balance carried forward	£9,000	

2.24 Fixtures — Entitlement to capital allowances

Special rules apply to clarify who is entitled to capital allowances where machinery or plant is installed in a building and becomes a fixture. The plant may be treated as belonging to you, for capital allowances purposes, even though you are not the owner.

Under the rules, which in general apply after 11 July 1984, if you lease out a piece of equipment and it becomes a fixture at a building, you only obtain capital allowances if you make a joint election with the lessee. If you pay to be granted a lease which includes a fixture on which the lessor would otherwise obtain capital allowances, you can jointly elect that you receive the allowances.

2.25 Short-life assets

Regarding short-life plant and machinery which you buy for your trade after 31 March 1986, you can elect to have the writing down allowances calculated separately from your 'pool'. This is known as de-pooling. The election must be made within two years of the year of acquisition and does not normally apply to assets leased to non-traders, or to cars or ships.

Selling the assets gives rise to a balancing charge or allowance. However, if the machinery or plant has not been sold within five years, it must be transferred to your pool at its tax written down value.

2.26 Example: Short-life assets — De-pooling

Jack Box makes up his business accounts to 31 December and buys plant for £1,000 on 30 June 1987, for which he makes a de-pooling election. The plant is sold for £100 on 15 May 1991. The capital allowances computations are as follows:

Year ended 31 December		£
1987	Cost	1,000
	25% writing down allowance	250
		750
1988		188

1989		562
		141
		421
1990		105
		316
1991	Sale proceeds	100
	Balancing allowance	£216

Note: If the plant had not been disposed of by 31 December 1991, the written down value would be transferred to the general plant pool.

2.27 Motor vehicles

If you buy a car for use in your business, you obtain the 25% writing down allowance. However, special rules apply to cars costing over £8,000; in this case your allowance for any year is restricted to 25% × £8,000, ie £2,000. Each car costing more than £8,000 must be treated as a separate 'pool'. When any such car is sold, it gives rise to its own balancing allowance or balancing charge. Cars costing no more than £8,000 are all put into a separate pool. (This pool also includes assets acquired before 1 April 1986 which you lease out and which did not qualify for first year allowance).

Where your car is leased through your business and its equivalent retail cost price exceeds £8,000, the rental deduction from your taxable business profits is correspondingly restricted. To find the actual deductible rental, you multiply the true rental by $(£8,000 + \frac{RP - 8,000}{2})$ and you divide by RP, the retail price of the car when new.

2.28 Hire purchase

The acquisition of plant or machinery on hire purchase entitles you to full capital allowances as soon as you bring it into use in your business. Allowances are given on the capital proportion of the total instalments. The interest proportion is allowed against your business profits in the year that the respective instalments are paid. For example, suppose that the cash cost of a machine is £5,000, but you buy it under a hire purchase agreement and are paying a total of £7,400 over three years. You get capital allowances on £5,000 as soon as you start to use the machine, ie 25% writing down allowance. You would also deduct the interest of £2,400 from your profits for the three years during which you pay off the instalments (ie about £800 each year).

2.29 Machinery for leasing

In general, you now obtain 25% writing down allowance on machinery which you buy for leasing out. However, the rate is restricted to 10% if you lease the assets to non-residents. Similarly, writing down allowances of only 10% are available where ships or aircraft are let on charter to non-residents.

2.30 Industrial buildings

The cost of new industrial buildings that are used in your business qualifies for writing down allowance at 4% of the original cost. Examples of qualifying buildings are factories, warehouses and some repair shops. If any of the expenditure was incurred before 6 November 1962, the allowance is only 2% of the original cost.

Expenditure incurred prior to 1 April 1986 attracted initial allowances as follows:

Expenditure incurred before	11 March 1981	50%
	14 March 1984	75%
	1 April 1985	50%
	1 April 1986	25%

In general, initial allowances are no longer available, apart from expenditure in Enterprise Zones (2.31).

Note that up to 25% of the capital cost of an industrial building is allowed to relate to a non-qualifying use without restricting the allowances.

The sale of an industrial building will give rise to a balancing charge or allowance. This is computed by comparing the sale proceeds with the balance of original cost, less initial allowances and writing down allowances obtained. This applies even if you had ceased to use the building for industrial purposes. You must disregard any excess of the proceeds compared with the original cost. However, this may give rise to a capital gain.

2.31 Enterprise zones

Enterprise zones are designated by the Government. One of their attractions is that expenditure on industrial and commercial buildings qualifies for 100% initial allowance. Unusually, for this purpose, shops and offices are included and also integral plant and machinery. You are able to claim less than the full initial allowance, in which case 25% writing down allowance (straight line) is obtained on the original expenditure until it is used up.

2.32 Agricultural buildings

As the owner or tenant of farm or forestry land (see below), you obtain allowance for expenditure on certain constructions on the land. These include farm or forestry buildings, farmhouses, cottages, fences, etc. The allowance consists of a writing-down allowance on your original expenditure. For expenditure between 11 April 1978 and 1 April 1986, there was an initial allowance of up to 20% and the balance was eligible for writing down allowance of 10% of the original cost for each year including the first. There is no initial allowance for expenditure after 1 April 1986, and only 4% writing down allowance applies.

In general, expenditure after 31 March 1986, which attracts a 4% writing down allowance is written off over a 25 year period. However, if within that time you sell or demolish the building, you have the right to elect for a balancing allowance or charge to be made. This election must be made within two years after the end of the relevant year of assessment.

Where the expenditure is on a farmhouse, the maximum allowance is generally limited to one-third of the total cost to take account of personal benefit. Expenditure on forestry buildings normally only attracts writing down allowance prior to 20 June 1989. However, transitional relief is available until 5 April 1993 in certain cases.

2.33 Hotel buildings

Prior to 1 April 1986, there was an initial allowance of 20% on the cost of constructing or improving certain hotel buildings. Also, in every year there was a 4% writing down allowance based on the original cost. Subsequently, only the 4% writing down allowance applies. Special rates apply in enterprise zones (2.31). These include 100% initial allowance.

Among conditions for obtaining the allowance, the hotel must have at least ten bedrooms for letting to the public. Also breakfast, together with an evening meal must be offered as normal facilities. Furthermore, the hotel must be open for at least four months in the season, which extends from April to October inclusive.

2.34 Scientific research allowance

If you incur capital expenditure on scientific research for the purposes of your trade, this is wholly allowed in the year when it arises. Also, any revenue expenditure will be allowed as a charge against your taxable profits. This applies if it is related to your trade or is medical research concerning the welfare of your employees. After 31 March 1985, the 100% allowance does not apply to the cost of land and houses.

2.35 Patent rights (and know-how)

Expenditure which you incur after 31 March 1986 on patents for use in your business and 'know-how' obtains a 25% writing down allowance. Previous expenditure is treated differently, depending on whether it relates to patents or 'know-how'. However, costs in connection with creating and registering your own patents are treated as deductible revenue expenses in any event.

Expenditure prior to 1 April 1986 on patents obtained a writing down allowance of 1/17th of the expenditure for each of the 17 years starting with when you made the purchase. A sale may give rise to a balancing charge or allowance. However, where the proceeds exceed the original cost, you are assessed to income tax under Case VI of Schedule D on the excess, normally spread over six years or the remainder of the patent if less. Payments prior to 1 April 1986 to obtain 'know-how' for your business or profession carry a writing down allowance of 1/6th of the expenditure for each of the first six years.

Regarding 'know-how' used in your business which you sell, the proceeds are taxed as trading receipts. However, if you cease to trade within the six years, you are allowed to charge the balance of your 'know-how' expenditure against your profits in the final trading period.

2.36 Mines, oil wells and dredging

Expenditure after 31 March 1986 on dredging generally qualifies for a 4% writing down allowance on a straight line basis. Prior to that date, expenditure attracted an initial allowance of 15% as well as the 4% writing down allowance.

Expenditure before 1 April 1986 on mines and oil wells attracted initial and writing down allowances related to output, etc. Expenditure after that attracts a writing down allowance of 25% or 10%, depending on the type of expenditure involved. In general, pre-1 April 1986 balances qualify for the new reliefs.

2.37 Assured tenancies

Special relief is available for certain expenditure incurred before 1 April 1992 on acquisitions under contracts entered into before 15 March 1988. Writing down allowances are given on dwellings let on assured tenancies by bodies approved by the Secretary of State for the Environment under the Assured Tenancies Scheme. Only approved bodies obtain the allowance.

The expenditure on each house or flat qualifying for allowance is limited to £40,000 (£60,000 in Greater London). Regarding expenditure after 4 May 1983 (unless under existing contracts) only landlords which are companies qualify for the allowance.

2.38 Safety at sports grounds

If relief is not otherwise available, you can claim capital allowances at 25% on the reducing balance on certain safety expenditure at sports grounds. You must be trading and the grounds designated under the safety of Sports Grounds Act 1975. From 1 January 1989 this is extended to include 'regulated stands' (broadly providing covered accommodation for 500 or more spectators).

2.39 Security assets

Expenditure after 5 April 1989 on 'Security assets' may qualify for capital allowance (25% on reduicing balance). You must acquire the assets to meet a special threat to your personal security which arises by virtue to your trade or profession. Partnership and sole traders are covered by the rules.

2.40 Class IV National Insurance contributions

For 1985–86 and subsequent years, relief may be claimed for half of your Class IV contributions. Your total income is accordingly reduced. Further details of the contributions, which are payable if you are self-employed, are contained later in this chapter (2.51).

2.41 Earnings basis and cash basis

Where you carry on a trade, you will normally be taxed on an 'earnings basis'. Your sales for each accounts period will be included as they arise and not when you receive the money. Generally, sales arise when they are invoiced. However, in a retail shop, sales normally arise as customers pay at the till. Similarly, your expenses are deductible on an arising basis and the date of payment is irrelevant.

However, should you carry on a profession or vocation, the Revenue may tax you on a 'cash basis', by reference to the actual cash received, ignoring uncollected fees at the end of each accounts period. This basis is usually used for barristers. Other professions are generally required to prepare their opening accounts on an earnings basis, having the option of switching to a cash basis later. Expenses are generally calculated on an arising basis. However, in some small cases, the actual expense payments are used ignoring accruals.

2.42 Post-cessation receipts

Post-cessation receipts are amounts received relating to your trade, profession or vocation after it has permanently ceased. An example is where you receive a late fee payment that had not been included in your accounts because they were prepared on a cash basis or the fee was not included in your debtors. Post-cessation receipts are generally taxed under Case VI of Schedule D and treated as earned income. You cannot set off unrelieved losses and capital allowances from before your cessation. However, you can elect that any post-cessation receipts for the first six years after cessation should be added to your income from the business, on its last day of trading.

A special relief applies if you were born before 6 April 1917 and were in business on 18 March 1986. Only a fraction of your post-cessation receipts will be taxed, varying between 19/20ths and 5/20ths. The latter fraction applies if you were born before 6 April 1903. If you were born before 6 April 1904 the fraction is 6/20ths and so on.

2.43 Losses

Special rules apply where your adjusted results show a loss. If you have an adjusted deficit of income compared with expenditure for any year, then your assessment under Case I or Case II of Schedule D will be nil for the related tax year. For example, if your annual accounts run to 31 December and you make an adjusted loss of £10,000 for 1989, your 1990–91 assessment will be nil. The 1989 loss of £10,000 must be augmented by your 1990–91 capital allowances (say £2,000) and the resultant loss of £12,000 is available for relief. This is applied:

(a) First against your other income for the tax year in which you suffer the loss. (This income includes your business assessment on the profits for the year prior to the loss.)
(b) Then against your income for the following tax year.

Although the rules require you to apportion your loss to the actual tax years that span your accounts year, the Revenue normally allows you to allocate the loss for a given accounts year to the tax year in which it ends. (This does not apply to the first year of trading.) Thus the £12,000 loss for the year to 31 December 1989 is allocated to 1989–90, your relief being set against other income for 1989–90 and 1990–91.

You must follow a strict order of set-off. The loss is first set against your other earned income for the year and then against your unearned income, followed (up to 5 April 1990) by your wife's earned income and lastly her unearned income. This loss relief is given under TA

1988, s 380 and must be claimed within two years of the end of the tax year to which it relates, by election to your Inspector of Taxes. Should your loss not be completely relieved in this way, you can claim that the balance is carried forward and set against your future profits from the same trade, profession or vocation (TA 1988, s 385).

You are not allowed to carry a loss forward from one trade to another. Remember this, should you change businesses. However, a move to a nearby shop in the same trade may be in order.

Concerning your first year of assessment of a new business, pre-trading expenditure of a revenue nature augments your losses. This applies to individuals and partnerships concerning expenditure within five years before trading commences.

Loss relief is given before personal reliefs, etc which cannot be carried forward. This may result in allowances being lost through your income being absorbed by losses. To avoid this, carry the losses forward where possible, so that your allowances are not wasted.

Losses on certain disposals of unquoted shares in trading companies by the original subscribers (6.13) may qualify for income tax relief. Such losses take precedence over claims under s 380.

2.44 Example: Relief for losses

Jack Box made a loss of £20,000 in his business for the year to 31 December 1988 having made a profit of £6,000 for 1987. In 1989, his profit is £20,000. His only other income is taxed dividends (including tax credits) amounting to £5,000 for 1988–89, £5,500 for 1989–90 and £6,000 for 1990–91. Loss relief can be obtained by Jack as follows:

Jack's loss of £20,000 for the year to 31 December 1988 will be allocated to the year 1988–89 (2.43).

	£
1988–89 loss relief (s 380)	
(1) Against 1988–89 Schedule D Case I assessment	6,000
(2) Against 1988–89 dividends	5,000
	£11,000
1989–90 loss relief (s 380)	
Against 1989–90 dividends	£ 5,500
1990–91 loss relief (s 385)	
Against 1990–91 Schedule D Case I assessment	£ 3,500

(Case I assessment for 1990–91 becomes £20,000 − £3,500 = £16,500).

2.45 Loss in new business

A special relief is available where you carry on a business or profession personally or in partnership. The relief applies to any loss in your first year of assessment or any of the next three years. A written claim is needed within two years of the end of the year of assessment. The losses include capital allowances and certain pre-trading expenditure. They are set against your income for the three years of assessment prior to that in which the losses are made, taking the earliest first.

2.46 Terminal losses

You are able to obtain relief for a 'terminal loss'. This is an adjusted loss made in your last complete year of trading, where you have ceased to carry on a trade, profession or vocation. The relievable loss is augmented by your capital allowances apportioned to your last 12 months of trading. Your terminal losses are allowed against your business assessments for the three years prior to that in which you ceased to trade.

2.47 Farming

Carrying on farming or market gardening business in the UK is treated as carrying on a trade, assessable under Schedule D Case I (2.9). As well as the normal Schedule D Case I rules, some special ones apply, including the following:

(1) Should you have more than one farm, they will all be assessed as one business.
(2) Grants received under various Ministry of Agriculture, Fisheries and Food grant schemes are treated as either capital receipts or revenue receipts for tax purposes according to their nature. For example, field husbandry grants are revenue and grants concerning the reclamation of waste land are capital.
(3) Where deficiency payments are received from the Government in respect of certain crops, etc, by concession these are included in your taxable profits for the year when they are received, rather than when the crop is sold.
(4) A special *agricultural buildings allowance* is available (2.32).
(5) Livestock is normally treated for tax purposes as stock in trade. However, if you have any 'production herds', you can elect for the 'herd basis' to apply. 'Production herds' are those kept for the purpose of obtaining products from the living animal, such as milk, wool etc. A 'herd basis' election must be made within two years from the end of your first year of assessment. Where an election has been made, the initial cost of the herd is not charged against your profits, but capitalised with the cost of any

additional animals. You also capitalise the cost of rearing the additional animals to maturity. Sale proceeds are taxable and the cost of replacement animals is deducted from your taxable profits. Where you sell your entire herd, you are not taxed on the proceeds.

(6) Loss relief is restricted if you carry out 'hobby farming' without any reasonable expectation of profit. Generally, subject to certain relaxations, a restriction applies when you made your sixth consecutive annual loss, so that you are no longer allowed relief against your other income. However, you are still able to carry your unrelieved farming losses forward to set against future farm profits.

(7) Where your farming profits fluctuate, relief is available. This applies to partnerships as well as individuals. You average the profits of any pair of consecutive years of assessment, provided you make a claim to this effect within two years of the end of the second year. If the taxable profits for either year are later adjusted, the original claim is set aside but a new one can be made by the end of the tax year following that in which the adjustment is made. Averaging is only allowed where the profits for the lower year are no more than 70% of the profits for the better year. (Limited spreading is allowed if the lower profits are between 70% and 75% of the higher ones.) If a loss is made, for the purposes of the spreading rules, the profits are treated as nil and the loss relieved as usual.

2.48 Sub-contractors

Should you be an independent or self-employed contractor (not engaged under a contract of employment), you will be taxed under Schedule D Case I and not Schedule E. Generally, this should prove advantageous since you will be able to deduct various expenses such as travelling from your home or other base of operations to the site, etc where you are working. Special rules apply to payments made by a building contractor, etc to a sub-contractor concerning building and construction work. These extend to non-building firms whose average annual construction expenditure on a three-year basis exceeds £250,000.

The contractor must deduct tax at 25% from each payment made to the sub-contractors who work for him, unless they have exemption certificates. (Before 1 November 1988 the percentage deduction was 27%). This tax must be paid over to the Revenue. When the sub-contractors prepare their own accounts under Schedule D Case I, they are credited with the tax already paid.

As a sub-contractor in the building trade, you are able to apply for an exemption certificate from your Inspector of Taxes. Requirements include having a regular place of business in this country and having been employed (or undergoing full time education or training) or being in business in the UK, making full tax returns for the three years up to the application.

2.49 Authors' copyright sales and royalties

Where patent royalties are paid to individuals, basic rate income tax (25%) is generally deducted. However, copyright royalty payments to authors, etc are made gross without the deduction of income tax. If you receive such amounts as an author or composer, then your royalties will normally be taxed under Schedule D Case II as part of your professional earnings (2.9). Otherwise, the royalties may be assessed under Schedule D Case VI.

Any sum that you receive for assigning the copyright in the whole or part of a work is taxable by reference to the tax year or accounting period when received. However, a spreading election can normally be made to the Revenue, as follows:

(1) Spreading depends on the time that you took to prepare the work of art. If this was more than 12 but less than 24 months, half of your proceeds is taxed as if received when paid to you and the other half one year earlier. If the preparation time was more than 24 months, you are taxed on 1/3rd of the proceeds as if received when paid to you, 1/3rd as if received one year earlier and the remainder one year earlier still.
(2) Where you assign the copyright of an established work not less than ten years after its first publication, you can spread any lump sum received. This relief also applies where you grant an interest in the work for a period of at least two years, and the sum which you receive may be spread over the lesser of six years or the duration of the grant or licence.

2.50 The assessment and payment mechanism

Detailed coverage of how your income tax is assessed is included in the *Allied Dunbar Tax Guide*. In general, assessment will follow the submission of your income tax return, business accounts and tax computations. You have the right to appeal against an assessment within 30 days of its issue, or longer in special circumstances.

The due date for paying income tax is normally 1 January in the year of assessment (ie tax for 1990–91 is payable on 1 January 1991). However, income tax assessments under Schedule D Case I and II on your business and professional income are payable in equal instalments on 1 January

Tax on business income 37

in the year of assessment and the following 1 July, as is Class 4 National Insurance (2.48). Higher rate income tax on your 'taxed investment income' is payable on 1 December following the year of assessment. (If an assessment is issued later than 30 days before the above dates, the tax payment date is normally 30 days after the assessment is issued.)

Interest is payable on overdue tax at $12\frac{1}{4}\%$ from 6 July 1989 (for earlier interest rates see 4.6). However, the Inland Revenue normally excuse you interest if it is less than £30 in total for one assessment. (This figure is subject to future updating). If you obtain an income tax overpayment, you may qualify for a repayment supplement (4.6).

2.51 Class 4 National Insurance

As a person who is self-employed or otherwise liable to Schedule D income tax under Cases I and II you may be charged an earnings related amount under Class 4. This is in addition to your normal flat-rate Class 2 (self-employed) contributions (£4.25 per week for 1989–90 — see 9.29). The following should be noted:

(1) The contribution rate for 1989–90 is 6.3% which applies to your Cases I and II income between £5,050 and £16,900. The maximum is thus 6.3% × £11,850 = £746.55.
(2) The rate for 1988–89 was 6.3 per cent, which applied to the income between £4,750 and £15,860.
(3) Class 4 is payable on your Schedule D assessments under Cases I and II for the tax year, after capital allowances, but with no deduction for personal allowances, pension contributions etc. Your share of partnership income is thus included.
(4) If your wife has self-employed earnings, these are also charged to Class 4 as if her earnings were separate from yours.
(5) Class 4 does not apply to men over 65 at the end of the previous year of assessment and women then over 60.
(6) Your contributions for each year of assessment are normally collected through your Case I or II Schedule D income tax assessment. Thus it is payable in two instalments.
(7) It is possible to defer your Class 4 payments in certain cases, such as where you also pay Class 1 contributions.
(8) Class 4 only applies if you are UK resident.

3 Partnership taxation

3.1 Introduction

The simplest form in which you can carry on a trade or profession is as a sole trader. However, your business may grow and you may wish to take in others as partners. A particular example would be your husband or wife, when tax advantages are likely (3.10). It is also possible that several individuals commence trading in partnership at the outset. Regardless of the circumstances, special tax rules apply to partnerships and these are considered below.

3.2 Partnership defined

Partnership is the relationship which exists between two persons carrying on business together with the object of making profits (5.90). It is not necessary to have a written partnership agreement. However, the partnership must exist in fact and if none actually operates, a written agreement would not make the partnership exist.

The Revenue will seek to establish whether a partnership actually exists. Particular points to consider include:

(1) The existence of a written partnership agreement.
(2) Whether the partners' names appear on business stationery.
(3) The arrangements existing for dividing the profits; also the assets on dissolution.
(4) Whether the partners can close down the business.
(5) Whether or not the partners are personally liable for the debts.

3.3 The taxation of partnership income

The partnership profits are adjusted in accordance with the rules which apply to businesses (2.9). A joint assessment to income tax is then made under Case I or Case II of Schedule D on the partners in respect of the adjusted partnership profits. The assessment covers both basic rate (25%) and higher rate (if any). The rules as for individuals are generally followed in respect of the opening years (2.13), closing years (2.15) and capital allowances (2.19). Special rules apply concerning partnership changes (3.6). Each year, a joint return must be made for the partnership, normally by the senior partner.

If any investment income has been included in the partnership accounts, this must be split between the partners in their profit-sharing ratios but it does not form part of the trading profits. The partners personally pay any income tax arising.

When the partnership trading or professional income has been determined, it must be split between the partners according to the way in which they share profits during the tax year. This provides the split of the Schedule D Case I or Case II assessments.

It should be noted that the proportions in which the assessments are split between the partners are not always the same as the profit sharing ratios for the year when the profits were made.

For example, if Jack and Jill are in partnership and make £20,000 in the year to 30 April 1989, when they split profits three to two, their partnership assessment for 1990/91, which is on the preceding year basis, is £20,000. This is split in the ratio in which they divide profits for the year to 5 April 1991. If the ratio is altered so that they divide profits equally from 1 May 1989, they will each be assessed on £10,000 for 1990/91.

Where a partner is remunerated partly by salary and partly by a profit share, the salary is not normally assessed under Schedule E. It is included in the profit share assessable under Schedule D Case I or Case II. Similarly, interest paid to partners on their capital is also treated as part of the profit shares and assessed under Schedule D, Case I or II. This interest is not an annual payment and it is not taxed as investment income.

3.4 Example: Partnership assessments

Jack, Jill and George trade in partnership sharing profits equally after the interest and salary allocations shown below. They prepare accounts to 5 April showing the following:

		Interest		Salary	
	Profits	Jack	Jill	Jill	George
5 April 1990	£16,000	£500	£500	£1,000	£2,000
1991	£20,000	£400	£600	£2,000	£2,000

The 1990-91 assessment under Schedule D Case I is as follows:

			TOTAL £	Jack £	Jill £	George £
Net profit (preceding year) — year ended 5 April 1990			16,000			
Add:	Interest	Jack	500			
		Jill	500			
	Salary	Jill	1,000			
		George	2,000			
			£20,000			
Less:	Interest	Jack	400	400		
		Jill	600		600	
	Salary	Jill	2,000		2,000	
		George	2,000			2,000
			5,000			
Balance split equally			15,000	5,000	5,000	5,000
Total assessment			£20,000	£5,400	£7,600	£7,000

Notes:

(1) In addition to the above, the normal Schedule D Case I adjustments must be made.
(2) The interest and salaries for the year to 5 April 1990 are added back to the profits.
(3) The 1990-91 assessments split includes the interest and salaries for the year to 5 April 1991

3.5 Losses

Where in any accounting period a partnership has an adjusted loss, this is split between the partners in the same proportions as a profit would have been. This means that the loss is split in the profit sharing ratios applicable to the year of assessment corresponding to the tax year when the loss is made. Thus, a loss made in the year to 5 April 1990 is split between the partners in their profit sharing ratios for 1990-91 (assuming that the preceding year basis of assessment is applicable).

Each partner is free to use his losses as he chooses, according to the rules. He can thus claim for his partnership loss to be relieved against his other income tax assessments for the year of assessment in which the loss is actually made or the following year. As a result, relief can be obtained against the previous year's partnership profits. (This applies even if the partnership had been treated as discontinued, because of a partnership change.)

You may be a limited partner, in which case your risk is generally limited to the capital which you have invested. Losses arising to limited partners after 19 March 1985 are broadly restricted to the capital which they have invested.

3.6 Changes of partners

Subject to a continuation election, which is described below (3.7), if there is any change in the make-up of a partnership, it is treated as ceasing for taxation purposes. Such changes include where a partner leaves or dies or a fresh partner joins.

A cessation caused by a change of partners has similar effects to any other Schedule D Case I or Case II cessation (2.15). The assessment for the final year is based on the actual profits. Furthermore, the Revenue have the option to increase the assessments for the two previous years to the actual profits for those years.

For changes after 19 March 1985, the first four years are assessed on an actual basis. The previous year basis then applies unless you elect for years five and six to be on an actual basis. This is subject to a continuation election (3.7).

3.7 Continuation election

Where there is a change in the members of a partnership, the old partnership is normally treated as having ceased to trade and the new one as having just started. However, within two years of the change, an election can be made to the Inland Revenue (under TA 1988, s 113) that the partnership should be taxed on a continuation basis. This election, which is often made, needs to be signed by all of the partners in both the old and new partnerships. Another requirement is that at least one of the partners (not being a company) in the old partnership remains as a partner in the new one.

As a result of the election, the partnership is not treated as ceasing for tax purposes at the date of the change. What happens is that the Schedule D Case I or Case II assessment for the tax year when the change takes place is apportioned up to the change. Thus, the old partners are assessed on their share of the assessment apportioned up to the change. Similarly, the new partners are assessed on the proportion after the change.

3.8 Overseas partnerships

Special rules apply concerning partnerships which are treated for tax purposes as being non-resident. This happens if you are in partnership carrying on a trade or business and the control and management is

Partnership taxation

outside the UK. The partnership is then regarded as being non-resident, even if you or some of your other partners are resident here and some of the business is carried on in this country.

Where a partnership is non-UK resident, any profits arising from its trade or business in this country are assessed here under Schedule D Case I, in the name of any partner resident in the UK. Partnership profits earned abroad are assessable on the partners resident in the UK, in respect of their profit shares, according to the special rules concerning Schedule D Case V. In general, this applies even where, under a double tax agreement, the profits arising abroad are exempt from UK tax.

3.9 Partnership capital gains

The assets of a partnership are regarded as being owned by the partners. Thus, when an asset is sold in circumstances that would have given rise to capital gains tax, had it been owned by an individual, this tax is assessed on the partners according to their shares in the assets. For example, if a capital gain of £15,000 is made from the sale of a partnership property on 1 January 1990 and Tom, Dick and Harry share equally in all the partnership assets, a capital gain of £5,000 must be included in the capital gains tax assessments for 1989–90 for each of them.

If a partnership share changes hands, a share in all of the assets is treated for capital gains tax purposes as also changing ownership. This might give rise to capital gains or losses for any partner disposing of his share. For example, if Tom, Dick and Harry are equal partners and Tom sells his partnership share to Jim, Tom is regarded for capital gains tax purposes as disposing of a one-third share in each partnership asset to Jim. However, in certain circumstances, concessional Inland Revenue treatment introduced in 1975 (SP/D12) may apply. (Various concessions were introduced at that time, concerning partnership capital gains tax, which are considered beyond the scope of this book.)

3.10 Husband and wife partnerships

For the sake of convenience, this section reflects a husband taking in his wife as a partner. However, the reverse may well take place.

If you are in business, it is beneficial from a tax point of view to employ your wife. However, it is necessary that she performs sufficient work to justify the salary which she is paid. Otherwise, the Revenue may seek to disallow part or all of her salary as a deduction from your taxable business profits.

44 Allied Dunbar Business Tax and Law Guide

It is particularly beneficial for your wife to receive earned income, so that she obtains the benefit of the wife's earned income allowance (maximum £2,785). Of course, if she already has another job, this allowance would normally be absorbed in any event.

If her work for you justifies a larger salary and particularly if she also has other sources of earned income, an election for the separate taxation of her earnings will be worthwhile. This will involve your losing your married man's allowance. You will each obtain the single allowance, however, and the election is normally worthwhile for 1989–90 if your combined incomes total £30,511 of which your wife's earned income is £7,026. The higher the incomes, the greater the savings, which are brought about because your wife's earned income is subjected to a separate set of tax rates, so that she has £20,700 at the 25% basic rate and so on. (From 6 April 1990, the income of husband and wife will be taxed separately in any event.)

In order to make the most of the wife's earnings election, the wife should have as large an earned income as possible. However, as mentioned above, it may be difficult to demonstrate that she does sufficient work to support this. In these circumstances, it is most helpful if she is a partner. Provided that she can be shown to take part in the management of the partnership, it will not be necessary that she works full-time. There should be a properly drawn partnership deed, stipulating her share in the capital and revenue profits and losses (3.2).

In general, the level of the wife's National Insurance contributions will be diminished if she is a partner. As an employee, she will be liable to pay her own contributions and the employers will do likewise. However, as a partner, she will be responsible for paying her own Class 2 and Class 4 contributions, whilst half of the latter will be deductible for Schedule D income tax purposes.

3.11 Example: Husband and wife partnership

Jack and Jill are husband and wife. Jack is in business as a sole trader and his assessable profit for 1989–90 is £38,000 after paying a salary of £2,000 to Jill for limited assistance. The following illustrates (a) the income tax and (b) the National Insurance contribution effects if instead Jill is an equal partner and an election for the separate taxation of her earnings is made.

(a) *Income Tax 1989–90*

	Jack – Sole Trader		Jack and Jill Partnership	
	Jack	Jill	Jack	Jill
	£	£	£	£
Earnings	38,000	2,000	20,000	20,000

Partnership taxation

	£	£	£	£
Less: 50% Class IV Contributions (below)	374		374	374
	37,626	2,000	19,626	19,626
Personal allowances:				
Married	4,375			
Wife's earnings		2,000		
Single			2,785	2,785
	£33,251	Nil	£16,841	£16,841

Income Tax	£		£	£
20,700 at 25%	5,175.00		4,210.25	4,210.25
12,551 at 40%	5,020.40			
£33,251	£10,195.40		£4,210.25	£4,210.25
				£8,420.50
INCOME TAX SAVING				£1,774.90

Note: When Jack employs Jill at a salary of only £2,000, an election for the separate taxation of her earnings is not beneficial. However, that level is below the National Insurance contributions threshold of £43 per week.

(b) *National Insurance contributions 1989-90*

	Jack – Sole Trader		Jack and Jill Partnership	
	Jack	Jill	Jack	Jill
	£	£	£	£
Class 1		Nil		
Class 2	221.00		221.00	221.00
Class 4 (maximum)	746.55		746.55	746.55
	£967.55		£967.55	£967.55

Additional contributions payable by Jill as a partner	£ 967.55
Saving in income tax as in (a) above	£1,774.90
Net saving	£807.35

Note: If instead of being a partner, Jill is employed by Jack at £20,000 per annum, an election for the separate taxation of her earnings will produce commensurate income tax savings. However, she will need to work full-time and demonstrate that her services are of special value. Otherwise, the Revenue may seek to restrict the deduction from Jack's taxable profits.

The National Insurance contributions for Jill will be far higher. Assuming she has not 'contracted out', she will pay 9% on £325 per week as an employee

46 Allied Dunbar Business Tax and Law Guide

under Class 1 for 26 weeks and then, from 4 October 1989, 2% on £43 and 9% on £282 for the remaining 26 weeks. This makes £1,442.74. At the same time, Jack as employer will pay 10.45% on £20,000, making £2,090. However, £2,090 will be deductible from his taxable profits and so his income tax bill in this example will be reduced by £2,090 at 25% = £522.50. Thus the partnership route is significantly better regarding National Insurance contribution levels.

4 The taxation of companies

4.1 Introduction

Unlike individuals and partnerships, companies are taxed separately from their owners. In other words, whilst partners pay income tax on the profits made by their partnership, in the case of a company the shareholders or directors generally only pay tax on their dividends or remuneration. The company itself pays corporation tax on its profits.

4.2 Corporation tax

All the income assessable on a company for a year is subject to corporation tax, at the present rate of 35%. This rate is reduced if the taxable profits are less than £750,000 (less if there are associated companies — see 4.4). Profits for corporation tax purposes include capital gains. (Before 17 March 1987, only a fixed fraction of a company's capital gain was liable to corporation tax.)

Corporation tax is charged on a company's actual income assessable for each accounting period (4.5), according to the rules of the various cases of Schedule D (2.2) and other applicable Schedules. The corporation tax rate is fixed by Parliament in the Finance Act each year, for the preceding 'financial year'. Such a year commences on 1 April so that the financial year 1989 is the year to 31 March 1990. The 35% rate has applied since 1 April 1986, prior to which it was 40% for one year, 45% for one year, 50% for one year and 52% back to 1973.

4.3 Small companies rate

A special reduced corporation tax rate called 'small companies rate' is charged on company profits not exceeding certain limits. For the purposes of these limits, both profits on which corporation tax is to be paid, and 'franked investment income' (4.9) must be taken. The rate has recently moved in line with the basic rate of income tax and is 25% from 1 April 1988, having been 27% for the previous year and 29% for the year before that.

Small companies rate of 25% is charged on the profits of a company, provided these do not exceed £150,000 and there are no 'associated companies' (4.4). Where profits are between £150,000 and £750,000, marginal relief is available. The tax is then broadly the full 35% corporation tax rate on the profits, less a fixed fraction of the amount by which they fall short of £750,000. The fraction was 3/200 for financial year 1986 1/50 for financial year 1987 and 1/40 for 1988 and 1989. This means that for 1989, there is a marginal rate of 37.5% which applies within the £150,000–£750,000 profit range, assuming that there are no 'associated companies' (see below).

The figures of £150,000 and £750,000 mentioned above must be divided by one plus the number of 'associated companies' connected with the company in question. For example, if three associated companies comprise a group, they will each pay 25% corporation tax on their profits for the year to 31 March 1990, if these are no more than £50,000 (£150,000/3) each. Where any of those companies have profits between £50,000 and £250,000 (£750,000/3), marginal relief is obtained.

The limits of £150,000 and £750,000 apply for the financial year 1989 (ending 31 March 1990). For prior years, lower figures have applied, being £100,000 and £500,000 most recently. Small companies rate does not apply to close investment holding companies (4.26) for chargeable accounting periods beginning after 31 March 1989.

4.4 Associated companies

Associated companies are those which are under common control or where one controls the other. Control broadly means voting power or being entitled to the greater part of the profits or of the assets on liquidation.

For the purposes of common control, the shares held by husband, wife and minor children are considered as one. However, if you control one company and a more distant relative, such as your brother, controls another, the two companies are not generally regarded as being 'associated' unless there is a large amount of inter-company trading.

4.5 Accounting periods and payment dates

Profits for corporation tax purposes are computed for 'accounting periods'. Such periods normally coincide with those for which a company draws up its annual accounts. However, 'an accounting period' must not be longer than 12 months in length. Where accounts are prepared for a longer period, of say 18 months, the first 12 months constitute one accounting period. The other six months are regarded as a second accounting period.

The normal payment date for corporation tax is nine months from the end of an accounting period or, if later, 30 days from when the assessment is issued. However, where a company traded before April 1965, there may have been a longer interval between the tax due date and the company's accounting date.

The rules for companies formed before April 1965 were changed for accounting periods starting after 16 March 1987. After a three year transitional period, corporation tax will be payable nine months after the end of each accounting period. The payment interval during the transitional period will be reduced to nine months in three equal stages. Thus, a company with a payment interval of 21 months and an accounting period ending 31 March has successive payment dates as follows:

Accounting period	Payment interval	Payment date
1.4.86–31.3.87	21 months	1.1.89
1.4.87–31.3.88	17 months	1.9.89
1.4.88–31.3.89	13 months	1.5.90
1.4.89–31.3.90	9 months	1.1.91

Under new rules resulting from proposals by the Keith Committee, which are to take effect no earlier than 1993, a 'pay and file system' will operate. This will involve companies paying corporation tax nine months after their accounting dates, whether or not assessments have been raised. Accounts will be required to be submitted to the Revenue within 12 months of the accounting date, otherwise, penalties will be charged where there is no excuse. Tax paid late or repaid by the Revenue will carry interest from the required payment date.

4.6 Interest and repayment supplement

If corporation tax is not paid when it is due, interest may be charged at $12\frac{1}{4}\%$ (from 6 July 1989). If, however, you appeal and obtain a postponement (ie permission to hold over some of the tax), interest on that part may not be payable until 15 months after the end of the accounts period.

If your company receives a tax repayment more than a year from when corporation tax is due for the accounting period, a repayment supplement generally arises. The tax-free repayment supplement is calculated from one year after the due date for paying the corporation tax until 'the tax month' in which the repayment is made. 'The tax month' ends on the fifth day of the following month. The interest rates for repayment supplements are the same as those payable on overdue tax and recently have been as follows:

From	Rate %
6 April 1987	9
6 June 1987	8¼
6 September 1987	9
6 December 1987	8¼
6 May 1988	7¾
6 August 1988	9¾
6 October 1988	10¾
6 January 1989	11½
6 July 1989	12¼

4.7 The imputation system

The present system of corporation tax is known as 'The Imputation System'. This is because shareholders are imputed with tax of currently 25/75ths of their dividends. Thus, as a shareholder, you would normally obtain a tax credit of this amount and are only liable for tax at the higher rate if applicable. When a company pays dividends, these are paid gross to the shareholders and tax of 25/75ths of the dividend is paid over to the Inland Revenue. This is known as 'Advance Corporation Tax' (ACT). (The ACT rate was 27/73rds for 1987-88 and 29/71sts for 1986-87). The ACT can be deducted from the company's corporation tax bill.

As a UK shareholder, you obtain a tax credit of 25/75ths of your dividends, but pay higher rates on your dividends plus tax credits. For example, if you receive a dividend of £75, you are imputed with a tax credit of 25/75ths × £75 = £25. If your income is sufficiently high, you will pay higher rates of tax on £75 plus £25 = £100. However, the £25 tax credit will be deductible from your total tax bill.

4.8 ACT on dividends etc

Companies pay advance corporation tax (ACT) on their dividend payments and other 'qualifying distributions' (4.9). Prior to 5 April 1986, the rate was 3/7ths. For the year to 5 April 1987 it was 29/71sts and then 27/73rds. For 1988-89 and 1989-90 ACT is 25/75ths.

Companies must account to the Inland Revenue for ACT, normally on a 3-monthly basis to 31 March, 30 June, 30 September and 31 December. However, if the company accounting period does not end on one of those dates, the company must submit an additional return for the period from the end of the last quarter to the end of the accounting period.

ACT returns must include 'franked payments' (4.9), and 'franked investment income' (4.9) received, together with the amount of ACT payable and certain other details. In calculating the ACT due for payment, tax credits on receipts of 'franked investment income' during the period may be deducted.

4.9 Distributions and franked payments

Distributions are classified as being either qualifying or non-qualifying. *Qualifying distributions* are dividends and similar payments. *Non-qualifying distributions* are particular types of shares, carrying potential future claims on the company's profits etc. For example, bonus debentures or bonus redeemable shares would come within this category.

Qualifying distributions are subjected to ACT. However, no ACT is payable by a company in respect of non-qualifying distributions which it makes. As a shareholder, you would obtain no basic rate tax credit and would not be liable to the basic rate on the distribution. However, you would still be liable to the excess of your higher rate tax over the basic rate on the actual value of your non-qualifying distribution.

When a company makes a qualifying distribution this, together with the relevant ACT, is defined as a *'franked payment'*. For example a qualifying distribution of £7,500 carries with it ACT of £2,500 and together, they make up a franked payment of £10,000.

A similar term is *franked investment income*. This consists of income from a UK resident company comprising distributions in respect of which tax credits are obtained. A company's franked investment income is the amount including the tax credits. For example, a company receiving a dividend of £750 has franked investment income of £1,000 (£750 + £750 × 25/75).

4.10 Setting off ACT

ACT is a pre-payment of the 'mainstream' corporation tax bill of a company. The 'mainstream' tax is only ascertained when accounts are submitted to the Inland Revenue for each accounting period. At that stage, the full corporation tax is calculated and any ACT paid is set off. However, there is a limit to the amount of ACT which can be set off in this way. The limit is the ACT which would have been paid on a full distribution of the company's pre-tax profits, taking account of the notional ACT payable.

For example, if a company makes adjusted profits of £1 million before tax for the year to 31 March 1990, the maximum ACT set-off is £250,000. On a distribution of £750,000, ACT would be paid amounting to £750,000 × 25/75 = £250,000. As a result, the entire profits of the company would be absorbed. The mainstream corporation tax assessment would be £1,000,000 × 35% = £350,000, from which £250,000 ACT would be deducted, leaving a net amount payable of £100,000.

An important change concerning capital gains took effect from 17 March 1987. For accounting periods beginning on or after that date, but not earlier, ACT may be set off against corporation tax on capital gains (4.17). For accounting periods straddling 17 March 1987, only tax on gains after that date qualifies for set-off.

4.11 Surplus ACT

ACT which is not relieved against the corporation tax payable for the accounting period when the relevant distribution is made because of the restriction rules (see above) is known as 'surplus ACT'. This can be carried back and set off against corporation tax payable for any accounting period beginning in the six years preceding that in which the distribution is made. To make this set-off, you must make a claim within two years of the end of the period for which the surplus ACT arises. The surplus ACT will then be allocated to one or more earlier periods (starting with the latest), resulting in a reduction in corporation tax payable or a repayment. Surplus ACT not carried back may be carried forward indefinitely, for setting off against future corporation tax payable.

4.12 Computing the assessable profits

The income assessable under each schedule, as well as under each case of Schedule D, must be computed and aggregated with any capital gains, in order to find the total amount chargeable to corporation tax. However, all corporation tax assessments are made on an actual basis, instead of the preceding year basis that sometimes applies for income tax. The profits shown by the accounts will need adjusting in accordance with rules which follow, with some modifications, those applicable for income tax assessments (2.9). For example:

(1) Deduct any franked investment income.
(2) Add back payments for non-business purposes.
(3) Add back capital losses and payments. Deduct capital profits and capital receipts. Compute the capital gains less losses for the accounting period according to the capital gains tax rules (4.17).
(4) Add back business entertaining unless in connection with overseas customers or the company's own staff. (Gifts of advertising articles of less than £10 value to each customer are also allowable.)
(5) Add back depreciation and amortisation of fixed assets charged in the accounts.
(6) Adjust interest payable and receivable to the actual gross payments and receipts during the accounting period.
(7) Deduct capital allowances for the accounting period (4.13), adding back balancing charges and deducting balancing allowances.
(8) In some cases, notional income tax at the basic rate must be added to any building society interest received. This is calculated by multiplying the actual interest received by 25/75. The notional tax is then deducted from the total corporation tax payable.

4.13 Capital allowances

The capital allowances rules for businesses (2.17) apply to companies subject to certain special rules including the following:

(1) Where a company obtained first year allowance (2.20) in respect of capital expenditure, if this resulted in an adjusted corporation tax loss, the loss could be carried back and set against profits for the three preceding years. (Expenditure after 31 March 1986 generally no longer attracts first year allowance.)
(2) Where one company takes over all of the assets and business of another company, the former continues to receive exactly the same capital allowances on the assets transferred as the old company would have obtained. For this to apply, there must be a 'company reconstruction' without change of ownership. This takes place if at any time during the two years following the reconstruction, no less than 75% of the acquiring company belongs to the same people who owned no less than 75% of the old company.

4.14 Example: Corporation tax computation

Box Ltd has no associated companies and prepares its accounts to 31 March each year. Its pre-tax profits for the year to 31 March 1990 amount to £80,000 which includes a dividend of £800 received in December 1989 which comprises its only franked investment income for the year. Also included is a profit on asset sales of £10,000 in respect of which a chargeable gain (4.17) of £8,800 has been computed. The profit is after charging £6,000 depreciation. Capital allowances of £9,000 are due for the year. A dividend of £2,300 was paid for the year in December 1989.

Assuming no other taxation adjustments are required apart from those noted above, compute:

(a) The corporation tax liability of Box Ltd for the year to 31 March 1990.
(b) Its ACT liability.

Box Ltd

(a) Corporation tax computations—
Accounting period to 31 March 1990

	£	£
Profit per accounts		80,000
Add: Depreciation		6,000
		£86,000
Less: Franked investment income		
(excluding tax credit)	800	
Capital allowances	9,000	
Profit on asset sales	10,000	
		19,800
Schedule D Case I assessment		66,200
Chargeable gain		8,800
Assessable profits		£75,000
Corporation tax payable at 25%		
(small profits rate)		£18,750

(b) ACT liability

	£
Dividends paid	
December 1989	£2,300
Less: Dividends received	
December 1989	800
	£1,500
Net ACT due £1,500 × 25/75	£ 500

Note: ACT of £500 will normally be payable with the return for the three months to 31 December 1989 by 14 January 1990. The remainder of the corporation tax of £18,250 (£18,750 — £500) will normally be due on 1 January 1991.

4.15 Losses

Where a trading loss results for an accounting period of a company, after the necessary corporation tax adjustments, a repayment of the tax on an equal amount of the profits (of any description) for the previous accounting period is obtainable under TA 1988, s 393(2). Note that a loss for a period can only be set against a profit from a previous period of equal length. Thus, where a loss is made in a nine month period, it can only be set against profits for the previous nine months. The time limit for making claims to the Inland Revenue is within two years of the end of the accounting period of the loss.

As an alternative, tax credits on dividends can be reclaimed by offsetting trading losses.

For the above purposes, trading losses are effectively augmented by capital allowances and annual charges. Any unused balance is available for carrying forward to be set against trading profits for future years.

Where there is a 'company reconstruction without change of ownership' (4.13), so that one company takes over the trade and assets of another, any trading losses are carried over with the trade. This broadly applies where the two companies are under at least 75% common ownership. However, the unused tax losses may not be fully available if the original company is insolvent when the trade is transferred.

4.16 Terminal losses

Relief for terminal losses is available (under TA 1970, s 394) to a company in much the same way as for an individual ceasing to trade (2.43). A company is therefore able to make a claim to set off a loss incurred in its last 12 months of trading against the profits for the three prior years.

4.17 Capital gains and losses

From 17 March 1987 capital gains realised by companies are charged to corporation tax at the normal rates. Thus, if a company has £1 million profits, it will pay 35% corporation tax on its capital gains. However, a gain of £20,000 made by a company with say £50,000 other taxable profits carries the small companies corporation tax rate (25%) on the gain.

In any accounting period, capital losses may be offset against gains and only net gains are taxable. An accounting period straddling 17 March 1987 was regarded as being two separate accounting periods, one before and one starting on that date for capital gains purposes. Allowable capital losses in the second period could be carried back to set against gains in the first.

Gains realised before 17 March 1987 effectively were taxed at 30%. This was achieved by charging a fraction of the gain to corporation tax at the full rate. Thus, 6/7ths of capital gains were so charged for the period from 1 April 1986 to 16 March 1987.

Capital gains can be relieved by setting off capital losses in the same period or those brought forward from previous periods. Trading losses may be offset against capital profits of the same or the previous period. Capital profits can also be offset by group loss relief claims (4.19). However, note that trading losses brought forward from previous periods can only be set against future trading profits and not against future chargeable gains.

Where a company incurs capital losses, these can only be set against its capital gains for the same accounting period or a future one. However, unused capital losses can be carried forward to future years, even after the company ceases to trade. This contrasts with trading losses which can no longer be carried forward if a company ceases trading.

Normally, overseas companies are not liable to UK corporation tax on their capital gains realised abroad. However, under CGTA, s 15, any shareholders resident and domiciled in the UK can have capital gains apportioned to them if the overseas company would have been close (4.21) if it were resident in the UK. This also applies to UK beneficiaries of an overseas trust owning shares in an overseas company.

4.18 Groups of companies

A variety of special provisions relate to groups of companies, broadly parent and subsidiaries. A subsidiary company is classified according to the percentage of its ordinary capital owned directly or indirectly by its parent company. In particular, a 51% subsidiary is owned as to more than 50% by its parent and a 75% subsidiary is not less than 75% owned by its parent.

4.19 Group loss relief

In a group comprising a parent company and 75% subsidiaries, the trading losses (including capital allowances) of the group members can be offset by way of group relief against the profits of other group members. Points to watch include:

(1) A claim must be made to the Inland Revenue within two years of the end of the accounting period.
(2) For full relief, there must be a group relationship throughout the respective accounting periods of the loss-making and profit-making companies. Otherwise, profits and losses are apportioned on a time basis to the period during which the group relationship exists.
(3) Parent and subsidiaries must all be resident in the UK.
(4) The parent company must have at least a 75% interest in each of the subsidiaries, and be entitled to at least 75% of the distributable profits of each subsidiary and 75% of the assets available on liquidation.
(5) Group relief also applies to a consortium of UK companies which, subject to the rules, owns 75% or more of the loss-making company. No member of the consortium may own less than 5% and thus the maximum number of members is 20. In addition, losses made by consortium companies can be surrendered down to a company which is jointly owned.
(6) If a company joins or leaves a group during its accounting period, a time apportionment basis is normally applied in calculating group relief. However, this can be set aside if it operates unfairly. A 'just and reasonable method' is then used.
(7) No group relief is now available for the losses of dual-resident investment companies.

4.20 Groups — Other reliefs

As well as group loss relief (4.19) various other reliefs are available for groups of companies including the following:

(1) Dividend payments from 51% subsidiaries to their parent may be made without having to account for ACT. In fact there needs also to be a group relationship in an economic sense. A prior election to the Revenue is needed, however. A similar rule relates to inter-group interest payments. (In both cases, the companies must be resident in the UK.) Payments from a consortium-owned company to the consortium members are included, provided the consortium owns at least 75% of the ordinary shares.
(2) Subject to certain rules, a parent company can transfer to its subsidiary relief for ACT. Thus, if the parent pays a dividend of £7,500, it obtains £7,500 × 25/75 = £2,500 ACT relief. However, instead of taking this itself, it can surrender the relief to its subsidiary which then deducts £2,500 from its corporation tax bill. It is necessary for the parent company to hold more than 50% of the ordinary shares of the subsidiary and to be entitled to more than 50% of the distributable profits and more than 50% of the assets on liquidation. If the subsidiary ceases to be owned by the parent company, any unused ACT will be lost. However, after

13 March 1989, this does not apply if the companies remain in the same overall group.
(3) No capital gains tax generally arises where assets are transferred within a group consisting of a parent and its 75% subsidiaries (all UK resident). However, when the asset leaves the group, capital gains tax is paid on the entire chargeable gain whilst it was owned by any group company.
(4) Capital gains tax 'rollover relief' (6.24) applies to a UK group consisting of parent company and 75% subsidiaries. The gain on an asset arising to one trading company may be 'rolled over' against the purchase of an asset by another trading company in the group. For these purposes, property holding companies which hold assets used for trade by trading companies in the group are also included. New rules applying broadly from 14 March 1989 restrict schemes to reduce the tax on selling subsidiaries.

4.21 Close companies

Special rules relate to 'close' companies. These are broadly those under the control of five or fewer persons and their 'associates' (or the directors). The term 'associates' includes close family, such as husband, wife, father, mother, brother and sister. A quoted company is not 'close', however, if the general public own at least 35% of its voting shares.

A UK subsidiary of an overseas parent company is 'close' if the overseas parent would have been a close company itself if resident in the UK. Thus, most small or medium companies are likely to be 'close' companies unless they are subsidiaries of non-close companies. In particular, most 'family companies' are 'close'. Although the rules concerning close companies are not nearly as harsh as they were, it is still important to have regard to these provisions, some of which are noted below.

4.22 Apportionment of income

For periods beginning *before 1 April 1989*, the Revenue may apportion the excess of the 'relevant income' of a close company over its distributions for an accounting period among its shareholders. However, no apportionment will be made for a trading company or member of a trading group, if the excess is under £1,001. Furthermore, by concession, no apportionment is made for a property investment company whose excess is under £251. Also, an individual is exempt from apportionment if his or her share of the total apportionment amount is less than both 5% and £1,000. For accounting periods beginning after 31 March 1989, *apportionment no longer applies.*

The taxation of companies

'Relevant income' consists of not more than the company's 'distributable investment income' plus 50% of its estate (property) income (subject to abatement — 4.23) and in certain cases 50% of its trading income. 'Distributable investment income' is calculated after tax interest and dividends (without tax credits). Dividends from companies in the same group, known as group income, must be included. A deduction is made from the investment income of the lower of £3,000 and 10% of the company's trading and property income.

The trading income of a trading company or member of a trading group is excluded from its 'relevant income'. (This applies for periods ending after 26 March 1980). However, 50% of the property income is still included.

If a company can prove that it cannot distribute its 'relevant income' because the money is needed for business purposes, a reduction might be obtained by negotiation with the Revenue. Business purposes include expansion and the acquisition of a business as well as the repayment of loans originally obtained for these purposes. If, however, a property investment company spends its profits purchasing land or buildings (not farm or market garden improvements) this money is regarded as available for dividends and thus apportionable. However, income which cannot be legally distributed is excluded from apportionment.

If a company pays dividends within a reasonable time, these are set against the 'relevant income' in arriving at the amount to be apportioned. For these purposes, 'a reasonable time' is accepted by the Revenue to be not less than 18 months after the accounting period.

4.23 Abatement

In order to understand how abatement works, it is easier first to consider periods ending prior to 27 March 1980, when trading income for trading companies was liable to apportionment. However, if a close company had no 'associated companies' (4.4) the first £25,000 of the company's trading or property income after tax was not regarded as 'relevant income' (4.22). If such after-tax income was between £25,000 and £75,000, you reduced this income by half of the difference between it and £75,000. This is known as abatement.

Where a company had one or more 'associated companies' (4.4), excluding dormant and non-trading companies, the amounts of £25,000 and £75,000 were reduced by dividing them by one plus the number of 'associated companies'.

For periods ending after 26 March 1980, a proportionate amount of abatement can be obtained. The limits of £25,000 and £75,000 mentioned above must be reduced in the ratio of the estate income (ie property income) to estate and trading income. Thus, if a trading company (without associated companies) has trading income of £30,000 and estate income of £20,000 after tax, it obtains abatement of 1/2 (£75,000 × 2/5–£20,000) = £5,000. The rules for reducing abatement by reference to the number of 'associated companies' remain as previously.

4.24 Close companies — Loans and distributions

Where close companies make loans to their 'participators' or associates of 'participators' the companies are charged to tax at 25/75ths of the amounts. For example, if a company makes a loan of £7,500 to a participator, the company will be assessed to tax amounting to 25/75 × £7,500 = £2,500. This rule extends to loans by companies controlled by or subsequently acquired by close companies.

A 'participator' broadly means a person having a share or interest in the capital or income of a company. This includes, for example, a shareholder or loan creditor.

The tax is repaid when the loan is repaid to the company. However, the Revenue may assess loans even if they have been repaid, in which case a repayment would follow later. Where a close company lends money to a participator or his associate and then releases the debt, higher rate tax is assessed. This is based on the grossed-up equivalent of the loan. Thus in the above example, if the company releases the participator from his debt, he will pay higher rate tax on £10,000 but will deduct the basic rate tax of £2,500 from the amount which he pays.

In the case of close companies, the term 'distribution' is extended to include living expenses and accommodation, etc provided for a 'participator', unless taxed as a benefit (9.14).

Where a payment is treated as a distribution, it is not deductible from the taxable profits of the company. Furthermore, in the case of a 'qualifying distribution' (4.9) ACT is payable to the Revenue, although offsettable against 'mainstream' corporation tax.

4.25 Cessations and liquidations

Prior to 27 March 1980, if a close company ceased to trade, its distribution requirement included all of its trading and property income after abatement for its final chargeable accounting period and any other chargeable accounting periods ending within a year of the date of cessation. For subsequent periods, trading income is excluded from the distribution requirement but the rule still applies to property income. For accounting periods beginning after 31 March 1989 there is no distribution requirement, since the previous close company apportionment rules no longer apply.

4.26 Close investment holding companies (CICs)

New provisions have effect for accounting periods beginning after 31 March 1989 which impose harsher taxation on certain close investment holding companies (CICs). CICs will be subject to 35% corporation tax regardless of their level of profits. They do not obtain the benefit of the 25% small companies rate.

A CIC is a close company which is normally neither a 'trading company' nor a member of a trading group, nor a property investment company. Broadly, a trading company is one which exists wholly or mainly for the purpose of trading on a commercial basis. Dealing in property or shares does not cause a company to be a CIC. Similarly, mixed property dealing and investment companies are not CICs.

If a shareholder waives, or does not receive, a dividend, the extent to which someone else is entitled to be repaid a tax credit may be restricted. The Revenue may request information and make 'just and reasonable' restrictions in certain cases. Where a CIC takes out a life assurance policy after 13 March 1989, profits subsequently realised will be taxed, subject to the rules.

4.27 Non-resident companies

From 15 March 1988, a new rule for determining the residence of a company applies. Subject to transitional provisions (see below), a company which is incorporated in the UK is treated for tax purposes as being resident here. Prior to 15 March 1988, a company was deemed to be resident where its central control and management were carried out. This was not necessarily where the company was registered although normally the central control and management would be exercised in the country in which the company was registered. If, however, a company simply had its registered office here but carried on all its business from offices abroad and held its board meetings abroad, it was non-resident. Such companies will not come within the new rules for determining residence until 15 March 1993, provided they were already non-resident on 14 March 1988 or became non-resident later with Treasury consent. (In general, such companies must continue to carry on business.)

If a company registered abroad transacts some of its business in this country, it will not normally be treated as being UK resident provided its management and control are exercised abroad, which includes all board meetings being held abroad.

TA 1988 s 765 contains penal provisions to prevent a UK company from becoming non-resident without Treasury consent being obtained. Such consent is also required to transfer part or all of its business to a non-resident and for certain share transactions. From 15 March 1988, such consent is no longer needed (except for certain share transactions) and it is replaced by a tax charge on unrealised gains. Companies intending to emigrate must notify the Inland Revenue in advance providing an estimate of their UK tax commitments including tax on unrealised gains, and details of arrangements to settle such tax. If the tax is not paid, penalties may be charged. Furthermore, former directors and group companies can be held responsible for tax and interest.

Where a non-resident company trades in this country through a branch or agency, corporation tax is charged in respect of the profits of the branch or agency. However, if those profits are also subject to tax in the country of residence of the company, double tax relief might be available.

4.28 UK companies with overseas income

UK resident companies are subject to corporation tax on the gross amount of their overseas income, if any. However, double tax relief is frequently available where overseas income is taxed both in the UK and abroad. Special rules apply where a UK company receives a dividend from an overseas company from which tax at source has been deducted (withholding tax). The gross dividend is included in the taxable profits which are subject to corporation tax and, normally, double tax relief for the withholding tax suffered is given against the corporation tax payable.

If the company owns at least 10% of the voting capital of the overseas company, relief is given for the 'underlying tax' (the proportion of the total tax paid by the foreign company attributable to its dividends). The rate of double tax relief is limited to the UK corporation tax rate (35% etc).

4.29 Controlled foreign companies

Anti-avoidance rules enable the Revenue to impose extra tax on UK companies with interests in controlled foreign companies which are under overall UK control, subject to certain rules including the following:

(1) The overseas company must be subject to tax in its own country of less than half that payable if it were UK resident.
(2) The UK company (together with its associates) must have at least a 10% interest in the overseas company.
(3) The charge is excluded if there are acceptable dividend payments. (Only counted if made by a company which is not resident in the UK at the time of payment.) In broad terms, 50% of the available profits of a trading company are required to be paid as dividends and 90% for investment companies.
(4) The charge is excluded if the controlled foreign company satisfies an 'exempt activities' test. This involves having a business establishment where the company is resident and being managed there; also being broadly a trading company or qualifying holding company.
(5) Exclusion is also obtained through a motive test. Requirements are that the foreign company's transactions are carried out for commercial reasons and not for the main purpose of saving UK tax or diverting profits from the UK.
(6) Certain foreign companies quoted on foreign Stock Exchanges are excluded.
(7) No charge is made if the foreign company's profit for the year is less than £20,000.
(8) The profits of the overseas company are apportioned to any UK companies having at least a 10% interest and corporation tax is charged at the appropriate rate for each. A deduction from the UK tax is then made for an appropriate proportion of the overseas tax and relief is given where dividends are paid by the overseas company.
(9) Under the controlled foreign company rules, where a company is resident abroad, it is necessary to establish in which country. Broadly, it is regarded as resident in the country where it is liable to tax because of its domicile, residence or place of management.
(10) The Inland Revenue has published a list of excluded countries which will not be regarded as low tax countries for the purposes of the above rules. In general, the list excludes tax havens.

4.30 Demergers

Where two or more trading businesses are carried on either by a single company or in a group of companies, there are special rules to assist in splitting up those businesses. Subject to the detailed provisions, the demerger rules include the following:

(1) Where a company distributes to its shareholders shares in a 75% subsidiary (4.18) this is not treated as a distribution for tax purposes and so no ACT nor income tax arises for the company or its shareholders.
(2) Where one company transfers a trade to a second company which in turn distributes its shares to the shareholders of the first, relief is also available.
(3) Any distribution which you receive in the above circumstances is relieved from capital gains tax until you sell the actual shares.
(4) Anti-avoidance provisions apply to counter, for example, the extraction of tax-free cash from companies, subject to a procedure for advance clearance.

4.31 Unquoted company purchasing its own shares

Company law enables a company to purchase its own shares and issue redeemable equity shares in certain circumstances. If the proceeds exceed the original cost, the surplus would be a distribution and the company would pay ACT at 25/75ths on the excess. An individual receiving the payment would pay higher rate tax on the grossed-up excess less a tax credit. However, relief is provided in certain circumstances so that the company pays no ACT and the shareholder's liability is restricted to capital gains tax (unless he is a share-dealer, in which case the gain is treated as his income). Application for advance clearance may be made to the Revenue.

There are various conditions for relief. For example, the company cannot be quoted and must be a trading company or the holding company of a trading group. The purchase or redemption of the shares must be mainly to benefit the trade of the company or its 75% subsidiary. The shareholder selling back his shares must be UK resident and ordinarily resident, having normally owned the shares for at least five years, and if he keeps part of his shareholding, it must have been substantially reduced (broadly by at least 25%). Furthermore, after selling back his shares, the shareholder must not be 'connected' with the company, which means holding with 'associates' 30% of the shares, etc.

4.32 Business expansion scheme

The business expansion scheme (BES) provides a useful method for suitable companies to raise capital. At the same time, investments carry income tax relief. Thus, if your income is high, you should consider making appropriate BES investments.

The detailed rules are involved and beyond the scope of this book. However, particular points to note include the following:

(1) Both investment in new unquoted companies and the issue of shares by established unquoted trading companies satisfying certain conditions are included.
(2) The scheme excludes employees, paid directors and any shareholder owning more than 30%.
(3) Your maximum investment in BES schemes is limited to £40,000 in any tax year. The minimum investment in any company is £500 unless made through approved investment funds. You may now elect to carry back to the previous tax year part of your investment if made prior to 6 October. The carry-back is limited to half such investment or £5,000, if less. Your total relief for any tax year, including the amount carried back, may not exceed £40,000.
(4) In general, you must hold the shares on which relief has been claimed for at least five years.
(5) The relief does not normally reduce the cost for capital gains tax purposes and shares issued after 18 March 1986 are exempt from capital gains tax when first disposed of.
(6) Share capital issued in excess of £50,000 in total in any tax year does not qualify for relief if the company broadly has more than half the net value of its assets consisting of land and buildings.
(7) In order to issue shares under the business expansion scheme, the company must exist to carry on one or more *qualifying trades*. Such trades are, with some exceptions, broadly manufacturing, wholesale and retail business but not leasing and financial activities, etc.
(8) For BES shares issued after 15 March 1988, no more than £500,000 of capital raised by a company each year qualifies for relief. However, there is a £5,000,000 limit for ship chartering and assured tenancies (below).
(9) From 29 July 1988, BES relief extends to companies buying properties for letting under assured tenancies over at least a four-year period from when the BES shares are issued. Properties valued at over £125,000 in Greater London and £85,000 elsewhere are excluded.
(10) Tax relief for interest on loans to buy shares in a close company (2.6), issued after 13 March 1989, is not given if BES relief is available.

4.33 Deciding whether to incorporate

If you are trading successfully as a sole trader, or in partnership, you should consider seriously whether or not to incorporate. Trading as a limited company has various advantages compared with trading as a sole trader or partnership and also certain disadvantages, such as the need to disclose more about your business to the world at large.

The non-tax advantages and disadvantages, such as the protection afforded by limited liability are dealt with elsewhere (1.13). This section considers only the taxation and National Insurance contribution position.

If your business is not incorporated, you will pay income tax on the profits at the basic rate (25%) and possibly higher rate (40%). However, if you are incorporated, any profits which you retain in the company will normally bear corporation tax at the small companies rate of 25% or a higher rate, ranging up to the full corporation tax rate of 35%. If you are considering incorporation, it is likely that your profits are below the small companies rate limit (normally £150,000) and thus the company would pay no more than 25% corporation tax (4.3). This indicates a tax advantage for incorporation, if you are a sole trader with profits of say £35,000 and thus a top income tax rate of 40%. In particular, this will help you to accumulate money in the company, for development.

Once you have incorporated, you will probably become a director of the company and draw out money for your living expenses, by way of director's remuneration. To the extent that you do this, the income tax position will be the same as if you were not incorporated. However, a balance of income is likely to be left in the company where it will simply bear corporation tax. Furthermore, you may be able to regulate the salary which you take from the company, so that the income tax borne is at more moderate rates.

So far as the comparison between income tax on an unincorporated business and corporation tax on a company is concerned, the latter is generally more favourable. However, the position is counterbalanced to some extent by the extra burden of National Insurance contributions on the directors' remuneration, compared with the charge on sole traders and partners.

Directors' remuneration is charged to National Insurance contributions under Class 1 (9.30), whereas sole traders and partners pay contributions under Classes 2 and 4 (2.48). The latter cases carry a strictly limited charge but Class 1 involves substantial contributions for the employee and unlimited ones for the employer. The maximum employers' contribution is 10.45%. This is relieved for corporation tax purposes,

The taxation of companies

but the overall effect of National Insurance contributions on directors' remuneration is significant.

Another factor is the additional tax cost when accumulated money is withdrawn from a company. If this is done on liquidation, capital gains tax will be paid by the shareholders, subject to indexation. Thus, even though such tax may not be payable in the foreseeable future, the contingency should still be kept in mind.

Another way in which profits may be extracted, either in the year when they are earned or at a future time, is by way of dividend. This may increase the tax burden for shareholders liable to higher rate income tax. However, there is the advantage, compared with directors' remuneration, that no National Insurance contributions are payable.

Thus, it is apparent that evaluating whether or not to incorporate is highly complicated. Many facets need to be considered and it is difficult to give an exact level of profits at which incorporation is beneficial from a tax viewpoint. However, a sole trader earning at least £30,000 per annum and a two-man partnership earning over £60,000 may well gain tax advantages from incorporation. The following example illustrates the position.

4.34 Example: Saving tax by incorporating

Jack Box is single and carries on business as a sole trader. His assessable profits are £35,000. Assuming that he has no other income, his income tax liability and National Insurance contributions for 1989–90 would be:

	£	£
Assessable profits		£35,000
Less personal relief	2,785	
50% of Class 4 NHI contributions	374	3,159
		£31,841
Income tax 1989–90		
20,700 at 25%		5,175.00
11,141 at 40%		4,456.40
£31,841		9,631.40
National Insurance contributions		
Class 2		221.00
Class 4 (maximum)		746.55

Total income tax and National Insurance   £10,598.95

If Jack incorporates his business and makes the same profits in his company, his tax and National Insurance contributions are shown below, assuming he draws salaries of (a) £10,000 and (b) £20,000.

	£	£ (a)	£	£ (b)
Profits		35,000		35,000
Salary	10,000		20,000	
Employer's National Insurance	1,045	11,045	2,090	22,090
		£23,955		£12,910
Corporation tax 25%		£5,988.75		£3,227.50

Jack's income tax and National Insurance

	£		£	
Salary	10,000		20,000	
Less personal relief	2,785		2,785	
Income tax at 25%	£7,215	£1,803.75	£17,215	£4,303.75

	£		£
Class 1 National Insurance			
at 9% (part at 2%)		821.74 (maximum)	1,302.34
		£2,625.49	£5,606.09

Thus, a reduction in total tax and National Insurance contributions is obtained by Jack forming his business into a company, depending upon his salary level as follows:

	(a)	(b)
Salary	£10,000	£20,000
Income tax on salary	1,803.75	4,303.75
National Insurance — Jack	821.74	1,302.34
— Company	1,045.00	2,090.00
Corporation tax	5,988.75	3,227.50
	9,659.24	10,923.59
Total tax and National Insurance if not incorporated	10,598.95	10,598.95
SAVING (EXTRA COST)	£ 939.71	£ (324.64)

Notes:

(1) The savings tend to reduce as Jack increases his salary because higher income tax rates and extra National Insurance are encountered. In fact, there is no saving as his salary approaches £20,000.

(2) If Jack takes dividends instead of more salary, the extra National Insurance is saved. Thus the benefits of incorporation are enhanced. However, it is wise to have a sufficiently high salary to support a good pension scheme.
(3) Future capital tax liabilities must be kept in mind. Capital gains tax may arise on retained profits, whilst if dividends are paid, this may well increase the value of the company shares for inheritance tax purposes.

5 Company and partnership law

Part A Company law

5.1 Introduction

The following discussion is an outline of some of the main features of company law. It has to be selective and non-exhaustive because of the sheer size of the subject (CA 1985 alone (which is not the only relevant statute) runs to 747 sections). Of necessity, then, certain rules and concepts and detail generally are omitted from this chapter. Finally, as with partnership law (5.89) Scottish law has slightly different rules, on occasions, from those set out here. Northern Ireland legislation virtually mirrors legislation in Great Britain but by Order in Council and the legislation headings and numbering of provisions are usually different. Northern Ireland legislation is also not always enacted contemporaneously with Great Britain's legislation; sometimes there is a delay in enacting the relevant Order in Council (insolvency law reform being a recent example).

There can be various types of companies, those limited by shares (both public and private), those limited by guarantee and unlimited companies. In this chapter we discuss *limited* companies as this is usually the type of company adopted by businesses trading with a view of profit.

5.2 Public companies

A public company is defined as one which carries the name 'public limited company' or 'plc' or, if its registered office is in Wales, 'cwmni cyfyngedig cwhoeddus' ('ccc'), which has a minimum issued share capital of £50,000 (a quarter of which must be fully paid up) and which is otherwise subject to more stringent rules in CA 1985 concerning maintenance of capital and other procedures that do not apply to private companies.

5.3 Private companies

A private company is one which is not a public company. Also, no private company may apply for admission to the Stock Exchange Official List nor (unless falling within an order issued by the Secretary of State) may a private company issue an advertisement offering securities to be issued by that company. These rules, presently contained in the Financial Services Act 1986, are a restatement of the long standing principle that a private company should not be allowed to offer its shares to the public.

5.4 The de-regulation of private companies

The distinction between public and private companies is further illustrated by the de-regulatory proposals contained in the Companies Bill. These are potentially valuable for private companies and, if enacted, will introduce an elective regime designed to trim down the procedural requirements applicable in company law in certain areas. The principal measures whereby this is proposed to be achieved are as follows.

Private companies to be allowed to make decisions by written resolutions

A new section 381(A) will provide that anything which could be done by a resolution of the company in general meeting or by a resolution of a meeting of any class of members of the company may be done without a meeting, and without any previous notice being required, by a resolution in writing signed by or on behalf of all the members of the company who at the date of the resolution would be entitled to attend and vote at such meeting. This is discussed in more detail later in the text.

Private companies to be allowed to elect to dispense with certain procedural requirements

(1) Private companies will be allowed to elect (by elective resolution (defined later in the text)) that the provisions of CA 1985 section 80 (see below) may be modified, in that authority to directors to allot shares may be given for an indefinite period or, alternatively, for a fixed period as specified in the resolution. It is proposed that such authority may be revoked by the company in general meeting. Alternatively, it may be renewed. When renewed, it must state the amount of securities which may be allotted and whether the authority is renewed for an indefinite period or a fixed period. If an election ceases to have effect,

the authority then in force which was given for an indefinite period or a fixed period of more than five years expires forthwith if it was given five years or more before the election ceases to have effect. In any other case it takes effect as if it had been given for a fixed period of five years.

(2) A private company will be allowed to elect to dispense with annual general meetings (again by elective resolution). However, here, any member of the company may, by notice to the company not later than three months before the end of the year in which an annual general meeting would otherwise be held, require the holding of an annual general meeting in that year. If the election ceases to have effect, the company will not be obliged to hold its annual general meeting in that year if, when the election ceases to have effect, less than three months of the year remain.

(3) A private company will be allowed to elect (by elective resolution) that references to 95% of members of the company being required to consent to short notice of meetings may be read as not less than 90%.

(4) Private companies will be allowed to make an election to dispense with the laying of accounts and reports before the general meeting (again by elective resolution). This is without prejudice to the obligation to send out accounts and reports under section 238 of CA 1985.

However, it is proposed that before the end of the period of 28 days beginning with the day on which the accounts and reports were sent out in accordance with section 238, any member or auditor of the company will be able by notice in writing to require a general meeting to be held for the purpose of laying the accounts and reports before such meeting. If the directors do not within 21 days of deposit of such notice hold a meeting, the person sending the notice can convene a meeting. The notice of meeting must not purport to convene a meeting more than three months after the date of its notice.

(5) Private companies will also be able to elect to dispense with the requirement to appoint auditors annually.

Most of these proposals will be picked up again at appropriate points in the text but it seems appropriate to draw attention to this recent development when dealing with basic definitions. Part of the thrust behind the development arises from two White Papers published by the Government, *Lifting the Burden* (Cmnd 9571, July 1985, and *Building Businesses . . . Not Barriers* (Cmnd 9794, May 1986) which recommended a lifting of administrative burdens on smaller companies.

5.5 Company law in general

Much of this chapter is common to both public and private companies, although significant differences are highlighted where thought appropriate. It is beyond the scope of this book to discuss certain aspects of company law, such as mergers, takeovers and reconstructions of both private and public companies, securities regulation, Stock Exchange rules and specialised rules that apply to public companies only. Nor does this book give any detailed treatment of the Financial Services Act 1986 except as far as is directly relevant to the discussion of company law in this text.

5.6 Starting up

It is possible to commence formation of a company undertaking all of the procedural steps yourself (or, preferably through a skilled lawyer). But there is another method which is simpler. Companies are often started up by purchases of 'off the shelf' or 'ready made' companies. This means that instead of preparing all the formalities yourself, you, or your professional adviser, can contact a company registration agent who may have a number of 'ready made' or 'off the shelf' companies available for purchase. The registration agent will already have completed much of the formality necessary in setting up one of these companies. The following is a brief description of the procedures to be followed in any event.

5.7 Name

First, you have to choose a *name*. The rules here are set out in Part C at the end of this chapter. A 'ready made' company will already have a name. Undoubtedly this will be one not entirely of your own choosing, but it can be altered by special resolution later, or, alternatively, you can keep the name with which the company was registered on incorporation and trade under a different, business name. The rules applicable to that situation can be found in Part C.

5.8 Documents to be delivered

On incorporation you have to deliver to the Registrar of Companies a memorandum and articles of association, a statement of first directors and secretary, a notice of accounting reference date, a notification of registered office address and a statutory declaration of compliance with incorporation procedures. (see, in more detail, below). The fee for incorporation is currently £50.

In this chapter we refer to the use of certain forms. Mostly, certain types of form are prescribed for lodging information with the Registrar of Companies. These are laid down by the Companies (Forms) Regulations 1985 as amended by the Companies (Forms) (Amendment) Regulations 1986, the Companies (Forms) (Amendment) Regulations 1987 and the Companies (Forms) (Amendment) Regulations 1988. The Registrar may reject forms which do not comply with the rules. But you can get the forms from your professional adviser or from a law stationer.

5.9 Memorandum and articles of association

The memorandum and articles of association are the constitutional documents of the company.

The memorandum contains the following:

(a) the company name;
(b) the country in which the registered office is situated;
(c) the objects clause;
(d) a statement that the liability of the company is limited;
(e) a statement of the authorised share capital of the company.

The memorandum must be signed by each subscriber in the presence of at least one witness, who must attest the signatures.

The articles of association are more to do with internal regulation of members' rights and procedures which companies have to follow to make decisions and to manage their day-to-day affairs. They include provisions about meetings, appointment of directors, company secretary and auditors, sale of shares, borrowing powers, appointment of managing director and procedures for the removal of directors. A model form of articles is contained in Table A of the Companies (Tables A to F) Regulations 1985. If a company does not incorporate its own articles expressly it will, by default, incorporate those articles in Table A. These are suitable for most purposes but not all. In particular, they may not be suitable for small partnership or joint venture companies (see below). Special articles would, in that case, have to be drafted at the outset, or subsequently adopted by special resolution. Legal advice is necessary here. The legislator appears to have recognised the inadequacy of Table A as a universal set of rules by providing, in the Companies Bill, clause 121, that the Secretary of State may introduce regulations laying down a model set of articles (Table G) for a partnership company which may be adopted if so desired (the Bill defines a partnership company as one where shares are intended to be held to a substantial extent by or on behalf of employees — but it is to be stressed that, in our view, this is not the only situation where special articles are necessary and the definition of a partnership company in the Bill is far from comprehensive — so consideration of tailor made articles is still very important)

Most companies' articles adopt Table A for the main part but make some modification where some standard provisions of Table A are considered unsuitable for the particular company in question. A company adopts the Table A relevant to the legislation under which it was incorporated. If your company was incorporated under an earlier Companies Act its articles may be based on an earlier (and different) Table A, eg CA 1948, Sched 1, Table A. In this chapter, when we refer to Table A, the reference is to Table A under the 1985 Regulations. The articles must also be signed by the subscribers to the memorandum, as above.

The memorandum and articles will be discussed in more detail later in this chapter (5.28, 5.36).

5.10 Statement of first directors and secretary

Every company must have at least one director (and a public company must have at least two). It is common to have more directors than the legal minimum. In the case of a private company, if there is a sole director, that sole director cannot also be company secretary. A form (Form 10) must be signed by the intending directors/secretary showing their consent to act and this must be sent to the Companies Registry.

5.11 Subscribers' shares

As stated, the memorandum and the articles (see above) should be signed by the two subscribers whose signature must be attested by at least one witness. Subscribers automatically become members. With the abolition by the Finance Act 1988 of capital duty formerly payable on all shares issued in the amount of £1 per £100, there is no need to file Form PUC1, which was formerly required to be filed in respect of the initial subscribers' shares.

5.12 Accounting reference date

The company must send to the Registrar of Companies within six months of the date of incorporation a notice (on Form 224) of its accounting reference date, ie the date up to which its annual accounts are to be prepared. If it does not, the date of 31 March will automatically be fixed.

5.13 Registered office address

The company must send to the Registrar of Companies (on Form 10) a notice of its intended registered office address (not simply the country in which the address is situated).

Company and partnership law 77

5.14 Statutory declaration of compliance with procedures

There must be filed with the Registrar of Companies a statutory declaration sworn either by a solicitor engaged in the formation of the company or by a director or by a secretary that the provisions of the Companies Acts in relation to formation have been complied with. Form 12 is used.

5.15 Certificate of incorporation

Once all this has taken place and been approved, the Registrar of Companies will issue a certificate of incorporation. The company, if it is a private company, is then ready to trade. If the company is a public company it must also apply to the Registrar of Companies (using Form 117) for a certificate of compliance with the capital requirements of CA 1985 as applicable to public limited companies. Before then it may have been incorporated but it cannot trade.

5.16 Minimum membership requirement

It is important to bear in mind that the company must have a minimum of two members at all times. If a company carries on business without having at least two members for more than six months, the sole member, if he is aware of the fact that there is only one member, will be liable jointly and severally with the company for the company's debts thereafter. Reduction of the members below two will also give the court jurisdiction to wind the company up under the provisions of the Insolvency Act 1986.

5.17 First meeting of directors

The company will now have directors and a company secretary and may have issued shares to the original subscribers. These can be transferred to the real members of the company if, in fact, the original subscribers are merely members of the company registration agency and further shares can be issued to the members of the company if desired. If further shares are issued this is done usually at the first meeting of directors of the company which should take place after incorporation. Any further shares issued are recorded on Form 88(2) (replacing Form PUC 2) which is then sent to the Registrar of Companies.

Rules about directors' authority to issue shares and pre-emption rights relating to share issues referred to in the section on raising capital, below, should be observed. Capital duty is no longer payable on any shares issued following its abolition by the Finance Act 1988. The first meeting of directors should also deal with the appointment of solicitors and accountants, the appointment of additional directors, appointment of managing director, chairman of the company and any other business.

5.18 Suggested minutes of first directors' meeting

Note:
The following contemplates the formation of a company by three proprietors, Mr Black, Mr Brown and Mr White, each of whom is to have an equal shareholding, each of whom is to be a director and of which Mr White is to be secretary. The proprietors have bought a company off the shelf and have now received statutory books, a company seal, certificate of incorporation, resignation of the first secretary and first directors (who will usually be members of the company registration agency) and transfers of the two initial subscribers' shares from the company registration agents (Mr South and Mr North). A different procedure of course applies if the subscribers are not third parties and are intended to remain members, in which case, no transfer of subscribers' shares need take place. There is no need to *issue* initial shares to subscribers. On subscription they automatically become members of the company.

Ordinarily directors must have authority from the articles of association or from the General Meeting to allot shares (CA 1985 s 80 (see below)). In this case it is assumed that the articles of association have been drafted to include such an authorisation. If not, there has to be a company meeting authorising the directors to issue shares. Finally, if shares are to be issued to shareholders in differing proportions it should be ensured that the directors are empowered to ignore the pre-emption rights conferred by CA 1985, s 89 (see below) either by a pre-existing provision in the memorandum or articles (in a private company) or by special resolution. Note that the requirement to have a company seal becomes optional after the Companies Bill comes into force.

Suggested Precedent:

Company No. 0000

XYZ COMPANY LIMITED

Meeting of Directors held at 12 High Street, Newtown, Anywhere on the 1st day of December 1989

Present:
      Mr A Black

Mr B Brown
Mr C White

In Attendance:
Mr D Pink (of Litigators, solicitors)

(1) IT WAS RESOLVED that Mr Black be elected Chairman of the meeting.

(2) Mr Brown produced documentation, the formalities of which had been dealt with by the company registration agents, ie the Certificate of Incorporation No 0000 dated the 1st day of November 1989, the two transfers of the subscribers' shares, the notice of appointment of Messrs Black Brown and White as new directors and the resignation of first directors, the notice of resignation of the first secretary and appointment of Mr White as new secretary and resolution of change of registered office. It was noted that Form 287 and Form 288 concerning respectively the change in registered office and change in directors and secretary had been filed at the Companies Registry by the company registration agents on 20 November 1989.

Note: the changeover of officers will have been handled by the company registration agents while still competent to act as directors and members.

(3) IT WAS RESOLVED that Messrs Litigators be appointed solicitors to the Company.

(4) IT WAS RESOLVED that Messrs Abacus & Co be appointed auditors to the Company.

(5) IT WAS RESOLVED that the common seal of which an impression is made hereon be adopted as the common seal of the Company.

(6) IT WAS RESOLVED that Mid South Bank plc of 47 High Street Newtown be appointed bankers of the Company. Bank mandate forms were produced and completed, the appropriate resolutions required by the Bank passed, and the Company Secretary was instructed to remit them to the Bank.

(7) IT WAS RESOLVED that the following transfers of shares be approved and registered in the books of the Company:

(i) The transfer of 1 Share of £1 numbered 1 from Mr South to Mr Black
(ii) The transfer of 1 Share of £1 numbered 2 from Mr North to Mr Brown

(iii) that the sum of £1 on each such share be called up and paid forthwith by the respective transferees to the Company, and that the stock transfer forms be sent for stamping.

Note: It is required by CA 1985, s 182 (2) that shares be distinguished by numbers. But this can be dispensed with if all shares are fully paid up and rank *pari passu* for all purposes and remain so.

(8) IT WAS RESOLVED that Ordinary Shares of £1 each be allotted to the persons set out below and be payable forthwith in cash at par:

>   Mr Black   32 Shares
>   Mr Brown   32 Shares
>   Mr White   33 Shares

(9) IT WAS RESOLVED that the accounting reference date of the Company be fixed at 6 April and the Company Secretary be requested to arrange for the filing of Form 224.

(10) IT WAS RESOLVED that the Company Secretary be requested to arrange for the filing of the Return of Allotments (Form 88(2)) in respect of the allotments referred to in paragraph (8).

(11) IT WAS RESOLVED that the seal of the Company be affixed to the Certificates relating to the aforesaid shares when the Certificates were prepared by the Company Secretary and that such Certificates be handed over to the persons entitled thereto.

(12) There being no further business the meeting dissolved.

Approved this 10th day of December 1989

Mr A Black
Chairman

Note: The above is simply a guide. More business may be added if thought appropriate. It is essential that a director declares his interest in any contract with the company to the board as required by Table A, Article 85 (which allows such an interest provided disclosure takes place), otherwise the contract may be avoided and the director will be in breach of CA 1985, s 317 (discussed later in the text). A contract in which a director might be interested at this stage could include, for example, a sale or lease of property. Also the articles may prohibit such a director from voting on the contract and from being counted in the quorum present at the meeting (see Articles 94 and 95 of Table A) — although it is possible that the articles may allow this (Article 96). Finally, the articles should always be checked — if there is no article like Article 85 the contract will be voidable if the director takes an interest.

5.19 Capital structure, borrowing, and other questions

The following is a brief synopsis of how companies are structured. Also explained are a few expressions that are peculiar to company law.

5.20 Capital

We have seen that a company must state in its Memorandum that it has an *authorised* share capital of a certain amount. The *authorised* share capital is also often known as the *nominal* capital (the two expressions have the same meaning). The *authorised* or *nominal* capital is simply a figure of capital which the company may achieve by the issue of shares to that value if it wishes. Thus, if a company is registered with a nominal share capital of £5,000, this means that the company can, if it wishes, issue shares (commonly, these will be of £1 each) of a total value of £5,000. It does not mean that it *has* done so, nor is it obliged (if it is a private company) to do so beyond the issue of one share each to the two minimum members. The authorised share capital can be raised by ordinary resolution.

When a company does issue shares the value thereof is known as the *issued* or *allotted* share capital. As we have seen, a company can have as little as two members and, therefore, a company could have an issued share capital of as little as £2, assuming shares are of a par value of £1 each.

A further twist is that not all of the issued share capital (at least in a private company (contrast requirements in relation to a public company (5.2)) needs to be paid up. So issued share capital is not necessarily *paid up* share capital. Naturally, the company can make a call upon members to pay up what is outstanding on the share capital issued but, in the case of a private company, it does not have to do so. Shares can be issued for cash or non-cash consideration (eg property or a business). But in the latter case, where public companies are concerned, there are procedural rules about obtaining valuations or independent reports (except in relation to share exchanges and mergers).

5.21 Limited liability

A member's liability is limited to the amount paid up on shares issued to him or if unpaid, to the amount outstanding on those shares. This makes the limited liability company an extremely attractive proposition for the proprietors of a business. There is no liability beyond this for the company's debts unless specific rules either in legislation (5.87 and 5.104 for example) or, occasionally, under the general law (5.61) are broken. There is a fuller discussion of limited liability and its origin in chapter one.

However, with the capital requirement being so low in the case of private companies this can also lead to abuse. There are many instances of overtrading by under-capitalised companies with resulting hardship for creditors who do not get paid when those companies fold.

In practice though, the concept of limited liability in the case of small businesses can sometimes be illusory. A company without assets and capital may have difficulty in borrowing without personal guarantees being given by its directors. These may even have to be backed up by the security of their own homes to the bank. If such companies fold, the directors may stand to lose their personal assets notwithstanding the use of a limited company as a trading vehicle.

Finally, limited liability does not mean limited responsibility. The text will reveal how onerous, for example, certain statutory and common law rules about directors' duties can be. And, subject to certain de-regulatory measures proposed in the Companies Bill affecting private companies, there are a vast number of provisions in CA 1985 and elsewhere obliging companies to disclose to and file documents with the Registrar of Companies and to hold meetings and pass resolutions. Breach can give rise to criminal liability of officers of the company in default. The Department of Trade and Industry Annual Report *Companies in 1987–88* shows us there were, in the year ended 31 March 1988, 2,770 prosecutions of company officers and 1,574 convictions. Custodianship and management of companies must not be undertaken lightly.

5.22 Raising capital

A company ordinarily raises capital either by issuing shares in return for money paid by subscribers, or by borrowing. Some companies start up and fund themselves entirely by subscription for shares. It is also possible for companies to ask for further money to be injected into the company by shareholders at a later date. This is sometimes done by means of what is known as a *'rights issue'*, that is to say, an offer of shares giving an equal chance for all to participate in the issue of shares of the company pro rata to their existing shareholdings.

The power to issue shares has traditionally been vested in the board of directors, but under CA 1985, s 80 the power may not be exercised unless the board is authorised by the company in general meeting or by the articles. Authorisation can be for a particular issue or generally, but cannot be for longer than five years. It is renewable.

Directors must also follow any pre-emption rights in articles, ie provisions which stipulate that, on a share issue, shares must be offered to members pro rata in accordance with the proportion of the company's shares they hold. Pre-emption rights are important in the context of minority rights in that they can stop discriminatory share issues that might otherwise have the effect of freezing out a minority.

Listed companies are, in any case, obliged to follow the practice of observing pre-emption rights by virtue of the provisions of the Admission of Securities to Listing.

CA 1985, ss 89–96 also implies this for all companies, so, on a share issue, members must be given the opportunity to subscribe pro rata to their holdings. This does not apply if the shares are to be paid up, wholly or partly, otherwise than in cash. Private companies may exclude the rules by provision in the memorandum or articles. Public and private companies may, when authorising directors to allot shares under CA 1985, s 80, provide by special resolution that the pre-emptive rights under s 89 do not apply to an allotment. Certain information must be given to shareholders when notice of the proposed resolution is circulated.

Otherwise, the company looks to lenders of money for capital. That lender may be a bank or some other financial institution. Some companies exist to provide venture capital to other companies. The Business Expansion Scheme can also be a useful method of raising capital (4.32).

Some lenders may take *debentures* in return for the loan. *Debenture holders* are often contrasted with *shareholders*. Shareholders and debenture holders are, however, very different. Thus:

(1) A shareholder is entitled to participate in capital gains of the company and a debenture holder is not.
(2) A shareholder is a member of the company with constitutional rights under the articles of association. A debenture holder is not.
(3) A shareholder may be given a dividend annually on his shares which is not fixed and which is at the discretion of the directors (although preference shareholders often have a fixed dividend). If the company cannot afford to pay a dividend, it should not be declared. This may leave a shareholder with no return on capital.

A debenture holder, however, usually receives interest on sums lent to the company at a fixed rate.

(4) A shareholder cannot be repaid his money. He must sell his shares to another or, very exceptionally under certain circumstances, ask the company to repurchase the shares under special provisions in the CA 1985 (5.78). However, a debenture evidences a loan and a loan is repayable under its own terms.

Being a debenture holder might be seen in some ways to be a safer prospect than being a shareholder since the money invested is always repayable and the return on capital fixed. Although a shareholder stands to enjoy capital gain and also to enjoy a reasonable dividend if the company is doing well, he nonetheless stands the risk also of capital loss and no dividend at all if the company is doing badly.

However, lending monies to a company can have its own risk. For a loan will only be repaid as long as the company survives and has the money to do so. Therefore, debenture holders who lend large amounts of money to the company should back up their loan with the security of a charge either *fixed* on the company's real property (such as its land or factory) whether freehold or leasehold or *floating* (5.23). This type of security may be incorporated into a standard debenture document.

5.23 Floating charges

A *floating charge* can only be given by companies (see chapter 1) and is a useful additional form of security to offer a lender. A floating charge is basically a charge on moveables such as stock in trade, furniture and other assets, but can also include, for example, book debts. The advantage of a floating charge is that, as its name implies, it does not actually fix itself to any particular asset or assets. Whilst the charge is in place the company is free to trade normally and even turn over its stock and other assets which are the subject of the charge. Only upon the occurrence of certain events, for example, the liquidation of the company, does the floating charge *crystallize*, ie become fixed. It then fixes on all the assets the subject of the charge existing at that time.

A floating chargee comes lower in the priority of creditors than a fixed chargee, even if the fixed charge is created later (assuming registration requirements (see below) have been complied with). After all, if a company holding assets may sell such assets the subject of a floating charge, what is to prevent it specifically charging them ahead of the interests of a floating chargee? Thus, most lenders, such as banks, play doubly safe by taking a fixed and floating charge.

5.24 Registration of company charges

A company charge should be registered in a company's own register of charges kept with its statutory books and it should keep a copy of the charge at its registered office. Also, particulars of charges (using form 395), together with the original instrument, have to be registered with the Register of Companies. The types of charge registrable with the Registrar of Companies are specified by CA 1985, s 396(1) as being:

(1) a charge for the purpose of securing any issue of debentures;
(2) a charge on uncalled share capital of the company;
(3) a charge created or evidenced by an instrument which, if executed by an individual, would require registration as a bill of sale;
(4) a charge on land (wherever situated) or any interest in it, but not including a charge for any rent or other periodical sum issuing out of the land;
(5) a charge on book debts of the company;
(6) a floating charge on the company's undertaking or property;
(7) a charge on calls made but not paid;
(8) a charge on a ship or aircraft, or any share in a ship;
(9) a charge on goodwill, or a patent, or a licence under a patent, or a trademark, or on a copyright or a licence under a copyright.

A charge must be registered by the company (in practice the initiative is taken by the lender or holder of the charge) within 21 days of its creation. Otherwise it is void against a liquidator or administrator or any creditor of the company. The court may grant an extension of time if satisfied the lapse was accidental, or due to other sufficient cause, or will not prejudice creditors or shareholders, or is otherwise just and equitable. The court order, however, will provide that acceptance of late registration is subject to rights of parties (ie other chargees) acquired during the period between the date of creation of the unregistered charge and the date of its actual registration. There are also criminal sanctions for failure to register.

There are extensive modifications to the rules about registration of charges in the Companies Bill. These include changes to the rules about delivery of particulars, the effect of non-registration and late registration and other matters. When law, these new rules should be consulted in a specialist work. Finally, it is to be stressed that the operation of the law and practice of company charges should always be entrusted to a professional adviser.

Constructive notice of company charges

The traditional position is that the world at large has constructive notice (see 5.34) of all charges registered with the Registrar of Companies. This makes it vital for a potential chargee and anyone dealing with the company (eg buying any of its assets) to search the register to see if there are any existing or prior charges. However the Companies Bill proposes a new section 397(6) CA 1985 which states that a person shall have notice of matters on the register if he 'ought' to have inspected the register (and this includes a chargee for value). This means that although constructive notice is proposed elsewhere in the Bill to be abolished (5.34) it is retained in a modified form here. In other words you should still search the register.

5.25 Receivers appointed by debenture holders

A debenture holder (very commonly, your bank) is also usually entitled, under the terms of his debenture, to appoint a receiver and manager (an administrative receiver under the nomenclature introduced by the Insolvency Act 1986) to look after the security that has been given by the company. A receiver is usually appointed upon the occurrence of some event specified in the debenture, generally when there is default or threatened default in repayment of the loan or breach of some other provision in the debenture. A receiver's job is to take charge of the company for the time being and get in debts owed to the company, and possibly to sell assets (sometimes this may mean selling the whole undertaking of the company) to raise money to pay off the debenture holder.

5.26 Stamp duty

Stamp duty is payable on transfers of shares for value at the rate of $\frac{1}{2}\%$ rounded up to the nearest 50p. There are reliefs on reconstructions and reorganisations but the conditions are very complicated and specific advice is necessary. Certain dispositions are exempt and these cases are specified on the rear of the printed stock transfer form used under the Stock Transfer Act 1963. A certificate is required to qualify for this treatment.

Stamp duty reserve tax, introduced by FA 1986, catches certain agreements to transfer securities and the rate of duty in such cases is presently $\frac{1}{2}\%$.

Stamp duty will also be payable on property transactions by companies and different rates apply.

5.27 Transfer of shares

Shares are ordinarily freely transmissible although the directors usually have a discretion to decline to register a share transfer. This is a fiduciary power and must be exercised for proper purposes (5.70). However, in smaller private companies, articles often have pre-emption provisions restricting the transfer of shares to outsiders without first offering the shares to the other members. These provisions will not be in Table A and special articles will have to be adopted to give effect to this. It is very wise for members in small private companies to provide for pre-emption rights. After all, a small company is like a partnership and you do not really want to be a partner with a stranger without consenting to it.

Shares are ordinarily transferred by using a standard stock transfer form signed by the transferor on which stamp duty will ordinarily be payable (5.26). Movements of shares must be recorded in the register of members in the statutory books. A member is entitled to a share certificate which is handed over on sale and a new one issued to the transferee.

Different rules apply, of course, in relation to dealings in shares of public companies, a subject outside the scope of this book.

5.28 The memorandum of association and the doctrine of *ultra vires*

This area, as in the case of the area of authority of directors to bind the Company, is subject to change proposed by the Companies Bill. At present, it is not known precisely when the provisions of the Bill will take effect and an account of the law prior to the implementation of the proposals contained in the Bill is included as well as the provisions in the Bill.

5.29 The doctrine of *ultra vires*

The memorandum of association which is filed with the Registrar of Companies must contain what is known as an objects clause. Being a creature of statute, a company can only do those things which it is set up to do as provided in its objects clause. In theory, if a company strays outside its objects clause and does something which it is not set up to do, then it acts *ultra vires*. An *ultra vires* act can, in the absence of statutory protection, have very serious consequences for the company, for its directors and for third parties dealing with the company.

Under the law prior to the implementation of the Companies Bill, objects have to be stated very specifically. As will be seen below, after the Companies Bill, s 4 of the Companies Act 1985 will provide that the objects of a company may be stated in any manner. But until then specific objects must be stated and of course many companies after the implementation of the Companies Bill will still have objects clauses which are specific (and the practice of lengthy objects clauses may continue anyway).

At common law an *ultra vires* contract is void and unenforceable. So at common law a third party who has delivered goods to the company cannot sue for the money due for those goods and vice versa. And in situations where the company has parted with assets or money under an *ultra vires* arrangement the directors themselves may be guilty of breach of fiduciary duty and may have personally to reimburse the company for any loss. There is some statutory protection for third parties in CA 1985, s 35 but until altered by the Companies Bill, the protection in that provision is not perfect. It is therefore of considerable importance that the company stays within its objects clause.

It has been stated that an *ultra vires* contract is void. This will happen where a company makes a contract and there is nothing in the memorandum to authorise it.

Example A

XYZ Co Limited is formed to run farms. It contracts to purchase some silicon chips for its unauthorised computer business. The contract is *ultra vires* and void.

However if a company exercises a power which is present in the memorandum and misuses that power, ie uses it for an unauthorised business and not its main object, the contract will not be *ultra vires*. It will be voidable as a misuse by directors of the power in the memorandum. (Powers in the memorandum such as borrowing, giving guarantees, writing cheques and buying land must only be used in furtherance of the main object of the company). That is to say the company can avoid the contract if the third party knew of the improper purpose of the transaction, eg:

Example B

ABC Co limited is formed to run farms. It borrows money from its bank to buy silicon chips for its unauthorised computer business. There is a power to borrow money in the memorandum. The contract is not *ultra vires*. But it may be avoided against the bank if the bank knew of the purpose to which the loan was being put. If the bank was ignorant of the purpose it can enforce the contract.

These rules are complicated by the doctrine of constructive notice at common law (see below). This says a third party dealing with the company is deemed to have notice of certain documents registered with the Registrar of Companies, such as the memorandum of association, articles of association and special resolutions. Therefore, you are deemed to know the objects of the company with which you deal. Thus in Example B, if the bank knows of the purpose of the loan, ie to buy the chips, it will stand the risk of the contract being avoided. The bank may well not actually appreciate that the company should not be buying chips. But it will be deemed to know it is set up to run farms and will be deemed to appreciate that it should not deal in computers. Therefore the doctrine of constructive notice at common law can catch out unwitting third parties. The traditional position as to constructive notice will change after inplementation of the Companies Bill (see below).

5.30 Protection of third parties by section 35 of the Companies Act 1985

There is some limited statutory protection in the law prior to the implementation of the Companies Bill which deals with the *ultra vires* and constructive notice problem. CA 1985, s 35, as originally drawn, gives protection to third parties dealing with the company. If it applies, the third party will not be deemed to know the objects of the company and can thus enforce any contract with the company even if the company is acting *ultra vires*. It therefore reverses the common law rules set out above as far as third parties are concerned (the provision does not apply in favour of companies).

However there are certain conditions to this protection:

(1) A person dealing with a company must deal 'in good faith'. Thus, for example, if the third party actually knows that the company with which it is dealing is acting *ultra vires*, it is suggested that good faith might be absent and the third party cannot claim protection under the provisions.
(2) The transaction in question must have been decided upon by the directors. On a literal reading, this implies that there must have been a board meeting approving the particular transaction in question before the section operates (although some commentators have argued for a wider view). This is, however, often absent in practice. If so, the section will not apply.

5.31 The Department of Trade consultative document

Because of the problems outlined above, the doctrine of *ultra vires* has always been the subject of much criticism. A couple of years ago the Department of Trade and Industry issued a consultative document entitled *Reform of the Ultra Vires Rule*. It was written by Dr Dan Prentice, a Fellow of Pembroke College, Oxford, after receiving representations from consultees. Among the recommendations that Dr Prentice made were that:

(1) there should be no restriction on corporate capacity;
(2) a company should have the capacity to do any act whatsoever;
(3) a third party dealing with the company should not be affected by the contents of any document merely because it is registered with the Registrar of Companies or with the company (this could be made subject to appropriate exceptions);
(4) a company should be bound by the acts of its board or of an individual director;
(5) a third party should be under no obligation to determine the scope of a company's board or of an individual director or the contents of the company's articles or memorandum;
(6) a third party who had actual knowledge that a board or an individual director did not possess authority to enter into a transaction on behalf of the company should not be allowed to enforce it against the company but the company should be free to ratify it. The same result should obtain where a third party had actual knowledge that the transaction falls outside the company's objects but in this case ratification should be by special resolution;
(7) knowledge in this context would require an understanding and it would only be knowledge of the individual entering into the particular transaction which would be relevant;
(8) the proposal to protect third parties should be modified where the third party is an officer or director of the company where constructive knowledge of the capacity of directors should render the transaction unenforceable and for this purpose constructive knowledge means the type of knowledge which may reasonably be expected of a person carrying out the functions of that director or officer of that company.

As will be seen below, many, although not all, of Dr Prentice's proposals have been included in the Companies Bill. These are now discussed below in relation to *ultra vires*. Some of the above proposals are of course relevant to a director's authority and these are discussed later.

5.32 The position under the Companies Bill

The scope of objects clauses

After implementation of the Companies Bill s 4 of the Companies Act will provide that the objects of a company may be stated in any manner. And a statement that the object of the company is to carry on business as a general commercial company will mean that the object of the company is to carry on any trade or business whatsoever. In such a case the company will have power to do all such things as are incidental or conducive to the carrying on of any trade or business by it. New companies incorporated after the coming into force of the Act based on the Bill may therefore be advised to adopt such wide ranging permissive objects clauses, thus out-flanking the effect of the *ultra vires* rule altogether (although shareholders may have an interest in having specific objects if they do not wish the directors to speculate in any business they choose). Companies formed before that date will in practice have more specific objects clauses. But the Companies Bill provides that a company may by special resolution alter its memorandum with regard to the statement of its objects at any time (cf the rather stricter position under existing law: 5.35). This is subject only to an application to the court by the holders of not less than 15% in nominal value of the company's issued share capital to have the alteration cancelled. If the alteration is confirmed by the court it will take effect notwithstanding the objection. On the other hand, the court may decline to approve the alteration.

Capacity of the company

A proposed revision of s 35 will mean that the validity of an act done by the company shall not be called into question on the ground of lack of capacity by reason of the fact that it is beyond the objects of the company as stated in the memorandum of association. Therefore protection of the third party against want of capacity of the company itself will be complete.

However it is expressly provided that the proposed new section will not affect any right of a member of the company to bring proceedings on the ground of incapacity of a company to enter into a transaction in order to restrain the commission of such a transaction and nor will the proposed new section affect any liability incurred by the directors by reason of such an act having been done. This is dealt with immediately below.

5.33 A director's responsibility for *ultra vires* acts

A director of a company who purports to commit the company to an *ultra vires* contract or other act and causes the company loss, can be liable for breach of fiduciary duty and liable to reimburse the company. A member of the company will have standing to restrain the commission of an *ultra vires* act and to take action against the directors on behalf of the company if the company declines to do so.

In exceptional circumstances under CA 1985, s 727, a court may grant an officer of the company relief from liability for breach of fiduciary duty if in the opinion of the court he has acted honestly and reasonably and that in the circumstances he ought fairly to be excused.

5.34 Constructive notice

Although the proposals in the Companies Bill if implemented, will take care of the problem of constructive notice for the purposes of *ultra vires,* the Companies Bill also proposes to abolish the rule as it is presently understood for other purposes, (save for the existence of charges registered at Companies House (5.24)). A new section 711(A) of CA 1985 will state that 'a person shall not be taken to have notice of any matter merely because of its being disclosed in any document kept by the Registrar of Companies. However this does not affect the question of whether 'a person is affected by notice of any matter by reason of a failure to make such enquiries as ought reasonably to be made'. In spite of the provision the proviso at the end of this clause leaves an area of doubt.

5.35 Alteration of the memorandum

Certain strict procedures apply in relation to permitted alteration of the memorandum. The following are the rules:

(1) The name of the company may be altered by special resolution. This often occurs after you buy a company off the shelf or when you take over a company. You may want to adopt a name different from that chosen by former shareholders. There is a fee payable to the Registrar of Companies of currently £40.
(2) The situation of the registered office cannot be altered. This means you cannot change the country in which the office is situated. You can change the address itself within that country by directors' resolution (using Form 287 to notify the Registrar of Companies).
(3) Under CA 1985 as originally drawn, the objects clause in the memorandum can only be altered under certain circumstances,

and for limited reasons, by special resolution. The Companies Bill, clause 103 provides for a proposal that a company may by special resolution alter its memorandum in respect of the statement of objects at any time, apparently for any reason. The right of alteration both pre and post the implementation of the Companies Bill proposals is subject to an application to the court by the holders of not less than 15% in nominal value of the company's issued share capital to have the alteration cancelled. If the alteration is confirmed by the court, it takes effect notwithstanding the objection. On the other hand, the court may decline to approve the alteration.
(4) Under certain circumstances, liability of directors can be made unlimited.
(5) The capital of the company can be raised by ordinary resolution and reduced by special resolution (in the latter case, with the consent of the court).

If the memorandum is altered a reprinted copy as altered should be filed at the Companies Registry.

5.36 The articles of association

The articles of association are mainly concerned with the regulation of members' rights as between themselves and with other internal company procedures.

5.37 The articles as a contract

The articles of association form a contract between the members and the company and between the members. This is the way in which the articles may be enforced by the company against its members (eg if the company wanted to sue a member for the amount unpaid on his shares), by a member against the company (eg if the company were to refuse to pay a dividend that the directors have already declared is due) or by a member against another member (eg if one member refuses to sell his shares to another member if required by the articles of association).

However, this contract differs from ordinary contracts (see chapter 12) in some significant ways:

(1) Not all of the terms of the articles are enforceable. For example:
    (a) Only membership rights can be enforced, ie only shareholder rights and not rights attaching to an individual in his capacity other than by reason of his capacity as shareholder. Thus in the case of *Eley* v *Positive Government Security Life Assurance Co* (1876) Mr Eley was unable to sue the company to enforce

his appointment as the company's solicitor in the company's articles since this was an attempt to enforce outsider rights and not rights given to him as shareholder (though of course he might have a separate contract with the company and could certainly sue under that).
(b) The court will also not enforce *all* membership rights. The courts are reluctant to allow an action to complain of a mere procedural irregularity. Normally the courts require you to show that there has been a substantial infringement of your personal proprietary rights.
(2) The remedy of rectification which may be available in some other contractual situations (chapter 12) is not available where the articles of association are concerned.

5.38 Alteration of the articles

The articles of association can be altered freely by special resolution subject to special rules which apply on alteration of class rights (5.40). A printed copy of the altered articles should be filed at the Companies Registry.

5.39 Shareholder protection and the articles

Articles of association can be a useful vehicle for safeguarding shareholder rights (5.37 and 5.40). For this reason companies, especially smaller ones, may wish to depart in significant ways from Table A in order to ensure that the articles are more tailor-made and contain express provisions to prevent disputes arising and to protect minorities. For example you could provide that all shareholders are entitled to be offered a chance to buy shares whenever there is a share issue. Similarly, you could stop another shareholder selling his shares to an outsider without first offering them to you. You could make sure that certain types of resolution (5.57) are needed for certain types of business, creating a right of veto for a minority. It would be wise also to provide that a chairman does not have a casting vote at company or board meetings. So there is a strong case for adopting special articles.

It is also possible to provide for this sort of protection in a separate shareholders agreement, and this has the advantage of being private, as it would not have to be registered (although it would not bind shareholders not a party to it).

It is strongly recommended that you take advice on this aspect when forming a company.

5.40 Class rights

One special feature of articles is that they sometimes contain what are known as 'class rights'. This occurs where there is more than one class of shares in the company and the rights attaching to the various classes of shares are different. A common example is the division of share capital between ordinary shares and preference shares. (A preference share commonly has different rights from an ordinary share, such as prior right to a dividend at a certain rate.)

If there are shares in different classes the rights attaching to those shares can only be altered by special procedures, usually in the articles or otherwise implied by CA 1985. Usually these will be that a member of a class whose rights are proposed to be varied is entitled to vote at a separate class meeting on whether he approves the variation of his rights. Only members of the class are entitled to participate in that vote and, usually, unless there is a three-quarters consent of the members of the class to the proposed alteration the amendment cannot be made *even if* there is the appropriate majority in the general meeting. Sometimes a simple consent by three-quarters of the class shareholders in writing will do (it is wise to check the articles of association and CA 1985 with the help of your adviser before implementing any procedures).

This is illustrated as follows:

Example

XYZ Co Ltd has two classes of shares, 'A' shares and 'B' shares. The A shares have three votes per share and the B shares have two votes per share. The A shareholders own 85% of the issued share capital of the company. A proposal is made by one of the A shareholders that the B shareholders have their voting power reduced from two votes to one vote per share. A special resolution may be carried by the A shareholders in general meeting as the necessary majority (75% for a special resolution: 5.57) is there (they have 85%). But the members of the B class who constitute only 15% of the company have, nonetheless, the right at their own class meeting to decide whether or not to approve the variation of their rights and, if less than three-quarters of them consent, the special resolution cannot take effect.

Class rights are thus a very valuable method of entrenching shareholder rights. If the class rights are contained in the memorandum of association of the company their position is even more secure. As an extreme example, class rights which are contained in the memorandum (although this is fairly unusual) and where there is no provision for variation in the memorandum or articles, can only be altered by the consent of all the members of the company.

5.41 Company officers, their appointment, tenure and removal

Each company must have at least one director (a public company must have at least two) and a company secretary. A sole director in a private company cannot be company secretary as well. The directors are appointed by the company in general meeting under the terms of the articles of association (for example under Articles 73 to 80 and 84 to 86 of Table A). The directors may appoint and (subject to 5.44) remove a managing director. Form 288 should be filed on change of officers.

A 'director' is defined under CA 1985, s 741 (1) as 'a person occupying the position of director, by whatever name called.' It is important to note that a number of provisions in legislation apply also to 'shadow directors' (eg provisions about long term directors' employment contracts and substantial property transactions, certain disclosure obligations and wrongful trading). A shadow director is defined by CA 1985 s 742 (2) as being a person in accordance with whose directions or instructions the directors of the company are accustomed to act (excluding those giving advice in a professional capacity).

5.42 The secretary

Article 99 of Table A provides that the directors shall appoint a secretary for such term and on such remuneration and on such conditions as they think fit and any secretary can (subject to 5.44) be removed by them. A secretary in a public company must have, by virtue of CA 1985, s 286, certain qualifications. A secretary customarily is responsible for issuing notices, eg of meetings, keeping records and filing material at the Companies Registry. But he can be employed to do other things.

5.43 The director

A director is ordinarily obliged to retire by rotation (Article 74, Table A) and, as a result, offer himself for re-election (this may not apply in the case of a managing director or other executive: Article 84, Table A). This can be inconvenient and the requirement is often (though not always) excluded in private companies.

A director may be removed by the shareholders in general meeting and, if so, this may be effected by ordinary resolution under CA 1985, s 303. Special notice (28 days) to the director is however necessary before he can be removed under that provision and he is entitled to attend the meeting concerned, whether or not he is a member,

Company and partnership law 97

and to circularise the members of the company with a statement protesting against his removal. Although a director is freely removable under CA 1985, s 303 this is, of course, without prejudice to any claims he may have for breach of a separate contract with the company, for example a contract of employment or any statutory employment claims such as unfair dismissal (5.44 and chapter 10).

Article 81 also provides that the office of a director has to be vacated automatically in certain cases, for example, if he becomes bankrupt, becomes mentally ill, resigns, absents himself for more than six months from directors' meetings and the directors resolve that the position is vacated, or if he is prohibited by law from being a director.

Directors can be disqualified now for sometimes long periods for various reasons under The Company Directors Disqualification Act 1986, for example for unsatisfactory conduct and involvement in insolvent companies and for persistent failure to file annual returns and other documents at the Companies Registry.

There are provisions in most sets of articles for fixing expenses (Article 13, Table A), gratuities and pensions (Article 87, Table A), and remuneration (Article 82, Table A) for directors and there are also, usually, provisions dealing with the appointment of alternate directors.

Table A deals with procedures of directors at board meetings. These are generally less formal than company and general meetings (5.58).

5.44 Contractual or other liability to company officers for dismissal

Although directors, managing directors and company secretaries may be removed under the procedures in 5.42 and 5.43 it is not uncommon for these individuals to have separate contracts of employment or service agreements. Summary termination of these agreements without good cause can lead to considerable claims against the company both for damages for wrongful dismissal and compensation for unfair dismissal (chapter 10).

5.45 Third party protection against internal irregularities and the authority of officers of the company to bind the company

This is another area subject to change proposed by the Companies Bill and a version of the law as it stands prior to the implementation of the proposals in the Bill is covered as well as the proposals in the Bill itself.

There are two problems at common law. The first is the doctrine of constructive notice which can affect a third party and give him notice of the limitation of the authority of the board of directors or of individual directors that may be contained in the public documents of the company such as in the articles of association, special resolutions and the like. The second question relates to whether an individual officer or employee has authority to bind the company in the absence of any particular restriction in the memorandum and articles of association and in the absence of an express conferment of authority. The first problem is mitigated at common law by the so-called 'indoor management rule' and the second point is dealt with by agency principles in relation to companies.

5.46 The indoor management rule

The common law doctrine of constructive notice deems a third party dealing with the company to have knowledge of matters published at the Companies Registry, namely the memorandum of association, articles of association and special resolutions, at least. It can be very unfair for third parties (although, even before the amendments proposed to be introduced by the Companies Bill, CA 1985, s 35 protects a third party to a certain extent).

However, the counterpart to this doctrine is that anything *internal* and *not* required to be published at the Companies Registry is *not* deemed to be published to a third party. And, further, a third party may *assume* that those internal matters are all in order and does not have to enquire. Such internal matters would include discussions or resolutions at board meetings of directors and even ordinary resolutions at company general meetings, because most ordinary resolutions do not have to be lodged at the Companies Registry (but cf for example, the case of an ordinary resolution increasing capital). This is the so-called 'indoor management' rule.

It is illustrated by the leading case of *Royal British Bank* v *Turquand* (1856). There a company under its articles gave power to its directors to borrow only such sums as were authorised by a 'general' resolution of the company (now this would be an ordinary resolution). But the directors borrowed £2,000 from the Royal British Bank without such resolution having been passed. It was held that the bank was entitled to assume that the resolution had been passed. It had no way of knowing whether or not the resolution had been passed since that sort of resolution was not required to be published at the Companies Registry.

However, the rule does not apply in the following situations:

(1) Where a third party has actual or constructive notice of the

irregularity, ie where he actually knows the matter is irregular or where the defect is or would be apparent from the inspection of the company's documents.
(2) Where there are suspicious circumstances, ie where a third party is put on enquiry.
(3) Where there is a forgery.
(4) 'Insiders' cannot rely upon the rule. The term insiders does not have a fixed definition but has been held to include company directors (although exceptionally, a newly appointed officer who has relatively little inside knowledge about the company might not be an insider for these purposes).

5.47 Statutory provisions protecting a third party against internal irregularities

In addition to the common law indoor management rule there are also some specific statutory provisions protecting third parties against internal irregularities.

(1) Companies Act 1985, s 285 provides that the acts of a director or manager are to be valid despite any defect that may afterwards be discovered in his appointment or qualification. However, it is thought that this does not apply where there has been no appointment at all.
(2) Companies Act 1985, s 382(4) provides that where minutes at any general meeting of the directors are made in accordance with s 382 (which provides for proper books to be kept and for minutes to be signed by the chairman) then, until the contrary is proved, any meeting is deemed to have been properly and duly held and all business properly transacted thereat, including the appointment of directors, managers or liquidators.
(3) The Law of Property Act 1925, s 71(1) says a purchaser may assume a deed has been duly executed by a company if its seal has been attached and affixed to the deed in the presence of and attested by its secretary and a member of the board of directors. (However this only applies in favour of a purchaser for value from the company and only in relation to a deed and not to other situations.)

The Companies Bill clause 123 proposes a new section 36(A) for the Companies Act 1985. This will state that a company need not have a company seal and that a document signed by a director and secretary and expressed to be executed by the company will have the same effect as if it were made under the company's common seal. If it is expressed to be a deed and intended to be a deed, it will take effect as a deed. In favour of a purchaser a document signed by persons who appear to hold the office of director and secretary will be deemed to be duly executed, but here again a purchaser will mean a purchaser in good faith for valuable consideration.

5.48 Protection under section 35 of the Companies Act 1985 prior to the implementation of the Companies Bill

The Companies Act 1985 section 35 mentioned above in relation to *ultra vires* may also apply to protect a third party where there is some doubt as to whether the director with whom he is dealing has authority. It says that when you deal with a company you are not deemed to know about any restrictions placed upon the authority of directors in the memorandum and articles.

However the same conditions apply before it protects the third party, that is to say, the third party must be in good faith and the transaction must be one decided upon by the directors. The provision is rarely helpful in a case where you are basically deciding whether one individual has authority to act on his own initiative. In a case where the board of directors has in fact decided upon the transaction, there is usually no want of authority anyway. In that case there is no need for s 35 to apply but, ironically, due simply to bad draftsmanship, the section only applies in such a case!

5.49 The Department of Trade consultative document

Dr Prentice's report made several recommendations relative to the authority of the board which have been discussed above in relation to *ultra vires*. The proposals below in the Companies Bill differ in one important respect: the report favoured making a company bound by the acts of the board *or* an individual director. The Companies Bill however simply refers to the board or those authorised by the board. Agency principles in relation to companies, ie the principles about usual or ostensible authority will therefore govern third party protection in relation to acts of other individuals, eg unauthorised single directors or others not authorised by the board (see below).

5.50 Section 35(A) of the Companies Act 1985 as proposed by the Companies Bill

Section 35 as it relates to the authority of directors is proposed to be replaced by section 35(A) which will provide that in favour of a person dealing with a company in good faith, the power of the board of directors to bind the company or authorise others to do so shall be deemed to be free of any limitation under the company's constitution. For this purpose a person will be deemed to deal with the company if he is party to any transaction or other act to which the company is a party. Secondly, a person will not be regarded as acting in bad faith by reason only of his knowing that an act was beyond the powers of the directors under the company's constitution and, thirdly, limitations under a company's constitution include limitations deriving from a resolution of the company in general meeting or of a unanimous resolution of members otherwise than in general meeting.

A party to a transaction with a company will not be bound to enquire whether it is within the objects of the company to enter into it or about any limitation on the powers of the board of directors to bind the company or authorise others to do so.

However, the requirement of good faith should mean that a person who actually knows that an act is beyond the authority of the directors or who in effect turns a blind eye to that fact, cannot bind the company to the transaction.

Such a transaction, even if beyond the powers of the directors and not binding on the company because of the absence of good faith on the part of the individual, should be ratifiable by the company (by ordinary resolution) if it wishes. Sometimes, however, the directors will have exceeded their authority because of a limitation flowing from the objects of the company. We have seen above that the doctrine of *ultra vires* will be modified so that as far as third parties are concerned, the capacity of the company should not affect the transaction concerned. It is further proposed that where, in relation to an act of the company the board of directors exceeds any limitation on its powers which flows from the objects of the company stated in the memorandum of association and is not binding on the company because of absence of good faith on the part of the third party, the act may also be ratified by the company but this time by special resolution. The logic here is that a special resolution would have been necessary to alter the memorandum (so as to permit the transaction) in the first place.

The proposed section 35(A) will not affect the right of any member of the company to bring proceedings to restrain the doing of an act which is beyond the powers of directors nor will it affect any liability incurred by the directors or any of them by reason of anything done.

This proposed new version of section 35 meets some of the criticisms about section 35 as originally drafted. For example, it will clarify the concept of dealing with the company. Previously, dealing with the company was thought to mean only transactions for consideration but the proposed new section 35(A) is certainly wider and seems to cover gratuitous transactions. On the other hand, the requirement of 'good faith' has been retained and could lead to some uncertainty. But now it will at least expressly provide that a party shall not be regarded as acting in bad faith by reason only of knowing that an act is beyond the power of the directors under the company's constitution.

Finally, it was thought that it was unfair to give directors dealing with the company the same protection in cases of lack of authority of the board as enjoyed by third parties. In such a case the Consultative Document suggested retaining constructive notice of limitations of a board's authority, in a modified form (see above). The Companies Bill clause 102 goes further and proposes (in a new CA 1985 s 322A) that when a director of the company or of its holding company or a person connected or a company associated with such director deals with the company in a case where the board of directors exceed their authority the transaction is *void* unless ratified by the company.

The new section 35(A) deals with the power of the board of directors to bind the company or at least those authorised by the board to bind the company. It does not deal with individual directors who are not authorised or indeed other company officers or employees who are not authorised by the board of directors. In which case, the common law rules about agency principles in relation to companies are still relevant and will decide the question in practice. These are dealt with below.

5.51 Constructive notice

Although the proposals in the Companies Bill discussed above deal with the question of constructive notice for the purposes of the authority of the board, it is worth mentioning that the doctrine is proposed to be modified for other purposes: see the discussion on *ultra vires* above.

5.52 Agency principles in relation to companies

A director or other officer of the company may bind the company to a third party when he has authority to do so. The three types of authority that a third party can rely on to enforce a contract with the company are:

(1) *Actual express authority*
An example of this is where John, a managing director of XYZ Co Ltd is told by XYZ Co Ltd, to make a specific contract for the purchase of a computer with ABC Co Ltd on XYZ's behalf.

He now has *actual express* authority to do so. This is a matter of agreement between the company and the managing director.

(2) *Actual implied authority*

An example of this type of authority would be where John is given no specific instructions by XYZ Co Ltd. But since he is managing director he has, from that position, an implied authority to do everything that is usual for that type of officer to do (5.53). As the actual implied authority of a managing director is extensive (5.53), he would have authority to buy the computer from ABC Co Ltd even without being told to do so by the Board. He would be able to bind the company by virtue of his actual implied authority. The actual implied authority of other officers such as individual directors and secretaries and managers is, however, much more limited than that of a managing director (5.53).

(3) *Apparent or ostensible authority*

Suppose John was never appointed managing director at all or, alternatively, was once managing director but no longer occupies that post. If he contracts with ABC Co Ltd without getting an express mandate from the XYZ Co Ltd he may nonetheless still be able to bind the company. You may find this remarkable, but it may happen where he has been 'held out' or represented by the company as being a particular type of officer and the third party relies upon that holding out or representation.

So if, for example, he has been held out as a *de facto* managing director he may have *ostensible* power to bind the company even if the company does not wish to enter into the contract at all. A 'holding out' or a representation could be by inclusion of a person's name on company notepaper or simply by conduct, in allowing that person to act as if he is managing director even if he is not.

The authority of officers and employees can be clearly limited by a company under the terms of an employee's service agreement or other instructions if issued to an employee or officer. If an employee or officer exceeds such authority, then he may be liable to the company. But if a third party is ignorant of such an express limitation of an officer's authority, that third party may be entitled to assume that the person with whom he is dealing has the authority that that type of company officer normally enjoys under the general law (see (2) above).

So the moral of this discussion is that the company must be very careful about its selection of directors, managers and employees because putting them into a certain position may clothe them with some sort of authority to do certain things (depending on their position) on their own initiative.

5.53 The actual implied authority attaching to various posts

It is unwise to generalise about what you would ordinarily expect of a typical company officer. But some examples can be given. The actual implied authority of a *managing director* is very wide and extends to many transactions short of selling the company or its business. Reported cases include instances of employing a firm of architects and surveyors (*Freeman and Lockyer* v *Buckhurst Park Properties (Mangal) Ltd* (1964)) and entering into guarantees and indemnities (*Hely Hutchinson* v *Brayhead Ltd* (1967)).

An *individual director* acting as such has very little actual implied authority but persons specifically appointed to posts of an executive nature (eg a 'sales director' or a 'technical director') may have some authority implied from that executive function.

As to a *company secretary*, the traditional view was that he was merely a 'servant' who served the Board of Directors as such and had no power himself to contract with third parties on his own initiative (*Barnett Hoares & Co* v *South London Tramways Co* (1887)). This is now probably not the case and it is thought that the actual implied authority of a company secretary extends at least to entering into contracts of an administrative nature on his own initiative.

Example

In *Panorama Developments (Guildford) Ltd* v *Fidelis Furnishing Fabrics Ltd* (1971) the company secretary of a company, without express authority, ordered self-drive cars apparently for the purposes of his company's business. It was held that the company was bound by the secretary's actions. According to the court, he had 'ostensible' (see above) authority to bind the company. However, as it was held that this was the sort of task ordinarily expected of company secretaries, being of an administrative nature, the court probably meant, it is thought, that he had actual implied authority.

Finally a *chairman* of a company usually has no greater authority (in the absence of express authority) to contract than any other director.

5.54 Meetings and resolutions

Company law is complex and very procedural. This applies especially in the area of the law of meetings and resolutions. The reason for this is that companies operate on the principle of majority rule. If majority rule is to prevail then matters should be conducted properly so that all members, including a minority, have a perfectly fair opportunity to receive notice of a meeting and participate in the making of any decision.

It has been held that, in some situations, company decisions can be made informally without the need for meetings at all. However, for this principle to apply, the incorporators must be unanimous, and it is not entirely clear, anyway, whether *all* types of company decisions may be validly effected by an informal unanimous resolution of this type (for example, recently, in *Re Barry Artists Ltd* (1985) it was doubted whether a unanimous resolution without a meeting could take the place of a special resolution ordinarily required to be passed in order to reduce share capital (5.35)). And rarely, save in the smallest of companies, will the consent of the members be unanimous.

So, as a general rule, the procedures laid down in CA 1985 and the articles of association of the company must be strictly followed.

However, the Companies Bill, clause 106 proposes a new s 381A to be included in CA 1985 providing that a private company may make decisions by written resolutions, without a meeting and without any previous notice being required. This may be effected by a resolution in writing signed by or on behalf of all of the members of the company who at the date of the resolution would be entitled to attend and vote at such a meeting. This proposal is part of the Government's drive towards an element of de-regulation of private companies (see 5.4).

5.55 The Annual General Meeting

Every company must have an Annual General Meeting, the first to take place not later than eighteen months after the date of incorporation. In any event, Annual General Meetings should take place each calendar year and not be more than fifteen months apart. An Annual General Meeting should adopt the accounts of the company, reappoint auditors and deal with any other outstanding business.

However, the Companies Bill, clause 108 proposes a new s 366A to be included in CA 1985 to the effect that a private company may elect by elective resolution to dispense with Annual General Meetings. This will be subject, however, to the right of any member of the company giving notice to the company not later than three months before the end of the year in which an Annual General Meeting would otherwise be held to require the holding of an Annual General Meeting in that year. For more discussion, see 5.4.

5.56 Extraordinary General Meetings

Any other meeting of the company is called an Extraordinary General Meeting. An Extraordinary General Meeting is usually convened by the secretary at the instance of the board of directors. If the directors do not convene a meeting the holders of not less than one-tenth of the issued share capital of the company have the right to requisition a meeting.

The length of notice of meetings is governed by the length of notice required under CA 1985 and under the articles of association of a company, depending mainly on what sort of resolution is proposed to be passed at the meeting.

Meetings at which it is proposed to pass ordinary and extraordinary resolutions require 14 days' notice and, in the case of special resolutions, require 21 days' notice. An Annual General Meeting requires 21 days' notice. Some resolutions require special notice (ie 28 days' notice) to be given to the subject of the resolution such as in the case of the removal of a director from office under CA 1985, s 303 (5.43).

5.57 Types of resolution

There are three types of resolution, an ordinary resolution, an extraordinary resolution and a special resolution. An *ordinary* resolution will do to effect any decision unless the provisions of the Articles or CA 1985 say otherwise. An ordinary resolution is one which can be carried by a simple majority (ie by 51%).

Both *extraordinary* and *special* resolutions require 75% approval. Companies Act 1985 and/or the Articles of Association will normally stipulate when an extraordinary or special resolution is required. Extraordinary resolutions are less frequently required than special resolutions. Special resolutions are required, for example, to alter the Articles of Association, to decrease capital, to amend the objects of the company, and generally to effect the more important of company decisions.

It is important to note that copies of special and extraordinary resolutions must be filed at the Companies Registry. So must an ordinary resolution increasing capital (with Form 123). You can often dispense with notice of extraordinary general meetings (other than in cases where special notice is required) if 95% of the members entitled to vote and holding at least 95% in nominal value of the shares giving a right to vote consent to short notice. This is often quite helpful. Under the Companies Bill, clause 108, it is proposed that a private company may by elective resolution (see below) allow the requisite percentage majority to be 90% instead of 95%.

Finally, members usually have one vote per share held, but the articles could create shares with more votes per share (such as in the case of class rights (5.40)).

The Companies Bill

(1) Written resolutions

The Companies Bill proposes a new section 381(A) of CA 1985 to provide that anything which could be done by a resolution of the company in general meeting, or by a resolution of a meeting of any class of members of the company, may be done without a meeting and without any previous notice being required by a resolution in writing signed by or on behalf of all the members of the company who at the date of the resolution would be entitled to attend and vote at such meeting. Furthermore, it is proposed that the signatures of the members concerned need not be on a single document provided that each is on a document which accurately states the terms of the resolution. The only exceptions will be that a resolution under s 303 of CA 1985 removing a director from office or under s 391 of CA 1985 removing an auditor from office cannot be effected by such a written resolution.

The Bill also proposes certain detailed procedural adaptations in relation to decisions that can, in the future, be effected by written resolutions, for example in relation to disapplication of pre-emption rights, in relation to approval of financial assistance for purchase of a company's own shares or those of a holding company, in relation to authority for an off-market purchase or contingent purchase contract of the company's own shares, for approval for payment out of capital, for approval of a director's service contract and for funding of a director's expenditure in performing his duties.

Finally, though, a copy of any written resolution proposed to be agreed to in accordance with this new s 381 (A) will have to be sent to the company's auditors. If the auditors are affected by the resolution, they may within seven days from the day on which they receive the copy, give notice to the company stating their opinion that the resolution should be considered by the company in general meeting or, as the case may be, by a meeting of the relevant class of members of the company. The written resolution will not have effect unless either the auditors notify the company of this and in their opinion the resolution does not concern them as auditors or does concern them but need not be considered by a company in general meeting or by a class meeting, or if the period for giving notice by the auditors has expired. The requirement to notify the auditors arguably detracts from the aim behind the written resolution proposal, ie decreased formality.

There are proposed provisions for recording the resolution in the company's books in the same way as minutes of proceedings of the general meeting of the company. And written resolutions on subject matter that would ordinarily require a special or extraordinary resolution will still have to be filed with the Registrar of Companies (see above).

(2) *Elective resolutions*

The Companies Bill also includes a proposed new s 379(A) of CA 1985. This will introduce *elective resolutions*. These are elections by a private company for the purposes of:

(a) CA 1985, s 80 (election as to duration of authority to allot shares)
(b) CA 1985, s 252 (election to dispense with laying of accounts and reports before general meeting)
(c) CA 1985, s 366(a) (election to dispense with holding of annual general meeting)
(d) CA 1985, s 369(4) or s 378(3) (election as to majority required to authorise short notice of meeting); or
(e) CA 1985, s 386 (election to dispense with appointment of auditors annually).

Such elections will have to be made by resolution of the company in general meeting. An elective resolution will not be effective unless at least 21 days' notice in writing is given of the meeting stating that an elective resolution is to be proposed and stating the terms of the resolution. The resolution will also have to be agreed to at the meeting in person or by proxy by all the members entitled to attend and vote at the meeting. However the company will be able to revoke an elective resolution by passing an ordinary resolution to that effect. An elective resolution will also cease to have effect if the company is re-registered as a public company. An elective resolution may be passed or revoked in accordance with the rules applying to it and have effect notwithstanding any contrary provision in the company's articles of association. An elective resolution or a resolution revoking such a resolution will have to be registered with the Companies Registry.

It may be that further subjects will be added to the list of the elective resolutions by the Secretary of State.

5.58 Procedure at meetings

The chairman of the company acts as chairman of any company general or board meeting and, if there is none, a chairman of the meeting is elected before the meeting commences. Votes at a general meeting are conducted by a show of hands unless a member requires a poll. (A poll means that the actual votes attaching to the shares held by those present are counted.)

For a board meeting, no particular notice is required (although you do have to give notice). At the meeting votes are by a show of hands and a simple majority commonly suffices for a decision. However, the articles can lay down a different procedure and even provide for blocking powers in favour of some directors.

The chairman will have a casting vote both in the general meeting and at board meetings if the standard provisions of Table A are adopted. So these provisions are often excluded.

The articles will stipulate what quorum is necessary for a meeting.

5.59 Relationship between the general meeting and the board of directors

Generally, it is not possible for the general meeting to pass resolutions interfering with the day-to-day management of the company by the board of directors unless it does so by special resolution. It has always been thought good policy that there be a separation of functions between the board of directors and the general meeting so that the board of directors is not prone to interference by the general meeting unless there are special circumstances. Having said that, there was a long running controversy in relation to *how* the general meeting could interfere, ie whether by special resolution or ordinary resolution. This was due to the drafting of Article 80 of Table A in CA 1948, sched 1. The balance of authority suggested that interference could only be by special resolution; but the wording of the article itself suggested an ordinary resolution. The doubt is resolved by Article 70 of Table A of the Companies (Tables A to F) Regulations 1985 which provides: 'Subject to the provisions of the Act, the memorandum and the articles and to any directions given by *special resolution*, the business of the company shall be managed by the directors, who may exercise all the powers of the company' (emphasis added). However, companies incorporated under a Companies Act before CA 1985 may still have the earlier version in their articles; if this is thought unsatisfactory, the modern version can always be adopted by change of articles.

But the general meeting has, of course, a powerful residual sanction against the board in the sense that it has the power to remove directors by ordinary resolution if it wishes (5.43).

5.60 Books, records, accounts and returns

A company must keep proper books and accounting records. Its statutory books (eg register of members and minute book) must be written up and available for inspection by members at the registered office of the company.

A company must prepare and file annual accounts for members and lay them before the company in general meeting (subject to the elective provisions proposed by the Companies Bill). The accounts should include a profit and loss account and balance sheet, directors' report and auditors' report. These must then be delivered to the Registrar of Companies. The accounts must be approved by the general meeting. Directors of small or medium-sized private companies (as defined by CA 1985) may deliver accounts to the Companies Registry in a modified form. Where appropriate, group accounts have to be prepared. The Companies Bill contains proposals for further modifications and adjustments about the procedure for laying and delivering of accounts and about the content thereof including relaxations in the context of group accounts for small and medium sized groups.

Under CA 1985 an unlimited company may avoid delivery of accounts if, during the financial year in question, it was not a subsidiary of a limited company or a holding company of a limited company; if the majority of its shares were not held nor its board controlled by limited companies; and provided it was not the promoter of a trading stamp scheme. The Companies Bill, clause 17 proposes to change this formulation in some detail.

There are numerous criminal penalties that can attach to directors for failure to observe the law about books, records and accounts, and this is a matter essentially best handled by your professional adviser.

Another obligation to note is the duty each year to file an annual return with the Registrar of Companies. This must be complete as at the fourteenth day after the Annual General Meeting and must be filed within 42 days of the Annual General Meeting. There is a fee, currently of £20. Default can result in criminal liability, and frequently does.

5.61 Directors' duties

One of the main differences between a company and a partnership is the sometimes quite daunting duties placed on directors by both the common law and, more recently, by statute. The extent of these duties often goes unappreciated by those who take on a directorship. It must be remembered that breach can lead to *personal* liability.

5.62 Duties of skill and care

There are said to be three main principles:

(1) A director need not exhibit a greater degree of skill and care than may be reasonably expected of a person of his knowledge and experience. A higher duty may therefore apply to a director who is a solicitor or an accountant than a director who has no experience of professional matters.
(2) A director is not bound to give continuous attention to the affairs of his company. However, this is a very old rule and somewhat unrealistic in many modern situations. Many directors are appointed under service contracts or are otherwise executive directors and, if so, would be required to give proper time and attention to their company.
(3) A director is, in the absence of grounds of suspicion, justified in delegating matters to some other official and justified in leaving that official to it. However, this principle does not mean that the directors can abdicate all responsibility. In *Dorchester Finance Co Ltd* v *Stebbing* (1980) it was held that directors who signed blank cheques and did not verify for what these cheques were being used had broken their duties of skill and care. This was especially so as the directors involved had some accountancy experience (see (1) above).

5.63 Fiduciary duties

A director is a fiduciary and, generally, this will mean that he has a duty not to let his own interest and that of his company conflict. The sections below illustrate some specific examples of this.

5.64 A director's interest in a contract with the company

A company director may avoid a contract between it and its director because of the conflict of interest that arises. However, it may approve such a contract if the director discloses fully to the general meeting and the general meeting ratifies.

This rule of disclosure to the general meeting is usually modified by Table A, Article 85, which allows a director to be interested in a contract with a company if he discloses his interest to the *board*; however the articles should always be checked, for if there is no article like Table A Article 85 and the director takes an interest, the rule about voidability (above) applies. Also, there may be rules in the articles prohibiting a director from voting on the contract or being counted in the quorum present at the meeting (see Articles 94 and 95 of Table A), though this can be allowed if the articles permit (see Article 96). Again it is vital that the articles are checked. There is also an obligation under CA 1985, s 317 (see below) to disclose such an interest to the board at a board meeting. The rule applies to shadow directors, too. They should disclose by notice to the board.

5.65 Secret profits

A director may not make a secret profit from his position with the company. Thus a director may not take a bribe, secret commission or kick back and if he does so, this will be recoverable from him.

5.66 Corporate opportunities

There is a strict and severe rule that a person in a fiduciary position such as a director cannot profit from that position. If he does so, he is liable to account to the company for any profits made thereby. If a 'corporate opportunity' arises, that opportunity belongs to the company and cannot be secretly taken up by the director himself.

Examples

In *Regal (Hastings) Ltd* v *Gulliver* (1967) Regal owned a cinema. It was desired that two more be acquired and the whole then disposed. A subsidiary company was formed for that purpose. A lessor required the subsidiary's share capital to be paid up to £5,000. Regal could only manage half, of that, so Regal's directors subscribed and paid for the remainder. The subsidiary was sold and a profit of £3 per share was made by Regal and the directors. Subsequently the new owners of Regal sued the directors for their profits. It was held they were entitled to recover. A profit had been made by the directors out of their position and it had not made any difference that this had been in good faith.

In *Cook* v *Deeks* (1916) three directors diverted to themselves a contract in which their company was interested. It was held that this belonged to the company and they were liable for breach of fiduciary duty.

In *Industrial Development Consultants Ltd* v *Cooley* (1972) a director was employed by a company which was trying to get contracts from the Eastern Gas Board. He entered into negotiation with the Gas Board but the Board indicated to him that it would not deal with his company. So he resigned and took the contract on himself. It was held he was in breach of his fiduciary duty. It made no difference that the company might not have received the contract itself and therefore had suffered no loss.

A director can be liable even if he acts in good faith, and even if the company suffered no loss. If the director acted in good faith, however, he may escape liability by having the transaction approved by the company in general meeting (and see also the reference to CA 1985, s 727 at 5.33). Ratification in general meeting would have saved the directors in *Regal* (above). However, some breaches are not ratifiable, it is thought, including breach of the duty of good faith and expropriation of corporate property. Thus although the directors in *Cook* v *Deeks* purported to approve their wrongdoing, their breach was probably not ratifiable because the contract they had diverted to themselves belonged to the company in equity. The majority of shareholders (who comprised the delinquent directors) could not vote themselves a present of the company's property.

In spite of some authority to the contrary, the rule is that ratification, in a case of ratifiable breach, *must* be by the general meeting. Ratification by the directors meeting alone is not sufficient.

5.67 Misapplication of the company's property

Theft from the company would not only be a breach of fiduciary duty but also a criminal offence. But other examples of misapplication of the company's property giving rise to breach of fiduciary duty can occur when some of the intricate provisions of CA 1985 preventing disposition of corporate property, or the making of contracts without certain procedures being followed, are broken by the directors.

For example, any money paid over by way of unlawful financial assistance to someone for the purchase of shares in a company as prohibited by CA 1985 (5.78) would be a misapplication of company funds and would give rise to a breach of fiduciary duty on the part of the directors. Other examples could be:

(1) A payment of compensation for loss of office made to one of the board without disclosure to and approval by the members (5.71).
(2) Where directors have disposed of the company's assets in a manner which is *ultra vires* (5.28).
(3) Where directors make a payment to a third party that is not necessarily *ultra vires*, but is, nonetheless, in breach of fiduciary duty, or not for the benefit of the company.

5.68 Acting *bona fide* and for the benefit of the company as a whole

A director must make decisions *bona fide* and for the benefit of the company as a whole. He must not therefore act *mala fide*, dishonestly, or otherwise for a non-corporate purpose.

5.69 What is 'the company as a whole'?

Generally (and primarily) this means the shareholders as a body but there can, exceptionally, be other considerations to be taken into account. First, especially where the company is near to insolvency there may be, in effect, a duty also to take into account creditors' interests. Whether the fiduciary duty here discussed actually extends to a duty towards creditors is a matter of some controversy. But undoubtedly the wrongful trading provisions of the Insolvency Act 1986 also indirectly create an incentive to directors to behave responsibly to creditors (see 5.87). Secondly, CA 1985 requires directors also to have regard to the interests of employees.

5.70 The duty to apply powers for their proper purposes

Powers of directors are numerous and these must be exercised *bona fide* and for the benefit of the company as a whole and *not* for an ulterior purpose. This applies, for example, to powers to allot shares, forfeit shares, make gifts or gratuities, or to approve transfers of shares.

5.71 Some statutory rules governing directors' duties and fair dealing by directors

There are certain statutory rules concerning the conduct of directors which include:

(1) A director must declare his interest in a contract with a company to the board of directors (CA 1985, s 317).
(2) A payment to a director or the transfer of property to a director for compensation for loss of office must be approved by the company in general meeting (CA 1985, ss 312–316).
(3) A company cannot give a director a service contract for more than five years without its being approved by the general meeting (CA 1985, s 319). The provision covers unapproved agreements where during that period of more than five years the tenure of the director cannot be terminated by the company by notice or where it can only be terminated in specified circumstances (eg misconduct). A term incorporated in an agreement in contravention of the section is void and the agreement will then be deemed to be terminable on reasonable notice only. As defined

by common law, this will be drastically shorter, certainly no more than a year and on the authorities, and more likely no more than three to six months. So the sanction is quite effective.
(4) Certain shareholder approvals must be obtained in relation to substantial property transactions involving directors and a company (CA 1985, ss 320–322).
(5) There are certain restrictions on loans to directors and persons connected with them (CA 1985, ss 330–344).
(6) A director may not deal in share options in a company (CA 1985, s 323). This extends to a spouse and infant child.
(7) A director must disclose shareholdings in his own company (CA 1985, s 324). This also extends to the interests of a spouse and infant child. A listed company must notify the Stock Exchange of such matters.
(8) In the context of public companies, under the Companies Securities (Insider Dealing) Act 1985 a director may not indulge in insider dealing in listed securities.

5.72 Collective abuse of shareholder power against minorities

Shareholders, when voting on resolutions in general meeting can, in the main, consider their own interests.

However the passing of resolutions by majorities against minorities can very exceptionally amount to what is known as a 'fraud on the minority' where the outcome is oppressive to the minority. The courts will impugn a resolution where the majority can be said not to have acted *bona fide* and for the benefit of the company.

As, ordinarily, the courts consider it is for the majority themselves to determine *bona fide* what is for the benefit of the company (unless they have formed a view which is so unreasonable that no reasonable majority would have adopted it), few cases are successful.

A different approach however is illustrated by the case of *Clemens v Clemens Bros Ltd* (1976). There 45% of the shares in a company were held by a minority shareholder and 55% by her aunt. The aunt caused the directors to raise the company's capital and issue new shares to the other directors and to a trust for employees but to the exclusion of the niece. This had the effect of diluting the niece's shareholding and losing her the 'negative control' (ie the right to block a special resolution) that she already possessed. The court clearly thought this was wrong and held it was a fraud on the minority. In doing so the court probably applied the wrong test by looking at the issue too much from the minority, as opposed to majority, view.

But it illustrates perhaps a different approach to small quasi partnership companies where equitable considerations may make it unjust that strict powers held by the majority are used to diminish a minority's rights and expectations. A pre-emption clause in the articles about share issues (see above) would of course have prevented the aunt's action in the first place, a salutary reminder of the usefulness of articles (or shareholder agreements) as a mode of regulating shareholder power by contract (see also CA 1985, ss 89–96 discussed earlier: 5.22).

5.73 Statutory protection for minorities

The discussion at 5.72 paints a gloomy picture of shareholder rights to challenge majority action at common law, but there are also remedies under statute. These are, first, winding up under the just and equitable ground and second, the statutory petition under which you can claim 'unfair prejudice'.

5.74 The statutory petition to wind up under the just and equitable ground under section 122(g) of the Insolvency Act 1986

Under this heading the company may be wound up at the instance of a member: for example, where the main object of the company has failed or where there is no *bona fide* intention on the part of the directors to carry on the business in a proper manner.

Also, and very importantly, it can be wound up where there has been a breach of an understanding between the members as to the equal rights of participation in management and other matters, and confidence between the parties has broken down. In those circumstances it might be 'just and equitable' to wind the company up.

5.75 Example: Winding up under the just and equitable ground

The leading case is *Re Westbourne Galleries Ltd* (1973). In this case A and B were partners with equal shares in a carpet business. They formed a company to adopt the business. A and B were the first directors and each held an equal shareholding. Later, B's son, C, was made a director and A and B each transferred some of their shares to him. The company made profits which were distributed by way of directors' salary and no dividends were paid. Later, A and B fell out, and when the dispute came to a head, C sided with B and, at a general meeting, C and B procured an ordinary resolution (because their shares gave them the necessary majority (5.43)) to remove A from office.

As a result, A ended up in a position whereby, because of pre-emption provisions in the Articles, he could not transfer his shares outside the company without the other directors' consent. Also he was receiving no dividend and he was excluded from management. It was held that it was 'just and equitable' to wind the company up.

Although these facts are not exhaustive of the situations in which a court will wind the company up under the just and equitable ground (other examples include lack of probity and failure of the company's substratum), the case forms a very useful example of how the winding up petition can be applied in practice to intra-corporate disputes.

On the other hand, using the winding up petition has been described as using a 'sledgehammer to crack a nut'. It is a drastic remedy and sometimes it may not even be the remedy that the partners would themselves choose as a solution to their dispute, if there were alternatives available. It is sometimes more constructive to try and sort out the dispute rather than dissolve the company. The next section provides an alternative solution.

5.76 The unfair prejudice petition

Under CA 1985, s 459 a member of a company may complain of 'unfair prejudice' by a petition presented to the court. This is a far more versatile legal action than winding up. A petitioner must show that there is an act or omission of the company which is unfairly prejudicial to him or that the company's affairs are being or have been conducted in a manner which is unfairly prejudicial to the interests of some part of the members (including himself at least). There has been some speculation as to the meaning of the concept of prejudice to 'some part' of the members. Does this mean that a petition will only succeed if one faction of the membership has been discriminated against?

In *Re Carrington Viyella plc* (1983) a petition was brought *inter alia* on the basis that a company had broken its promise to the government not to acquire more than a certain percentage of shares in another company. The petition was rejected partly on the ground that such conduct affected all shareholders equally and, in the opinion of the trial judge, the basis of the petition was, instead, that some *part*, not all of the members had to be prejudiced. This decision has been greatly criticised. But the Companies Bill sched 18 proposes a substitution of the words 'unfairly prejudicial to the interests of its members generally or of some part of its members' for 'unfairly prejudicial to the interests of some part of the members', and this amendment should close off the loophole.

There have been a great many cases on s 459 already and it is probably futile to set out the facts of all of these. Examples of conduct relied on in successful petitions or in cases where the court has refused to strike out a petition at an early stage (thereby approving the conduct alleged as *prima facie* unfair prejudice) include a seven month delay in convening a meeting on requisition of shareholders, an exclusion of a director who was also contributor of capital from management (see below), a proposal of a rights issue in which a minority shareholder was, in practical terms, unable to participate because he needed to save his funds to pursue a section 459 petition against the company that he had just issued, a continually low payment of dividends (although the facts were unusual — the conduct extended over 37 years), payment of excessive remuneration to a director who was a majority shareholder, and a misappropriation of corporate assets.

If the petition is successful the court may order or grant such relief as it thinks fit. But it can specifically, for example, regulate the conduct of the company's affairs in future, require the company to refrain from doing something complained of in the petition, allow a shareholder to bring a civil action against someone in the company's name, or provide for the compulsory purchase of a member's shares.

There is some doubt as to whether the petition would apply to the facts of *Re Westbourne Galleries Ltd* (5.75) as the petition seems to comtemplate that a petitioner must complain of prejudice to his *member's* rights. It is not certain whether this would cover a complaint of loss of directorship without more. However, case law is still developing on the meaning of the petition and a number of cases have held that the petition ought to cover cases of exclusion of a member from management. Thus in *Re A Company No 00477 of 1986 (1986)* it was held that a director who had put capital into the business might be unfairly prejudiced if dismissed as director and removed from management. Although the petition *was* concerned with members' rights the court could look at this in its widest sense.

5.77 Department of Trade investigations

It may sometimes be possible for the Department of Trade inspectors to investigate the affairs of a company and take action arising therefrom in cases of suspected fraud, misfeasance or withholding of information from shareholders, to investigate ownership or control of a company, to investigate directors' share dealings, or to investigate insider dealing. An inspector has powers to call on persons to produce books and records and to require attendances before him. The powers of inspectors are proposed to be enlarged by the provisions of the Companies Bill, clauses 54–87 *inter alia* in relation to companies affairs generally, company ownership matters under CA 1985, in relation to persons who carry on investment business under the Financial Services

Act 1986 and in relation to insider dealing under the Financial Services Act 1986.

5.78 Some rules about maintenance of capital

Capital rules are complicated and too detailed to describe in full here. The following, however, indicates the strictness with which the subject is treated.

A company may increase its capital by ordinary resolution and reduce it by special resolution if allowed by the articles. Reduction requires notice to creditors and the approval of the court.

Subject to the below, a company may not purchase shares in itself, or in its holding company, nor (subject to a limited defence, where the principal purpose of the company in giving assistance is not to finance the purchase, but is an incidental part of some larger purpose and the assistance is given in good faith in the interests of the company) give financial assistance for the purchase of shares in itself or its holding company. A company may not repay share capital to members. There are also strict rules concerning what money is available to pay dividends, which, in any event, cannot be paid out of capital and can normally be paid only out of realised net profits. A company cannot issue shares at a discount. All these rules are to maintain the company's capital. However:

(1) A company may give financial assistance for the purchase of shares under certain limited conditions, eg in relation to an employee share scheme, and a private company may give financial assistance if approved by a special resolution and if there is a detailed statutory declaration of solvency.
(2) It is possible (if a company is authorised by its articles) to issue redeemable shares (although there are strict rules about financing the redemption).
(3) It is possible for a company (if authorised by its articles) to repurchase its shares with the approval of the members of the company. Ordinarily this must be financed out of distributable profits or the proceeds of a fresh issue of shares; but a private company (subject to strict safeguards) may finance the repurchase out of capital. There are also other very detailed rules about procedure in relation to the type of approval concerned (depending on whether the purchase is an off-market or market purchase), and otherwise. (4.31).

Even stricter rules, generally about capital, apply in the case of public companies, eg a duty to alert members to a serious loss of capital; to ensure that there is a minimum issued share capital of £50,000, a quarter of which is paid up; and to ensure that there are valuation safeguards on payment for shares by transfer of non-cash assets.

5.79 Corporate insolvency

It is ironically appropriate to close this part of the chapter by discussing the subject of termination of businesses. In this section we look at three stages of insolvency, ie, receivership, administration and liquidation, some of these conditions being more terminal in nature than others.

Before doing this, it may be noted that under the Insolvency Act 1986, it is possible for a company in difficulty to propose a voluntary arrangement with its creditors in composition of its debts or a scheme of arrangement of its affairs. A nominee (who must be a licensed insolvency practitioner) must supervise such a proposal. It may be made either by the directors, before administration or winding up (see below) or by an administrator (5.81) or a liquidator (5.82). If a certain proportion in value of creditors vote in favour of such a scheme it will be binding on all creditors and the company may obtain a new lease of life.

5.80 Receivership

A receiver of a company may be appointed at the instance of a debenture holder (5.22) when the terms of the debenture allow this. This will usually arise as a result of breach of the provisions of the debenture. The receiver appointed by the debenture holder may then enter the company and take charge of its affairs. He will normally be a receiver *and manager* and, for the purposes of the Insolvency Act 1986, will usually be an *administrative* receiver.

He takes charge of the company's business and has the authority to dismiss and engage staff. His function is to get in the company's debts and to realise the company's assets in order to raise as much money as possible (or as is necessary) to discharge the company's liability to the debenture holder. This may in practice involve selling a substantial proportion of the company's assets. Sometimes he may have to sell the entire company's undertaking on the basis that an undertaking or part thereof sold as a going concern is more valuable to a purchaser (and therefore will cost more) than a bundle of assets alone.

Receivers (or indeed administrators) who are selling businesses as a going concern must be aware of the Transfer of Undertakings (Protection of Employment) Regulations 1981 which may, because of their provisions about automatic transfer of employment and other matters, discourage potential purchasers who are unwilling to inherit staff employed in the ailing business. This subject is more fully discussed in chapter 10.

When the exercise is completed, the receiver will pay the debenture holder, observing the order of priorities of payment in insolvency prescribed by the Insolvency Act 1986 and set out at 5.88. Then, in theory, he is free to hand the company back to the members to deal with as they think fit. In practice, though, there is usually nothing to hand back and the company inevitably proceeds into liquidation. A receiver may also be appointed by the court, but this is comparatively rare.

5.81 Administration order

A new regime was instituted by the Insolvency Act 1986 as a possible means of rescuing an insolvent company otherwise than by receivership and of saving it from liquidation. A court may make an administration order if:

(1) the company is or is likely to become unable to pay its debts;
(2) the court considers that the making of an order would be likely to achieve one or more of the following purposes, viz, to secure:
   (a) the survival of the company as a whole or any part of its undertaking as a going concern;
   (b) the approval of a voluntary arrangement;
   (c) the sanctioning of a compromise or arrangement between the company and its creditors;
   (d) a more advantageous realisation of the company's assets than would be effected on a winding up.

An application may be made by petition presented by either the company or the directors or by a creditor or creditors including any contingent or prospective creditor or creditors, or by all or any of those parties together or separately. Upon the making of the administration order an administrator has similar powers to an administrative receiver. An administrator may take control of the affairs, business and property of the company, prepare a statement of affairs, make proposals and eventually seek to be discharged as an administrator.

It is hoped that administration, combined with the possibility of a voluntary arrangement with creditors under the Insolvency Act 1986, may lead to an extension of the life of companies that otherwise would have no alternative but to proceed into liquidation.

5.82 Liquidation

A liquidator deals with the dissolution of the company, that is to say, the (terminal) stage beyond either receivership or administration. Liquidation means a winding up and there are two modes, voluntary and compulsory.

5.83 Voluntary winding up

There are two sorts of voluntary winding up, a *members'* voluntary winding up and a *creditors'* voluntary winding up. This is commenced by special or extraordinary resolution (the latter resolution applying where a company cannot carry on its business by reason of its liabilities). For a member's voluntary winding up to continue, the directors must file a declaration of solvency. If this is not possible, the voluntary winding up *has* to take the form of a creditors' voluntary winding up and a creditors' meeting must be convened within 14 days of (but this often takes place at the same time as) the members' meeting to pass the resolution to go into liquidation.

5.84 Compulsory winding up

The ways in which the court can compulsorily wind up a company are set out in s 122 of the Insolvency Act 1986 and are as follows:

(1) The company has resolved by special resolution that it be wound up by the court.
(2) The company is a public company which was registered as such on its original incorporation and has not been issued with a certificate of compliance with the capital requirements of CA 1985 (5.15) and more than a year has expired since it was so registered.
(3) The company is an old public company within the meaning of the Companies Consolidation (Consequential Provisions) Act 1985.
(4) The company has not commenced its business within a year from incorporation or it has suspended its business for a whole year.
(5) The number of members has fallen below two.
(6) The company is unable to pay its debts.
(7) It is just and equitable that the company should be wound up.

It is case (6) which is most relevant here. The other cases do not necessarily mean there is an insolvency. Cases (5) and (7) are discussed at 5.11 and 5.74 respectively.

5.85 Choice of liquidator

In the case of a voluntary winding up, the liquidator is elected by the members or creditors as the case may be. In the case of a compulsory winding up the official receiver takes over as liquidator in the first instance. He may or may not be replaced as liquidator by a liquidator voted in by the first creditors' meeting. If the first creditors' meeting does not elect its own choice of liquidator the official receiver will, in practice, continue as liquidator.

5.86 An administrator's or liquidator's powers

An administrator or liquidator can apply to the court to avoid certain transactions if he thinks fit. For example:

(1) Under the Insolvency Act 1986 he can apply to avoid *transactions at an undervalue* (Insolvency Act 1986, s 238) at 'a relevant time' (see below). Transactions at an undervalue are either gifts or transactions where the company is agreed to be entitled to receive no consideration or transactions where the value of the consideration is significantly less than the consideration provided by the company. A court must not make an order in relation to a transaction at an undervalue if it is satisfied:

   (a) that the company entered into the transaction in good faith and for the purpose of carrying on its business and
   (b) that at the time it did so there were reasonable grounds for believing that the transaction would benefit the company.

(2) He can also apply to avoid *preferences* (Insolvency Act 1986, s 239), again at 'a relevant time'.

   A company gives a preference to a person if:

   (a) that person is one of the company's creditors or a surety or a guarantor for any of the company's debts or other liabilities and
   (b) the company does anything or suffers anything to be done which (in either case) has the effect of putting that person into a position which, in the event of the company going into insolvent liquidation, will be better than the position he would have been in if that thing had not been done.

   A court must not make an order in respect of a preference unless it is satisfied the company was influenced by a desire to prefer. However, where the preference has been given to a person connected (otherwise than by reason only of being its employee (see below)) with the company, the company is presumed to have been so influenced unless the contrary is shown.

   The '*relevant time*' in relation to transactions at an undervalue and preferences is:

(a) in the case of a transaction at an undervalue or of a preference which is given to a person who is connected with the company (otherwise than by reason only of being its employee): *two years* before onset of insolvency;
(b) in the case of a preference which is not a transaction at an undervalue or given to a connected person *six months* before the onset of insolvency;
(c) in either case any time between the presentation of a petition for the making of an administration order in relation to the company and the making of an order.

Where a company enters into a transaction at an undervalue or gives a preference at a time as mentioned in (a) or (b) above the time is not treated as a 'relevant time' unless the company

(a) is at that time unable to pay its debts or
(b) becomes unable to pay its debts in consequence of the transaction or preference.

However, this is presumed, unless the contrary is shown, in relation to any transaction at an undervalue which is entered into by the company with a person connected with the company.

A person is 'connected' if he or it is a director, an associate (1.8) or an associated company.

(3) A floating charge will be invalid except to the extent of any consideration given at the time of or after creation of the charge, if, when the charge was created, the company was unable to pay its debts or became unable to pay its debts in consequence of the transaction under which the charge was created. This is so if it is made within 12 months of the onset of insolvency. Where the charge was given to a person connected with the company, the period is two years, and in that case it is not necessary to show that the company was unable to pay its debts. In any event, the charge will be invalid to the extent described above if given at a time between the presentation of the petition for making of an administration order in relation to the company and the making of an order.

(4) Transactions at an undervalue aimed at putting assets beyond the reach of claimants can also be attacked where it is considered appropriate during a winding up. Unlike in the case of the provisions on transactions at an undervalue discussed at (1), a court is not restricted to a two year period before insolvency if these circumstances apply.

5.87 Wrongful and fraudulent trading

Liability can also attach to individuals for wrongful and fraudulent trading if the circumstances appear to support this during the course of a liquidation.

Fraudulent trading (Insolvency Act 1986, s 213) occurs when it appears that any business of the company has been carried on with an intent to defraud the creditors of the company or creditors of any other person or for any fraudulent purpose. Any persons who were knowingly parties to the fraudulent trading can be made to contribute personally to the company's assets.

Wrongful trading (Insolvency Act 1986, s 214) applies to a person who is or was a director of a company and occurs when the company has gone into insolvent liquidation and at some time before the commencement of the winding up of the company that person knew or ought to have concluded that there was no reasonable prospect that the company would avoid going into insolvent liquidation and that person was a director (or, importantly, a shadow director (5.41)) of the company at that time.

Again the court can order a contribution to the company's assets as it thinks fit. That is to say, it can make the individual personally liable. Both provisions are important exceptions to the concept of limited liability of members of a company (5.21).

The concept of wrongful trading is much more important in practice because it is easier to establish. In effect it imposes a duty on directors to consider creditors' interests on penalty of having personally to contribute to the company's assets. Liability can be avoided if the court is satisfied that the director in question took every step with a view to minimising the potential loss to the company's creditors that he ought to have taken. The conclusions a director ought to have reached and steps he ought to have taken are those which would have been reached or taken by a reasonably diligent person having both

(1) the general knowledge, skill and experience that may reasonably be expected of a person carrying out the same functions as are carried out by that director in relation to the company and
(2) the general knowledge, skill and experience that that director has.

The test is mainly an objective one envisaging in limb (1) a reasonable director. But some regard can be had to a director's qualification and experience in limb (2).

There is no indication as to what steps a director ought to take to avoid liability. But he should take professional advice (or cause the board to do so) if concerned, and the board, rather than adopt a 'Micawber' like attitude, should consider administration or liquidation earlier rather than later if the facts dictate.

The first reported case indicates how the provision works. In *Re Produce Marketing Consortium Ltd* (1989) the company went into liquidation in October 1987 with debts amounting to £317,694. The company had been making a loss since 1980. The position deteriorated further in the summer of 1986. From November 1986 the bank started to dishonour cheques. The accounts for 1986 were late and not available until January 1987. They showed heavy losses. The company carried on until October. It was held the directors were liable. They argued that they did not have the benefit of accounts until 1987. But s 214 posed an objective test and required scrutiny not only of what they knew but what they ought to have known. And they were involved in the business intimately. The directors were therefore held to pay £75,000 towards the company's assets.

Fraudulent trading (whether or not arising in a winding up) is a criminal offence under s 458 of CA 1985, and there are numerous penalties for fraud and malpractice arising before and during winding up contained in the Insolvency Act 1986.

5.88 Order of distribution of assets

The order of distribution of assets on insolvency is as follows:

(1) Costs of the winding up.
(2) Rights of a fixed chargee.
(3) Rights of preferential creditors, viz:
 (a) PAYE debts due to the Inland Revenue;
 (b) debts due to Customs and Excise;
 (c) debts due to the DSS by way of Social Security contributions;
 (d) contributions to occupational pension schemes;
 (e) arrears of remuneration of employees (subject to limits).
(4) Rights of a floating chargee.
(5) Rights of ordinary trade creditors.
(6) Rights of shareholders to return of capital.

It is important to note that certain individuals may take priority over the above order. These include, for example, those entitled to the benefit of retention of title (or 'Romalpa') clauses in relation to goods delivered to a company but not yet paid for. Those entitled to the benefit of reservation of title clauses may come above (3) to (6) above because the beneficiary of the clause may have the right to reclaim the goods himself (although an administrator (5.81) has a power of sale under the Insolvency Act 1986 subject to accounting to the beneficiary of the clause for the net proceeds). As those under (3) to (6) can only claim proceeds of sale of assets of the company, those entitled to the benefit of reservation of title clauses may transcend this order because the goods which are the subject of the clause have never been the company's assets (see chapter 12).

In an insolvent compulsory liquidation it is of course most unlikely in practice that shareholders will receive any reimbursement of their capital.

Part B Partnership law

5.89 Introduction

The following is a brief account of partnership law. The discussion is based on English law; in Scotland there are certain differences which should be separately checked if need be.

5.90 Indicators as to whether a partnership exists

A partnership is defined as the relationship which subsists between persons carrying on business in common with a view of profit (Partnership Act 1890, s 1). A business includes a trade, occupation or profession.

The Partnership Act 1890 lays down some rules to help determine whether or not a partnership exists. Thus:

(1) Common ownership of property of itself does not create a partnership even if there is sharing of profits.
(2) Sharing of gross returns does not of itself create a partnership.
(3) Receipt of a share of the profits of a business can be evidence that a person is a partner in the business but does not *of itself* create a partnership. Thus:

  (a) Receipt of a debt by instalments from profits of a business does not necessarily make the recipient a partner.
  (b) Remuneration by a share of the profits of a servant or agent of a person engaged in a business does not of itself make the recipient a partner.
  (c) If a widow or child of a deceased partner gets an annuity paid from part of the profits that does not of itself make the widow or child a partner.
  (d) If a lender who makes a loan to a person engaged or about

to engage in business gets interest on the loan variable with the profits or interest taking the form of a share of profits, this does not necessarily make the lender a partner (provided that the contract is in writing and signed by or on behalf of all the parties).
  (e) Receipt by a person who has sold the goodwill of a business of part of the profits in payment for the sale does not make that person a partner as such.

Commonly, of course, intending partners sign up to an express partnership agreement (5.93), thus avoiding doubt about the matter.

5.91   Size of partnerships

A firm consisting of more partners than the statutory limit is not permissible. The statutory limit in most cases is 20 (but this limit does not apply to partnerships between solicitors, accountants, persons carrying on business as members of the Stock Exchange or other (mainly professional) partnerships specified in orders made under CA 1985).

5.92   Rules implied by the Partnership Act 1890

Some of the rules implied by the Act are as follows:

(1) Every partner is an agent of the firm and has authority to bind the partners unless this is countermanded by the other partners and the person with whom the partner is dealing knows of the lack of authority.
(2) Every partner in a firm is liable jointly with the other partners for its debts (and, in Scotland, also severally) whilst he was a partner (and after his death his estate is also liable) and is liable jointly and severally for torts and other wrongs for which the firm is liable.
(3) If a partner commits a wrongful act or omission either within his apparent authority or in the ordinary course of the business of the firm any liability attaches to the firm as well as to the partner committing the act (5.94).
(4) Where a partner misappropriates the property of another received in the course of the firm's business the firm is liable to make good the loss (5.94).
(5) All partners are entitled to share equally in the capital and profits of the business.
(6) All partners must contribute equally towards losses of capital or losses otherwise sustained by the firm.
(7) A partner is not ordinarily entitled to interest on capital agreed to be subscribed by him (but see (8)).

(8) A partner making any payment or advance beyond the capital he has agreed to subscribe is entitled to interest at the rate of 5% per annum from the date of payment.
(9) Every partner can take part in the management of the partnership business.
(10) A partner cannot receive remuneration for acting in the partnership business.
(11) No person can be introduced as a partner without the consent of the existing partners.
(12) On ordinary matters relating to partnership business decisions may be made by a majority of partners but no change in the nature of the partnership business can be effected without the consent of all the existing partners.
(13) The majority of partners cannot expel any partner unless a power to do so has been conferred by agreement.
(14) A partnership is determinable at will by any partner giving notice of his intention to do so to all the other partners.

The rules which are implied by the Partnership Act 1890 and which affect partners' relations with each other may well be inconvenient to you. But the Partnership Act 1890 provides that rules about partners' relations with each other (but *not* rules about their obligations to *third parties*) may be modified by express agreement between the partners. That is when an express partnership agreement is useful. An express agreement allows you to settle the terms between you and your colleagues in some detail in accordance with your real wishes.

5.93 Partnership agreements

No special form is required for a partnership agreement as a partnership can arise from oral agreement, or even by implication (5.90, 5.92). But you would be well advised to put your agreement into writing.

Partnership agreements can, and very often do, include the following. This, however, is merely a list of common terms and is not exhaustive by any means:

(1) The name of the firm and what it does (as to its name, see Part C of this chapter).
(2) The date the partnership started and how long it is to continue.
(3) The proportions in which the partners are to put in capital.
(4) The firm's bankers and which partners may sign cheques.
(5) Whether all or only some of the partners manage the business, and to what extent, and whether any partner is to be a 'sleeping' partner.
(6) Details of the firm's accountants and solicitors.
(7) Details of holidays and procedures for taking holidays.

(8) How profits are to be shared and what provision there is for drawings.
(9) What provision, if any, there is about private income.
(10) Provision for keeping regular accounts and books and records.
(11) What happens on the death or retirement of partners.
(12) A clause allowing for expulsion of a partner and providing what cases will justify expulsion.
(13) A clause providing that a partner may only retire by notice and specifying the length of notice.
(14) An arbitration clause.
(15) What restrictions, if any, apply to prevent a departing partner from competing with the firm (note here, though, the potential of the doctrine of restraint of trade discussed in chapters 10 and 12).
(16) What provisions apply as to length of maternity leave for a woman partner and what share of profits she should receive during her absence.
(17) What length of absence through sickness is permissible before the other partners may require retirement through ill health and what share of profits applies during such absence.
(18) A provision requiring partners to sign a continuation election for tax purposes on a change in the composition of the firm (3.7).
(19) Finally, any special provisions or rules relevant to particular partnerships such as doctors, accountants or lawyers' practices. Every partnership is different, it must be remembered, and what may be appropriate for inclusion in a deed of partnership for farmers, for example, may not be appropriate for estate agents.

5.94 A partner and third parties

A partner is an agent of the firm and of the other partners to do any act for the carrying on of the firm's business unless he has no authority to do the act concerned and the person with whom he is dealing knows about this. A partner has authority to make the firm liable on a range of matters. This would not include, for example, execution of a deed or giving a guarantee in the firm's name or submitting a dispute to arbitration or making his partners partners with others. But in a trading partnership his authority is otherwise quite wide. It therefore goes without saying that partners should be chosen with care.

A firm can also be liable for a tort (chapter 12) or other wrongful act to a third party committed by a partner. This is provided that it was committed within the apparent authority of the partner or that it was committed in the ordinary course of the firm's business. Partners can also be liable for fraudulent misappropriation of monies received from a third party in the course of the business if the fraudulent partner is acting within the scope of his apparent authority or where the firm has in the course of its business received money or property of a third person and such money or property is misapplied by a partner while it is in the custody of the firm.

Liability of partners for the firm's obligations is joint in contract, and joint and several in tort and for other wrongful acts and misappropriations, and this is one of the big disadvantages of being a partner in a partnership (chapter 1). Limited liability is possible in a limited partnership formed under the Limited Partnerships Act 1907, but as discussed in chapter 1, the conditions attaching to this type of structure mean that relatively few of this sort of partnership exist.

5.95 Liabilities of new and retiring partners

Under the Partnership Act 1890 a new partner does not take on liability for obligations incurred by the firm before he became a partner. Nor does a retiring partner cease to be liable for obligations incurred whilst he was a partner once he leaves. A retiring partner ceases to be liable for obligations incurred after he has left.

However, if a third party who has been dealing with the firm before and after its change has no notice of the change, he may be entitled to treat all apparent members of the old firm as still being members. So if you retire from a partnership you should ensure that the letterheading is changed to reflect this and that people you deal with (say as a consultant) know about your retirement. A circular giving actual notice of retirement to customers or clients of the firm is desirable. A notice in the *London Gazette* will be sufficient notice of the change in the case of persons who have not previously dealt with the firm.

It is possible for a retiring partner to be released from liability to a creditor entirely and a new partner liable in his place under a contract of 'novation', ie a three-party agreement between the retiring partner, the firm newly constituted and a creditor. Such an agreement can be express or implied (eg by conduct), although it would not be easy to infer an implied agreement. A new partner would not be advised to enter into such an agreement.

5.96 Partners' duties of fair dealing to one another

Partners must deal fairly with one another. For example, partners are bound to render true accounts and full information of all matters affecting the partnership. A partner must account to his colleagues for any benefit received by him without their consent from any transaction concerning the partnership or from using the firm's name, property or connection. And if a partner carries on a competing business of the same nature without the consent of his colleagues he must account for the profits he makes.

Finally, the provisions of the Sex Discrimination Act 1975 (chapter 10) apply to partnerships in that it is unlawful for a firm to discriminate against a person on ground of sex or marital status in relation to a position as partner in the firm:

(1) in the arrangements they make for the purpose of determining who should be offered that position, or
(2) in the terms on which they offer her that position, or
(3) by refusing or deliberately omitting to offer her that position, or
(4) in a case where the woman already holds that position

    (a) in the way they afford her access to any benefits facilities or services, or by refusing or deliberately omitting to afford her access to them, or
    (b) by expelling her from that position, or subjecting her to any other detriment.

Race discrimination in the same context is similarly prohibited under the Race Relations Act 1976, but in that case, at the time of writing, anomalously, only partnerships of six or more partners are covered.

5.97 Partnership property

Property acquired on account of the firm or for the purposes of and in the course of the business or with partnership money will be partnership property subject to any agreement (express or implied) to the contrary. But there can be difficult borderline cases. So ownership of partnership property is best dealt with by express agreement and this is another good reason why an express partnership agreement should be drawn up (5.93).

5.98 Dissolution of partnerships

Under the Partnership Act 1890, a partnership is dissolved:

(1) by expiry of a fixed term;
(2) by termination of the object for which the venture was set up;
(3) by death or bankruptcy of a partner;

Company and partnership law

(4) by one of the partners giving notice to the other or others in a partnership at will;
(5) upon the happening of an event which makes it unlawful to carry on the partnership business;
(6) by an event specified in an express clause, eg dishonesty, insobriety, fundamental disagreement;
(7) if a partner causes his share of the partnership property to be charged for his separate debt, if the other partners so elect to dissolve on that ground.

It is important to note that the above rules can be modified by consent usually in a formal partnership agreement (5.93). In particular, partners often provide that a partnership cannot be determined by a notice given by one of the partners only, or provide that a minimum period of notice is required (contrast (4) above), and it is often provided that partners may expel another under certain circumstances (eg misconduct) (a power of expulsion is not implied by the Partnership Act 1890).

Dissolution may be ordered by the court in the cases set out below, in case (1) under the Mental Health Act 1983 and, in the other cases, under the Partnership Act 1890:

(1) if a partner is incapable by reason of mental disorder of managing his affairs;
(2) if a partner other than the partner suing becomes in any way permanently incapable;
(3) if a partner other than the partner suing is guilty of conduct calculated to prejudice the business;
(4) if a partner other than the partner suing is guilty of wilful or persistent breaches of the partnership agreement or other conduct which makes it not reasonably practicable for the other partners to carry on in partnership with him;
(5) if the business can only be carried on at a loss;
(6) if it is just and equitable.

5.99 Order of application of assets on dissolution

On dissolution, assets, including contributions to make good losses of capital, are applied:

(1) in paying the firm's creditors;
(2) in repaying advances by partners;
(3) in repaying capital to partners in accordance with their entitlement;
(4) in dividing any balance as profit.

Losses (including losses of capital) must be made good:

(1) out of profits;
(2) out of capital;
(3) by the partners in the proportion in which they share the profits.

If the losses are too great for all the partners to bear, the result will be insolvency. There are specialised rules relating to partnership insolvency. But at the end of the day, because a partner may be personally liable, the final result in cases of serious indebtedness may be personal bankruptcy. The horrors of this are described in our discussion at 1.8.

5.100 Limited partnerships

Limited partnerships, set up under the Limited Partnerships Act 1907, have been briefly described in chapter 1.

Part C Company and business names

5.101 Company names

A company, if private, must have the suffix 'Limited' or 'Ltd' or, if public, 'public limited company' or 'plc' or the Welsh equivalent ('cyfyngedig') if appropriate (ie if the company's registered office is in Wales).

Private companies limited by guarantee with restricted objects, for example for the promotion of commerce, science, art, religion, charity or any profession, and whose profits have to be applied therefor, and which prohibit payment of dividends to members and require assets on a winding-up to be transferred to a similar body, can omit the suffix 'Limited' or 'Ltd'.

A company name:

(1) must not be the same as one on the Register already;
(2) must not constitute a criminal offence;
(3) must not be offensive;
(4) must not have a suffix other than 'Limited' 'Unlimited' 'public limited company' or the Welsh equivalent.

A company name must not give the impression that the company is connected with national or local government nor include any word or expression specified in the Company and Business Names

Regulations 1981 without the approval of the Secretary of State. The Regulations contain a schedule of such words and the relevant government department or other authorised body to contact for permission in each case. This is too long to set out here in full but, for example, any use of the word 'midwife' would require the consent of the Central Midwives Board; use of the word 'dental' would require the permission of the General Dental Council and so forth. The list ought to be consulted if you are in any doubt.

5.102 Change of name

A company can change its name by special resolution (5.35). A company *has* to change its name if it is, in the opinion of the Secretary of State, the same as or 'too like' a name already on the Register. The Secretary of State may direct this within 12 months of incorporation. The Secretary of State may also direct a change of name if it gives so misleading an indication of the company's activities as to be likely to cause harm to the public. A person who or which is not a public company is guilty of an offence if he or it carries on any trade, profession or business under a name which includes the suffix 'public limited company' or its Welsh equivalent. A public company may, on the other hand, commit an offence if it gives a material impression to someone that it is a private company.

5.103 Directors' names

It is optional as to whether the names of directors go on a company's notepaper. But if you do put directors' names on the notepaper all of the names must go on, together with the directors' Christian names or initials.

5.104 Use of company name

A company has to paint or affix its name on the outside of every office or place where it carries on its business. A company's name has also to appear:

(1) in all business letters;
(2) in all its notices and other official publications;
(3) in all bills of exchange, promissory notes, endorsements, cheques and orders for money or goods;
(4) in all its bills of parcels, invoices, receipts and letters of credit.

Although contraventions of the company and business name rules carry criminal liability and fines there is an important civil sanction in relation to use of the company's name on paperwork. For if the company omits its name from, or misdescribes it on, any bill of exchange, promissory note, endorsement, cheque or order, the signatory can be personally liable to the holder if there is default by the company. This is an important exception to limited liability.

Examples

In *Blum* v *OCP Repartition S.A.* (1987) B was a director of an English company called Bomore Medical Supplies Ltd which imported pharmaceutical products. OCP were a French company which supplied Bomore with products. Bomore paid for these with cheques which bore the name 'Bomore Medical Supplies' signed by B. Later Bomore was wound up and the cheques were not honoured. Because of the omission of the word 'limited' from the company's name B was personally liable to OCP.

In *Lindholst & Co A/S* v *Fowler* (1987) Lindholst contracted with Corby Chicken Co Ltd for the supply of equipment. In payment, F and H, directors of Corby Chicken signed bills of exchange addressed to 'Corby Chicken Co'. Corby Chicken went into receivership and F and H were sued by Lindholst for over £170,000 on four bills of exchange. It was held that because of the misdescription, F and H were personally liable.

At the time of writing, under CA 1985, every company must have a company seal with its name legibly engraved. However clause 123 of the Companies Bill proposes that a company need not have a company seal and that a document signed by a director and the secretary expressed to be executed by the company has the same effect as if it were under the company's common seal. It is also proposed, though, that if a company does have a seal it must have its name legibly engraved as above.

A company has to have the following information on any business letters or order forms:

(1) the company's place of registration and its number;
(2) its registered office address;
(3) if it is an investment company under CA 1985, that fact;
(4) if it is a limited company with permission to omit 'limited', the fact that it is nonetheless a limited company.

If you state the company's share capital on such documentation (although this is rarely done), this has to be a reference to paid-up share capital.

Finally, where the name of a company which is a public company includes, as its last part, the equivalent in Welsh of the words 'public limited company' ('cwmni cyfyngedig cyhoeddus') or in the case of a private company 'cyfyngedig' as the last word the fact that the company is a public limited company or a limited company respectively must be stated in English and in legible characters:

(1) in all prospectuses, bill-heads, letter paper, notices and other official publications of the company and
(2) in a notice conspicuously displayed in every place in which the company's business is carried on.

5.105 Business names

There used to be a Register of Business Names under the Registration of Business Names Act 1916. But it was abolished in 1981 and there is now no central register of business names which you can search.

5.106 Companies and business names

A company can trade under a business name which is different from that with which it is registered (its corporate name). The Business Names Act 1985 is the source of rules about this subject, as it applies to companies as well as to individuals and partnerships (see 5.107). There are similar restrictions to those discussed at 5.101 about the use of names which give the impression that there is a connection with local or national government or which are specified in the schedule to the Company and Business Names Regulations 1981. Further, a company using a business name must still carry its corporate name on letters, written orders for goods and services, invoices, receipts and written demands for payment together with an address for service. It must also display its corporate name and address for service at premises where the business is carried on and to which customers and suppliers have access. This information must also be given by written notice to any person with whom anything is done or discussed in the course of business upon request.

5.107 Business names for individuals and partnerships

The Business Names Act 1985 provides that if you carry on business under a name which is different from your own, or in the case of a partnership, does not consist of all surnames of the partners, the provisions of the Act apply. Certain words and expressions are restricted (see the Company and Business Names Regulations 1981) and require the Secretary of State's approval as in the case of companies (5.101).

If a partnership, you have to include the name of each partner (and if an individual, the individual's name) on all letters, written orders for goods or services, invoices, receipts and written demands for payment of debts. There must also be address for service. There must also be a notice displayed in a prominent position in any premises where the business is carried on and to which the customers or suppliers have access containing such names and addresses for service.

This information must also be given by written notice to any person with whom anything is done or discussed in the course of business upon request.

A partnership of 20 or more individuals may exclude the names of partners from its notepaper if no partner's name appears at all other than in the text or as signatory, and if the letter heading states its principal place of business and that a list of the partners' names is available for inspection at that address.

Breach of the business name provisions may lead to a novel civil remedy if a person dealing with the firm or individual suffers loss as a result of the breach. This is, that if the firm or individual in breach sues someone, the defendant to the action can plead the breach and ask that the claim be dismissed because of the breach. The court will allow this defence unless it thinks it is 'just and equitable' to permit the claim to be continued.

5.108 Passing off and trade marks

You must also ensure that a trading name does not infringe another's trade or service mark or amount to the tort of 'passing off' (eg by the use of a name similar to an existing name the similarity of which will be injurious to another because it is likely to cause confusion in the minds of the public and lead the public to believe that the goods or services that you trade in or provide are the goods or services of another). Infringement of trade or service marks and 'passing off' could lead to expensive court action.

6 Capital gains tax

6.1 Introduction

This chapter provides a brief summary of capital gains tax, particularly dealing with special rules and reliefs relating to businesses. Fuller details concerning other matters are contained in the *Allied Dunbar Capital Taxes and Estate Planning Guide* and the *Allied Dunbar Tax Guide*. Most references throughout this chapter are to CGTA 1979 which consolidated the relevant legislation from FA 1965 onwards.

6.2 Capital gains tax and businesses

Capital gains arise both within businesses and on the sale of businesses. Thus, the sale of a business asset might give rise to a capital gain. If you are trading as a sole trader, the capital gain is assessed on you personally and if you are in partnership, you will be charged to capital gains tax on your proportion of the gain (3.9). In either case, the rates of tax are the same as for income tax (25% and 40%). Prior to 6 April 1988, the capital gains tax rate was generally 30%.

The position regarding a company is different. Companies are taxed as separate entities and so a company is liable to tax on its capital gains (less losses). The rate of tax is the normal company's corporation tax charge (4.17). However, where you have been trading through a company which is sold, you will personally be liable for capital gains tax on the sale of your company shares.

6.3 Liability to capital gains tax

Any taxpayer is liable to capital gains tax on gains accruing in a year of assessment during any part of which he is resident or ordinarily resident in the UK. Even if he is neither resident nor ordinarily resident here, a taxpayer carrying on a trade in the UK through a branch or agency is generally liable to capital gains tax accruing on the disposal of assets in this country used in his trade; or assets held here and

140 Allied Dunbar Business Tax and Law Guide

used for the branch or agency. This rule has been extended to professions and vocations (as well as trades) regarding gains accruing from 14 March 1989. Similar rules apply to companies and partnerships etc.

Should you be resident or ordinarily resident in the UK during a tax year, you are liable to capital gains tax on asset realizations worldwide. However, an exception applies if you are not domiciled here. Your capital gains tax liability then only extends to gains which you remit here. For these purposes, a non-Sterling bank account is treated as located outside the UK unless the account is held at a UK branch and you are UK resident.

6.4 Annual exemptions for individuals

If you are in business as a sole trader or partner, your annual net gains (after losses) are not charged to capital gains tax if they do not exceed the annual exemption. The basic rules are as follows and the rate shown is that for 1989–90:

(1) The first £5,000 of your net gains is exempted from capital gains tax. This applies no matter how high are your total business or other gains for the year. Any gains of your wife are included unless you are separated.
(2) Losses for previous years (6.14) are offset, but so as to leave £5,000 of net gains to be exempt. This results in your exemption being protected and it increases your losses to carry forward. However, all losses for the year must be deducted in arriving at the net gains.
(3) As an example of set offs, suppose you have £8,000 of losses to carry forward from 1988–89 and your gains for 1989–90 are £10,000, with losses of £1,000. You must set off the losses of £1,000 leaving £9,000 of net gains for 1989–90. This is then reduced to £5,000, by setting off £4,000 of losses from the previous year. This leaves £4,000 of losses to carry forward.
(4) The annual exemption is to apply for future years, subject to indexation in line with the increase in the retail price index in the December before the year of assessment compared with the previous December. This applies unless Parliament directs otherwise. For 1988–89 there was, in fact, a reduction to £5,000. The annual exemptions in previous years have been:

1984–85	£5,600
1985–86	£5,900
1986–87	£6,300
1987–88	£6,600
1988–89	£5,000

(5) At present, husband and wife only normally have one capital gains tax annual exemption between them. However, starting with 1990–91, each will have a separate exemption, as a result of separate taxation.

6.5 Capital gains tax rates

The system of charging capital gains tax by means of a single rate of 30% was changed from 6 April 1988 as follows:

(1) Indivduals now suffer capital gains tax at 25% and 40%.
(2) The rate for accumulation and maintenance trusts and discretionary settlements is 35%. Other trusts in general pay 25%.
(3) The capital gains of companies continue to bear corporation tax at the appropriate rate.
(4) To find the rate or rates payable by individual, you take the total gains less losses for the tax year, deduct losses brought forward and the annual exemption, considering this together with taxable income after reliefs and allowances. (Note, however that income tax losses cannot be set against capital gains.) The first £20,700 attracts 25% and the remainder 40%.

Thus, if your taxable income after allowance for 1989–90 is £15,700, you have £20,700–£15,700 = £5,000 of your 25% rate band unused. This means that if your net capital gains for 1989–90 are £15,000, this is reduced to £10,000 by your annual exemption (£5,000). Your capital gains tax is thus:

£5,000 at 25%	1,250
£5,000 at 40%	2,000
	£3,250

(5) Husband and wife must be considered together for the above rules for 1988–89 and 1989–90, but not subsequently, when they will be treated separately. This represents a substantial improvement after 5 April 1990.

6.6 Liable and exempt assets

Subject to certain exemptions (6.6) all forms of property are regarded as 'assets' for capital gains tax purposes including:

(1) Investments, land and buildings etc.
(2) Options and debts.
(3) Currency other than Sterling.
(4) Property created by the person disposing of it or otherwise coming to be owned without being acquired. (This would cover articles

made or works of art created by you, but not normally in the course of your trade or profession.)

6.7 Table — Assets exempted from capital gains tax

The following are some of the main types of assets exempted from charge to capital gains tax, subject to the rules:

(1) Private motor vehicles.
(2) Your own home.
(3) Certain Government savings arrangements, such as National Savings Certificates, Defence Bonds, Development Bonds, Save-as-you-Earn etc.
(4) Foreign currency obtained for personal expenditure abroad.
(5) Decorations for gallantry unless purchased.
(6) Wins on pools, lotteries and premium bonds etc.
(7) Compensation for any wrong or injury which you suffer to your person or in connection with your profession or vocation.
(8) British Government Securities and qualifying corporate bonds, as well as futures and options concerning them.
(9) Life assurance policies and deferred annuities provided you are the original owner or they were given to you. Certain policies assigned after 25 June 1982 may give rise to income tax instead of capital gains tax.
(10) Chattels sold for £6,000 or less.
(11) Assets gifted to charity.
(12) Certain gifts of historic houses, works or art, etc to the nation.
(13) Tangible movable property which is a wasting asset (ie with a predictable life of 50 years or less). This includes boats, animals, etc but not land and buildings, nor assets qualifying for capital allowances.
(14) Disposals by a close company (4.21) of assets which it holds on trust for the benefit of its employees.
(15) The sale of a debt by the original creditor is not liable to capital gains tax, unless it is a 'debt on security' (a debenture etc).
(16) Business expansion scheme shares issued to you after 18 March 1986 provided you are their first holder (4.31).

6.8 Disposals for capital gains tax purposes

Examples of circumstances in which you will be treated as making a disposal or part disposal of an asset include the outright sale of the whole or part of an asset. The gift of an asset constitutes a disposal although there is some scope for electing to hold over the gain (6.23).

The destruction of an asset, for example, by fire is treated as a capital gains tax disposal. Another example is if you sell any rights in an asset such as by granting a lease. This is a part disposal, although if you obtain a fair rent, there is normally no capital gains tax liability.

Another example of a disposal is where you receive a capital sum in return for the surrender or forfeiture of any rights. For example, if you receive a sum of money for not renewing a lease, although you had an option to do so.

Gifts or sales of assets to your spouse are not treated as disposals for capital gains tax purposes, provided he or she is living with you during the relevant tax year. Furthermore, the transfer of an asset as security for a debt or to someone else to hold as a nominee does not count as a capital gains tax disposal, provided you retain the beneficial ownership.

6.9 The computation of chargeable gains

(1) In general, you must take the consideration received for each of your disposals during the tax year. (Accounts period for a company 4.5.)
(2) Deduct from the disposal consideration in respect of each asset the original cost, together with any incidental expenses in connection with your original acquisition and with the disposal of the asset. Also deduct any 'enhancement expenditure', ie the cost of any capital improvements to the assets not including any expenses of a revenue nature. For disposals after 5 April 1988 of assets owned at 31 March 1982, you normally deduct the value at that date, if it gives a better result. This is known as 're-basing' (6.10).
(3) Your incidental costs of acquisition and disposal include surveyors', valuers' and solicitors' fees, stamp duty and commission in connection with the purchase and sale; also the cost of advertising to find a buyer and accountancy charges in connection with the acquisition or disposal. However, no expenses may be deducted if they have already been allowed in computing your taxable revenue profits.
(4) Deduct (if applicable) indexation allowance (6.11).
(5) Special rules apply in the case of leases and other wasting assets (6.22).
(6) Special rules also apply regarding assets originally acquired prior to 7 April 1965 (6.15).
(7) In certain circumstances, it is necessary to substitute the open market value of the assets for the proceeds (if any). Such circumstances include gifts of assets, transfers of assets by gift or sale to persons *connected* with you including your business partner and close relatives other than your wife; also, other disposals of assets not at arm's length. A further example is where transactions are such that the sale proceeds cannot be valued.

6.10 Re-basing to 31 March 1982 values

If you dispose of an asset after 5 April 1988, which you owned on 31 March 1982, its base value is automatically taken as its value at that date, provided this exceeds the cost. Thus, if you bought some shares for £1,000 in 1970 and they are worth £4,000 on 31 March 1982, you use £4,000 as their base value for capital gains tax purposes. Assuming you sell the shares for £10,000 in August 1989, your capital gain is £10,000 – £4,000 = £6,000 (ignoring indexation).

Re-basing to 31 March 1982 does not increase a gain or loss compared with what it would have been under the old rules. Furthermore, where there is a gain under the old system and a loss through re-basing, or vice versa, the transaction is treated as giving rise to neither gain nor loss.

The existing rules for assets held at 6 April 1965 can themselves give rise to disposals being treated as producing no gain and no loss (6.16). This is not affected by re-basing.

Even if you did not hold an asset at 31 March 1982, it may still qualify for re-basing if you received it from someone else in circumstances that there was neither a gain nor loss under the rules and their acquisition was before that date. A particular example is where you acquire an asset from your spouse.

If you held assets at 31 March 1982, but subsequently realised them in curcumstances such that your gain was deferred, rebasing does not apply. However, special relief is available regarding disposals after 5 April 1988 (excluding no gain/no loss disposals). Provided you make a claim to the Inland Revenue within two years of the end of the year of assessment in which the disposal is made, your original held-over, rolled-over or deferred gain is halved (FA 1988 S97 & Sch 9).

You have the right to elect that all of your assets are re-based as at 31 March 1982. There is a two year time limit for this irrevocable election (ie before 6 April 1990). However, this is extended to two years after the end of the tax year in which you make your first sale after 5 April 1988.

6.11 Indexation allowance

Indexation relief is available for disposals after 5 April 1982 (31 March 1982 for companies). The original cost and enhancement expenditure are scaled up in proportion to the increase in the retail price index (6.10) between March 1982 and the month of disposal. If the asset was acquired subsequent to March 1982, indexation runs from the month of acquisition until the month of disposal. After 5 April 1988, disposals are automatically re-based to their 31 March 1982 values if the assets were held at that time and if re-basing is beneficial. In that case, indexation is taken on the 31 March 1982 value.

The full benefit of indexation relief is available, even to the extent that it creates or enlarges a loss. (This did not apply prior to 6 April 1985.)

If you acquire an asset from your wife, your deemed acquisition cost is taken to be hers, augmented by any indexation allowance which she had accrued up to the transfer date. When you sell the asset, you calculate indexation allowance on your deemed acquisition cost from the date you took the asset over from your wife. Similar treatment covers transfers between companies in the same group (4.18) and certain reconstructions.

Special indexation rules cover assets which you held on 6 April 1965 (6.15) and 31 March 1982. The latter extends also to assets which you obtained subsequently on a 'no gain–no loss' basis from someone who had held them at that date. Within two years of the end of the tax year in which your disposal is made (accounting period for a company), you have the option of electing for your indexation relief to be based on the *market value at 31 March 1982* of the relevant assets, rather than cost. This applies only for disposals before 6 April 1988.

6.12 Table: Retail prices index

	1982	1983	1984	1985	1986	1987	1988	1989
January	310.6	325.9	342.6	359.8	379.7	394.5/ 100.0*	103.3	111.0
February	310.7	327.3	344.0	362.7	381.1	100.4	103.7	111.8
March	313.4	327.9	345.1	366.1	381.6	100.6	104.1	112.3
April	319.7	332.5	449.7	373.9	385.3	101.8	105.8	114.3
May	322.0	333.9	351.0	375.6	386.0,	101.9	106.2	115.0
June	322.9	334.7	351.9	376.4	385.8	101.9	106.6	115.4
July	323.0	336.5	351.5	375.5	384.7	101.8	106.7	115.5
August	323.1	338.0	354.8	376.7	385.9	102.1	107.9	115.8
September	322.9	339.5	355.5	376.5	387.8	102.4	108.4	116.6
October	324.5	340.7	357.7	377.1	388.4	102.9	109.5	
November	326.1	341.9	358.8	378.4	391.7	103.4	110.0	
December	325.5	342.8	358.5	378.9	393.0	103.3	110.3	

*Note: At January 1987 the index base was changed to 100.0. Thus assets acquired before January 1987 and sold after that time must be indexed using both scales. For example, the index figure for March 1987 is taken as 394.5 × 100.6/100 = 396.9.

6.13 Example: Capital gains tax – Indexation relief

John has a retail business and in January 1990 sells a freehold shop which he personally owns for £105,000 (legal and other expenses on sale £5,000). The cost including legal expenses, stamp duty, agents' fees, etc. in May 1978 was £50,000 and the value on 31 March 1982 was £75,000. In September 1980 he made capital improvements costing £10,000. Assuming the Retail Price Index is 300 for March 1982 and 450 (adjusted to previous base) for January 1990 and that John has no other gains in 1989–90, his capital gains tax will be as follows (on the basis that he is a higher rate income tax payer):

	£
Proceeds	105,000
Less legal and selling expenses	5,000
	100,000
Less cost	50,000
	50,000
Less indexation £75,000 × (450–300)/300	37,500
Chargeable gain	12,500
Less annual exemption	5,000
	£7,500
Capital gains tax liability at 40%	£ 3,000

6.14 Capital losses

Your chargeable gains during a tax year are reduced by any capital losses arising on disposals during that year. The capital losses are computed in the same way as capital gains and are augmented by indexation. Any remaining surplus of losses after setting-off all chargeable gains during the tax year are then carried forward to be set against future capital gains of your spouse and yourself.

The position regarding capital losses made by a company (4.17) is similar to those of an individual. However, the company's accounting period must be considered rather than the tax year. A further point to note is that whilst a company can set a trading loss against capital gains within the same chargeable accounting period or the previous one, an individual is only able to offset capital losses against capital gains.

6.15 Loss on unquoted shares in trading companies

Provided you or your spouse was the original subscriber of shares in a 'qualifying trading company', you can elect to obtain income tax loss relief for any loss on a fully priced arm's length sale. The same applies to a loss on liquidation. It is necessary to elect within two years after the tax year in which the relief is to be used.

Complicated rules define a 'qualifying trading company'. The requirements include trading for at least six years or from within one year of incorporation if less. The company must be unquoted and may not deal in land, shares or commodity futures. The company is permitted to have stopped trading within the previous three years provided it has not, meanwhile, become an investment company.

6.16 Assessment and payment of capital gains tax

Capital gains are treated as arising on the actual date of sale (or gift). Where there is a sales contract involved, such as regarding shares or land, the date of the contract applies rather than the completion date, if different. Your capital gains tax assessments are raised for each tax year, as soon thereafter as the Revenue obtain the necessary information. However, for a company, the gains are included in its corporation tax assessment which is due for payment according to the special company rules (4.5).

For individuals, capital gains tax assessments are due for payment on 1 December following the tax year in which the respective gains are made, or 30 days after the assessment is issued, if later. Thus, capital gains tax on disposals during 1989–90 are due for payment on 1 December 1990, provided they are assessed by 1 November 1990.

Interest at the normal rates (12¼% etc) is payable on overdue capital gains tax, generally from the earlier of 1 June following the next year of assessment or when the tax becomes due and payable. However, in no event does interest normally run from a date earlier than 30 days after the issue of the assessment.

In general, even if the sales consideration is paid by instalments, the gain is assessed for the tax year of disposal. However, if you can satisfy the Revenue that undue hardship would otherwise be suffered, payment of the tax can be spread over the period of the instalments up to a maximum of eight years.

6.17 Assets owned on 6 April 1965

The current system of capital gains tax only applies concerning sales after 6 April 1965. Rules therefore operate to relieve such part of your capital gains as relate to the period prior to 7 April 1965. However, following the introduction of the re-basing rules (4.10) these rules are far less significant (see below). The general rule is that you assume that your asset increased in value uniformly and you are relieved from capital gains tax on such proportion of the gain as arose on a time basis, prior to 7 April 1965.

The foregoing is known as the 'time apportionment' method and it operates as follows. If your gain is G on an asset which you have held for A months before 6 April 1965 and B months after that date until sale, your taxable chargeable gain is $G \times B/(A + B)$. The gain to which you apply time apportionment is net of any indexation allowance available and A is limited to 20 years.

The market value of an asset disposed of may be substituted for its cost instead of using time apportionment. In order to do this, it is necessary to make an election to the Revenue within two years of the end of the tax year in which the disposal is made. In the case of a company, however, the election must be made within two years of the end of the accounting period of the disposal. The election is not allowed to increase a capital loss. Furthermore, if it converts a gain into a loss, you are regarded as having made no gain and no loss on the transaction.

Following the introduction of 1982 re-basing (4.10) these rules are of far less importance since in most cases, a lower gain (or greater loss) will result from re-basing. However, if a better result is produced by applying the old rules, these are then used, unless you have elected for all of your assets to be valued as at 31 March 1982.

Note that the 'time apportionment' basis does not apply to quoted shares and securities (6.19), nor to land reflecting development value when sold. Also note that 'time apportionment' applies so as to reduce losses as well as gains.

6.18 Valuations

As has been seen, various circumstances require valuations to be made for capital gains tax purposes. These includes gifts, transactions between connected persons, valuations at 6 April 1965 and 31 March 1982. The general rule is to take the 'market value' of the assets at the relevant time. This means the price which the assets might reasonably be expected to fetch on a sale in the open market.

Only the assets being disposed of need to be valued, even though they form part of a larger whole. This is particularly vital concerning the shares in any non-quoted company. Suppose you hold 90% of the shares in such a company which are together worth £450,000. The gift of 10% of the company's shares to your son would not be worth £50,000 because whereas your 90% carried full control, 10% is a comparatively small minority holding. The true valuation of the gifted shares might be only £5,000, depending on the profits of the company and dividends paid. Note, however, that unquoted share valuations must take account of all information which a prudent arm's length purchaser would obtain.

Regarding the valuation of quoted securities, such as shares and debentures, you must normally take the lower of the two prices shown in the Stock Exchange official daily list plus one quarter of the difference between them; or half way between the highest and lowest prices at which bargains (other than at special prices) were recorded in the shares or securities for the relevant day. (A slightly different basis is used at 6 April 1985.) Apart from quoted shares, valuations normally require to be agreed with the Inland Revenue valuation officers such as the District Valuers, who are concerned with valuing land and buildings, and the Shares Valuation Division.

6.19 Quoted shares and securities

Complicated rules apply concerning identification of the shares which you sell out of a holding which you have built up over a period. Broadly, regarding sales from 6 April 1985 (after 31 March 1985 for companies), these are identified with your acquisitions of the same shares on a 'last in–first out' basis. You must keep separate pools of shares acquired after 5 April 1982 and those obtained from 6 April 1965 to 5 April 1982. Also, acquisitions before 6 April 1965 must be kept separately (unless you have made a pooling election in which case they are included in the 31 March 1982 pool).

Sales after 5 April 1985 are first identified with your post-5 April 1982 pool and then with your pre-6 April 1982 holdings; finally with your unpooled pre-6 April 1965 holdings. (For fuller details, reference should be made to the *Allied Dunbar Tax Guide* or *Capital Taxes Guide*.)

Indexation must be calculated separately on the different parts, additional purchases carrying indexation relief from the date of purchase (or 31 March 1982 if later) until sale.

6.20 Company reorganizations and take-overs

If your company has a capital reorganization, in the course of which you receive shares of a different class, either instead of or in addition to your original shares, you are not normally charged to capital gains tax on any of your existing shares which you exchange for new ones. Capital gains tax is only payable when you sell your new holding. These rules include bonus issues which you may receive.

Where you take up 'rights' to subscribe for additional shares in a company of which you are a shareholder, your new shares are treated as having been acquired at the same time as your original shares and the cost of the rights shares is added to the original cost of your shareholding. Selling your rights on the market without taking up the shares is treated as a 'part disposal' and accordingly charged to capital gains tax (6.20). However, any new consideration is treated effectively as a new acquisition for indexation purposes.

Anti-avoidance rules prevent you from obtaining capital gains tax loss relief artificially. Any increase in the capital gains tax acquisition value of shares obtained through a reorganization is limited to the actual increase in value.

To the extent that you receive shares or loan stock, etc in the acquiring company in a takeover situation, you will not normally be liable to pay capital gains tax until you actually sell your new shares or loan stock. However, there are certain conditions and anti-avoidance rules. One of the conditions is that the acquiring company already held, or obtains as a result of the takeover, at least 25% of the ordinary share capital of the other company. The Revenue are empowered to set aside the relief and thus charge capital gains tax on the value of shares which you receive, if they can show that the transactions had as a main object the saving of tax. However, there are clearance provisions. If the company provides full details to the Revenue, they are required to state within 30 days whether or not clearance is granted.

6.21 Unquoted shares

Many of the special capital gains tax rules apply to quoted and unquoted shares alike. However, some are only of application to unquoted shares and these particularly concern holdings at 6 April 1965, where for example the 'time apportionment' rule applies (6.17). This is not the case for shares in quoted companies.

6.22 Part disposals

Should you dispose of part of an asset, the cost applicable to this part must be computed. (This includes part of a 'pool' holding of shares in a particular company.) You multiply the original cost by the fraction $A/(A + B)$ where A is the consideration for the part disposed of and B is the market value of the remainder at the date of the part disposal. This formula is applied before computing the indexation allowances which is not calculated on the cost attributed to the undisposed of part until that is sold.

A special rule covers part disposals of land where the proceeds do not exceed one-fifth of the total market value. Provided the proceeds during the tax year do not exceed £20,000, you may deduct them from your base cost rather than pay now.

6.23 A series of disposals

If you split up an asset or a collection of assets by having transactions (including gifts) etc with two or more connected persons (6.8) all of the assets are valued together in order to find the relevant proceeds. The transactions must be within a total period of six years and must particularly be watched regarding unquoted company shares. For example, if you have 90% of the shares in the company and gift 20% to each of your three sons, the shares must be valued on a control basis of 60% rather than as minority holdings of 20%. (However, you might be able to make a gifts election — 6.25.)

6.24 Leases and other wasting assets

A 'wasting asset' is defined as an asset with a predictable life not exceeding 50 years. This excludes freehold land and buildings, etc. Leases with no more than 50 years to run are separately treated for capital gains tax. The original cost must be written off according to a special formula under which the rate of wastage accelerates as the end of the lease is reached. Should you sell the property and lease back the premises at a lower rent for less than 15 years, you may be taxed on all or part of the proceeds, either as a trading receipt or under Schedule D, Case VI (Miscellaneous Income).

'Wasting assets' which are also moveable property (chattels) are generally exempted from capital gains tax. Regarding other wasting assets apart from leases, the original costs must be reduced on a straightline time basis over the lives of the assets. For example, if you buy a wasting asset for £20,000 with an unexpired life of 30 years and sell it after 15 years for £30,000, on the assumption that the residual value after 30 years would have been nil, your allowable cost is £20,000 × 15/30 = £10,000. Thus your chargeable gain is £30,000 − £10,000 = £20,000.

6.25 Relief for gifts

Originally, gifts relief only applied to business assets. However, general relief applied for gifts, made prior to 14 March 1989, subject to an election being made by both donor and donee. The gain is then reduced to nil and the recipient deducts the original capital gain from his acquisition value for the asset. (Gifts to a settlement only require an election by the donor.) If you received any consideration, the claim only covers the gift element, if this is less than the total gain. Where you are entitled to retirement relief (6.28) this reduces the heldover gain.

The general gifts relief covered gifts between individuals, from individuals to trusts and from trusts to individuals. However, it did not cover gifts to non-residents.

With the removal of general gifts relief from 14 March 1989, the business gifts relief has been expanded so that it now includes other items. The relief is only available if the donee is UK resident and/or ordinarily resident and it applies to the following:

(1) Business assets used in a trade profession or vocation carried on by the giver or his family company. etc.
(2) Certain agricultural property (normally where the giver has vacant possession).
(3) Shares and securities in family trading companies or non-quoted trading companies. (These categories include the holding companies of trading groups.)
(4) Gifts which give rise to an immediate charge to inheritance tax, for example, into a discretionary settlement (7.20). Potentially exempt transfers (7.3) do not qualify for this relief. However, if a gift is covered by the nil rate band and exemptions for inheritance tax but would otherwise be taxed, the gifts election is available.

The relief is also available on certain occasions when beneficiaries benefit from accumulation and maintenance trusts (7.20).
(5) Gifts of heritage property and to maintenance funds; to political parties which qualify for inheritance tax exemption; and subject to an election by donor and recipient, gifts to a housing association.
(6) Certain assets not mentioned above, which are not eligible for gifts relief may qualify for the tax on disposal to be paid by instalments.

6.26 Replacement of business assets — Rollover relief

One of the main capital gains tax reliefs for businesses is the facility of 'rolling-over' gains on business assets by purchasing new ones. This applies to individuals, partnerships and companies. Gains realized on sales of assets used in your business may be rolled-over against further business assets purchased within one year preceding and three years after the sale. The effect is that no tax is paid until the new business assets are sold, unless they, in turn, are replaced.

In order to obtain full roll-over relief, you must reinvest the entire proceeds within the time limit. If only part is reinvested, it is taken to be that part of the proceeds excluding the gain, before the gain is covered. Thus, suppose you sell a factory used in your business for £100,000, making a capital gain of £50,000. If you then buy a warehouse for £50,000, by itself this has no effect on your £50,000 capital gain. However, if you now buy a further warehouse for £30,000, within the time limit, this will reduce the original capital gain to £20,000.

Only 'qualifying' assets attract the relief. This means that the old and new assets must be within the following main categories:

(a) Land and buildings (apart from trading stock).
(b) Fixed plant and machinery not forming part of a building. This excludes items such as motor vans, fork-lift trucks and moveable machines.
(c) Ships, aircraft and hovercraft.
(d) Goodwill.

Both the old and the new assets must be used in the same business. However, if you carry on several trades, they are treated as one for this purpose. By concession, this still applies if there is a gap of no more than three years between one trade ceasing and another starting. Furthermore, rollover relief applies regarding your purchases and sales of personally owned assets used in your 'family company' (6.28).

You can obtain rollover relief by purchasing wasting assets (6.24). However, unless they are replaced by non-wasting assets within 10 years, the rolled over gains become chargeable. This also applies to assets which will become 'wasting' within 10 years, such as a lease with 59 more years to run.

If you are non-resident and replace a business asset chargeable to UK tax with one which is not, roll-over relief is generally no longer available. This rule normally applies where you dispose of the old asset or acquire the new one after 13 March 1989; but not if the new asset was acquired before that date and the old asset disposed of within one year.

6.27 Transferring a business to a company

If you transfer your business to a company, as a going concern, wholly or partly in exchange for shares, you obtain a form of rollover relief. All of the assets of your business must be transferred, except that you need not pass its cash over to the company. The relief applies to the transfer of a partnership business to a company but not one already carried on by a company.

If your consideration consists entirely of shares in the company, your total gain is rolled over and you pay no tax until you sell some of the shares. However, if part of your consideration takes another form, such as cash, you will be immediately liable for the capital gains tax attributable to that part of the consideration. Thus, if your total gain is £20,000 and your consideration is shares worth £30,000 and cash of £20,000, you will pay tax now on £20,000 × £20,000/£50,000 = £8,000, the remaining £12,000 being rolled over.

6.28 Business retirement relief

If you have reached age 60 and dispose by gift or sale of the whole or part of a business which you have owned for the past 10 years, you are exempted from capital gains tax on the first £125,000 of any gain arising in respect of the 'chargeable business assets' of the business. If you have several businesses, your total relief is restricted to £125,000 together with up to £375,000 at 50% (see below).

For disposals after 5 April 1988, not only is the first £125,000 of gains exempted from capital gains tax; the next £375,000 is given 50% relief. Thus if you are over 60 (having used no retirement relief previously) and sell your business, giving rise to a chargeable gain of £405,000, £125,000 of this is exempted from capital gains tax, as is 50% × (£405,000

− £125,000) = £140,000. You are taxed on only £405,000 − (£125,000 + £140,000) = £140,000.

'*Chargeable business assets*' includes those used for the trade, of the business and goodwill. Assets held as investments are not classified as chargeable business assets, however. Also excluded are assets which could not attract any capital gains liability if you sold them, such as trading stock debtors or cash.

You do not actually need to retire to obtain the relief. However, after 5 April 1985 you are able to obtain relief if you retire younger than age 60 for reasons of ill health. You will need to obtain a medical certificate and must show that you are likely to remain incapable of performing your previous work.

Retirement relief also covers any disposal of shares in a trading company which has been your 'family company' for at least the last 10 years, during which time you have been a 'full-time director' of the company. A *family company* is one in which you have 25% of the voting rights or your immediate family has at least 50% including 5% held by yourself. You are a *full-time working director* if you are required to devote substantially the whole of your time to the service of the company (or group) in a technical or managerial capacity.

Only the proportion of the gain on the shares attributable to the 'chargeable business assets' of the company compared with its total chargeable assets qualifies for the relief. Since 6 April 1985 (but not previously), the subsidiary trading companies in a group are regarded as chargeable business assets.

The relief also applies where you dispose of an asset which you personally owned and which has been used rent-free by your 'family company' in its trade. You must have been a full-time working director throughout your period of ownership of the asset. Limited relief is available if you receive less than a market rent. Assets owned by partners and used in the partnership business attract similar relief if sold.

Where you dispose of the whole or part of a business which you have owned for less than ten years, you obtain 10% of the full relief if you owned the assets for at least one year prior to disposal, 20% relief for at least two years of ownership and so on, adding a further 10% for each year up to 100%.

If your wife complies with the requirements, she is eligible for the relief if she disposes of her business or shares in a 'family company'. The relief also covers disposals by a settlement of assets used by a beneficiary for his own business or that of his 'family company'. This also applies to shares in a family trading or holding company. The beneficiary must retire and have an interest in possession in the settlement (ie be entitled to the income).

Capital gains tax retirement relief is of great value and can be maximised by simple planning. For example, if you are approaching 60 years of age, you should delay disposing of your business until you reach that age. Similarly, you should aim to maximise the proportion of chargeable business assets in your company. If you have reached age 60 but worked in your business for less than 10 years, it might be worthwhile working for a few more years, in order to maximise the relief. A further point is to ensure that your directorship of a family company involves you in working sufficient hours to be treated as a 'whole time working director'.

7 Inheritance tax

7.1 Introduction

This chapter deals with inheritance tax, with particular reference to businesses. It covers some basic rules and then outlines special reliefs relating to businesses, including shares in companies.

The following is only a brief outline of a most complicated subject. Furthermore, only details of the present rules are given. Thus, no mention is made of capital transfer tax, which applied for transfers and deaths before 17 March 1986. However, it should be mentioned that many of the old capital transfer tax rules have been incorporated into the present system and the main legislation is to be found in The Inheritance Tax Act 1984, originally known as the Capital Transfer Tax Act 1984.

7.2 Property chargeable

Subject to various reliefs (7.10 et seq), inheritance tax is charged on transfers which you make during your lifetime unless they are exempt or potentially exempt transfers (PETs) (7.3). Also, the value of your estate will be charged to inheritance tax when you die, if it is sufficiently large. Lifetime transfers are evaluated by taking the decrease in value of your assets less liabilities which you suffer as a result of any transfer of your assets and this is known as a 'chargeable transfer'.

Normally, arm's length transactions are ignored if they are not intended to confer any gratuitous benefit. Any capital gains tax which you pay is ignored in calculating the decrease. If you are domiciled in the UK or deemed domiciled here (7.5), inheritance tax applies to all your property wherever situated. Otherwise, it only applies to your property in this country.

7.3 Potentially exempt transfers

If you make gifts after 17 March 1986 to other individuals, or certain trusts, they are classed as 'potentially exempt transfers' (PETs). As a result, inheritance tax is not payable on these gifts unless you die within seven years. However, if this happens, the PETs (less exemptions) become 'chargeable transfers'. Your tax is then recalculated using the rate scale applying at death and subject to possible tapering relief (see below).

Gifts to accumulation and maintenance settlements are classed as PETs, as are those to trusts for disabled persons and interest in possession trusts. The latter are broadly trusts where one or more beneficiaries have the income or use of property as of right. Transfers out of such trusts are also PETs, except on death.

7.4 Tapering relief

Where an individual dies within seven years of making a PET, a proportion of the full tax is payable as follows:

Death in years	%
1–3	100
4	80
5	60
6	40
7	20

7.5 Deemed domicile

You are deemed to be domiciled in the UK if you were domiciled here on or after 10 December 1974 and within the three years preceding the date of the chargeable transfer. You are also deemed domiciled if you were resident here on or after 10 December 1974 and in not less than 17 of the 20 years of assessment ending with that in which you make the chargeable transfer.

7.6 Rate scale

Inheritance tax is charged according to the following table (7.7). This is applied to 'chargeable transfers' and property passing on death after 5 April 1989. Lifetime gifts which are not PETs (7.3) are charged at 50% of the rates shown in the table. This basically covers transfers into discretionary settlements, charges on such settlements and chargeable transfers arising from close company transactions.

Inheritance tax is payable on chargeable transfers soon after they are made, cumulating them with other such transfers within the previous seven years in order to calculate the amount. However, where death occurs within three years, the tax is adjusted using the full rates. Furthermore, the full rates are applied subject to possible tapering relief (7.4) where death occurs in years 4, 5 and normally 6.

Where death occurs within seven years of a PET (7.3), tax must be calculated by treating the PET as a chargeable transfer and cumulating it with any earlier chargeable transfers within seven years before the PET. Inheritance tax is computed using the value of the gift when made. However, you must use the rate scale current at the date of death. Gifts made more than three years before death would qualify for tapering relief (7.4).

7.7 Table: Inheritance tax rates after 5 April 1989

Slice of cumulative chargeable transfers	Cumulative total	% on slice	Cumulative total tax
The first £118,000	£118,000	Nil	Nil
The remainder		40	

7.8 Valuation

The general rule is that for inheritance tax purposes, your assets are valued at their open market value at the transfer date. Where the value of an asset which you keep is affected by the transfer, you need to value your estate both before and after the transfer, taking account of your liabilities also, in order to calculate the fall in value.

Regarding quoted securities, any sold for less than their probate value within 12 months of death attract special relief. Those liable to pay the inheritance tax can claim that the total of the sale proceeds should be substituted for the original probate values of the investments. However, if the proceeds are reinvested in the same quoted shares or unit trusts and within two months after the last sale, the relief may be reduced or lost.

Where land is sold for less than probate value, within three years of death, the person paying the inheritance tax can claim that the sale proceeds are substituted in calculating the tax liability. There are various conditions, including the requirement that the shortfall is at least the lower of £1,000 and 5% of the probate value of the land.

7.9 Valuation of related property

Related property is that belonging to your spouse or in a settlement in which you or your spouse has an interest in possession. Also included is property transferred by either of you after 15 April 1976 to a charity or charitable trust.

Where the value of any of your property is less than it would have been if you had taken into consideration any 'related property', your own property must be valued as the appropriate proportion of the whole, including the related property.

This rule is particularly important regarding unquoted shares. For example, if your spouse and yourself each have 40% of the shares in an unquoted company, the value of 80% of the shares is normally much higher than twice the value of 40% of the shares. This is because the 80% holding carries full control of the company. Thus, the related property rule makes the values of your respective shares much higher for inheritance tax purposes.

7.10 Exempt transfers

Various transfers are exempt both during your lifetime and on death. The following are examples:

(1) Transfers between your spouse and yourself. However, the exemption does not apply if the recipient of the property is not domiciled or deemed domiciled (7.5) in the UK. In that case, only the first £55,000 transferred to the non-domiciled spouse is exempt.
(2) Transfers in the course of trade are exempt, if allowed as deductions in computing the profits for income tax purposes. This applies equally to professions and vocations.
(3) Gifts to charities are exempt, including to settlements for charitable purposes.
(4) Gifts to political parties are wholly exempt. (For gifts made before 15 March 1988 exemption was limited to £100,000 if made more than a year before death.)
(5) Gifts for national purposes to certain bodies such as the National Trust, gifts for public benefit and property deemed by the Treasury to be of outstanding scenic, historic, scientific or artistic merit and PETs of property held for national purposes are generally exempt.
(6) Gifts of shares to an employee trust are exempt provided amongst

other things the trust will then hold at least half of the ordinary shares of the company.
(7) Gifts or sales at undervalue, to housing associations, of land after 13 March 1989.

7.11 Exempt transfers — Lifetime gifts

The following transfers are only exempt if made by an individual and do not normally apply to transfers made by trustees or assets passing on death. In any fiscal year to 5 April, your spouse and yourself can make all of these exempt transfers cumulatively. Furthermore, the rules apply not only to chargeable transfers but also to PETs (7.3). If you make an exempt transfer, which would otherwise be a PET, it will not attract inheritance tax even if you die within seven years.

(1) Transfers each year up to a value of £3,000 are exempt. If you do not use up the full allowance in one year, you can carry the unused part forward for one year only. Should your transfers taken against this exemption reach £3,000 in one year, you will have nothing to carry forward, even though you may have the £3,000 carried forward from the previous year.
(2) Outright gifts to any one person not exceeding £250 for each year to 5 April are exempt. However, the £250 exemption cannot be used against gifts larger than this amount.
(3) Normal expenditure out of income is exempt. This means that there must be an element of regularity and the transfer must come out of your after-tax income and leave you with enough to maintain your usual standard of living.
(4) Gifts in consideration of marriage made to one of the partners of the marriage or settled on the partners and their children etc are exempt. The limits are £5,000 if the donor is a parent of the bride or bridegroom; £2,500 if a grandparent or great-grandparent or one of the parties themselves, and otherwise £1,000.

7.12 Example: Inheritance tax

Jack Box, having made no gifts relevant for capital transfer tax or inheritance tax, gives £56,000 to his son on 30 June 1988 and £100,000 to his wife on 15 September 1988. He dies on 31 January 1990 leaving an estate valued at £300,000, including £50,000 to his wife, £30,000 to charity and the remainder to his son, including his controlling interest in a family company valued at £120,000.

Inheritance tax is payable as follows:

	£	£
30 June 1988 — gift to son		56,000

		£	£
Less Annual exemption 1987/88			
	brought forward	3,000	
	Annual exemption 1988/89	3,000	6,000
Potentially exempt (7.3)			£50,000

15 September 1988 — gift to wife is exempt provided she is UK domiciled (7.10)

Estate at death 31 January 1990		300,000
Less Bequests free of inheritance tax:		
To wife	50,000	
To charity	30,000	80,000
		220,000
Less business property relief (7.14)		
50% × £120,000		60,000
		160,000
Potentially exempt transfer 30 June 1988		50,000
		£210,000

		£
Inheritance tax on £210,000 : £118,000	Nil	–
£92,000	40%	36,800
		£36,800

7.13 Administration and collection

Chargeable transfers must be reported to the Inland Revenue within twelve months from the end of the month of transfer or death. Tax chargeable on death must be paid on at least an estimated figure before probate is granted. Inheritance tax on death is payable out of the residuary estate unless there is a contrary direction in the Will. However, property situated outside the UK bears its own tax. Recipients of PETs are primarily responsible for the relevant tax.

Interest on unpaid tax runs from when the tax is due. The due date is six months after the end of the month in which death occurs. For lifetime transfers, it is six months after the end of the month in which the transfer is made. However, for transfers between 5 April and 1 October, the due date is 30 April in the following year. The rate of interest on overdue inheritance tax is 6% from 6 June 1987, 8% from 6 August 1988, 9% from 6 October 1988 and 11% from 6 July 1989.

Inheritance tax on death on certain assets may be paid by annual instalments over 10 years. This applies to land and buildings, controlling holdings of shares in companies and certain other unquoted shares; also business assets. PETs which become chargeable only qualify for the instalments basis if the recipient keeps the property until the death of the donor.

Provided instalments are paid on time concerning the shares and business assets mentioned above, they are free of interest. Land and buildings only qualify for this relief if they are held as business assets. Otherwise, interest is payable, currently at 11%. Inheritance tax in respect of property qualifying for agricultural relief (7.14) may also be paid in interest-free instalments.

The above provisions extend to lifetime transfers if the donee bears the tax; also to settled property which is retained in a settlement. The interest-free category includes lifetime disposals of timber. In the case of minority holdings of unquoted shares, these must be worth at least £20,000 in order to qualify for the instalments option, also being at least 10% holdings. The instalments basis may also be allowed where paying the tax in one sum would cause undue hardship and the recipient keeps the shares.

7.14 Relief for business property

Business property relief applies to 'relevant business property'. The latter includes:

(1) A business or part of a business.
(2) Shares owned by the controller of a company.
(3) Unquoted minority shareholdings.
(4) Land, buildings, plant and machinery used in your partnership or in a company which you control.
(5) The business of UK stock jobbing and 'market making'.
(6) Investment company and land or share-dealing company shareholdings generally do not qualify.

For the purposes of business property relief, the control of a company includes shareholdings which are 'related property' (7.9) in relation to your shares. Normally you must own the business property (or property which has directly replaced it) for at least two years prior to the transfer, otherwise no relief is due.

The relief is given by reducing the value of the assets concerned as follows:

(1) The whole or part of a business — 50%.

(2) Company shares to be valued on a control basis — 50%.
(3) From 17 March 1987, holdings over 25% in an unquoted trading company — 50%.
(4) Property transferred by you which is used in a trade by a company controlled by you or your partnership — 30%.
(5) Shares in an unquoted trading company to be valued on a minority basis (prior to 17 March 1987) — 30%.
(6) Shareholdings of 25% and under in an unquoted trading company from 17 March 1987 — 30%.
(7) The transfer of land or buildings owned by a trust provided that immediately before the transfer, the assets were used in his own trade by a person beneficially entitled to an interest in possession in the trust — 30%.

Before 17 March 1987, shares dealt in on the USM qualified for business property relief. However, this no longer applies (unless forming part of a controlling holding).

An important rule applies regarding PETs. Business property relief is available against any PETs which fall into charge following the donor's death within seven years. However, the relief is lost if the recipient disposes of the property before the donor's death. To avoid losing the relief, it is permissible to replace the original gifted business property with other qualifying assets within one year. Furthermore, the property must remain 'relevant business property' during the seven years. The relief is proportionately reduced if the conditions are only satisfied for part of the property. Where part of an estate is left to the surviving spouse, thus attracting no tax, and part to others, the allocation of business property relief and relief for agricultural property (7.15) is subject to special rules. Specific gifts of such property must be reduced by the business or agricultural property relief. Otherwise, the relief is spread proportionately over the estate.

7.15 Relief for agricultural property

Special relief is granted in respect of the valuation of agricultural property for inheritance tax purposes. In order to qualify, you must have either occupied the property for the purposes of agriculture for at least two years before transferring it, or owned it for seven years up to that time with others farming it. The rules are relaxed where you inherit the property or have replaced one agricultural property by another.

If you enjoy the right to vacant possession of the land or can obtain this within the next 12 months, you obtain relief of 50%. Otherwise, it is normally 30% which applies to tenanted situations, etc.

The grant of a tenancy of agricultural property is not treated as a transfer of value if made for full consideration. Similar rules apply to those relevant for business property relief, regarding lifetime gifts within seven years of death and the allocation of relief to partially exempt estates. Thus, if agricultural property is disposed of within seven years of the gift and before the death of the donor, agricultural property relief could be lost.

7.16 Woodlands

Inheritance tax relief against the charge at death on growing timber is available, provided you either owned the woodlands for at least five years or acquired them by gift or inheritance. Inheritance tax is not charged on the timber on your death, provided the inheritor elects within two years of your death. However, should the timber be sold or given away before the recipient dies, tax is charged on the proceeds or value of the gift. The tax rate is found by adding the proceeds to the estate at your death. The relief only applies to the timber and not the land on which it grows; however, the latter may qualify for business property relief.

7.17 Close companies

Although inheritance tax is predominantly of application to individuals, there are rules under which it is charged where a close company (4.21) makes a transfer of value. What happens is that tax is charged on the company as if each of the participators (4.24) had made a proportionate transfer, according to his or her interest in the company.

The rules extend to close companies owned by trusts or those which are the beneficiaries of trusts. Furthermore, transfers of value arising as above from alterations in the capital and associated rights in a close company may attract inheritance tax at once. Such transfers are not classified as PETs (7.3).

7.18 Anti-avoidance

There are a number of avenues which enable the Revenue to challenge arrangements designed to avoid inheritance tax. Two are mentioned here. The first concerns 'associated operations'. Two or more transactions related to a certain property may be treated by the Revenue as forming one 'chargeable transfer'. Where transactions at different times are treated as 'associated operations', the chargeable transfer is regarded as taking place at the time of the last of the transactions.

Another problem area concerns gifts with reservation. If you make a gift but reserve some benefit, this normally results in the property remaining yours for inheritance tax purposes on your death. However, if you subsequently release the reservation, you will be regarded as making a PET (7.3) or chargeable transfer at that time.

7.19 Deeds of family arrangement

Inheritance tax is not charged on certain variations in the destination of property passing on death. Nor is it charged on the disclaimer of title to property passing on death. However, the disclaimer or variation must be made within two years of the death. Furthermore, an election to the Revenue is required within six months after that.

7.20 Quick succession relief

This relief applies to reduce the tax payable on death where the deceased himself received chargeable transfers on which the tax was paid within five years of his death. The deduction is broadly a proportion of the original tax, being 100%, 80%, 60% 40% or 20%, depending on whether the period between the transfer and the death is one, two, three, four or five years or less in each case

7.21 Settled property

The rules concerning inheritance tax in relation to settled property are most detailed, and wider coverage is to be found in the *Allied Dunbar Tax Guide* and *Allied Dunbar Capital Taxes and Estate Planning Guide*. The following are a few brief notes:

(1) Broadly any settlement is subject to the inheritance tax rules on its worldwide assets, if at the time it was made the settlor was domiciled in the UK. Otherwise, only assets situated in this country are caught.
(2) The settlement of any property is treated as a chargeable transfer by the settlor. However, settlements on accumulation and maintenance trusts, or for the disabled are classified as PETs (7.3).
(3) Where you have an interest in possession in a trust (eg because you receive the income as of right), the relevant property is treated as yours for inheritance tax purposes. Thus, if your interest ends, you are treated as making a transfer of the value of the property concerned. From 17 March 1987, lifetime transactions involving interests in possession are classed as PETs. This covers gifts, setting them up and transfers out.
(4) If you obtain interest in property in which you previously had

an interest in possession, no inheritance tax is payable. However, this does not normally apply to discretionary settlements.
(5) Quick succession relief is given if an interest in possession comes to an end within five years of a previously chargeable transfer of the settled property. The relief is allowed against the tax due on the later transfer, etc but is calculated as a percentage of the tax payable on the first transfer. The percentage is 100%, 80%, 60%, 40% or 20% where the interval is not more than 1, 2, 3, 4 or 5 years respectively.
(6) Superannuation schemes and charitable trusts are normally exempted from inheritance tax, as are employee and newspaper trusts.
(7) Accumulation and maintenance settlements attract special reliefs and are most useful vehicles for inheritance tax savings. Provided that beneficiaries obtain interests in possession in all of the trust property by the time they attain age 25, no inheritance tax is then payable during the currency of the trust, nor when any beneficiary becomes entitled to the income at 25, nor to the capital at any future time.
(8) Complicated rules relate to discretionary settlements, including provisions for them to be charged to inheritance tax every 10 years, and on removals of capital. However, the rate of charge is 30% of half of the inheritance tax rates taken on the assets held on discretionary trusts. Furthermore, capital distributions from the trust during the 10 year period are charged at a correspondingly lower percentage of the full rates, depending on how early or late in the 10 year period they are made.

8 Value added tax

8.1 Introduction

Value Added Tax (VAT) is imposed in the UK at a rate of either 0% or 15% on:

(1) The supply (ie sale, hire, etc) of goods and services by a business in the UK;
(2) Imports of goods by any person into the UK; and
(3) The import of services by a business, in certain circumstances.

VAT is thus payable whenever goods or services pass from one business to another or to a private consumer. However, when VAT arises on the sale of goods or services from one business to another, it is frequently refunded. This is because each business is normally allowed a credit for the VAT on its 'inputs'.

The total VAT on the 'inputs' of a business is ascertained from the tax invoices given to it by various other businesses which have supplied it with goods or services. A typical tax invoice would show the VAT registration number (8.2) and, for example:

	£
Goods	100
VAT @ 15%	15
Price payable	£115

For VAT purposes, returns must be made to Customs and Excise of the inputs and outputs (supplies of goods and services) for an accounting period (generally three months). At the end of each accounting period, outputs and inputs must be totalled and included in the VAT return. A typical return for an accounting period might show the following:

Total outputs during the period	£100,000	
VAT thereon		£15,000

Total inputs for the period	£40,000	
VAT thereon		£6,000
Balance payable to Customs and Excise		£9,000

As a result of the credit mechanism, although VAT is charged on each business in the chain of import, production and distribution, each such business obtains a credit for the tax on its inputs. Thus, at the final stage, the whole tax is passed on to the consumer. Often, a business will not normally bear any tax, but merely acts as a collection agency. An effect of the credit mechanism is that it is normally neutral between supplies which go through a number of stages and those where the supplier is vertically integrated. In each case, the tax is borne on the amount of the final price to the consumer. However, businesses which make some 'exempt' supplies (8.10) obtain no credit for the VAT on their inputs relating to such supplies.

8.2 Registration

In general, businesses are normally required to be registered with Customs and Excise and have to make returns every three months (8.3). However, certain businesses which are likely to have repayments of tax are allowed to make returns monthly. Furthermore, certain small businesses can prepare returns annually (8.3). When you register, a Customs and Excise VAT officer will allocate to you a VAT registration number, which must appear on your invoices (8.1).

If your taxable supplies are less than £23,600 per annum, you are not liable to be registered, although you can apply to be registered voluntarily. The £23,600 registration limit applies from 15 March 1989, prior to which the level was £22,100. If you are not registered and your supplies exceed £8,000 in the preceding three months, you must notify Customs and Excise. They will register you unless you can show that your total supplies in the year will not exceed £23,600.

The effect of a small trader not registering for VAT is that he is put in the same position as a business making only exempt supplies. No VAT is chargeable to the customers and the small trader has to bear the input tax on his purchases, etc. If your supplies are all zero-rated, you can apply to be exempted from registration. You will not then be able to claim a refund of your input tax, but will be excused the administrative burden of making VAT returns.

From 1 June 1989, if Customs and Excise are satisfied that the taxable supplies for the ensuing year will not exceed £22,600, they will normally allow *de-registration*. (For the previous year this figure was £21,100.)

8.3 Accounts and administration

As mentioned earlier, most accounting periods for VAT purposes are three months in length. However, if your business is likely to have tax repayments, you may be allowed to make monthly returns.

A special scheme started in the summer of 1988. Businesses with annual taxable supplies (excluding VAT) of less than £250,000, which have been registered for at least one year are able to elect for annual VAT accounting. They are then only required to submit a VAT return once each year. It is also necessary to make nine equal monthly payments on account by direct debit and a tenth balancing amount with the annual VAT return. Such monthly payments are computed by the authorities with reference to your VAT for the previous year. Electing to come within the new scheme reduces your administrative burden but may be detrimental insofar as you will pay some of your VAT earlier.

In general, VAT returns should be completed for each quarter and the tax paid by the end of the following month. Thus, your return for the three months to 31 March 1990 should be submitted by 30 April 1990 and the tax paid by that date. Any repayments due to you will be paid but payments to you in error may be recovered by assessment. Where there is any unreasonable delay by Customs and Excise in making any repayment to you, a repayment supplement of 5% of the tax or £30 (if greater) will be due.

Rules govern the period into which supplies and inputs fall. For goods, it is normally the date when they are removed or made available. For services, it is the date of performance. Two exceptions should be noted. If an invoice is issued within 14 days of the time mentioned above, the date of the invoice is taken. In practice, this usually applies, so that the VAT return can be made up from the copy invoices. Another exception is for payments in advance, in which case the date of the invoice or payment counts. This is the only time when payment is relevant; normally it is the invoice date which matters, but note the position for bad debts (8.17). By arrangement with Customs and Excise, the last day of the calendar month or VAT accounting period can be used as the time of supply. Similar rules apply regarding the periods into which inputs fall. As a result, input tax relief is often available before the invoices have been paid. (The invoices should be kept as proof.)

There are special rules concerning *imports*. VAT is payable by the 15th of the month following importation. Payment must be by direct debit covered by bank guarantee. However, no tax is due so long as the goods are in a bonded warehouse. Taxable persons pay no VAT on temporary imports for repair, modification, etc provided ownership does not change. Where there are temporary exports for repair, modification, etc, VAT on the re-import only applies to the repairs, etc plus freight and insurance.

8.4 Penalties

There are severe regulations regarding the imposition of penalties in respect of certain VAT offences. The rules were significantly changed in 1985, although certain new provisions have not yet come into force.

Certain offences involve criminal proceedings which may only be initiated by Customs and Excise or a Crown law officer. Such proceedings must be started within three years of the offence.

On conviction or indictment, penalties of any amount may be charged and/or imprisonment can be demanded for up to seven years. (For offences committed before 26 July 1985, the maximum term is two years.)

On summary conviction, the penalty is limited to three times the tax and/or six months' imprisonment.

The offences for which the above penalties may be incurred include:

(1) Fraudulent evasion of tax.
(2) False documents and statements.
(3) Conduct which must have involved an offence (even though the particulars of the offence are not known).
(4) Knowing that evasion has been intended by someone who has supplied you with goods or services.*
(5) Failure to provide security when required to do so by Customs and Excise.*
(6) Bribery and obstruction of officers.*

*Lighter penalties apply.

In addition to the above, there is a wide range of civil penalties. One of the most important of these is the *default surcharge*. If Customs and Excise have not received your VAT return and tax by the required date (the end of the month following the period), you will be in default. If you are then in default regarding another accounting period ending no more than one year later than the first, you may be charged a default surcharge. Furthermore, if you are then in default regarding another accounting period, no more than one year from the second, a further default surcharge can arise.

The amount of the default surcharge is the greater of £30 and a specified percentage of the outstanding tax. This percentage is 5% for the first default in the surcharge period, 10% for the second default and so on, up to a maximum of 30% for the sixth and any subsequent period.

You will be treated as not liable to a surcharge if you can show that there is a 'reasonable excuse' for not sending the return or the tax; or that the return and/or tax were sent in such manner and at such time as to expect that they would be received by the Commissioners of Customs and Excise within the time limit.

From 16 March 1988, the penalties on late registration for VAT are 10%, 20% and 30% of the tax. These rates apply where registration is late by no more than nine months, 18 months and more than 18 months respectively.

As from early 1990, a 'serious misdeclaration penalty' operates at 30% of the tax. Furthermore, there is a 15% penalty on 'persistent misdeclaration resulting in understatements or overclaims'. This penalty will only be used where a person has under-declared or over-claimed tax twice within two years and a written warning has been issued.

The new zero rating rules (8.8) have given rise to additional penalty provisions. Giving incorrect certificates of entitlement to zero-rating regarding supplies of fuel and power, new buildings or construction services may result in a civil penalty.

8.5 Appeals

Independent VAT tribunals deal with appeals about the matters listed below. There are tribunals in London, Edinburgh, Belfast and Manchester. The tribunals consist of a chairman who can sit alone or with one or two other members. The chairman must be a barrister or solicitor of seven years' standing. The procedure is explained in a leaflet issued by the President of VAT Tribunals which is available from Customs & Excise VAT offices.

In general an appeal must be made within 30 days of the issue of the disputed assessment or other document. Normally, it is necessary to pay any disputed VAT in advance of the hearing. However, if this would entail hardship the requirement is sometimes set aside.

The matters over which the tribunals have jurisdiction include the folowing:

(1) Registration (including groups of companies).

(2) VAT assessments.
(3) The amount of VAT chargeable.
(4) The amount of input tax deductible.
(5) The apportionment of input tax by partly exempt persons (8.10).
(6) Special schemes for retailers (8.19).
(7) The value of certain supplies.
(8) Repayment of VAT on certain imports (8.3).
(9) Refunds to do-it-yourself builders.
(10) Bad debt relief.
(11) Voluntary registration of a person whose turnover is below the limit.
(12) Appeals against certain Commissioners' decisions arising from earlier unappealable decisions which they had made.

There is an appeal from the tribunal on a point of law (not fact) to the High Court and from there to the Court of Appeal. There is a final appeal to the House of Lords if leave to appeal is obtained. In Scotland appeals go to the Court of Session and thence to the House of Lords.

8.6 Groups of companies and divisions

A group registration may be made. This involves a group of companies being registered as a single business. As a result, supplies between members of the group will be ignored. One of the companies in the group is responsible for making returns for the group as a whole. Where a company is organised in divisions, each can be registered separately for VAT purposes.

The Commissioners of Customs and Excise are empowered to direct that separately registered businesses are treated as one for VAT purposes. This applies for companies and other traders. The object is to combat artificially splitting a single business to avoid registration, for example where a business with turnover of £30,000 is split into two businesses each with £15,000 turnover.

8.7 Business

The definition of 'business' is central to the VAT system, because the credit mechanism is applied only to a business. The definition includes any trade, profession or vocation; also clubs and associations such as sports clubs and members' clubs. The charging of admission fees is also taxable as a business, for example in the case of the National Trust. Subscriptions to political parties, trade unions or professional bodies do not normally attract VAT.

8.8 Zero-rated supplies

Not all the inputs and outputs of a business are taxable at a positive rate. Certain classes of supply are treated specially either because they are 'zero-rated' or because they are 'exempt'.

Where a supply is zero-rated, no tax is charged on it, but credit is given to the supplier for all tax on his inputs relating to that supply. Exports of goods, for example, are zero-rated. They leave the country free of VAT in the UK, although they may be liable to VAT in the country of importation if that country has a VAT system. Thus, where a business exports most of its products, its VAT returns for an accounting period will probably show more tax on inputs than on outputs, the majority being zero-rated. (The business can then claim back the difference from Customs and Excise.)

In general, EC countries operate a VAT system with a similar structure to our own. This is required by the EC although different rates are allowed. One of the reasons is that the similar treatment of imports and exports promotes equality between home-produced and imported goods. However, the range of zero-rated supplies is not uniform throughout the EC. For example, food is zero-rated in the UK but positive-rated in certain other EC countries. On 21 June 1988, the European Court of Justice ruled that certain UK zero ratings do not comply with EC law. As a result, changes have been made regarding groups 2,7,8 and 17 of the zero-ratings (8.9).

8.9 Table: Zero-rated supplies

The following is a list of the important items. Full details are contained in the General Guide (VAT Notice No. 700) available from Customs and Excise:

Group 1:	*Food.* All food except pet foods, alcoholic drinks and certain food products (such as ice cream, chocolate, soft drinks and potato crisps). Meals out are, however, taxable and this includes hot take-away food and drink.
Group 2:	*Sewerage services and water.* Water except for distilled water and bottled water; emptying cesspools. These items are standard-rated from 1 July 1990, if for industrial use.

Group 3: *Books etc.* Books, newspapers, magazines, music, maps. But diaries and stationery are taxable.

Group 4: Talking books and tape recorders for the blind and handicapped and wireless sets for the blind.

Group 5: *Newspaper advertisements.* Advertising in newspapers, periodicals and journals only, including advertising agency charges. From 1 May 1985, however, all of these items are fully taxable.

Group 6: *News services.* News services supplied to newspapers — fully taxable from 1 April 1989.

Group 7: *Fuel and power.* Coal, gas, domestic heating oil, lubricating oil, electricity (standard-rated if for non-domestic use).

Group 8: *Construction of buildings, etc.* Sale of the freehold or grant of a lease for more than 21 years of a building by a builder; construction and demolition of buildings but not repairs. Sales by a builder's merchant, and architects' and surveyors' fees are, however, taxable. (Construction of buildings is standard-rated if for industrial or commercial use). A person building his own house (not merely conversions and alterations) can reclaim tax paid on items purchased. Conversions, reconstructions, alterations and enlargements are standard rated and sales of reconstructed buildings are exempt.

Group 8A: *Protected buildings.* This includes alterations and reconstructions of listed buildings, ancient monuments and listed churches.

Group 9: *International services.* Exports of services, such as professional advice to non-residents (except individuals in a non-business capacity who are resident in the EC) and overseas insurance. In some cases, the 'import' of professional services is charged to VAT.

Group 10: *Transport.* Passenger transport (inland and international) including travel agents (except in relation to hotels in the UK or package tours) and international freight transport. Taxis and hire cars are, however, taxable, as are pleasure boats and aircraft.

Group 11: *Caravans and houseboats.* Caravans which are too large to be used as trailers on the roads (22.9 feet in length or 7.5 feet in breadth). But smaller caravans are taxable.

Group 12:	*Gold.* Transactions on the London Gold market.
Group 13:	*Bank notes.*
Group 14:	*Drugs, medicines, aids for the handicapped etc.* Drugs dispensed by a registered pharmacist on a doctor's prescription. Other drugs purchased without a prescription are taxable. Medical and surgical appliances for the disabled and certain donated computer and other equipment.
Group 15:	*Imports, exports, etc.* This group has limited application.
Group 16:	*Charities* (8.20) including certain equipment, vehicles and also drugs used in research.
Group 17:	*Clothing and footwear.* Clothing for young children, industrial protective clothing and motor-cyclists' crash helmets. (Protective boots and clothing are standard-rated if supplied to employers for their employees).

Export of Goods. This does not include exports to Northern Ireland, which is part of the UK, or to the Isle of Man.

8.10 Exemption

The exemption of a supply of goods or services is not as favourable as zero-rating. As with zero-rating, there is no VAT on the supply but no credit is allowed for the corresponding tax on the inputs of the business. For example, life assurance is one of the exempt items so that there is no VAT on any premium which you pay on a life policy, but the life assurance company gets no credit for the tax on those inputs which it uses for its life assurance business. This introduces a hidden tax cost to its business. Note that zero-rating has priority over exemption if a supply falls into both categories.

Where a business supplies taxable (including zero-rated) and exempt goods and services, it is classified as *partly exempt*. When claiming credit for the tax on its inputs from Customs and Excise, it is entitled to a credit for the tax on those inputs which it uses for its taxable supplies. However, it is not entitled to credit for tax on those inputs used for its exempt supplies.

Regarding a *partially exempt* business, VAT is only recoverable if attributable to:

(1) Taxable business supplies.
(2) Supplies outside the UK which would have been chargeable or zero-rated if made here.
(3) Business supplies of certain warehouse goods disregarded for VAT.
(4) Overheads supporting the above.

8.11 Table: Exempt supplies

The following is a list of the more important items. Full details are contained in the General Guide (VAT Notice No 700) available from Customs and Excise:

Group 1: *Land.* Sales, leases and hiring out of land and buildings (unless within zero-rating Group 8). But hotels (excluding conference facilities), holiday accommodation, camping, parking, timber, mooring, exhibition stands and sporting rights are taxable, as are the letting, sale and construction of new and non-residential buildings under the new rules.

Group 2: *Insurance.* All types of insurance and insurance related activities by brokers and agents. Both premiums and the payment of claims are exempt.

Group 3: *Postal services.* Post, except telegrams. But telephones and telex are taxable.

Group 4: *Betting, gaming and lotteries.* Bookmakers, and charges for playing bingo. But admission or session charges, club subscriptions and takings from gaming machines are taxable.

Group 5: *Finance.* Banking, buying and selling stocks and shares and from 1 May 1985 charges from credit card companies to retailers etc, accepting the cards. But stockbrokers' commissions and unit trust management fees are taxable.

Group 6: *Education.* Schools, universities, non-profit-making institutions teaching pupils of any age, or providing job training; private tuition by an independent teacher.

Group 7: *Health and welfare.* Doctors, dentists, dental workers, nurses, midwives, registered opticians (including spectacles supplied in the course of treatment), chiropodists, dieticians, medical laboratory technicians, occupational therapists, orthoptists, physiotherapists, radiographers and remedial gymnasts, hearing aid dispensers, registered pharmaceutical chemists, medical and surgical treatment (except health farms, etc). The supply of welfare services by a charity or public body (unless for profit).

Group 8:	*Burial and cremation.* Undertakers, crematoria.
Group 9:	*Trade unions and professional bodies.*
Group 10:	*Sports competitions.*
Group 11:	*Certain works of art, etc.*
Group 12:	*Fund-raising events of charities, etc.* Supplies from 1 April 1989 of goods and services by charities, etc in connection with fund-raising events.

8.12 Land and buildings

Originally sales of land and buildings were generally exempt (8.11), whilst the construction of buildings and their sale were normally zero-rated (8.9). However, subject to the new rules, the construction of buildings for industrial and commercial use after 31 March 1989 is standard rated (15%).

All contracts entered into before 21 June 1988 continue to be zero-rated. Owners of non-domestic property have the option to elect to charge VAT on rents, and on sales of certain used buildings, from 1 August 1989. An election made before 1 November 1989 can go back to 1 August 1989. Otherwise the election can take effect no earlier than the date when made. Owners can obtain no input tax relief before the election has effect, subject to transitional relief. Certain transactions in non-residential buildings may be treated as self-supplies giving rise to VAT (8.16).

Where the rent is payable by someone who was in occupation immediately before 1 August 1989, only half of the rent for the year to 31 July 1990 will carry VAT. However, for charities, greater relief starting at 80% and tapering over the five years to 1 August 1993 is available.

Exempt businesses will be adversely affected by the new rules but some relief will be obtained by phasing in VAT on rents over a period of time.

8.13 Motor cars

Special VAT rules apply to motor cars. In general, no deduction is allowed for input tax on cars required for use in your business. The same is true regarding the acquisition of hire cars and taxis, apart from London-type taxis. However, where a car is leased, the tax on the hire charge is available for credit as input tax. The definition of 'motor car' for this purpose excludes commercial vehicles, vans without rear side windows and vehicles accommodating only one person or more than 11.

By contrast, a car dealer can claim a credit for input tax in the normal way on car purchases. However, if he takes a car out of stock and uses it in his own business, tax must be paid which is not available for credit. The 'self-supply' rules (8.15) normally apply.

The input tax on petrol used for business purposes is deductible. However, if it is supplied free of charge or below cost for private journeys, a quarterly scale corresponding to the income tax figures (9.13) is used for each person concerned. The employers are then charged to VAT on the scale figures which counteract the appropriate input tax. The scale figures from 6 April 1987 are as follows:

Cylinder capacity	Scale (quarterly) £
Up to 1400cc	120
1401–2000cc	150
Over 2000cc	225

The scale charge does not apply where a car is wholly used for business purposes, nor where it is used entirely for private purposes, in which case input tax is not deductible. If the business buys any private petrol, it may elect that the scale charges should not apply. However, in that case no deductions of input tax are allowed on petrol and diesel, even for vans and lorries. The scale charge is halved if business mileage exceeds 4,500 miles per quarter.

8.14 Business entertainment

In general, input tax on business entertainment (including overseas customers from 1 August 1988) is not deductible. Entertainment includes meals, accommodation, sporting facilities and theatre visits, etc. But concerning subsistence expenses refunded to employees, deduction of input tax is normally allowed.

8.15 Second-hand goods

In general, second-hand goods are chargeable to tax in the normal way. However, dealers in certain qualifying items can pay tax under special schemes. These provide that VAT is payable only on the dealer's mark-up.

Second-hand schemes apply to cars, motor cycles, caravans, boats and outboard motors, original works of art, antiques over 100 years old, collectors' pieces, electronic organs, aircraft, firearms, horses and ponies. With the exception of cars, these provisions only apply when no tax was charged on the dealer's acquisition or when tax was charged on another dealer's mark-up. Full VAT is payable on new goods supplied even though goods are taken in part-exchange.

8.16 Self-supply and personal use

Since a business which makes exempt supplies obtains no input tax relief, it is normally advantageous for it to produce goods for its own use. However, certain rules have been introduced to prevent undue distortion in certain areas.

For example, printed stationery is charged to tax even though supplied to oneself, so that a bank, which is exempt, would be charged tax on the value of any stationery which it prints itself and could not obtain relief for the tax. Similarly, a rule applies to cars which prevents avoidance of the general non-deduction of input tax (8.12).

If you acquire goods in the course of your business and apply them to your own personal use, tax is payable on their market value. This would apply, for example, if you are a shopkeeper and take goods from the shelf. A similar rules applies to the temporary private use of a business asset other then a car.

Developers of certain non-residential *buildings* may be treated as making self-supplies in various circumstances. This applies where, for example, a lease is granted which is an exempt supply. Also, when the developer is not a fully taxable person and occupies the building. In such cases VAT is chargeable on the land and taxable construction costs subject to certain exclusions. These include where the value is less than £100,000 and where the construction was completed before 1 August 1989; also, if the freehold had already passed and the non-residential building is new.

8.17 Gifts

Gifts of services are not subject to VAT. However, business gifts of goods are taxable on the cost price. (Items costing under £10 in aggregate for each recipient can be ignored.)

8.18 Bad debts

Limited relief for bad debts applies where the debtor goes bankrupt or goes into liquidation. The amount excluding VAT is claimed from the liquidator, etc. The VAT must be reclaimed from Customs and Excise. Retailers operating special schemes (8.18) effectively obtain bad debt relief since they only account for VAT on the amounts received.

8.19 Retailers

Retailers are frequently unable to record each sale separately and so there are special schemes for calculating the amount of VAT which they pay. The schemes also deal with problems arising where retailers sell both zero-rated goods (eg food) and standard-rated goods (eg kitchen equipment). Details of the schemes are to be found in Customs & Excise Notice number 727 and supplements.

At present, there are nine retail schemes in operation. These may be used by anyone dealing mainly with the public and unable to issue tax invoices for all their sales. In all cases, gross daily takings must be recorded and used as the basis for computing VAT.

'Scheme A' is used where all supplies are standard-rated. You simply apply the fraction 3/23 to your gross takings and this gives the output VAT. Input VAT is taken in the normal way from your purchase invoices, etc. The other schemes are more complicated, dealing with situations where there is a mixture of standard-rated and zero-rated supplies.

8.20 Tour operators

Previously, the services of tour operators regarding overseas package holidays were not liable to UK VAT. However, new rules have introduced a special VAT margin scheme. As a result, UK based tour operators buying in services pay VAT on the margin between their buying and selling prices. This applies if the services are used in the EC (including the UK). The tour operators are not able to recover any VAT charged by suppliers for such services.

8.21 Charities

Widespread income tax, capital gains tax and inheritance tax reliefs apply for charitable gifts and to the charities themselves. However, in the case of VAT, reliefs are limited. Sales in charity shops or at fetes, coffee mornings, etc of donated goods are zero-rated if the charity is established for the relief of distress. Apart from this, the business supplies of a charity are treated in the normal way for VAT purposes.

Any non-business supplies by a charity, such as distributions of free goods are outside the tax (unless exported when they are zero-rated). If a charity has separate branches, they may each be able to benefit from the £23,600 registration threshold. However, the authorities have powers to stop this being exploited (8.6). Further details regarding charities may be found in the VAT leaflet 701/1/84 and the schedule of zero-rated items (8.10). From 1 April 1989, supplies of goods and services by charities in connection with fund-raising events are exempt (8.11).

8.22 Official literature

The main VAT legislation is contained in VATA 1983 together with subsequent Finance Acts. Also, a large number of statutory instruments have been made under powers contained in the various Acts, all of which are available from HMSO.

An abundance of helpful literature has been published by H M Customs and Excise and a list is given below of a selection of the Notices, which are available free of charge from VAT offices. It should be emphasised that, in general, these Notices are guides and they do not have any legal force. A notable exception is Notice number 727, 'Special schemes for retailers' and those parts of the Notices relating to second-hand goods, which deal with keeping records. Some of the Notices are supported by numerous leaflets on specific topics.

Number

700/1/89	Should I be registered for VAT?
41	Trade classifications
101	Deferring duty, VAT and other charges
200	Temporary importations into the EC
201	Temporary imports from the EC
480	Special import entry procedures — period entry
700	The VAT guide (the most helpful booklet of all)
702	Imports
703	Exports

704 Retail exports
705 Personal exports of new motor vehicles
706 Partial exemption
711 Second-hand cars
712 Second-hand works of art and antiques
713 Second-hand motor cycles
714 Young childrens' clothing and footwear
717 Second-hand caravans and motor caravans
719 Refund of VAT to 'do it yourself' builders
720 Second-hand boats and outboard motors
721 Second-hand aircraft
722 Second-hand electronic organs
723 Refunds of VAT to European community traders
724 Second-hand firearms
726 Second-hand horses and ponies
727 Special schemes for retailers
731 Cash accounting
741 International services
742 Land and property
744 Passenger transport, international freight, ships and aircraft
748 Extra-statutory concessions.

9 Tax and National Insurance for employees

9.1 Introduction

For the purposes of taxation, 'employees' normally includes directors. Thus, if you trade through a company, your own remuneration will be subjected to both income tax and social security contributions, on the basis that you are an employee. However, special rules may apply to you as a director, as described in this chapter.

As previously mentioned, if you are a sole trader or trade in partnership, you are subject to income tax under Case I or Case II of Schedule D. However, it should be noted that as a salaried partner, you may be treated as an employee for tax purposes. Income from employments or any office, such as a directorship, is normally taxed under Schedule E.

The distinction between Schedule D, Case I or II and Schedule E is sometimes very fine. For example, where you have a number of part-time employments and do some of the work at home. If you are able to show that you actually work on your own account and are self-employed, then you will be assessed under Schedule D, which normally results in your being able to deduct more of your expenses from your taxable income than if you were assessed under Schedule E. However, particularly where you do work exclusively for one company, etc, the Revenue may try to assess you under Schedule E.

9.2 The three cases of Schedule E

Schedule E is divided into three cases. Of most frequent application is *Case I*, which applies if you are both resident and ordinarily resident in the UK. Your assessment is usually on the actual income received during the tax year. This case also applies to work which you do wholly abroad (unless you work for a non-resident employer and you are not UK-domiciled).

If you are absent from the UK for a continuous period of 365 days or more, you are not charged to UK tax on your overseas earnings during that period. You are allowed to spend up to 1/6th of your time here without losing this relief.

Schedule E, Case II applies if you are not resident in the UK or where you are resident but not ordinarily resident here. In these circumstances, you will normally be assessed to tax under Case II on your earnings for duties performed here.

Case III applies if you are UK resident, working wholly abroad but remitting salary here during the course of your overseas employment. You are assessed on the actual amounts remitted to the UK in the tax year. However, if one of the other cases applies to the income, then Case III does not operate and it now normally only applies to non-UK domiciled people.

Up to 5 April 1989, you may have been assessed to income tax on your emoluments on what is known as the 'accounts basis'. This involved paying tax for a tax year based on your director's remuneration, etc, for the accounts year ending therein. Thus, if your remuneration for the year to 31 December 1987 was £25,000, this was assessed for 1987–1988.

From 6 April 1989, the earnings of *all* directors and employees are assessed for the year in which they are received and not for the year for which they were earned. (Pensions are to be assessed under Schedule E on an accruals basis.) However transitional provisions deal with situations where income is either taxed twice or not at all. In general, the earnings are taken out of assessment for the year when earned and taxed only in the year received, provided relief is claimed.

For the purposes of the new rules, you are regarded as receiving your earnings at the earliest of the following times.

(1) When actual payment is made (in whole or on account).
(2) When you become entitled to be paid.
(3) If you are a director, when sums on account of emoluments are credited to you in the company's books.
(4) The end of a period of account, where your director's emoluments are determined *before* the end of that period.
(5) *When* your director's emoluments are determined, if after the relevant period of account.

Where emoluments for an accounting period ending after 5 April 1989 are paid more than nine months after the end of that period, they must be added back in the employer's tax computations and only allowed as a deduction when paid. This applies where the remuneration relates to any period after 5 April 1989.

9.3 Schedule E income

For Schedule E purposes, any amount that you derive from your office or employment is normally included in your taxable income. This covers the value of payments in kind, as well as cash. The following list gives some examples:

(1) Your normal salary or wage and overtime pay.
(2) Holiday pay.
(3) Sick pay (including statutory sick pay and statutory maternity pay).
(4) Sickness insurance benefits paid to you (benefits are taxable immediately except to the extent that you have paid for these yourself).
(5) Luncheon vouchers in excess of 15p per day.
(6) Cost of living allowance.
(7) Christmas or other gifts in cash (excluding personal gifts like wedding presents).
(8) Annual or occasional bonus.
(9) Commission.
(10) Director's fees and other remuneration.
(11) Remuneration for part-time employment.
(12) Salary paid in advance.
(13) Tips from your employer or from customers or clients of your employer.
(14) Settlement by employer of debts incurred by employee.
(15) Payment of employees' National Insurance contributions by employer.
(16) Value of goods supplied cost-free by employer to employee.
(17) Share options (9.20).
(18) Job release allowances capable of beginning earlier than a year before pensionable age.
(19) Payment for entering into an employment.
(20) Salary in lieu of notice (often tax-free — see 9.27).
(21) Fringe benefits, such as travelling allowances and cars — according to the rules, amounts are frequently taxable (9.10).

9.4 The PAYE system

The 'pay as you earn' system (PAYE) applies to most Schedule E income tax payable on earnings from employment in this country. The employer is responsible for administering the PAYE on the wages of employees, including directors. From each wages or salaries payment which you receive, whether it be weekly or monthly, the employer deducts income tax at the basic and higher rates (if applicable). National Insurance contributions are also deducted. However, if income tax has previously been over-deducted by the employer (for example, where personal reliefs change following the Budget), you may receive a repayment of income tax through the PAYE system.

The employer pays the total PAYE income tax deductions (less refunds) and National Insurance contributions to the Collector of Taxes in respect of the previous month. If payment is not made by the time limit, which is the 19th day of the following month, the Collector may send an estimated demand which must be paid within seven days, unless (1) the correct PAYE is paid; (2) the Collector is satisfied that no more is owing; or (3) the Collector is invited to inspect the PAYE records.

9.5 Your code number

The PAYE system takes account of your income tax allowances and reliefs by means of 'code numbers'. The Inspector of Taxes allocates a code number to you which takes into account all the reliefs to which you are entitled, adjustment being made for other income being set off and any Schedule E income tax underpaid or overpaid for the previous year.

In general, coding notices are only sent out to cover changes. Otherwise, the code for the previous year is normally used at the beginning of the next tax year. The coding notice itemises your allowances and reliefs. Adjustments are also shown and then the balance of your allowances and the corresponding code number. The Inspector of Taxes normally obtains the details for your coding notice from your last income tax return. However, if your return is overdue, your code number may be understated.

To convert your total allowances and adjustments into your code number, you simply divide by 10 and round down to the nearest whole number. Thus, if your allowances, etc for 1989–90 total £2,945, your code number is 294. Your code number normally ends in L, H, P or V, depending on whether it includes respectively single, wife's earning's allowance, married allowance or single allowance plus additional personal allowance, full single age allowance, or full married age allowance. Whenever increases take place in these reliefs, the Revenue instruct employers to change codes ending in L, H, P or V accordingly. Revised coding notices are not then needed in those cases.

The above normally applies to your code number in respect of your main employment. However, where you have, for example, several directorships or employments, other rules apply to them. If the

Revenue consider that your net taxable earnings for 1989–90 will not exceed £20,700, you will be coded 'BR' regarding each of your other employments etc. This means that Table B (9.6) must be applied to your total earnings from each employment, except your main one. If, however, your earnings are likely to be more than £20,700, the Inspector of Taxes is likely to allocate you with 'D' codings (9.6) regarding your supplementary employments etc.

9.6 PAYE records and general operation

The employer is allowed to use computerised records. Otherwise, he may use the official deductions working sheet (form P11). These can be used for weekly or monthly paid employees. One form is used for each individual, and for a weekly paid person the following particulars are entered and calculated:

(1) National Insurance contributions.
(2) Gross pay for the week.
(3) Cumulative pay for the tax year to date.
(4) Total 'free pay' to date (see below).
(5) Total taxable pay to date (3–4).
(6) Total tax due to date (see below).
(7) Tax to be paid or repaid for the week (see below).

For monthly paid employees, similar details are entered for each month. Total 'free pay' to date is obtained from 'Table A' which is provided by the Revenue. This table shows for each week the 'free pay' applicable to each code number (9.5). Where your total pay is less than your 'free pay' to date, you pay no more tax for that week and normally receive a refund. You calculate the tax to be paid or repaid for the week (7 above) by subtracting the total tax due to date for the previous week from that for the current week (6 above). Total tax due to date is found each week from the tax deduction tables provided by the Revenue, which give the tax attributable to the relevant total taxable pay to date.

The PAYE tax deduction tables are designated B, C and D. Table B shows tax due for each week or month at the basic rate. Table C shows the amounts to be taxed at the higher rate, 40%. Both weekly and monthly tables are provided. Table C is effectively supplementary to Table B.

Where your earnings are substantial and you have more than one employment, etc, the Revenue normally direct that Tables B and C are used for your main employment. For your other employments, you are likely to be issued with Code D0 and you must refer to Table D. This lists the tax payable at 40% (Code D0). Thus, if you receive £10,000 from a directorship for which your code is D0, PAYE is deducted at 40% on your entire salary, making £4,000. This provides the Revenue with a very approximate means of collecting tax for your supplementary employments, directorships, etc. Once your income tax return is submitted, at the end of the tax year, your income tax is adjusted to the correct figure.

The Deductions Working Sheet (form P11) also provides columns for your earnings related National Insurance contributions. These are calculated either weekly or monthly and are collected through the PAYE system. The total Class I contributions (9.30) are entered together with the employee's amount. The figures are readily calculated from tables provided by the Department of Social Security.

9.7 Employer's PAYE returns

End of year returns P14 must be completed for each employee. These returns are filled in from the forms P11 or other records and should include the National Insurance number, date of birth, final code, total pay, tax and National Insurance contributions. The forms P14 are then sent to the Inspector of Taxes, together with form P35, which is a summary of the total tax due to be deducted for the tax year for all of the employees.The earnings related National Insurance contributions for each employee are also entered on the form P35. The details are obtained from the weekly or monthly records.

The total income tax due to be paid over by the employer is found by adding all of the tax entries on form P35 and the total of the actual payments made is deducted. A similar procedure is followed regarding the earnings-related National Insurance contributions except that the amount to be paid over also includes the employer's contributions. Any amounts shown owing for income tax and National Insurance earnings-related contributions should be remitted when submitting the form P35. (Conversely, any over-payment will be repaid.) Where forms P11D (9.25 are required for the tax year, they should be sent to the Revenue with form P35.

A further part of the year-end procedure is that the employer should issue to each of the employees a form P60. This is a certificate of gross earnings for the year and income deducted under PAYE and now actually forms part of the P14 pack, so that the bottom copy can be used for this purpose.

9.8 Change of employer

Where an employee leaves, the employer should complete a form P45 in triplicate showing the employee's name, district reference, code number, week or month number of the last entries in the tax deduction records, gross pay to date and total tax due to date. The old employer sends Part I of the form to his Inspector of Taxes and hands Parts II and III to the employee who must give these to the new employer.

On receiving form P45, the new employer enters the address and date of starting on Part III and sends it to his Inspector of Taxes. The new employer then prepares tax deduction records (P11) etc from the details on the form P45 and deducts PAYE from future wages, etc in the normal way.

If an employee is not able to provide the new employer with a form P45, the latter must normally deduct tax under the 'emergency' system. This assumes that the employee is single and has no other allowances. If this happens to you, make an income tax return to the Inspector of Taxes or supply the necessary details to him, so that he can issue you with your correct code number which your employer will then use, making any necessary tax payment to you. If an employee does not have a form P45 when starting a new job, it is possible to complete form P46. This form covers whether the employee is a school leaver, and whether it is his main job or an additional one. The P46 enables the employer to know whether to deduct basic rate tax or use an emergency code.

9.9 Fringe benefits

The term 'fringe benefits' is widely used to describe any benefit which you obtain from your employment which is not actually included in your salary cheque. Fringe benefits are taxable according to the rules outlined below. However, the rules provide scope for the emoluments of directors and other employees to be enhanced in a tax-efficient way.

Employees earning less than £8,500 each year, including the value of any benefits, are taxed on their fringe benefits in a comparatively favourable way. However, those earning over £8,500 or who are directors, are normally taxed more strictly on the actual value of the benefits obtained. If you fall into this latter class, then a form P11D (9.25) must be submitted for you to the Revenue each year, by the employer.

For these purposes, you are not treated as a *director* if you work full time for a company and do not own more than 5% of its shares. This includes shares owned by your relatives and other associates. (If you are a director of a charity, you do not need to work full time.) Where you work for a number of companies which are connected, these must be considered together for the purposes of these rules.

9.10 Table: Fringe benefits — Taxation 1989-90

The taxation of certain fringe benefits is summarised below according to whether or not you are a P11D employee (ie a director or earning over £8,500).

	Details	Non-P11D employee	P11D employee or director
(1)	Travelling and entertainment allowances	Generally tax-free if expenses actually incurred (9.11)	(9.11)
(2)	Free private use of motor vehicle supplied by your employers	Tax free (provided some business use is made)	Taxable (9.12)
(3)	Company house occupied rent free	Taxed on annual value of benefit (ie open market rental and expenses paid) unless you need to occupy house to do job properly	Taxed on annual value unless you live there to perform your duties (9.14)
(4)	Board and lodging	If you receive cash you are taxed on it. Otherwise tax free	Taxed on cost to employer of board and lodging subject to a limit (9.14)
(5)	Assets at employee's disposal	Normally tax free	Taxable (9.15)
(6)	Pension and death in service cover	Normally tax free (9.16)	Normally tax free (9.16)
(7)	Interest free loan	Tax free	Taxable subject to certain exceptions (9.17)
(8)	Loan to participator etc of close company	(not Schedule E benefit)	(4.24)
(9)	Employee shareholdings		(9.18)
(10)	Share options	Sometimes taxable (9.21)	Sometimes taxable (9.20)
(11)	Private sickness insurance cover	Tax free	Taxed on premiums paid by your employer
(12)	Working clothing — eg overalls	Tax free	Tax free
(13)	Suits and coats etc	Taxed on estimated second-hand value	Taxed on full cost to employer

(14)	Luncheon vouchers	Tax free up to 15p per day — excess taxable	Tax free up to 15p per day — excess taxable
(15)	Subsidised staff canteen	Tax free	Tax free provided facilities available to all staff
(16)	Employee's outgoings	Tax free	Normally tax free
(17)	Long service awards of articles of employer company shares; after 20 years' service; maximum £20 for each year	Tax free	Tax free
(18)	Cash vouchers	Taxable	Taxable
(19)	Season tickets and credit cards	Generally taxable	Generally taxable
(20)	Scholarship from employer for children of employee	Normally tax free	Taxable with some exceptions for pre 15 March 1983 arrangements and 'open' schemes
(21)	Security assets and services provided after 5 April 1989	Tax free	Tax free
(22)	Profit related pay (9.33)		

9.11 Travelling and entertainment allowances

Where your employer makes any allowance or advance to cover your travelling costs or entertaining or other services, in the course of the business, this is not taxable, provided you actually spend the money for these purposes. (The employer deducts the payments from his taxable profits. However, entertaining expenses are, in the main, not deductible.) Any excess amount which you are allowed to keep is treated as your taxable income.

As a P11D employee (including director, 9.9) allowances to cover your travelling etc are generally included in your form P11D which your company completes for you (9.25) and it will be treated as part of your income unless you actually make a claim for your business travelling expenses, etc to be set against it. However, in general, you are allowed no deduction for travelling costs between your home and your place of business. Thus, any allowance made by the employers towards this expense is wholly taxable in your hands.

The cost of travelling abroad on company business is allowable. However, if you have a holiday at the same time, an appropriate proportion of the cost of the trip is treated as a personal benefit. If your wife accompanies you and the company pays, her own trip would normally be taxed as your personal benefit (assuming she is not also an employee). However, in certain circumstances, some allowance could be obtained such as where she acts during the trip as your secretary or she needs to accompany you because your health is poor.

If you work abroad for at least sixty continuous days, no benefit is assessed on you if your employer pays for your family to visit you. This covers the actual journeys of your spouse and any children under the age of 18 on the outward journey; also journeys by your family in accompanying you at the beginning of your period overseas. The rule covers two return trips for each person in any tax year. Furthermore, provided you are UK resident and working abroad, any travel expenses paid by your employer covering journeys to and from the UK are tax-free.

9.12 Motor cars

Cars constitute one of the most sought after and important 'fringe benefits'. The following rules should be noted, if you are a director or an employee earning more than £8,500 (9.9) and a car is provided for you:

(1) If your employment carries a car, you are normally assessed to tax each year on a 'scale benefit' which is fixed according to the size of your engine and the price of your car when new (9.13). However, if your business use is 'insubstantial', you are assessed on 150% of the scale benefit appropriate to your car. Second cars are also treated in this way. 'Insubstantial' means no more than 2,500 miles each year.

(2) Where your business use exceeds 2,500 miles each year, you are assessed on the actual scale benefit figure (9.13). Thus, if you have a 1500 cc car costing less than £19,250, your scale benefit for 1989–90 is £1,850. this covers the provision of the car and any expenses borne by your employer except for petrol (see (4)). If your business mileage during the tax year reaches 18,000, your scale benefit is halved.

(3) Car pools are afforded favourable treatment. Provided you simply take a car from the pool and do not garage it at home overnight, you will not normally be assessed to any benefit. However, you must not have the use of any one particular car and any

Tax and National Insurance for employees 195

private use of the car must be merely incidental to your business use.

(4) Where petrol is provided by the employer, higher paid employees are taxed by applying an additional scale charge. This is equal to the scale benefit figures for new (less expensive) cars. This scale only applies if your employer bears any of the cost; thus the petrol charge can be set aside if you repay the cost of any petrol provided. Should your business mileage for the tax year reach 18,000, your scale benefit is halved.

(5) From 6 April 1988, the provision of *car parking facilities* near to the place of work is not assessed on an employee as a benefit. Furthermore, any open cases for earlier years are not pursued by the Inland Revenue, although no repayment is made of tax already paid.

9.13 Table: Car and fuel benefit scales 1988–89 and 1989–90

Cylinder capacity (original market value if no cylinder capacity)	Scale benefits assessed Cars under 4 years old		Cars over 4 years old		Fuel Benefit (both years)
	1989–90	1988–89	1989–90	1988–89	
Less expensive cars – cost up to £19,250					
1400cc or less (under £6,000)	£1,400	£1,050	£ 950	£ 700	£ 480
1401cc–2000cc (£6,000–£8,499)	£1,850	£1,400	£1,250	£ 940	£ 600
Over 2000cc (£8,500–£19,250)	£2,950	£2,200	£1,950	£1,450	£ 900
Cars costing more than £19,250					
£19,250–£29,000	£3,850	£2,900	£2,600	£1,940	£ 900*
(over £29,000)	£6,150	£4,600	£4,100	£3,060	£ 900*
*provided over 2,000cc					

9.14 Living accommodation

Where living accommodation is provided for you because of your employment, in general, you are taxed on the gross rateable value of the property or the actual rent paid by your employer, if this is more. However, anything which you pay towards the cost is deducted. Exemption applies in the following circumstances:

(1) In order to perform your duties properly, you have to live in the accommodation.
(2) In your type of employment, it is customary to have accommodation provided and it helps you to do your job better.
(3) The accommodation is provided with a view to your safety, because your employment involves you in a security risk.

Exemptions (1) and (2) do not apply to directors unless they own broadly no more than 5% of the company's shares and work full time or work for a charity, etc.

In the above circumstances, rates are also covered by the exemption. However, if you are a P11D employee (9.9), you are still assessed on payments made by your employer for heating, lighting, cleaning, repairs, maintenance and decoration, etc. You are also assessed on the value of domestic furniture and equipment provided (9.15). However, the charge for these items is limited to 10% of your net emoluments from your job, after deducting pension contributions, capital allowances and expense claims.

If you are provided with a house costing your employer more than £75,000, there is an additional benefit charge broadly based on the excess of the cost over that sum. This excess is subjected to the rate of interest in force regarding beneficial loans (now 15½%) at the start of the year of assessment (9.17). After you have occupied the house for six years, its market value is substituted for the cost in calculating the benefit. However, this only applies if you first occupied the property on or after 31 March 1983.

9.15 Assets provided for employee

If you are a P11D director or employee (9.9) and your employer places an asset at your disposal for your personal use, your annual taxable benefit is 20% of its market value when you first begin to use it. This does not apply to cars (9.12) nor land, for which 'annual value' is used. If you subsequently become the owner of the asset, you will have a taxable benefit of the excess over anything you pay for the asset, of the original market value less previous benefit assessments.

9.16 Pension and life assurance arrangements

As a director or other employee, you will need to make National Insurance contributions (9.28). These are not deductible from your taxable income. However, the employer's contributions are deductible from the taxable profits of the company, etc. On retirement, your state pension is taxed as earned income, according to the actual amount for each tax year. Any widow's pension payable to your wife is also taxable in this way. In addition to the basic contributions, there is an earnings related component in the state scheme. However, you may be 'contracted out' which relieves you and your employer of the obligation to pay higher rate National Insurance contributions.

You are taxed on any pension paid to you out of your employer's own pension scheme. The same applies to any retirement pension paid by your employer outside any scheme. In both cases, the pensions are treated as earned income.

If the employer bears the entire cost of a retirement scheme, it is known as 'non-contributory'. Otherwise, if the employee makes his own regular contributions to the scheme as well as the employer, it is known as 'contributory'. For larger companies, a separate pension trust is sometimes set up and investments made on which generally no UK tax is payable, either on income or capital gains. Any employees' contributions are deductible from their taxable earnings and amounts paid by the company are deductible from its taxable profits. No 'benefit-in-kind' assessments are made on the employees. However, Revenue approval is needed in order to obtain this taxation treatment (11.12).

Many employers arrange for their pension schemes to be operated by insurance companies. In return for annual premiums based on the salaries of the employees covered, the insurance company provides retirement pensions and also sometimes lump sum payments in the event of death in service. Subject to Revenue approval (11.12), the company deducts the contributions that it pays from its taxable profits and the employees deduct their contributions from their taxable earnings. Subject to the rules, part of the retirement benefits may be taken as a tax-free lump sum (11.12).

From 1 July 1988, *personal pension schemes* (11.13) are available for those not covered by staff superannuation schemes. The contributions may be paid by the employer or employee. Fuller particulars of these and other matters concerning pensions are contained in chapter 11.

9.17 Beneficial loan arrangements

If you are a P11D director or employee (9.9) and have a loan by reason of your employment at no interest, or at a lower rate than the 'official' one, you are taxed on the benefit of your interest saving compared with the 'official' rate, subject to the rules.

The above also applies to a 'relative' including parent, grandparent, child, grandchild etc, brother or sister; or your spouse, or the spouse of any of the relatives mentioned.

The 'official rate' varies periodically. Recent rates are:

From 6 April 1987	11½%
From 6 June 1987	10½%
From 6 September 1987	11½%
From 6 December 1987	10½%
From 6 May 1988	9½%
From 6 August 1988	12 %
From 6 October 1988	13½%
From 6 January 1989	14½%
From 6 July 1989	15½%

No charge to tax is made if the cash value of the benefit does not exceed £200 and no tax charge is made if tax relief would have been available for any interest paid on the loan.

9.18 Employee shareholdings

If you are a director or P11D employee (9.9) and acquire shares at an undervalue by reason of your employment, you are taxed on the shortfall of what you pay for the shares compared with their market value when you bought them, as though it was an interest-free loan (9.17). You are regarded as obtaining shares at an undervalue if you pay less than the market value of fully paid shares of the same class at that time, whether or not you are under any obligation to pay more in the future. This continues until the shortfall is ended, or you sell the shares, even if you cease your employment. Note that the shares need not be in the company which employs you, provided you obtain them at an undervalue by reason of your employment.

Share incentive schemes are arrangements under which you are allowed to purchase shares in the company where you work because of your employment or directorship and not simply because of a general offer to the public. If you obtain shares under such a scheme, you are assessed normally to income tax under Schedule E on the increase in market value of the shares between the time when you acquired them and the earliest of the following:

(1) seven years from your purchase;
(2) when in certain circumstances you cease to be a director or employee;
(3) when you sell the shares; and
(4) when your shares cease to be subject to any special restrictions.

Regarding relevant share acquisition after 25 October 1987, less stringent rules apply, which are contained in the 1988 Finance Act. In particular, there is only a charge to the extent that value is actually shifted preferentially into the employee shares by lifting or varying restrictions or attaching some new or enhanced rights to the shares.

Certain *profit-sharing schemes* etc are excluded, provided certain conditions are satisfied, including the following:

(1) the shares are publicly quoted or not in one company which is controlled by another or are shares in an authorised unit trust satisfying certain conditions;
(2) the shares are not subject to any special restrictions (apart from Stock Exchange 'insider dealing' rules);
(3) all employees of the company are allowed to belong to the scheme, provided they are aged 25 and over and have at least five years' continuous service;
(4) your shares are received as part of your earnings according to a pre-arranged basis, which is geared to the profits of the company;
(5) shares obtained through an approved share option scheme (9.22) are also excluded; and
(6) a further exclusion concerns offers to employees at the same time as offers to the public of at least 75% of the shares, provided any discount has been taxed under Schedule E.

9.19 Profit-sharing schemes

Tax relief is available for employees participating in a company share scheme approved by the Revenue. Under such a scheme, trustees are allowed to acquire company shares to the value of up to £2,000 for any employee in each tax year. This is increased to 10% of salary (excluding expenses) if higher. For this purpose, you take your salary for the current or previous year, whichever is the higher, but the maximum value of shares is £6,000 in any event. (Lower limits applied before 6 April 1989).

You must agree to keep your shares with the trustees for at least two years, unless you die, retire or become redundant. The scheme must be open to all employees who have been with the company or group for five years or more, although the employers can allow those with shorter service to join, at their discretion. Dividends on the shares are paid over to the participants.

If the trustees sell any of your shares, 100% is taxable if they had been held for less than four years, 75% if held for four years and the sale is tax-free if the shares are held for five years or more. The percentages are taken on the original value, or the proceeds of the shares if less. However, any capital receipts already charged to income tax are deducted. (The appropriate percentage of capital receipts is charged to income tax less an allowance of £100 maximum.) The charge is abated by 50% for employees who leave due to injury, disability, redundancy or reaching pensionable age.

9.20 Unapproved share option schemes

If you are granted an option to take up shares in the company for which you work, you are assessed to Schedule E income tax on a notional gain, when you exercise your option. (This does not apply to an approved scheme — 9.22.) You pay income tax on the notional gain as part of your earned income. The 'gain' is computed by taking the market value of the shares on the day when you exercise the option and deducting both the price you paid for the shares and the price (if any) you paid for the option. If you subsequently sell the shares at a profit, you will normally have a capital gain (chapter 6) equivalent to your proceeds less the value of the shares when you exercise the option. (For options granted before 6 April 1984, there are certain opportunities to pay the tax by instalments.)

9.21 Savings-related share option schemes

Notional or real gains which you make from an approved savings-related share option scheme are free of income tax, although some capital gains tax may be payable. Under the scheme, you are given an option to buy shares in the company which employs you or its controlling company. However, you are not eligible if you control more than 25% of the shares and the company is close (4.21). You must save the money to buy the shares through a special SAYE contract geared to produce the required cost of the shares on its maturity.

Normally, the option must not be capable of being exercised within five years. Early exercise of the option is only allowed in special circumstances, such as death, disability, retirement or redundancy. Early exercise is also allowed if the company or part of its business, in which you work, leaves the group operating the scheme.

Monthly contributions are now limited to £150 and no minimum monthly contribution can be stipulated above £10. The future purchase price of the shares must not be manifestly less than 80% of the market value of the shares when the option is granted. Because of the limitations, if larger benefits are sought, an approved share option scheme (9.22) is likely to be preferable.

9.22 Approved share option schemes

Where you obtain options under an approved share option scheme, the gain is only taxable when the shares are sold and capital gains tax, rather than income tax, applies. The scheme can extend to groups. Conditions for Inland Revenue approval include the following:

(1) You may hold options over shares worth no more than £100,000 at the time of their grant or four times your current or previous

year's emoluments if greater. (This limit is applied on a cumulative basis.)
(2) The share price contained in the option must not be much lower than the market value when the option was granted.
(3) You can only exercise your option between three years and ten years after its grant.
(4) When the option is granted to you, you must be a full time director or employee but you are allowed to leave before you exercise it.
(5) You are only allowed to exercise approved options once in every three years.
(6) The options must be non-transferable and the shares fully paid ordinary shares. Shares subject to special restrictions may not be used, although employees may be required to sell their shares when their employment ceases.
(7) Redeemable shares cannot be used except in the case of registered worker co-operatives.
(8) On a takeover, it is possible for a scheme to be transferred from one company to another, subject to certain conditions.
(9) No one with a 'material interest' (broadly 10% of the shares) in a close company or group (4.21) can participate.

9.23 Employee share ownership plans (ESOPs)

New tax relief for ESOPs applies to contributions made to qualifying trusts from 27 July 1989. The main features are:

(1) ESOP trusts may borrow to acquire their shares rather than relying on funds provided by the employer company.
(2) ESOP trusts may provide a market in unquoted shares and may distribute larger amounts of shares than under Profit Sharing Schemes (9.19).
(3) All employees of the company and its subsidiaries, who work 20 or more hours weekly and have been employed for a stipulated period must be beneficiaries of the ESOP trust. (The stipulated period is as contained in the trust deed and must be at least 1–5 years.) However, those with a 'material interest' in the company (broadly 5%) must be excluded.
(4) Beneficiaries may also include ex-employees and ex-directors within 18 months of leaving.
(5) Funds from the company must be used within nine months after the end of the company's accounting period in which they were received. The funds must be used in buying ordinary shares in the company, servicing and repaying borrowings, paying benefits and paying expenses.
(6) The shares must be distributed within seven years of their acquisition to all accepting beneficiaries on similar terms.
(7) Payments to an ESOP trust by the company or a subsidiary are

allowed for corporation tax. However, the trust itself is taxable on its income and capital gains. Also, employees receiving shares at less than market value will be liable to income tax.

9.24 Director's PAYE

If you are a director and your company accounts, other than at the proper time, for PAYE to the Inland Revenue in excess of the amounts which you suffer by deduction, this excess is treated as your income. However, this would not apply to you if you work full time for the company and hold less than 5% of its shares, nor in the case of a charity.

9.25 Form P11D

Forms P11D must normally be completed for each tax year for directors and higher paid employees, in respect of all benefits in kind and expense payments made to them or on their behalf. However, where any directors and higher paid employees do not receive benefits, it is merely necessary for employers to complete a confirmation that all necessary forms P11D have been prepared and returned to the Revenue.

Form P11D requires details covering a wide range of benefits including the following:

(1) Cars owned or hired by the employer.
(2) Cars owned by the employee — allowances from employer.
(3) Entertainment — allowances and reimbursements.
(4) General round sum expense allowances not exclusively for entertaining.
(5) Travel and subsistence — fares, hotels, meals etc.
(6) Subscriptions, private medical and dental care and insurance.
(7) Educational assistance including scholarships awarded after 14 March 1983 to you or your family.
(8) Goods and services supplied free or below market value.
(9) Work done to your home or other assets by employer.
(10) Domestic staff provided by employer.
(11) Vouchers and credit cards given by employer.
(12) Living accommodation provided by employer.
(13) Assets provided by employer.
(14) Home telephone — cost of rental and calls.
(15) Beneficial loans.

The amounts are entered on form P11D according to the instructions and then the employer deducts the amounts of any of the expenses that have been repaid and the amounts included above, from which tax has been deducted under PAYE.

Other information required includes details of payments of remuneration for previous years included in the current form P35 (9.7) and payments relating to that year, to be made after it. Confirmation must be given that PAYE has been paid to the Collector regarding emoluments, including bonuses and commissions for the year in question; otherwise the amounts not deducted but later paid to the Revenue should be detailed.

9.26 Deductions from income

As an employee or director, you may claim any expenses incurred wholly, exclusively and necessarily in performing the duties of your employment, excluding:

(1) Travelling between home and work.
(2) Business entertainment except where disallowed in computing the employer's tax assessment.

Directors or P11D employees (9.9) should make a claim to the Revenue regarding allowable expenses included in the form P11D. The claim should certify that the expenses were incurred 'wholly, exclusively and necessarily' in performing the duties of the employment. Provided the claim is accepted, the payments escape tax, whether made to the employee or third parties.

Any expenses that you personally incur as an employee or director in connection with your employment should be included in your income tax return, including:

(1) Overalls, clothing and tools.
(2) Travelling.
(3) Business use of car including capital allowances (2.27).
(4) Home telephone and other expenses.
(5) Professional fees and subscriptions relating to your work.
(6) Your own contributions to any superannuation scheme operated by the employers.
(7) In certain employments (entertainment industry etc) expenses such as hairdressing, make-up, clothes cleaning, etc.

9.27 Compensation for loss of office

Where a 'golden handshake' payment is made to you on your retirement, resignation, redundancy or removal from a directorship or other employment, £30,000 will normally be tax-free. The excess is taxed as your earned income. 'Golden handshake' payments are normally deductible so far as the employer is concerned, unless, for instance, they are abnormally high payments to controlling directors. It would also be very difficult to obtain any deduction where the payments are in connection with a sale of the actual business or made just before it ceases to trade.

Payments to you arising out of your contract of employment are taxable. For example, if you have a service contract providing for a lump sum payment when you leave your employer, this is liable to income tax.

Prior to 6 April 1988 and subject to the rules, the first £25,000 was exempt, the next £25,000 was taxed at half the marginal income tax rate of the recipient and the next £25,000 at 75% of the marginal rate. In other words, 100% relief was obtained on the first £25,000, 50% relief on the next £25,000 and 25% relief on the next £25,000, the remainder being fully taxed.

Due to faultily drafted legislation, the Inland Revenue conceded that up to 3 June 1986, higher relief was due. The first £25,000 was exempt, for the next £50,000 the tax was reduced by half and for the next £25,000, the tax was reduced by 25%. As a result, recipients of 'golden handshake' payments from 6 April 1982 to 3 June 1986 may have qualified for tax repayments. New legislation took effect from 4 June 1986 so as to apply the rules as originally intended.

Certain payments are normally tax-free including the following:

(1) Ex gratia payments on the death or permanent disability of an employee.
(2) Terminal grants to members of HM Forces.
(3) Ex gratia payments on the termination of an employment where the employee worked abroad, either:

   (a) For three-quarters of his entire term of service or
   (b) For the whole of the last 10 years or
   (c) If the total service exceeds 20 years, half of the total service period including any 10 of the last 20 years.

9.28 National Insurance contributions

Contributions are payable under four categories known as 'Class 1' (employees), 'Class 2' (self-employed), 'Class 3' (voluntary) and 'Class 4' (self-employed earnings related). Classes 2 and 3 are flat rate contributions and Class 4 is dealt with earlier (2.50).

Tax and National Insurance for employees

9.29 Table: National Insurance contributions for 1989–90

	Employee	Employer
The four classes of contributions are as follows:		
'Class 1' — employees aged 16 & over:		
Lower earnings limit (LEL) pw	£43.00	
Upper earnings limit (UEL) pw	£325.00	
(a) earnings less than LEL:	Nil	Nil
(b) earnings LEL or more and contracted out: up to LEL on balance up to UEL		See Table 9.31
(c) earnings at least LEL and contracted in: on earnings up to UEL		
'Class 2' — self-employed pw		£4.25 (lower earnings limit £2,350)
'Class 3' — voluntary pw		£4.15
'Class 4' — self-employed earnings related		6.3% on annual earnings between £5,050 & £16,900

9.30 Class I National Insurance contributions

(1) Contributions are graduated according to earnings up to a certain level and are collected together with income tax under the PAYE system (9.4). They are not allowable for income tax purposes.
(2) The employer supplements each employee's contributions. Employer's contributions are deductible for tax purposes.
(3) No contributions are payable if the weekly earnings are less than £43 but once this level is reached, your entire wages (up to £325) carry percentage contributions (9.31). Note that a more equitable system operates from 5 October 1989 in that your first £43 each week only attracts contributions of 2%.
(4) There is no upper earnings limit for employers. They pay contributions on the total earnings of employees.
(5) If the employers operate an approved pension scheme, they are allowed to contract out of the state scheme. Similarly employees can be contracted out if they have appropriate Personal Pension Plan arrangements (11.13) which result in lower contributions.
(6) Retired employees who have passed normal retirement age (60 for a woman and 65 for a man) do not have to pay contributions. Those still working beyond age 65 are not liable for contributions, although their employers remain liable.

9.31 Table: Class I National Insurance contributions for 1989-90

Weekly Earnings Band* 1989-90(a)	Employee Not contracted out %	Employee Contracted out %‡	Employer Not contracted out %	Employer Contracted out %‡
Under £43.00	Nil	Nil	Nil	Nil
£43.00–74.99	5.0	3.00	5.0	1.20
£75.00–114.99	7.0	5.00	7.0	3.20
£115.00–164.99	9.0	7.00	9.0	5.20
£165.00–325.00	9.0	7.00	10.45	6.65
over £325.00	9.0 of £325	9% on first £43. 7% on earnings between £43 and £325	10.45	10.45 on first £43. and earnings over £325. 6.65 on earnings between £43 and £325

1989-90(b) Employee	Not contracted out	contracted out		
Earnings below £43	Nil	Nil		
Earnings above £43				
0–£43	2%	2%		
£43.01–£325	9%	7%		
£325 or more	No further liability			

Notes: (a) Employers 6 April 1989 to 5 April 1990. Employees 6 April 1989 to 4 October 1989.
(b) Employees only 5 October 1989 to 5 April 1990
*Contributions at the rates shown for each band are levied on all earnings if they reach the beginning but do not exceed the top of the band.
‡Applies only to earnings between LEL and UEL. Non-contracted out rates apply to part up to LEL. (5%, 7%, etc.)

9.32 Statutory sick pay

Employers generally pay up to 28 weeks statutory sick pay for each employee in any period. (The employee does not need to have paid National Insurance contributions.) Only after that is any sickness benefit paid direct by the State (10.64). Employers can deduct their statutory sick pay payments in any month from the total National Insurance contributions which they pay. A similar scheme operates regarding maternity pay (10.63).

For 1989–90 statutory sick pay is paid at the following weekly rates (daily rates are calculated proportionally):

Normal weekly earnings	Weekly rate
Less than £43.00	Nil
£43.00–£83.99	£36.25
£84.00 or more	£52.10

9.33 Profit-related pay

The profit-related pay (PRP) system provides useful tax relief as follows:

(1) Half of your PRP is free of income tax up to £4,000 each year. (Before 1 April 1989, this figure was £3,000). However, a further limitation of 20% of your PAYE pay also applies. Thus if your pay is £10,000, your tax-free amount is limited to £1,000.
(2) The employer gives tax relief through the PAYE system.
(3) PRP payments qualify for relief only if made under a scheme registered with the Inland Revenue before the start of the first profit period it is to cover.
(4) PRP schemes can be registered for groups, companies, firms or sub-units of any of these.
(5) Certain employers are excluded — mainly those under the control of central or local government.
(6) The rules must show a clear relationship between PRP and profits. Normally, eligible employees will share in a pool representing a stated percentage of the profits. Alternatively, a fixed sum might be stipulated which varies with future profits.
(7) Controlling directors, with interests amounting to 25% or more of the company, must be excluded. Recruits with less than three years' service and part-timers who work less than 20 hours per week may be excluded. Otherwise, in general at least 80% of the employees in an employment unit at the beginning of each period must be eligible for PRP.
(8) Independent audits are required for both the registration application and the general running of the scheme.

10 Employment law

10.1 Introduction

As a business grows, it will inevitably need a workforce. Although, sometimes, a workforce may comprise self-employed sub-contractors, it is, in practice, usually composed of employees. The legal relationship between an employer and his workforce can be extremely complex and impose on him a broad range of obligations. This chapter concentrates on the main features of individual employment law as this is the area with which the business will immediately, and often exclusively, have contact; considerations of space prevent us from including a discussion of trade union law and the law of industrial conflict.

10.2 Recruiting employees

It is at this stage that an employer has most freedom of choice as to whom he wants to work with. There are, however, some important rules about freedom of recruitment.

10.3 Sex and race discrimination and recruitment

Recruitment must not infringe the law relating to sex and race discrimination in respectively the Sex Discrimination Act 1975 and the Race Relations Act 1976. Discrimination generally is dealt with below (10.48). Here we concentrate on some recruitment issues only. In considering these, it is important to note that, unlike in the case of much other employment protection law, this legislation applies to applicants for employment *and* to those who provide a service on a self-employed basis.

Unlawful discrimination on the ground of sex or marital status or on racial grounds (defined later) in the employment field on recruitment can occur:

(a) in the arrangements the employer makes for the purposes of determining who should be offered employment;

(b) in the terms on which he offers a person that employment; or
(c) by refusing or deliberately omitting to offer a person that employment.

A major pitfall for employers is the possibility of discriminatory arrangements for the purposes of determining who should be offered employment which are contrary to the Acts (case (a), above). This could occur if discriminatory job questions are asked at interview. Some examples follow.

In *Gates v Wirral Borough Council* (1981) the applicant, a woman, was asked at her job interview, among other things, about her relationship with her husband, whether she was a Miss or a Mrs, whether she was legally separated from her husband and whether she intended to have a family in the near future. These questions were not asked of male applicants. The industrial tribunal found that the questions were discriminatory and the employer had unlawfully discriminated against the applicant under section 6(1)(a) of the Sex Discrimination Act in the arrangements made for the interview for determining who should be appointed to the post.

In *Bryce v J Sainsbury plc* (1980) Bryce, a woman, applied for a job as a management trainee. At interview she was asked if she planned to get married and have a family. All single applicants, male and female, were asked whether they were planning to get married but no single male was asked whether there were any plans to have a family. The industrial tribunal found that the employers had discriminated in the arrangements they had made for selection under section 6(1)(a) of the Sex Discrimination Act.

Similar principles arise in relation to race discrimination. In *McKenzie v West Lambeth Health Authority* (1987) McKenzie, who was black, applied for the post of nurse tutor at a nursing school. There were two other candidates, both white, with similar but less relevant experience. At the interview McKenzie, who happened to be a Justice of the Peace, was asked by one of the interview committee whether she was a Magistrate because she was black and whether she knew how many black community nurses there were within the Health Authority's area. McKenzie was unsuccessful in her job application. Her complaint of racial discrimination succeeded. The tribunal said that the questions were irrelevant and were not asked of the other white candidates and that there had been unlawful discrimination. The arrangements for determining who should be offered employment were discriminatory and contrary to the Race Relations Act.

Finally, a discriminatory attitude at interview could raise an inference of discrimination under case (c) above ie of a predisposition to not to offer a job to a person of a particular race or sex which leads to a refusal or deliberate omission to offer the job for discriminatory reasons.

Generally, in order to comply with the letter and spirit of discrimination law, questions at interview in particular should be asked along neutral lines relevant to the job, free of race or sex bias and asked of both men and women or all races, as the case may be.

Under the Acts, it can be unlawful directly *or* indirectly to discriminate on grounds of sex or marital status or race or ethnic origin. Direct and indirect discrimination are discussed again later but it may be useful to illustrate the distinction here, in relation to recruitment.

The discussion about job interviews illustrates what is probably direct discrimination, ie direct discriminatory treatment of one sex or a particular race compared with another. Indirect discrimination is more subtle. This is where a condition or requirement is imposed which seems applicable to all but the proportion of one sex or racial group which can comply with it is considerably smaller than in another sex or racial group. As an example, suppose the following instructions were sent to the Jobcentre by an employer:

(1) 'Shorthand Secretary/Typist required (male or female). Must wear a smart blouse and skirt at all times';
(2) 'Wanted: Mature canteen assistant (age 40 or below) (male or female). Must have at least 15 years' uninterrupted experience since leaving school'.

Both of these instructions impose conditions which apply equally to both sexes. But in the first example, the number of men who can comply with the condition imposed will be fewer than women and, in the second example, the number of women who can comply with the conditions (because of time out of employment through child rearing) may be fewer than men. These conditions could be unlawful unless they were justifiable on objective grounds unrelated to sex (see, in detail, 10.50). In the extreme examples quoted it would be unlikely that the conditions would be regarded as justifiable.

Liability for discrimination can attach to the employer of the interviewer or recruiter as an employer is vicariously liable for an act done by his employee in the course of employment whether or not it was done with the employer's knowledge or approval. Individuals can also be liable if they give instructions to discriminate or put pressure on someone to discriminate or if they aid another person to commit unlawful acts of discrimination. An employer has a defence to vicarious liability if he has taken such steps as were reasonably practicable to prevent the employee from doing that act or from doing, in the course of his employment, acts of that description. The formulation and positive implementation of an equal opportunities policy and training of interviewers and recruiters has an important role to play here and this may be a very prudent and constructive measure for an employer to take.

There is a limited defence to discrimination where sex or race is a genuine occupational qualification for the job. This is discussed in more detail at 10.51. Remedies for breach and other aspects of the Sex and Race Discrimination Acts are discussed in more detail later.

10.4 Rehabilitation of offenders and 'spent' convictions

The Rehabilitation of Offenders Act 1974 provides that certain 'spent' convictions need not be disclosed. This could apply in favour of a person seeking a job with an employer. The type of conviction that is deemed to be 'spent' under the Act tends to be of the more minor variety, and certain offences cannot be spent, for example, sentences of life imprisonment, custody for life and terms of imprisonment extending beyond 30 months. The rehabilitation periods required before a conviction is spent are set out in the Act and vary according to the type of offence. Certain persons are excluded from the protection of the Act. These include medical practitioners, barristers, solicitors, accountants, doctors, dentists, nurses, midwives and the like.

10.5 Disabled persons

There is a limited protection for disabled persons on recruitment and whilst they are employed. Under the Disabled Persons (Employment) Acts 1944 and 1958 and regulations thereunder a disabled person can apply to be a registered disabled person. If this happens he can receive what is commonly known as a 'green card'.

The Act controls recruitment in two ways. First, in certain employments it is an offence not to take on a registered disabled person unless a permit is obtained from the Department of Employment. So far this only applies to lift operators and car park attendants.

Secondly, the 1944 Act introduced what is known as the 'quota' system. This applies to all employers employing 20 or more employees. An employer has to seek to ensure that not less than 3% of his workforce comprise registered disabled persons. For the purposes of calculating the number of employees in employment, any employee working less than 10 hours a week is ignored, any working between 10 and 30 hours per week counts as half an employee and any other employee counts as one. It is a criminal offence to fill a vacancy that arises with an able-bodied person unless the quota is already filled. This can, however, be avoided if permission to employ nonetheless is obtained from the Department of Employment. It is also an offence

Employment law   213

to dismiss a registered disabled person without reasonable cause, if that dismissal causes the quota to drop below 3%. An employer can obtain a (renewable) permit to ignore the quota from the Department of Employment.

Finally, under CA 1985, companies employing on average 250 employees per week are required to give details in the directors' report in their annual accounts of such policy as the company has applied in relation to disabled employees in the preceding year. Employers even of this size are not actually required to *have* a policy about disabled employees and their recruitment, but it can be argued that the provision indirectly creates an incentive to have one.

10.6 Future laws on discrimination: new trends

As can be seen from the above, the law interferes in only a limited way in the employer's freedom to hire what labour he chooses; but will this change?

First, the Government has invited views on a proposal to legislate to prevent employers discriminating against individuals who apply for jobs on the ground of an individual's non-membership of a trade union or on the ground of an individual's refusal to become a trade union member after employment has commenced (*Removing Barriers to Employment*, Cm 655, March 1989). This may be the subject of legislation in the near future. The proposal does not extend to outlawing discrimination before employment on the ground either that an individual *is* or *proposes to become* a trade union member (although the Report of the Committee of Experts of the International Labour Organisation (1989) says that the UK should consider such a provision (such discrimination during employment is outlawed: see 10.25).

Secondly, there is considerable pressure to have legislation prohibiting age discrimination and discrimination against Aids carriers or those who are HIV positive. Although less imminent, this may happen one day.

10.7 The status of your workforce: employees or self-employed persons?

Your labour force may well comprise either employees or self-employed contractors, or both. Although most businesses employ employees (and this is the norm), it is possible, to a certain extent, to make a choice in employing one or other of these two different kinds of worker. Does the difference matter? The answer is that employing employees generally involves an employer in far greater responsibilities and overhead costs than engaging self-employed sub-contractors. Against this, however, you must compare the advantages of the integration of workers into your business and the relationship of command and subordination which is inherent in an employer/employee relationship as opposed to an employer/self-employed sub-contractor relationship.

There are a number of important points to note if you are employing employees:

(1) The duties on the part of both parties under a contract of employment are more extensive than under a contract for self-employment (10.11, 10.12).
(2) Employment status gives employees important statutory rights under the Employment Protection (Consolidation) Act 1978 (EP(C)A) and other employment legislation, such as unfair dismissal and redundancy (10.18 onwards). However *both* employees *and* self-employed persons working for an employer enjoy protection under the 'employment' provisions of the Race Relations Act 1976 and the Sex Discrimination Act 1975 (10.48), and under the Equal Pay Act 1970 (10.58) and the Wages Act 1986 (protection against wrongful deduction from 'wages') (10.47). This is because the definitions of the persons covered are wider than under the EP(C)A and include not only persons who work under contracts of employment but also under contracts personally to execute work or labour.
(3) Your responsibility as an employer for the deeds of an employee (called, in law, vicarious liability) is considerably wider in the case of employees than in the case of independent sub-contractors. Employees can therefore expose you to more liability to third parties for their wrongful acts than can independent sub-contractors.
(4) Liability for accidents at work to the individual who works for you is greater in the case of an employee than in the case of an independent sub-contractor. Related thereto, an employer of employees must take out employer's compulsory liability insurance under the Employers' Liability (Compulsory Insurance) Act 1969.
(5) If you employ employees you will have to deduct tax at source and administer the PAYE system (chapter 9). And you will also have to administer certain other employment payments, responsibility for which has recently been put on the shoulders of the employer, such as statutory maternity pay (Social Security Act 1986) (10.63) and statutory sick pay (Social Security and Housing Benefits Act 1982) (10.64). If you employ employees you will also have to pay employer's National Insurance contributions (chapter 9).

(6) If you engage an independent sub-contractor it is possible to require him to be responsible for his own tax and National Insurance and he or she will not qualify for statutory maternity pay, statutory sick pay or any other payments arising out of an employment relationship.
(7) Sooner or later, you may well come under pressure to provide contractual benefits to an employee that may commonly be enjoyed by other employees in firms like your own, such as a pension scheme, a car, and so forth and you will also have, in any event, to provide employees with working tools, equipment and materials that a self-employed person might supply himself.
(8) The self-employed person should himself bear in mind that he will not qualify for state unemployment benefit during workless periods or industrial injuries benefit if injured at work.

10.8 How does the law distinguish between employment and self-employment?

Historically there have been a number of tests.

(1) First, the courts decided that the issue was best looked at solely by considering whether the employer *controlled* the worker. Employees could be controlled; the self-employed could not. This, on its own, soon became unsatisfactory as workers' skills became more sophisticated. It is, for example, difficult for an employer to control how a highly skilled employee such as a pilot or a surgeon actually does his job; but this may not mean they are not employees of an airline or hospital respectively.
(2) The courts then developed the so-called 'business integration' test. Under this theory if a worker is thoroughly integrated into the business, rather than appearing to be an outside contractor, he will be more likely to be an employee. But this test, again, does not, of itself, provide the answer in every case.
(3) Another question the courts have asked is whether the worker is in business on his own account. If he is, or he is 'his own boss', to use an expression from at least one of the cases, then it could be that he is self-employed rather than an employee.
(4) At the end of the day, it can appear that no single test is satisfactory because all businesses and all jobs are not exactly the same and may not respond well to a single test.

So the courts developed what was known as the 'multiple' test, ie you have to look at multiple factors to arrive at the answer. And this is, more or less, with some modifications, the approach adopted by courts and tribunals today. Nowadays it is recognised that, in practice, a large number of factors are relevant in deciding between employment and self-employment. These have to be enumerated and then it must be considered whether they are present or absent in the case in question. A useful checklist of the type of factors involved is set out below, the majority of which can be found in the case of *Addison v London Philharmonic* (1981). These include:

(1) The degree of control exercised by the employer.
(2) Whether the employee's interest in the undertaking involved any prospect of risk or loss.
(3) Whether the employee was properly regarded as part and parcel of the employer's organisation at the relevant time.
(4) Whether at the relevant time the employee was carrying on a business on his own account or carrying on the business of the employer.
(5) Who provides equipment?
(6) The incidence of tax and National Insurance in respect of any contracts.
(7) The traditional structure of the employee's industry or profession and arrangements within it.
(8) Whether the contractual terms are more consistent with a contract of service rather than a contract for services.
(9) What the parties intended.
(10) Also, more recently, in cases concerning the status of casual workers and home workers, the Court of Appeal has coined yet another relevant factor, namely, whether *mutuality of obligation* is present in the relationship, ie whether the worker and employer are mutually bound to each other.

A number of these factors are more helpful in some cases than others. For example the provision of equipment might be relatively unimportant in a white-collar case. 'Mutuality of obligation' is very important in the case of intermittent work provided by casual workers and home workers.

Three final points need to be emphasised.

(1) The label put on the relationship by the parties is not conclusive. On the one hand, all things being equal, the self description of the relationship may be decisive. But the parties may think there is a self-employed relationship whilst all along being mistaken because there may, in truth, be a contract of employment. It is thus possible to look beyond the apparent agreement of the parties.

Certainly, it seems it is not possible for an unscrupulous employer to attempt to get round employment legislation by imposing a putative self-employed status on an employee that is contrary to the true situation. This might be considered an attempt to contract out of the provisions of the EP(C)A and would be void. This is because section 140 of the EP(C)A prevents parties trying to exclude or limit the provisions of the EP(C)A or to preclude any person from presenting a complaint to or bringing any proceedings under EP(C)A before a tribunal (10.68).

Also, it is not only in the context of the EP(C)A that an inappropriate label put on the relationship can be removed. Thus, the Department of Social Security and the Inland Revenue will be keen to find an employment relationship if at all possible because collection of National Insurance and tax in relation to labour services is more convenient to the relevant authority in that case than if a worker is self-employed (chapter 9).

If what is thought to be a self-employed relationship turns out to be an employment contract for the purposes of tax and National Insurance, the fiscal consequences of unravelling the past arrangements (eg sorting out arrears of tax that should have been paid on a different basis and adjusting allowances that should not have been claimed) can be severe.

Thus, putting an atypical label on the relationship can be very dangerous indeed unless you are absolutely sure that it will stand up under scrutiny from such bodies. If in any doubt, when engaging workers, it is prudent to take advice from a lawyer or an accountant and also, possibly, depending on their advice, to clear the matter with the Inland Revenue (see, generally, chapter 9).

(2) As the issue of whether there is a contract of employment comes up in all sorts of different contexts such as taxation, National Insurance, a claim by an injured worker for accident compensation, unfair dismissal and other statutory rights, different policy considerations and different approaches can be taken by different bodies depending on the context. Our discussion has centred largely on the approach that an industrial tribunal might take if the issue of employment came up in a dispute between the employer and the worker as this tends to be the context in which the issue most commonly arises. But the Inland Revenue or Department of Social Security, for example, may approach the question slightly differently. One example illustrating this duality of approach by the law is the position of agency workers. For the purposes of statutory employment rights at least one case has held that temporary workers were not employees of the agency that placed them. Thus in *Wickens v Champion Employment* (1984) although there was a written agreement between the agency and the workers, the agency exercised minimum control and the workers received no holiday or sick pay and were free to work for other 'employers'. It was held the workers were not employees.

(Of course, other arrangements between agencies and their staff might well produce a different result — each case depends on its facts. And there is nothing to stop an agency creating an employment relationship expressly, by words used and the way it treats and affords benefits to workers). The tax position is however unequivocal. By TA s 134 an agency supplying labour to an employer has to treat remuneration paid by it to the agency worker as chargeable to income tax under Schedule E and tax it at source.

(3) A small business in particular might have to consider whether its proprietors themselves are employees or are self-employed. The principles discussed above will usually decide the issue. It is, however, useful to examine our three forms of trading vehicle which we discussed in chapter 1 to illustrate this.

 (a) A *sole trader* will be self-employed and cannot employ himself (although he can, of course, employ others including a spouse or other relation).
 (b) *Partners* will be self-employed and cannot be employed by the partnership firm. The firm can, of course, employ others.
 (c) The position of *company directors* is less straightforward and depends more on the facts of each case. In principle, even the smallest company can be an employer of a person even if, in effect, it is almost wholly owned by that person. This is because of the theory of separate corporate personality discussed in chapter 1. Thus, in Lee v Lees Air Farming Ltd (1961) the widow of a pilot who operated his business through his own company was able to claim compensation for his death under a workers' compensation law in New Zealand because Mr Lee was held to be employed by that company. In many, especially larger companies, where directors are executive directors and not solely proprietors, they will commonly be employees (and the Revenue very often will insist upon directors being treated as officers or employees for Schedule E tax purposes (chapter 9)).

 However, in smaller companies, the issue may be finely balanced. In *Albert J Parsons and Sons Ltd* v *Parsons* (1976) it was decided that the directors were self-employed and not employed. There the court was influenced by the fact that the directors took their remuneration by way of fees and not salary; they paid their own tax and National Insurance; there was no note of any service agreements at the company's registered office and, indeed, there were no service agreements at all. On balance, these directors were not employees.

10.9 The contents of the contract of employment

A contract of employment may be oral or in writing. Its terms may arise by express agreement of the parties, by implication or by incorporation from other sources such as collective agreements. Incorporation from collective agreements can arise by express reference in the contract of employment itself, by custom and practice and, very occasionally, (though not usually) by agency. Generally, terms in collective agreements must be considered appropriate for incorporation into an individual contract before they can be incorporated. Collective and policy issues, such as long-term planning agreements, are generally regarded as inappropriate. But individual matters such as payment terms and other benefits and conditions to be enjoyed by employees would be considered appropriate.

10.10 Terms of the contract

Every contract of employment has basic terms which, if not set out by the parties in writing would, in any event, be implied by the courts. These may usefully be separated into employer's obligations and employee's obligations. It is important to note that many of these can be modified by express agreement (10.13).

10.11 The employer's obligations

(1) An employer must pay *wages* or other remuneration. However:

    (a) This is not always the case when an employee is *sick*. Mostly, these days, sick pay entitlement is covered by express agreement and this is wise (10.14, 10.15). But if not, the position is as follows. For a long time the courts were quite generous and were willing to imply a term that wages should continue during sickness without limit. At one point it was thought that there was a presumption in favour of continuance of wages in the absence of express agreement to the contrary. Nowadays, however, this would be regarded as somewhat out of line with current industrial practice. The more modern view is that there is no such presumption in favour of continuance of wages. The court must have regard to all the circumstances including what the parties thought and what they said and did within the relationship. If there are no factors either way indicating whether such pay is applicable there may still be a residual presumption in favour of payment of wages. But, in practice, the facts and circumstances of the case will usually provide an indication of whether sick pay is available.

    It is also thought that if a court *does* imply a right to

continuation of wages during sickness, that right will only extend for a reasonable period.

Notwithstanding any right to wages during sickness under the *contract*, a qualifying employee may be entitled to Statutory Sick Pay (10.64). An employer would be advised, however, as well as limiting the duration of contractual sick pay, to provide by contract that contractual sick pay is only available to top up statutory sick pay (or state sickness benefit thereafter) to the level of an employee's normal wages.

Also, an employee may have rights to payment during his period of notice by virtue of the provisions of the EP(C)A, Schedule 3 even if he has exhausted or is otherwise not entitled to contractual sick pay.

(b) If an employee absents himself from work on account of a *strike* or other *industrial action* he will not be entitled to wages. The consideration for wages in a contract is the provision of work and if work is withheld in the context of an industrial dispute no wages are earned.

More complex are cases where the industrial action taken is more sophisticated and does not result in a complete absence from duty, such as in the case of a work to rule or a go slow. This might also affect the right to wages, certainly if an employer rejects the defective performance and indicates that only full performance will be paid for. Such an employer would be advised to notify employees proposing partial industrial action that partial or defective performance is rejected. He should state that an employee's attendance on site during such action is not required unless normal work is to be performed and that attendance without working normally (if in practice an employer cannot prevent this) should not be taken to mean that an employer condones the action or that he accepts partial performance.

Example:

In *Wiluszynski* v *London Borough of Tower Hamlets* (1989) council employees took action by boycotting enquiries from council members. Otherwise they proposed to work normally. The council informed the employees that they would only be paid for full work and attendance on site and performance of other duties during the dispute would be regarded as voluntary. It was held that as full performance was being withheld and partial performance rejected the employees were entitled to no pay at all even though they had performed *some* of their duties.

(c) Deductions of this sort are not covered by the provisions of the Wages Act 1986 which exclude deductions on account of a strike or industrial action from the protection of that Act (see below, (d) and 10.47). On the whole, though, you would be unwise to deduct from pay without taking legal advice as the position is so complex and an improper deduction could lead to an action for breach of contract on the part of an employee.

(c) When work is short, an employer may be tempted to lay off without pay. This may be possible within reasonable limits if there is an express power arising from the contract, from a collective agreement or from custom and practice. Nowadays though, it is most unlikely that a court would *imply* a power for the employer to lay off without pay. If he did so without express authority, this would probably be a breach of contract entitling the employee to claim arrears of wages and possibly, in due course, constructive dismissal (10.19). And there may even sometimes be an overlap with the law of redundancy where the right to a redundancy payment can arise, under certain complex conditions, after lay off or short-time working (10.32). Under the EP(C)A a qualifying employee may have the right to a modest guarantee payment when laid off (10.39). Collective agreements can also regulate lay off and short time.

(d) Deductions from wages generally are now covered by the Wages Act 1986 which provides a remedy for improper deductions from wages before the industrial tribunal (10.47).

(e) Employees on maternity leave may be entitled to Statutory Maternity Pay which is a payment administered by the employer by virtue of the Social Security Act 1986 (10.63).

(2) It is not clear whether an employer has to provide *work* to his employee as long as he pays *wages*. In fact the basic rule (although it is very old) implies that an employer is *not* obliged to provide work as long as wages are paid. In *Collier* v *Sunday Referee Publishing Co Ltd* (1940) the trial judge said: 'Provided I pay my cook her wages regularly, she cannot complain if I choose to take any or all of my meals out'. This implies that an employer can, in effect, lay off with pay. In more modern cases, courts have doubted whether this is always the case. In 1974 the Court of Appeal expressed the view that there is, by law, a 'right to work' which the employer would breach by laying an employee off even on full pay. But is is doubtful whether there is in fact such a generalised right to work.

Nonetheless, an employee may well have a right to work in certain situations where to carry on working is important to him, for example:

(a) To ensure his bonus, commission or piece work earnings are maintained by his continuing efforts or
(b) Where publicity is important to him (such as in the case of an actor) or
(c) Where reputation in the trade is important to him.

(3) An employer owes a duty of *safety* to his employees by providing competent staff, safe equipment and a safe system of work. This threefold duty was developed at common law but is also enshrined in the Health & Safety at Work Act 1974.
(4) An employee will be entitled to an *indemnity* against expenses incurred during the course of his employment on behalf of his employer.
(5) Recently, in the context of unfair dismissal cases, courts and tribunals have developed some very up-to-date implied terms. For example, it is now accepted that there is a duty on the employer to maintain 'trust and confidence' in the employment relationship and even, according to one case, to treat an employee as would a 'good and considerate' employer. Breach of these terms often comes up in the context of constructive dismissal (10.19), ie whether an employee is entitled to leave and claim unfair dismissal arising out of a constructive dismissal triggered by an employer's unacceptable conduct.
(6) Any contract, in the absence of an express provision, may be terminated by reasonable notice. So you are bound to give reasonable notice of dismissal to an employee (and *vice versa*) unless you have made an express agreement about length of notice. The length of notice required at common law is a question of fact in each employment case and it is not possible to generalise. In any event, under the EP(C)A an employee is entitled to a *minimum* period of notice of one week for each year of service (subject to a maximum of 12 weeks) (10.45).

10.12 Duties of the employee

(1) An employee is under a duty to *work*. This is the consideration he gives for his wages or salary. Not to work is a breach of contract. There are some problems that arise out of this:

(a) It is generally implied that an employee is not in breach of contract by failing to work when he has good excuse, for example, when he is absent through ill-health or sickness. An employer will, however, often provide that it will be a breach of contract not to notify the employer of the sickness and otherwise follow sickness procedures.
(b) In a case of a strike or industrial action, not to work may be a breach of contract and there will also be a breach of contract, even when work is done, if it is defectively

performed or performed in a way designed to disrupt the employer's business, such as in the case of a go-slow or a work-to-rule.

(2) An employee is under a duty to take reasonable care in and about the performance of his duties.
(3) An employee has to be competent in his job. However, only *gross negligence* will generally allow an employer to dismiss without due notice for incompetence at common law. This applies even more so under the law of unfair dismissal (10.18) and very rarely would a single act of incompetence allow an employer to dismiss fairly. One example however, is the case of *Alidair Ltd v Taylor* (1978) where a single act of negligence by a pilot of a passenger aircraft in landing badly and causing damage to the aircraft was held to justify dismissal (in this case, however, the issue was whether dismissal was fair under statute for unfair dismissal purposes (10.18); the case is not necessarily authority for any proposition that the employer would have been entitled to dismiss without notice — each case depends on its facts).
(4) An employee is under a duty to *obey reasonable commands* of the employer. But

   (a)   an employee is not obliged to follow an *unlawful* order of the employer.
   (b)   An employer cannot dismiss summarily for a single act of disobedience where the act is not serious and the intention of the employee is still, on the whole, to be bound by the contract.

(5) Every employee is under a duty of *fidelity* (faithfulness) that applies during the contract of employment and which may, to an extent, continue thereafter. An employee must be honest and must not steal from his employer. Nor must he take any secret profits or commissions arising out of his duties. During the employment the employee must not take up competing employment with another nor solicit the employer's customers. At first glance, however, there is nothing to stop an employee taking up spare time employment during his employment with the first employer. However, exceptionally, an employee might have a duty not to work for another in his spare time if there is a serious risk of leakage of trade secrets or confidential information to the part time employer.

Example 1

In *Hivac v Park Royal Scientific Instruments* (1946) employees who were skilled assemblers of hearing aids and who worked for a rival company on their day off were held to have broken their implied duty of fidelity.

The employees here had access to confidential information or trade secrets of the first employer and work for the second involved risk of such information and secrets being passed on to the competitor.

Example 2

In *Nova Plastics Limited* v *Froggatt* (1982) an odd-job man who did work for a rival concern in his spare time was not in breach of contract. He had no access to confidential information or trade secrets and there was no risk of such information being passed to a competitor.

It will also be a breach of the duty of fidelity to give away or make personal use of confidential information and trade secrets. But there is a distinction between the extent of the duty owed by an employee during the life of the contract and the extent of the duty thereafter. Both confidential information and trade secrets are protected during the course of the employment. But only trade secrets are protected thereafter.

The ground rules about post employment activity have been laid down by the leading case of *Faccenda Chicken Limited* v *Fowler* (1986) which holds that where the situation is governed by the implied term of fidelity the following principles apply. For example, it will be a breach of the duty if an employee makes or copies a list of customers of the employer for use after his employment ends or deliberately memorises such a list. And after the employment ends, any misuse of trade secrets generally may be enjoined. What is a trade secret depends on the facts of each case but it may include a secret process of manufacture, such as chemical formulae or designs or special methods of construction. The court indicated that the following additional matters might be relevant in determining whether information amounted to a trade secret. First, regard must be had to the nature of the employment. Relevant factors here include the sensitivity of the area in which the employee is employed. Secondly, the nature of the information itself must be assessed. A trade secret must, by definition, be *highly* confidential. How information is treated and regarded by the parties during the employment may be relevant as to whether it has acquired this highly confidential status.

Example 1

In *Roger Bullivant Ltd* v *Ellis* (1987) Mr Ellis left his employer and began working in competition with his former employer. It was discovered that a large number of documents belonging to the Company were in Mr Ellis' possession including a card index system of customers. It was held that the information on the card index was not a trade secret but merely confidential information. However it had been a breach of the contract of employment to make, memorise or copy a list of the employer's customers with the intention of using it after the termination of employment. An injunction was granted on that basis.

Example 2

In *Johnson & Bloy (Holdings) Ltd and Johnson & Bloy Limited v Wolstenholme Rink plc and Fallon* (1987) an employer discovered that a former employee had taken certain secret formulae about printing inks for use in future employment. This was a misuse of trade secrets and the employee could be injuncted.

Apart from a duty during the employment not to abuse confidential information or trade secrets and after the employment has ended, not to abuse trade secrets, an employee is, in theory, free to canvass former customers, solicit former employees (provided that this does not induce a breach of their contracts of employment) and indeed to set up in competition with his former employer, either as an employee or on his own account. Only an express restrictive covenant can stop this. Any employer in a competitive industry would be advised to consider imposing such a covenant on relevant employees.

However, the doctrine of restraint of trade applies to such covenants and they are invalid unless justifiable and necessary to protect the legitimate interests of the employer. These interests include the protection of trade secrets and trade connections. The higher the status of the individual and the more access to or influence over customers or suppliers and the more access to confidential information, the more likely it is that the covenant will be enforceable. Likewise the radius, duration and subject matter of the covenant must be closely geared to the status and position of the employee, his contact with customers and the nature and geography of the employer's business. Clauses are commonly attacked on the basis that they cover too wide a radius, cover activities that go beyond the legitimate interests of the employer which it is necessary to protect and endure for too long a time. There is no merit in drafting a clause which is too wide. It will be unenforceable. (The courts very occasionally enforce covenants that are too wide in a modified form, but it would be unwise to rely on this possibility). It is better to have a milder restriction which is enforceable than a fiercer one which is not.

Example 1

In *Mason v Provident Supply Company* (1913) the employer was a clothing supplier. The employee was employed as a canvasser based in Islington. But the employer imposed a restriction against competing employment after the termination of employment within 25 miles of London as a whole. It was held that this was unreasonable. It was not necessary to protect the employer's legitimate interests to that degree. The area around Islington would have done.

Unreasonableness can apply also to non-solicitation clauses.

Example 2

In *Gledhow Autoparts* v *Delaney* (1965) a sales representative in the car accessory trade was required not to solicit any customers or potential customers in the areas he had worked in for three years after the ending of his employment. The clause was not enforceable as it went beyond what was necessary: it extended to customers that neither he nor even the Company had ever dealt with.

Example 3

To be contrasted are the facts in *Spafax Limited* v *Harrison* (1980). There the employee was a branch manager of a company engaged in the wholesale of motor parts. A restriction stopped him soliciting his own customers and also any other customer which to his knowledge had been served by any member of his staff. This covenant was enforceable as it was held to deal with an interest which the employer was entitled to protect: it was possible for the branch manager to have influence over such customers.

Drafting such clauses, balancing the interests of the employer and employee, deciding whether to have a non-competition covenant, a non-solicitation of customers covenant or a non-solicitation of employees covenant (or all of them) and deciding on the radius of the covenant and its duration can be tricky. Legal advice is strongly recommended here.

(6) There are also rules about ownership of industrial property rights generated during employment. First, there are detailed rules applicable to *employee inventions* after 1 June 1978. This is provided for by the Patents Act 1977.

Under this Act, an invention belongs to an employer if

(a) it is made in the course of the employee's duties or
(b) it arises as a result of a specific assignment outside the

(c) employee's normal duties in circumstances such that an invention might reasonably be expected to arise or it is made in the course of the duties of the employee the nature and responsibilities of which impose a special obligation to further the employer's interests.

Otherwise, inventions belong to an employee. The terms of a contract between an employer and employee which purport to diminish an employee's rights are unenforceable.

Where a patent is granted in relation to an invention made by an employee but belonging to an employer under the above rules and the patent is of outstanding benefit to the employer (having regard amongst other things to the size and nature of the employer's undertaking) compensation may be payable where the compensation already paid to the employee (if any) is inadequate. An employee may make such an application for compensation at any time during the life of the patent and during one year thereafter. The court seeks to award a fair share of the rewards or benefits derived from the patent or which are reasonably expected to derive from the patent to the employer. Also to be taken into account are the nature of the employee's employment, the remuneration he has derived from his employment and a comparison of the effort and skill devoted to the invention by the employee and by any other person and the degree of contribution by the employer. There are also rules about possible compensation for employees who have assigned or licensed inventions or patents owned by them to employers, where the benefit to those employees arising therefrom is inadequate.

Secondly, *copyright* in a literary, dramatic or artistic work made by an employee during the course of his employment will belong to an employer (Copyright, Designs and Patents Act 1988, s 11(2)). Note that the test is different from that relating to employee inventions (see above).

Thirdly, *design right* in original designs made by an employee in the course of his employment will also belong to the employer (Copyright, Designs and Patents Act 1988, s 215(3)).

10.13 Should a contract of employment be in writing?

As has been seen, a contract of employment may exist orally or in writing, express or implied. If no terms are struck between the parties, the courts will imply some basic terms into the agreement for the parties (10.11, 10.12). However, the EP(C)A requires a *written statement* of main terms and conditions to be issued to an employee after 13 weeks of employment (10.14). And there is every merit in issuing a written document to an employee that goes further than the basic requirements of a statutory written statement. You may find it helpful and prudent expressly to provide for certain matters which the common law will not imply for you (for example a restraint on future employment with a competitor (see above)), or to modify common law rules, or to provide more fully about discipline, performance and about your firm's rules generally.

10.14 The written statement under the EP(C)A

Under the EP(C)A, s 1 an employer must give a written statement to an employee giving particulars of the major terms of his employment within 13 weeks of the commencement of employment. The items to be included are as follows:

(1) The name of the employer.
(2) The name of the employee.
(3) The date when the employment began.
(4) The rate of pay or method of calculating pay.
(5) The frequency of payment.
(6) Hours of work (including normal working hours).
(7) Holiday entitlement (also enabling the employee to calculate any accrued holiday pay on termination).
(8) Any terms relating to sickness and injury and sick pay.
(9) Pension terms.
(10) Length of notice.
(11) Title of employee's job.
(12) Any disciplinary rules applying to the employee or identification of a document where he can find them. (The Employment Bill, clause 11 proposes that firms with less than 20 employees shall be exempt from the requirement to include a note of disciplinary procedures in the written statement. The logic of this is not clear. After all (see below) the existence of disciplinary procedures is good industrial relations practice, is recommended by ACAS and may help in handling unfair dismissal cases, which may be brought against small, as well as large, firms.)
(13) Details of the person to whom the employee may appeal if dissatisfied with any disciplinary decision (but cf here, too, the Employment Bill, clause 11) or if he has any other grievance.
(14) A statement of whether there is a contracting out certificate in force in respect of the Social Security Pensions Act 1975.

Any change in the particulars must be notified in writing to the employee within one month of the change. If the employee does not receive a statement or if he does receive a statement which he alleges is inaccurate or incomplete he may complain to an industrial tribunal and the industrial tribunal may declare what the terms of the employment are or may correct the inaccurate terms (although the employee cannot get compensation from the tribunal for the employer's default).

The written statement is not a contract and is not necessarily conclusive of the main terms of the contract (hence the employee's right to go to the industrial tribunal to complain of any inaccuracy). It is therefore possible (albeit rare) that the written statement can conflict with other terms, eg in a collective agreement, letter of appointment and so forth. This conflict is less likely to arise where a written contract is used (10.15).

10.15 A written contract of employment

Although the written statement is often used in industry quite satisfactorily and is, very often, regarded as accurately reflecting the main terms of the contract (but see 10.14), it is possible to issue a written contract which both includes the requirements of the EP(C)A s 1 and which also covers much more additional ground. Alternatively, if the written statement format is preferred, there is nothing to stop you providing a contract of employment as well. A written contract could make express provision, for example, about:

(1) The way the job is to be performed.
(2) Secrecy and confidential information.
(3) Whether an employee may work for a competitor or solicit customers or suppliers or employees after the termination of employment — a very important issue — see 10.12.
(4) Sickness and reporting procedures.
(5) Holiday rules.
(6) Bonus calculations.
(7) Special rules in the business that you require to be observed.

Thus the merit of having a more comprehensive document than the minimum required by law can easily be seen. By including additional provisions in a contract you can make it much clearer to your employees what their obligations are to you (and, indeed, vice versa). To take one example, if you have no express agreement about notice, you will be thrown back on the common law which will imply a 'reasonable' period. This is vague in the extreme. You can instead (subject to the statutory minima specified in the EP(C)A (10.45)) declare what the notice on either side shall be and this will override the common law. A clear and express agreement may also be helpful in avoiding disputes and may even help you in unfair dismissal cases (10.18) because you have at least provided some employment rules to be followed.

A contract may not contain anything which is illegal or in restraint of trade. So, for example, a provision in an agreement whereby the parties agree to evade tax will not be enforceable. Further, if an employer tries to restrain an employee for too long and over too wide a radius from working for a competitor after the termination of employment, this may be beyond what is necessary for the protection of the business and what is reasonable and, therefore, may be unenforceable as an unlawful restraint of trade (10.12).

Under the Wages Act 1986 certain deductions from pay or demands for payment from workers are required to have the authority of a statutory provision or a provision of the worker's contract, or the consent of a worker before the making of the deduction. A provision in the contract of employment allowing for deductions or demands can make it easier for an employer to comply with the Act, provided he gives the worker a copy of the appropriate term before making the deduction or demand as the case may be (see 10.47).

Finally, in the case of contracts given to *directors*, a copy of any service contract, or a memorandum of the terms of any oral contract, must be kept at a company's registered office and be available for inspection by members of the company.

10.16 Statutory employment rights

As we have seen (10.7) statutory employment rights depend, in the main, on there being a contract of employment (but rights under the Equal Pay Act 1970, Sex Discrimination Act 1975, Race Relations Act 1976 and Wages Act 1986 are also available to others (10.7)). Many (although not all) such statutory rights depend also on the employee having worked *continuously* under the contract for a minimum period of time. This period is often called 'the qualifying period'. Our next paragraph therefore deals with the important concept of continuous employment.

10.17 Continuity of employment

The following is a (non exhaustive) table of the main statutory employment rights (many of which are discussed later) and the qualifying periods, comprising continuous employment, relating thereto.

Right	Qualifying period
Redundancy payment	2 years
Unfair dismissal	2 years

Sex discrimination, race discrimination and equal pay	None
Statement of reasons for dismissal	6 months (2 years when Employment Bill, clause 13 comes into force)
Right to return to work after maternity	2 years before beginning of 11th week before expected week of confinement
Guarantee payment	1 month ending with the day before payment is claimed or more than 3 months if engaged on a fixed term or specific task contract for 3 months or less
Written statement of terms and conditions	None, but has to be supplied within 13 weeks
Time off for union officers, union members or for public duties	None
Claim for remuneration under protective award	None
Time off for ante-natal care	None
Itemised pay statements	None
Remuneration on suspension on medical grounds	One month ending on day suspension begins or more than 3 months if engaged on a fixed term or specific task contract for 3 months or less
To complain of action short of dismissal on trade union grounds	None
Time off to look for work under notice of redundancy	2 years
Statutory sick pay	None
Statutory maternity pay	26 weeks before beginning of 14th week before expected week of confinement

It is important to note that these periods are subject to change from time to time.

Employment must be continuous under the rules contained in the EP(C)A Schedule 13. There is a presumption of continuity which has to be rebutted by an employer in any employment dispute. The basis of calculation was revised by the Employment Act 1982. First, the actual beginning and the actual end of employment should be identified. Secondly, it is to be assumed that employment is continuous between those dates (because of the presumption of continuity discussed above) unless otherwise proved. Thirdly, and lastly, the total number of calendar months or years of employment (for qualifying periods) or years (for notice, basic award and redundancy) achieved are calculated for the purposes of the statutory right in question. Employment commences on the day the contract commences and ends on the day the contract ends (but an employee who is dismissed without notice may for certain purposes, eg the qualifying period for dismissal claims, be treated as 'employed' until the expiry of the statutory minimum period of notice he should have received: (EP(C)A s 55(5) and (6) and s 90(3)).

Any week during which either 16 hours or more are actually worked or the employee works under a contract of employment involving ordinarily 16 hours or more per week to be worked will count and the basic rule is that other weeks will not, and will therefore break continuity. However, after 5 years of employment under a contract involving 8 hours or more work per week the number of qualifying hours required to make a week count reduces from 16 to 8 and there are other saving provisions for part time employees.

There are some cases, however, where intervals between employments will not break continuity. For example:

(1) Periods of up to 26 weeks may count notwithstanding a break due to absence from work in consequence of sickness or injury or wholly or partly because of pregnancy or confinement.
(2) In any case where there is absence from work on account of a 'temporary cessation of work' or absence from work in circumstances such that 'by arrangement or custom' an employee is regarded as continuing in the employment of his employer for all or any purposes, such absences may not break continuity.
(3) An employee who is dismissed and then reinstated or re-engaged pursuant to an industrial tribunal award or by a settlement through ACAS may have his continuous employment preserved notwithstanding the break between dismissal and reinstatement.
(4) There are also some complicated provisions preserving continuity notwithstanding that there has been a change of employer. This occurs in the transfer of a trade, business or undertaking, on a change in the composition of personal representatives, on a change in the composition of a partnership, on a transfer by Act of Parliament, upon transfers between associated employers, and upon transfers to and from local authority schools. The preservation of continuity of employment on business transfers is also dealt with below (10.79).
(5) When a woman returns to work after maternity leave under the EP(C)A then provided that she has complied with the statutory provisions about such leave, her period of absence counts towards continuous employment, even if there was no contract subsisting throughout the maternity leave.
(6) A strike does not break continuity but days on strike do not count. The effect of strike activity on length of employment is that the period of continuous employment is regarded as reduced by the

actual number of strike days which are deemed to be deducted from the period of employment by the artificial means of postponing the commencement of employment by the number of strike days in question.
(7) Weeks of employment overseas do not break continuity. But for redundancy purposes only (and not unfair dismissal) weeks overseas do not count.
(8) If an employee is re-engaged by an employer after service with the armed forces under the Reserve Forces (Safeguard of Employment) Act 1985 the interval between the ending of employment and re-engagement does not break continuity although weeks away from employment do not count. As with other non-counting weeks which do not break continuity, the beginning of employment is deemed postponed by such period.

10.18 Unfair dismissal

One of the most important statutory employment rights, one of the most commonly litigated and, arguably, the best known is the right of an employee not to be unfairly dismissed (24,916 of the 34,233 industrial tribunal cases registered in 1987–88 were complaints of unfair dismissal). The statutory source is part V of the EP(C)A which provides that an employee has the right not to be unfairly dismissed. The right was introduced by the Industrial Relations Act 1971. This controversial Act was itself repealed in 1974 but the unfair dismissal provisions survived subject to some amendments in the succeeding Trade Union and Labour Relations Act 1974 and other legislation. The roots of the legislation include the International Labour Organisation Recommendation No. 119 (1963) and the Donovan Commission Report (1968).

There are certain qualifying factors which have to be satisfied before a claim can be made. Amongst these are that an applicant must show:

(1) That he was an employee (10.7).
(2) That he worked long enough continuously (10.17) under a contract of employment, that is to say, two years ending with the effective date of termination of employment. This qualification does not apply in trade union membership and activities dismissals nor to sex and race discrimination claims (which can, of course, arise out of dismissals).
(3) That he is not among the excluded categories of workers not protected by the EP(C)A (eg those whose employment is wholly or mainly outside Great Britain; fishermen remunerated by a share of profits and policemen).
(4) That there has been a dismissal (10.19).
(5) That he has not attained the age of 65 or the normal retiring age in the firm (Note that the upper age limit of 65 applies to

both men *and* women since 7 November 1987). A claim must be affectively submitted to an industrial tribunal within that time. This qualification does not apply in trade union membership and activities dismissals.

(6) That he has claimed in time. There is a time limit of three months from the effective date of termination of the employment. This is extendable but only where the tribunal in its discretion considers that it was not reasonably practicable to present the claim within three months. The discretion is rarely exercised.

10.19 Dismissal

It may at first seem trite to say that an employee cannot claim unfair dismissal unless he has been dismissed but the position can be more complicated than it may appear at first sight. There are three kinds of dismissal, viz where:

(1) the contract under which the employee is employed by the employer is terminated by the employer, whether it is so terminated by notice or without notice or
(2) where, under that contract, the employee is employed for a fixed term, that term expires without being renewed under the same contract, or
(3) the employee terminates that contract, with or without notice, in circumstances such that he is entitled to terminate it without notice by reason of the employer's conduct.

Case (1) is what most people would understand as 'giving the employee the sack'. It is an express employer-initiated dismissal. Case (2) is unusual in that it *deems* there to be a dismissal when a fixed term contract comes to an end and is not renewed. Case (3) is what is known as a 'constructive' dismissal and merits some further explanation.

Constructive dismissal occurs where an employer's conduct is such that it amounts to a serious repudiatory breach of the contract of employment entitling the employee to resign. If he resigns in the face of such a breach he will have been constructively dismissed. A breach of this sort could be of an express term, eg a demotion, a unilateral reduction in pay, withdrawal of a bonus scheme (provided it is one which is contractually binding), unilateral change of location of work (where there is no term in the contract requiring the employee to be geographically mobile) and so forth. Or it could be a breach of an implied term, for example that the employee be given work to do or to maintain trust and confidence in the employment relationship (10.11). Examples of breach of the latter duty could be sexual harassment, an unjustified accusation of theft and/or continual

Employment law   235

undermining of the employee's position. These examples are far from exhaustive.

In relation to Case (2), and to fixed term contracts, section 142 of the EP(C)A allows an employer and employee by agreement in writing to exclude the right to claim unfair dismissal arising out of the non-renewal of the contract if the employee is employed under a fixed term of one year or more.

Finally, a contract may sometimes end by frustration (chapter 12), ie by operation of law without the need for action by either party. If so, there will be no dismissal. Frustration can occur in cases of imprisonment or long term illness where the employee's absence makes the contract impossible to perform. Because this doctrine, in effect, prevents an unfair dismissal claim, it is not popular with tribunals and it only rarely applies.

10.20   The test of unfair dismissal

When a claim is heard it is for the employer first to show an admissible reason for dismissal. Secondly, the industrial tribunal must be satisfied that the employer acted reasonably in relying upon that reason for dismissal.

10.21   Reasons

The permitted (or admissible) reasons are as follows:

(1) Capability or qualifications (EP(C)A, s 57(2)(a)).
    (This includes ill health as well as lack of qualifications and under-performance.)
(2) Conduct (EP(C)A, s 57(2)(b)).
(3) Redundancy (10.32) (EP(C)A, s 57(2)(c)).
(4) That the employee could not continue to work in the position which he held without contravention (either on his part or on that of his employer) of a duty or restriction imposed by or under an enactment (EP(C)A, s 57(2)(d)).
(5) Some other substantial reason (EP(C)A, s 57(1)(b)).
    This is seemingly a 'catch-all' reason, but applies in specific circumstances which are otherwise difficult to bring under heads (1) to (4). For example it has been held to cover dismissals arising from a personality clash which was not truly employee misconduct, and an employer's reorganisation of work which fell outside the definition of redundancy. Other examples have included dismissals for failure to accept new terms and conditions necessitated by proper business reasons and dismissals at the behest of third parties (eg customers of the employer).

10.22 Reasonableness

The statutory test of reasonableness of the decision to dismiss (and to rely upon one of the above reasons) is contained in EP(C)A, s 57(3) which states:

'... the determination of the question whether the dismissal was fair having regard to the reason shown by the employer shall depend on whether in the circumstances (including the size and administrative resources of the employer's undertaking) the employer acted reasonably in treating it as a sufficient reason for dismissing the employee; and that question shall be determined in accordance with equity and the substantial merits of the case'.

10.23 Establishing reasonableness

The test of reasonableness (and therefore, fairness) is a question of fact in each case. The industrial tribunal itself is the judge of what is fair and reasonable in all the circumstances and therefore the judge of what is good industrial relations practice.

To assist it in its determination of this question there are: 'A Code of Practice on Disciplinary Practice and Procedures in Employment' (1977) issued by ACAS and guidelines from time to time issued by the Employment Appeal Tribunal and the Court of Appeal.

(1) The Code of Practice was issued under the Employment Protection Act 1975 (EPA) and is admissible in evidence before an industrial tribunal. It has to be taken into account if relevant; but it is only *one* factor that has to be taken into account. It is however quite useful, stressing as it does, the need for fair implementation of disciplinary procedures. ACAS have recently issued an Advisory Handbook called *'Discipline at Work'* (1987) which, although not issued under the EPA, and not having the status of a code of practice, is intended to bring the existing Code of Practice up to date, and may well be influential.

(2) *Guidelines* issued by the Employment Appeal Tribunal and the Court of Appeal are of use but they must not be treated as rigid precedents and an industrial tribunal would go wrong in law if it slavishly followed guidelines in a particular situation without regard to the facts of each case. Recently the Employment Appeal Tribunal and the Court of Appeal have deprecated the use of guidelines even though many industrial relations specialists agree that guidelines are useful both for those implementing dismissals and those advising the parties as to the merits of particular cases. Many industrial relations pamphlets and periodicals report extracts from cases which can help those implementing dismissals. It is to be stressed, however, that industrial tribunals are supposed

to eschew legalism and many, if not most, cases depend on their own facts.

Generally, factors related to reasonableness include warnings, consultation, full and fair investigation before dismissal, clear disciplinary procedures and contractual rules (10.15), observation of mitigating circumstances, length of service and consistency. Very recently the House of Lords in *Polkey v A E Dayton Services Ltd* (1987) has reaffirmed the importance of procedures (including those in the Code of Practice) before dismissal in unfair dismissal cases. In fact Lord Bridge in the House of Lords stressed that dismissals in breach of procedure would usually be unfair by reason of a procedural lapse alone. He said: '... an employer having *prima facie* grounds to dismiss ... will in the great majority of cases not act reasonably in treating the reason as a sufficient reason for dismissal unless and until he has taken the steps, conventionally classified in most of the authorities as 'procedural' which are necessary in the circumstances of the case to justify that course of action.' And it is settled law that the employer's actions are to be judged at the time of dismissal. It is therefore no defence to say that, notwithstanding the procedural lapses before dismissal, the dismissal would have taken place in any event, even if evidence obtained subsequently might otherwise justify this conclusion. Thus procedure is all-important, even if the employer's case seems strong on the merits.

It may help to concretise the idea of reasonableness by setting out a few principles that the courts have developed in relation to specific cases of dismissal. It must be stressed that these are purely illustrative and not exhaustive and are no consideration for the facts of each case.

10.24 The test of reasonableness in unfair dismissal

A. *Ill health and absenteeism*

An important test was put forward by the Employment Appeal Tribunal in *Spencer v Paragon Wallpapers Ltd* (1976) that the basic question is whether in all the circumstances the employer could be expected to wait any longer and if so, how much longer. Relevant circumstances in answering that question are:

(i) the nature of the illness;
(ii) the likely length of the continuing absence;
(iii) the need of the employer to have the work done which the employee was engaged to do.

There are other procedural matters to be observed including the need to consult with the employee and, in most cases, with his medical adviser (*East Lindsey District Council* v *Daubney* (1977)). It is important to note that, certainly if the employee's own GP is used, the employee may have certain rights of access to the medical report under the Access to Medical Reports Act 1988. Use of another medical practitioner *may* avoid this problem (see below, 10.67). If an employee refuses his consent to be examined, or for a report to be made, the employer may have to make his decision on what information he has. Regard can also be had to the size and administrative resources of the employer's undertaking. Finally, even if the employee is unfit to do the job for which he is employed, a reasonable employer should also consider whether there is any alternative work for the employee to do that is within his capability.

Example

In *Todd* v *North Eastern Electricity Board* (1975), Mr Todd was a collector of arrears from customers. His job involved taking quite a lot of abuse from customers. As a result he developed a skin complaint which was a nervous reaction to the stress he was undergoing. He was declared unfit to do the job for which he was employed. However it appeared there was a clerical vacancy and it was also apparent that he had applied for a clerical vacancy in the past. He was suitable for that. He was nonetheless dismissed without consideration of alternative employment and it was held that the dismissal was unfair because of the failure to consider the possibility of employment in a different capacity.

In cases of absenteeism, particularly of an intermittent nature, a different approach is sometimes permissible and it may not always be necessary to take medical counsel in such circumstances. There would, however, have to be a warning to the employee to improve and clear indication of the possible sanction in the event of failure to improve.

B. Capability and performance

General principles were laid down by the National Industrial Relations court in *James* v *Waltham Holy Cross UDC* (1973) which included the following

(i) the employer should carry out a careful appraisal of the employee's performance and discuss his criticism with the employee;
(ii) the employer should warn the employee of the consequences of there being no improvement;
(iii) the employer should give the employee a reasonable opportunity to improve.

Finally, too, it may be appropriate to consider alternative employment, particularly if the failure to perform in the job is not the fault of the employee and a job which the employee could satisfactorily undertake is available.

Usually, in cases of under-performance, warnings and the opportunity to improve are essential. Very exceptionally indeed a prior warning may not be necessary if the under-performance amounts to gross negligence. The situation, however, must be extreme.

Example

In *Taylor v Alidair Ltd* (1978) a pilot was accused of landing a commercial aircraft rather badly on its descent into the Channel Islands. The passengers escaped unhurt but there was damage to the aircraft. The employers were able reasonably to conclude that the fault was that of the pilot and although no prior warnings about performance had been given, the exceptional circumstances that obtained meant that summary dismissal could follow without prior warning. The employers were not expected to tolerate the risk of the accident happening again. The case was eventually decided in the Court of Appeal. But, earlier in the proceedings, the Employment Appeal Tribunal laid down some guidelines particularly relevant to cases of severe shortcomings of professional judgement, saying: ' . . . there are activities in which the degree of professional skill which must be required is so high, and the potential consequences of the smallest departure of that high standard are so serious, that one failure to perform in accordance with those standards is enough to justify dismissal. The passenger-carrying airline pilot, the scientist operating the nuclear reactor, the chemist in charge of research into the possible effect of, for example, thalidomide, the driver of the Manchester to London express train, the driver of an articulated lorry full of sulphuric acid, are all in the situation in which one failure to maintain the proper standard of professional skill can bring about a major disaster.'

C. Conduct

In general cases of conduct, the following of procedures is extremely important. The existence of disciplinary rules spelling out the consequences of breach is also relevant. Generally it is not appropriate to dismiss for a criminal offence outside employment unless the commission of the criminal offence affects the ability of the employee to do his job properly or the confidence in the employer in the employee to do the job.

Only gross misconduct permits instant or summary dismissal. This could cover theft, violence or other grave conduct.

Example

In *C A Parsons v McLoughlin* (1978) McLoughlin was a toolroom grinder who had an argument with another employee. This turned into a fight. After the event McLoughlin, when questioned by the employer, claimed he did not start the fight but he was simply acting in self-defence. The employer was entitled to reject this defence as it was not credible on the facts. Nonetheless McLoughlin claimed the dismissal was unfair, partly because there was nothing in his contract which prohibited fighting. It was held that this was an act of gross misconduct and it should not be necessary for anyone to have it spelt out that fighting was a dismissable offence.

Difficult questions arise in the case of suspected misconduct. Does the employer have to prove beyond doubt that the misconduct occurred? The answer is no. While this may apply in the criminal courts, a more lenient test applies to industrial relations cases. The employer's belief does not have to be proved beyond doubt but simply 'on the balance of probabilities'.

The leading case is *BHS v Burchell* (1978) where it was stated that:

> 'first of all there must be established by the employer the fact of that belief; that the employer did believe it. Secondly, that the employer had in his mind reasonable grounds upon which to sustain that belief. And thirdly we think that the employer at the stage at which he had formed that belief should carry out as much investigation into the matter as was reasonable in all the circumstances of the case'.

Sometimes misconduct occurs and while the employer is sure that one employee committed the act concerned, he may be unable to determine which. Very exceptionally he may be entitled to dismiss all employees, any of whom could have been responsible for the act concerned, if he is unable to determine which employee in fact committed the alleged misconduct. In *Monie v Coral Racing Ltd* (1980) money disappeared from the employer's safe and the employer had reasonable grounds for believing that one of two employees was responsible. But he could not determine which. He therefore dismissed both. It was held that the dismissal was fair provided that the employer reasonably believed (which he did) that one of the two committed the misconduct, and the type of misconduct justified dismissal (See also *Whitbread & Co. plc v Thomas* (1988)). Extreme caution should be taken in applying this decision, though, and advice is necessary.

In all cases, even of serious misconduct, there must be a hearing at which the employee can state his case, the opportunity to appeal and, generally, a fair investigation must always be applied.

D. Redundancy

A redundancy dismissal can be unfair for a number of reasons, either for lack of consultation or notification, an unfair selection or a failure to search for alternative employment. A key case (which must not be applied too slavishly) is *Williams v Compair Maxam Ltd* (1982) where the principles were stated as being:

(1) The employer should seek to give as much warning as possible of impending redundancies so as to enable the union (if applicable) and employees who may be affected to take early steps to inform themselves of the relevant facts, consider possible alternative solutions and, if necessary, find alternative employment in the undertaking or elsewhere.
(2) The employer should consult the union (if applicable) as to the best means by which the desired management result can be achieved fairly and with as little hardship to the employees as possible. In particular, the employer should seek to agree with the union the criteria to be applied in selecting the employees to be made redundant. When the selection has been made the employer should consider with the union (if applicable) whether the selection has been made in accordance with those criteria.
(3) Whether or not an agreement as to the criteria to be adopted has been agreed with the union, the employer should seek to establish criteria for selection which so far as possible do not depend solely upon the opinion of the person making the selection but can be objectively checked against such things as attendance record, efficiency at the job, experience or length of service.
(4) The employer should seek to ensure that the selection is made fairly in accordance with those criteria and consider any representations the union and/or employees may make as to such selection.
(5) The employer will seek to see whether instead of dismissing an employee he can offer him alternative employment.

In summary, there must be warning to and consultation with a trade union if one exists, warning to and consultation with the individual, a fair selection and a search for alternative employment.

It is important to note that certain redundancy dismissals can be automatically unfair under section 59 of the EP(C)A where either the reason for the selection was for trade union membership or non-membership or that the employee was selected for dismissal in contravention of a customary arrangement or agreed procedure relating to redundancy and there were no special reasons justifying a departure from that arrangement or procedure in the employee's case.

E. *Where continued employment would contravene a statutory enactment*

Merely because a case occurs under this heading an employer is not absolved from adopting industrial relations procedures prior to the dismissal that are appropriate in the circumstances.

Example

In *Appleyard v Smith (Hull) Ltd* (1972) Mr Appleyard was required to drive his firm's vehicles as part of his job. He was disqualified from driving for 12 months. It was held his dismissal was not unfair: his disqualification meant he was prevented by law from driving vehicles. However, it is important to note that it was not an unfair dismissal because the employer *had* followed appropriate procedures, which in this case included considering the importance of driving as an element in the job and whether there was suitable alternative employment.

F. 'Some other substantial reason'

Some examples of dismissals that might fall under this heading have already been mentioned. In all cases appropriate procedures must be followed, failing which the dismissal will probably be unfair.

To illustrate, if an employer wished to impose new terms and conditions or to reorganise generally, and wished to dismiss an employee who failed to go along with the change, he would have, at the least, to demonstrate the genuineness of the proposal, to demonstrate the business need for it, to consult with an employee and offer only such terms as a reasonable employer should offer. (Employers must be careful in this area and legal advice is usually necessary; and it must be borne in mind that unless there is a dismissal with proper notice, acting without an employee's agreement could result in a breach of contract claim if an employee decided to resist the imposed change (see *Rigby v Ferodo* below)).

And, finally, if faced with a personality clash, he would have to seek in the first instance to resolve the problem by other means, consult, investigate and consider redeployment, before contemplating dismissal.

G. Conclusion on Procedures

The reminder here is that the *Polkey* case indicates that dismissal in breach of the *Code of Practice* or other procedures will usually be unfair and this aspect of unfair dismissal cannot be over-emphasised (10.23).

10.25 Dismissals relating to trade union membership or activities

It is *automatically* unfair to dismiss an employee on the ground either:

(1) That he was, or proposed to become, a member of an independent trade union; or
(2) That he had taken part or proposed to take part in the activities of an independent trade union at an appropriate time.

'Appropriate time' in relation to an employee taking part in the activities of a trade union means a time which is either outside his working hours or is a time within working hours when, in accordance with arrangements agreed with or consented to by his employer, it is permissible for him to take part in those activities.

Dismissal of an employee who refuses to become a trade union member or who refuses to remain a trade union member is also automatically unfair. In other words, it is not possible to enforce a closed shop agreement by dismissing an employee without the risk of an automatically unfair dismissal. Previously, in a closed shop context, although most dismissals for non-union membership would be automatically unfair, there were some exceptions, including where the closed shop had been introduced under certain complicated and continuing balloting requirements. However, the Employment Act 1988 swept the exceptions away and made all dismissals for refusal to become a trade union member automatically unfair. Also, dismissal of an employee for refusing to make a payment or have money deducted from his remuneration in lieu of joining a trade union is also automatically unfair.

It is also important to note that all trade union membership related dismissals carry additional awards of compensation over and above the ordinary levels (see below, 10.31). There is also protection in the EP(C)A to prevent action short of dismissal against an employee on trade union related grounds (see 10.42). And an employee dismissed on trade union grounds may also be entitled to interim relief (an order continuing the contract) before his case gets to a tribunal and the final remedy (see 10.31) is awarded. Finally, as previously mentioned, there is no qualifying period of continuous employment required to exercise these rights.

10.26 Pregnancy and dismissals

Dismissal for pregnancy is not a permitted reason for dismissal and so will be automatically unfair unless the employee:

(1) Is at the date of termination incapable, because of her pregnancy, of adequately doing her work; or
(2) Is, because of her pregnancy, unable to do her work without contravention (either by her or by her employer) of a duty or restriction imposed by some enactment

and in either case there is no suitable alternative vacancy to offer her. An employee dismissed by reason of pregnancy still needs the two year qualification period in order to claim unfair dismissal. However, there have been some cases that have held that dismissal of a woman by reason of her pregnancy could be an act of sex discrimination under the Sex Discrimination Act 1975. That would be if the employer is shown to have treated the woman less favourably than he would have treated a man. Thus, for example, if the employer's objection is to the woman taking maternity leave, and if in the same circumstances he would not have objected to a man taking leave say for an operation or other illness, this might be unlawful sex discrimination. Sex discrimination claims require no qualifying period.

10.27 Automatically unfair dismissals and the Transfer of Undertakings (Protection of Employment) Regulations 1981

It must be remembered (see below, 10.77) that a dismissal of an employee in connection with a transfer of an undertaking within the meaning of the Transfer of Undertakings (Protection of Employment) Regulations 1981 will, by virtue of Regulation 8, be automatically unfair unless for an economic, technical or organisational reason entailing changes in the workforce. Where there is an economic, technical or organisational reason for the dismissal entailing changes in the workforce the dismissal is deemed to be for 'some other substantial reason' under Section 57(1) (*b*) of the EP(C)A (10.21) and the fairness of the dismissal falls to be judged under general principles under section 57(3) of the EP(C)A (see above, 10.22). This aspect is discussed in more detail below.

10.28 Strikes and industrial action

Section 62 of the EP(C)A states that an unfair dismissal claim arising out of a dismissal during a strike, lock-out or other industrial action cannot be heard by a tribunal unless there are discriminatory dismissals or discriminatory non-re-engagement of strikers (ie not all those on strike or taking part in industrial action are dismissed or re-engaged as the case may be).

10.29 Written statement of reasons for dismissal

An employee is entitled to ask for a written statement of reasons for dismissal. As originally drawn, the EP(C)A requires six months' qualifying employment only for this right. But the Employment Bill, clause 13 will raise this to two years to equalise the period with that which applies for unfair dismissal claims.

If the employer unreasonably refuses to supply the reasons within fourteen days of a request, or if the reasons supplied are inadequate or untrue, a claim can be made to the industrial tribunal. If the claim is well founded a tribunal may make a declaration as to what the reasons actually were and it must make an award to the employee of an amount equal to two weeks' pay. It is important to note that a written statement provided by an employer is admissible as evidence in any proceedings, eg for unfair dismissal. It is important therefore that the statement is consistent with the employer's case before the industrial tribunal in the unfair dismissal proceedings.

10.30 Remedies for unfair dismissal

Complaint is to an industrial tribunal and the remedies available are:

(1) Reinstatement; or
(2) Re-engagement; or
(3) Compensation comprising

    (a) a basic award and
    (b) a compensatory award

(4) If either reinstatement or re-engagement are awarded but those orders are not complied with then the tribunal may make an additional award (see 10.31 below).
(5) Special awards may apply in the case of dismissals for trade union membership or activities or for non membership of a trade union in a closed shop context where statute provides for additional compensation (10.31(2)).

A basic award is calculated along the lines of a redundancy payment, ie is based on variables of age, length of service and the amount of a week's pay. The figure is the same as a redundancy payment, in effect (10.32), and when a redundancy payment has been made, an employee will not recover a basic award in subsequent unfair dismissal proceedings. The compensatory award is based on loss. Such loss can include loss of earnings, fringe benefits, such as BUPA, pension and loss of car, and also loss of statutory rights. The compensation maxima are stated below (10.31). The compensatory award may be made only to such extent as is 'just and equitable.' Compensation is the remedy commonly granted although the tribunal has a duty first of all to consider reinstatement/re-engagement.

10.31 Compensation levels

Note: the following levels are applicable from 1 April 1989. They are reviewed annually and different figures may apply from 1 April 1990.

(1) *Ordinary cases*
The maximum basic award is £5,160. The maximum compensatory award is £8,925. The additional award for failure to reinstate/re-engage will vary from £2,236 to £4,472 (ie 13–26 weeks' pay) or, in discrimination cases, £4,472 to £8,944 (ie 26–52 weeks pay).

(2) *Other cases*
In the case of dismissals for union membership and activities and dismissals for refusal to become or remain a trade union member the minimum basic award is £2,520 and the maximum award is £5,160. The compensatory award is the same as for ordinary cases, ie maximum £8,925. There is also a special award in these cases and the minimum and maximum for a special award which is available where there is no order for reinstatement or re-engagement are £12,550 and £25,040 respectively.

The minimum for the special award where there has been an order for reinstatement or re-engagement which has not been complied with is £18,795 but there is no maximum in this case as the award is 156 weeks' pay without limit as to the amount of a week's pay (normally £172) to be taken into account.

Awards may be reduced on ground of employee conduct or contributory fault, or, in the case of a compensatory award, on account of the principles relating to mitigation of loss (12.28).

10.32 Redundancy

An individual dismissed by reason of redundancy is entitled to a redundancy payment under the EP(C)A. There are qualifying conditions just as in the case of unfair dismissal (10.18), viz:

(1) The employee must have worked for at least two years.
(2) The employee must not fall within a number of excluded employments in the EP(C)A, eg overseas employees, share fishermen, public servants, those employed by overseas governments etc.
(3) As the provisions are drawn under the EP(C)A, a redundancy payment is not applicable in the case of a man aged 65 or over or a woman aged 60 or over (and the amount of a redundancy

payment diminishes in any event for a man between 64 and 65 and for a woman between 59 and 60 the closer the individual gets to retirement). This is obviously discriminatory and the Employment Bill, clause 14, when enacted, will equalise entitlement of men and women by providing that the entitlement to a redundancy payment ceases on reaching either a 'normal retirement age' below 65 which is the same for men or women, or, if there is no normal retiring age, 65 in each case. Years of work below the age of 18 do not count.
(4) There must have been a dismissal. The categories are the same as with unfair dismissal. As with the case of unfair dismissal, under EP(C)A, s 142 an employee working under a fixed term contract (here, of two years or more) may in writing exclude the right to a redundancy payment on non-renewal after its expiry (10.19).
(5) The dismissal must fall within the definition of redundancy in the EP(C)A s 81(2) which is as follows:

'An employee who is dismissed shall be taken to be dismissed by reason of redundancy if the dismissal is attributable wholly or mainly to

- (a) the fact that his employer has ceased, or intends to cease to carry on the business for the purposes of which the employee was employed by him or has ceased or intends to cease to carry on that business in the place where the employee was so employed, or
- (b) the fact that the requirements of that business for employees to carry out work of a particular kind or for employees to carry out work of a particular kind in the place where he was so employed, have ceased or diminished or are expected to cease or diminish'.

A redundancy occurs not only when there is a general closure of the business, but also where an employer ceases to carry on business at the place where the employee is employed, ie intends to change location of the place of work. If the work place is moved a redundancy payment may be applicable (subject to the rules about suitable alternative employment below).

However, if the employee is required to be mobile under his contract of employment, the place where the employee is employed to work is where the employer sends him. No redundancy would then arise.

Example

In *United Kingdom Atomic Energy Authority v Claydon* (1974) the employee was employed in Suffolk but the employer asked him to move to Berkshire.

He worked under a contract which required him to work anywhere in the UK. It was held there was no redundancy entitlement.

A redundancy also arises where there is a need to shed labour because there is less work; or where the work is rationalised so fewer employees are needed to do it; or where a job disappears entirely or changes so much that a different type of job holder is required.

Examples

In *Sutton v Revlon Overseas Corporation Ltd* (1973) a chief accountant was dismissed and his work re-allocated among his 3 colleagues. It was held that he was redundant as 3 as opposed to 4 employees were now needed.

In *Murphy v Epsom College* (1985) a plumber was dismissed and replaced by a heating technician because of changed requirements. It was held the old job of plumber had disappeared and Murphy was redundant.

A redundancy payment is based on variables including length of service, age and the amount of a week's pay (currently fixed at a maximum of £172). The employee is given 1½ weeks' pay for each year of employment when he was at the age of 41 and above, one week's pay for every year of employment when the employee was aged between 22 and 40 and ½ a week's pay for every year of employment when the employee was aged less than 22 but not less than 18 (subject to a maximum of 20 years' continuous employment). The current maximum redundancy payment possible under the statutory scheme is £5,160 (20 × 1½ × £172). These figures apply from 1 April 1989. They are liable to change annually. A redundancy payment must be claimed within six months of termination. Within those six months a claim in writing must have been made to the employer; or to the industrial tribunal; or an unfair dismissal complaint submitted to an industrial tribunal (thus the mode of claiming is more flexible than with unfair dismissal (see 10.18). Recovery of the payment, if refused, is from the industrial tribunal. There is a limited discretion for an industrial tribunal to hear late claims, but only for another six months after which the claim is absolutely time-barred. In proceedings there is a statutory presumption of redundancy which the employer has to discharge.

The right to a redundancy payment may be lost if the employer makes an offer of new employment on the same terms, or, if different, suitable alternative employment whether in writing or not before the ending of the old employment and this is unreasonably refused by the employee. If the offer of alternative employment is accepted the dismissal by reason of redundancy is deemed not to have taken place, and if the offer is taken up within four weeks of the ending of the old employment, employment is deemed to be continuous.

There is a four week trial period for an employee to try out the new terms and conditions if they differ from the old, and unless the decision to reject suitable new terms is unreasonable the employee may within the trial period reject the new terms and conditions, even after trying them out (see EP(C)A, s 84). The right to reject (and therefore the right to the redundancy payment) is lost if the employee stays on after the end of the trial period.

A redundancy in theory occurs where an employer sells his business. But it is important to note that where the Transfer of Undertakings (Protection of Employment) Regulations 1981 apply there should be no redundancy entitlement if the employee is transferred to the purchaser under Regulation 5 of the Transfer Regulations: in such a case dismissal is deemed not to have taken place. However if, for some reason, the employee is not transferred by the Transfer Regulations a claim can be made against the seller. Alternatively, there can be cases where the Transfer Regulations do not apply and yet redundancy liability is negatived nonetheless on a transfer from seller to purchaser. This is explained at 10.80.

There are modifications of entitlement to redundancy pay in the case of misconduct or strike action.

The EP(C)A also provides that an employee laid off or on short time (10.11) may be entitled to a redundancy payment after a number of weeks of lay off or short time have elapsed. But the conditions are complicated. Lay-offs or imposed short time working may in any event be a breach of contract at common law (at least if there is no term express or implied, allowing for lay off (10.11)) and trigger a constructive dismissal and therefore a 'redundancy' claim independently on that ground.

An employer is entitled to a redundancy rebate on a statutory redundancy payment (currently 35% of the amount of the statutory redundancy payment). But the rebate is now confined to employers with less than 10 employees. The Employment Bill, clause 15 provides for the abolition of the rebate altogether.

An employee who fails to receive a redundancy payment from an employer that is due to him may apply for reimbursement from the Secretary of State out of the Redundancy Fund where the employer is insolvent or has simply refused to pay it.

Redundancy dismissals also give rise to the right to claim unfair dismissal (10.18). Although redundancy is a permitted reason for dismissal, proper procedures must be followed, such as warning, notification, consultation, fair selection and consideration of possible alternative employment. Otherwise a redundancy dismissal might be unfair and attract unfair dismissal compensation (10.24).

Additionally, in multiple redundancies, the provisions of EPA, s 99 must be observed. Under those provisions a recognised trade union must be consulted about the redundancies. If 100 or more employees at one establishment within 90 days or less are proposed to be made redundant, the period of consultation is at least 90 days before the first of those dismissals takes effect. If 10 or more employees are proposed to be dismissed within 30 days or less the period of consultation is at least 30 days. In other, and indeed all, cases, consultation has to begin at the earliest opportunity.

An employer has to disclose in writing

(1) the reasons for his proposals
(2) the numbers and descriptions of whom it is proposed to dismiss as redundant
(3) the total number of employees of any such description employed by the employer at the establishment in question
(4) the proposed method of selecting the employees who may be dismissed and
(5) the proposed method of carrying out the dismissals, with due regard to any agreed procedure, including the period over which the dismissals are to take effect.

The employer has to consider a trade union's representations and reply to them, stating his reasons if he rejects them.

There is a defence to contravention of these obligations where there are special circumstances rendering it not reasonably practicable for the employer to comply; but this is very narrowly construed indeed and is rarely satisfied.

Complaint of breach of these provisions may be made to an industrial tribunal by the trade union concerned and if the complaint is upheld the tribunal may make a protective award (a minimum number of days' remuneration) in favour of affected employees.

There is a duty under EPA, s 100 to notify the Department of Employment of multiple redundancies by notice similar to that under s 99. A form is available from the Department of Employment for this purpose.

Failure to comply with the provisions of EPA, s 99 does not of itself make an individual dismissal for redundancy unfair, but failure to consult with an employee's trade union *may* be relevant to that issue in some cases.

Employment law 251

Under the EP(C)A, s 31 an employee under notice of dismissal for redundancy is entitled to reasonable time off during the employee's working hours to look for new employment or make arrangements for training for future employment. He is, during such time off, entitled to be paid remuneration by the employer for the period of absence at the appropriate rate. But here the EP(C)A limits the total liability of the employer (without prejudice to the employee's contractual rights to remuneration, if any) to two fifths of a week's pay. Complaint in the event of non compliance by an employer is to an industrial tribunal.

10.33 Wrongful dismissal and breach of contract claims at common law

So far, we have discussed possible claims arising out of dismissal under statutory employment law, principally unfair dismissal. In practice, this is likely to be the most common claim an employer will meet in the case of a dismissal which is contested by a former employee. But an employee may have a claim at *common law* in addition to unfair dismissal if he has been dismissed wrongfully, that is to say, summarily, ie without notice in circumstances where he was entitled to notice. In such a case the dismissal will have been in breach of contract because of the failure to give due notice.

The law thus operates two systems of dismissal compensation, unfair dismissal and wrongful dismissal. Unfair dismissal involves compensation for unfair dismissals under statute (10.17) irrespective of whether the employer complied with his notice obligations. Wrongful dismissal allows compensation to an employee for the fact that his employment has not been ended in accordance with the contract.

Under wrongful dismissal if he is dismissed without notice in circumstances which do not justify this, he will be entitled to compensation for loss of chance to earn wages during the notice period. In most employments, an employee's right to notice is fairly modest. Very often it follows the statutory minimum. So, in practice, suing an employer for unfair dismissal is the obvious choice for a former employee requiring compensation, as the compensatory award (maximum £8,925 at present) will usually far exceed the value of a payment in lieu of statutory notice.

However, an employee who has a more generous entitlement to notice (such as an executive with a two year notice entitlement earning £40,000 per annum) may find his wrongful dismissal compensation puts the unfair dismissal maximum compensatory award in the shade. And also employees who have not yet reached the qualifying period to present a claim for unfair dismissal may find a wrongful dismissal claim valuable.

Damages for wrongful dismissal can include compensation for loss of wages *and* other fringe benefits such as loss of pension contributions, use of car and so forth that would have been enjoyed throughout the notice period had notice been given. An employee is under a duty to mitigate loss (and this also applies to unfair dismissal) and if he does so (or fails unreasonably to do so) this may reduce his compensation claim.

Many contracts contain procedures that have to be followed before certain dismissals. If these are broken an additional claim for damages may apply.

Example

'D', a social worker, was summarily dismissed by the London Borough of Brent following the report of Louis Blom-Cooper QC about the handling of the Jasmine Beckford case. Under her contract she was entitled to the benefit of a disciplinary enquiry before dismissal but that was also dispensed with. The Court of Appeal upheld the High Court saying:

(a) not to give notice (her entitlement was eight weeks) was a breach of the contract and made the dismissal wrongful;
(b) it was a further breach of contract not to go through the disciplinary procedure.

D received wages equivalent to eight weeks' wages under (a) and a further eight weeks under (b) because it was established that a disciplinary enquiry, if set up, would have lasted about eight weeks and she had lost the chance to earn wages over that period (*Dietman* v *London Borough of Brent* (1988)).

A claim for damages for wrongful dismissal is ordinarily brought in the county court if less than £5,000 or in the High Court if greater.

In unfair dismissal, reinstatement and re-engagement are possible. In wrongful dismissal cases, the courts generally do not order specific performance (ie an order to the employer to continue employing the employee) of contracts for personal service. However, very occasionally, injunctions to restrain breaches of employment contracts and orders for specific performance may be granted where the employer is a large (often public) undertaking. But for an order for specific performance or an injunction having the same effect to be granted, the court must be satisfied that mutual confidence between employer and employee still subsists. This will of course be absent in many cases.

It is possible that there may be other types of breach of contract claim other than wrongful dismissal. For example an employee may wish to challenge a pay cut, or a unilateral variation in conditions or duties via a breach of contract claim rather than choose to resign (if the breach is serious enough), and claim constructive and unfair dismissal (10.19).

If an employee waits too long before taking action or otherwise appears to affirm the contract, though, he may lose his claim and be taken to have agreed what is in effect a variation of his contract.

But, in principle even if the breach is very serious, an employee can elect not to terminate the contract and, instead, sue for damages or, sometimes, in certain cases where arrears of wages under the contract are claimed, also in debt.

Example

In *Rigby* v *Ferodo Ltd* (1987) Mr Rigby was a lathe operator. His employer unilaterally reduced his wages. Mr Rigby continued to work but issued proceedings for damages for breach of contract. The employer's action was a serious breach of contract but the employee had not elected to end the contract — he wanted to keep it alive on the original terms. He could do this as he had not waived his rights: he had protested about the change and said he was not going along with it. He was therefore entitled to damages covering arrears of wages arising out of the wrongful reduction. The employer's argument that damages should be limited to the equivalent of his notice period was rejected: the employer had not purported to terminate the old contract by giving notice and therefore the claim was not restricted to a limited number of weeks — all the arrears could be recovered.

NB:

(1) It was important that Mr Rigby rejected the change by protesting and taking action; otherwise he might eventually have impliedly accepted the change by conduct;
(2) It seems the employer *could* have effected the change by giving due notice to terminate the old contract (and the old rates would have to be paid during notice) coupled with an offer of a new contract at the expiry of the old at the new rates. This would avoid a breach of contract but would, since it involves a dismissal, run the risk of an unfair dismissal claim which would have to be justified probably for 'some other substantial reason' and would have to be reasonable, to be fair (see above).

The process of altering terms and conditions carries considerable risk and should not be undertaken without advice and should preferably be done by agreement.

Simple breach of contract claims, like wrongful dismissal claims, as already mentioned, go to the County Court or High Court as appropriate. But a consultative document issued by the Department of Employment this year has invited comment on whether the Lord Chancellor should exercise his power in section 131 of the EP(C)A to confer breach of contract (which would also include wrongful dismissal) jurisdiction on industrial tribunals. If a favourable response is received, it may be that secondary legislation giving effect to that will be enacted in the near future.

10.34 Inter-relationship between wrongful and unfair dismissal summarised

(1) For a wrongful dismissal there has to be a dismissal in breach of contract. But a dismissal can be unfair even if the contract has been terminated with proper notice.
(2) Damages for wrongful dismissal (usually) compensate an employee over the notice period (if notice has not been given) but not beyond. Unfair dismissal can compensate for loss generally (even if beyond the end of the notice period) but only up to a limit (presently) of £8,925.
(3) There is, in unfair dismissal, additionally, a basic award based on past service. This does not apply to a wrongful dismissal alone.
(4) Reinstatement and re-engagement are theoretically available in unfair dismissal cases as an alternative to wrongful dismissal. But specific performance of contracts in a wrongful dismissal case rarely happens.
(5) Unfair dismissal claims go to an industrial tribunal, wrongful dismissal claims to the county court or High Court. (But note that industrial tribunals may also be given breach of contract (presumably including wrongful dismissal) jurisdiction soon (see above)).

10.35 Settling dismissal and other claims

A claim for compensation for unfair dismissal or for damages for wrongful dismissal can be settled 'out of court' and this commonly occurs. Sometimes the dispute between an employer and an employee is settled even before a tribunal claim or court action is instituted. Often the sums of money paid by employers under these settlements are referred to as 'ex gratia' payments, 'golden handshakes' or 'severance' payments. They have the same effect as settlements of actual or prospective court actions. A sum of money is usually paid in full and final settlement of the employee's claims. Both employers and employees often find settlements attractive for the purposes of avoiding the costs, publicity, stress, anxiety and delay involved in court or tribunal proceedings.

All claims within the jurisdiction of an industrial tribunal, including unfair dismissal, cannot be validly settled unless the settlement is effected through the auspices of the Advisory Conciliation and Arbitration Service (ACAS). Such a settlement is not binding unless the conciliation officer has 'taken action'. The reason for this is to ensure that individual unrepresented employees are made aware of their rights by an independent person when offered a sum of money by an employer and to ensure that, as far as possible (the ultimate decision is that of the employee) they are not being given less than, in the circumstances, they deserve. The procedure is quite important as, if an employer pays a sum of money over to an employee in supposed settlement of his claim, and if the settlement is not effected through ACAS, the employee can accept the money and still proceed to the industrial tribunal. In other words the settlement will not have been final.

There seems no reason why ACAS settlements, say, about unfair dismissal, cannot also deal with settlements of all other claims (not only other statutory claims but also claims for wrongful dismissal), and this commonly takes place. And, as mentioned, other statutory claims, eg under the EP(C)A or under the Sex and Race discrimination legislation can only be effectively compromised by using the ACAS procedure.

ACAS are also available to advise and conciliate in employment cases generally and (although this is not generally well known) they offer a free advisory service to employers on a wide range of issues from contracts of employment through to job evaluation.

Finally, a payment of compensation for loss of office as *director* must be approved by the general meeting of the company making the payment, under CA 1985 (chapter 5).

10.36 The taxation of ex gratia payments

The first £30,000 of payments which are widely known as 'golden handshakes' or terminal payments to former employees is tax free. The remainder is taxable. These rules apply to payments made after 5 April 1988 and differ considerably from those which obtained before (see TA ss 148 and 188). However, the key to this treatment is that the payment is a genuine termination payment. Making a payment or even making a contract to pay a sum during employment may prejudice this. You must therefore generally ensure the employment has ended before the deal is implemented. The rules are discussed in detail in chapter 9 (9.27).

10.37 Other significant statutory rights in employment

In addition to the right to claim unfair dismissal and redundancy an employee is entitled, if he or she works under a contract of employment, to enjoy certain other significant rights. These are set out below.

10.38 Maternity rights

(1) *Maternity leave*
Under the EP(C)A, provided that an employee has accrued two years' service and provided also that she works up to and including the 11th week before the expected date of confinement she has a right to return to work after confinement.
She must also comply with various notification requirements, viz:

- (a) informing her employer in writing at least 21 days before the beginning of her absence of her intention to take leave, to return and her expected week of confinement;
- (b) if requested by the employer not earlier than 49 days after the expected date of confinement, notifying her intention to return in writing within 14 days of the employer's request. The employer's notice must contain a statement of the effect of non-confirmation by the employee (ie that the right is lost);
- (c) notifying the employer in writing at least 21 days before the proposed date of return. The proposed date of return may be any time before the expiry of 29 weeks from the date of confinement.

She has a right to return to her job or, if not reasonably practicable because of redundancy, a right to return to suitable alternative, but no less favourable, employment. Failure to permit her to return to work is deemed to be dismissal save in employment where the employer employs less than five employees and it is not reasonably practicable to allow the employee to return. In larger employments the deemed dismissal will not apply if the employer can show it is not reasonably practicable to permit a return to the original job and suitable alternative but no less favourable work is offered and accepted or unreasonably refused.

(2) *Maternity pay*
An employee may qualify for statutory maternity pay (see 10.63).

(3) *Ante natal care*
An employee may be entitled to be paid time off for ante natal care. Such care must be on the advice of a registered medical practitioner, registered midwife, or registered health visitor and

an employer is entitled to a certificate from such that the employee is pregnant and evidence of an appointment. Complaint is to an industrial tribunal.

10.39 Guarantee payments

An employee who is laid off by reason of lack of work may, under the EP(C)A, be entitled to a guarantee payment for five workless days per quarter currently at the rate of £11.85 per day. Employees working under fixed term contracts of three months or less do not qualify.

10.40 Written statement of main terms and conditions

The employee is entitled to a written statement of main terms of conditions (10.14).

10.41 Payment during suspension on medical grounds

An employee who is suspended from work on medical grounds as a result of a requirement in legislation or a recommendation in a code of practice issued and approved under certain provisions of the Health and Safety at Work Act 1974 is entitled to be paid during the suspension for each week up to a maximum of 26 weeks.

10.42 Protection from action short of dismissal on grounds of trade union membership and activities

An employee has, under EP(C)A s 23, the right not to have action short of dismissal taken against him by an employer to prevent or deter him from or penalising him for:
(1) being or seeking to become a member of an independent trade union
(2) taking part in the activities of an independent trade union at an appropriate time
(3) not being or failing to become a member of a trade union
(4) declining to make payments in the event of failure to become or ceasing to remain a member of a trade union
'Appropriate time' has the same meaning as in trade union dismissal protection (see above 10.25). Complaint is to an industrial tribunal.

10.43 Itemised pay statements

An employee is, under the EP(C)A, entitled to an itemised pay statement or a standing statement of deductions. Complaint is to an industrial tribunal which may award an employee an amount up to the amount of unnotified deductions over 13 weeks prior to the application.

10.44 Time off for trade union and other reasons

Under the EP(C)A an employee is entitled to time off for trade union activities without pay. The time off must relate to the activities of an independent trade union recognised by the employer and the activities concerned are those of the union of which the employee is a member or in relation to which the employee is acting as a representative (excluding industrial action). The amount of time taken off must be 'reasonable'.

An official of a recognised trade union is entitled to time off with pay to carry out trade union duties concerned with industrial relations between his employer and any associated employer and their employees or to undergo training in aspects of industrial relations which is relevant to the carrying out of those duties and which is approved by the TUC or his union. The duties for which time off applies are potentially wide and may go beyond areas in which the union is recognised for collective bargaining purposes. But the Employment Bill, clause 12, proposes to amend the EP(C)A so that the duties for which time off must be allowed are limited to duties concerned with negotiations over matters in respect of which the employer recognises the union or duties concerned with certain functions the employer has agreed may be performed by the union. The rules relating to time off for training will similarly be limited to training relevant to those duties.

The amount of time taken off must, as with time off for trade union activities, be 'reasonable'. Whether trade union duties are concerned with industrial relations is hard to tell if union officials want to attend preparatory meetings or coordinating committees. The test is, according to *Adlington v British Bakeries (Northern) Ltd* (1989), whether the preparatory meeting or committee is 'sufficiently proximate' to negotiations with employers which constitute 'industrial relations'. This is a matter of fact and degree.

The case law on the meaning of 'time off' in trade union cases coupled in particular with the fairly lengthy statutory provisions means that legal advice should be taken when a difficult point arises. There is also an ACAS Code of Practice (No 3) *'Time off for Trade Union Duties and Activities'* (1977) which is of use and which is admissible in tribunal proceedings and specifically assists on what is 'reasonable' (see above).

A woman is entitled to time off for ante natal care (10.38) and safety representatives are also entitled to time off to do with their duties. An employee under notice of dismissal for redundancy may be entitled to time off to look for other work (10.32).

Employment law 259

An employee who is a justice of the peace, a member of a local authority, a member of any statutory tribunal, a member of a Health Authority, Health Board or Family Practitioner Committee, a member of a governing body of a school or college or of a water authority or river purification board has the right to unpaid time off during working hours to fulfil those public duties. The amount of time off must be reasonable having regard to the requirements of the office, the amount of time off an employee may already have had for trade union purposes and the effect on the employer's business.

Complaint in all these cases is to an industrial tribunal.

10.45 Statutory minimum periods of notice

As discussed (see above) after one month's employment every employee is, under EP(C)A s 49, entitled to not less than one week's notice of dismissal if he has been employed for less than two years and thereafter one week's notice for every year worked subject to a maximum of 12. An employee, after one month's employment, is obliged to give at least one week's notice of termination. It is important to note that these are minima and may be improved by contract, either by an express term or by the implied period of reasonable notice at common law. The statutory right itself operates as an implied term in the contract and therefore the remedy for breach is an action for damages for breach of contract.

10.46 Payment of wages — cash or cheque? The Wages Act 1986

Prior to the Wages Act 1986 employers could not pay wages otherwise than in coin of the realm unless the employee consented to it. Now, as from 1 January 1987 employees can be paid by cheque or credit transfer. The only pitfall might be that, whilst an employer can freely implement cashless pay in relation to new employees, the imposition of cashless pay on existing employees who already enjoy payment by cash might be a breach of contract and this could result in a constructive and, possibly, unfair, dismissal. Whether there was an unfair dismissal (10.18) would depend upon considerations such as consultation, facilities for encashment of cheques on site, and general issues of reasonableness (10.22).

10.47 Deductions from wages and the Wages Act 1986

With the repeal of the Truck Acts 1831 to 1940 the Wages Act 1986 also introduced a new system controlling deductions from workers' wages generally and also deductions on account of cash shortages and stock deficiencies in the case of retail employment.

It is important to note that the Act applies not only to employees but also to those working under a contract for services.

Under section 1 of this Act, deductions from wages may only be made if required or authorised to be made by virtue of any statutory provision or relevant provision of a worker's contract or if the worker has previously signified in writing his agreement or consent to the making of the deduction. Nor may an employer receive any payment from a worker unless these conditions are satisfied. A 'relevant provision' of a worker's contract means a provision contained in one or more written terms of the contract of which the employer has given the worker a copy on any occasion prior to the deduction being made or the payment received. Alternatively, it may be one or more terms of the contract, whether express or implied, and if express, whether oral or in writing, whose existence and effect in relation to the worker the employer has notified to the worker in writing on any such occasion. It is not possible to vary a contract or to make a *subsequent* agreement with an employee after an unauthorised deduction or payment in order to legitimise the deduction or payment retrospectively.

Section 1 does not apply to deductions or demands for payment in respect of any overpayment of wages or expenses; or to deductions or payments in consequence of disciplinary proceedings if the proceedings were held by virtue of a statutory provision; or where the employer is required to deduct in accordance with the determination of a public authority; or where under an arrangement with the worker, the employer deducts and pays over to a third party (eg the check off); or where the deduction or payment is on account of participation of a strike or other industrial action or, finally, where the deduction or payment is in pursuance of an order of a court or tribunal requiring payment of any amount by a worker to an employer.

Certain deductions or demands for payment are also outside the Act if they relate to payments which fall outside the definition of 'wages' in section 7. For example, the following are not treated as wages: any payment of an advance under an agreement for a loan or by way of an advance of wages; any payment in respect of expenses incurred by a worker in carrying out his employment; any payment by way of a pension, allowance or gratuity in connection with retirement or compensation for loss of office; any payment referable to a worker's redundancy; and any payment to a worker otherwise than in his capacity as a worker.

It is important to note that section 1 of the Act makes no provision about whether the deduction should be fair or reasonable (as did the Truck Acts) and there is no limit as to the *amount* of the deduction or demand, so long as the employer complies with section 1.

However, an additional regime applies to *retail workers* where it is provided that any deduction made (section 2) or payment required (section 3) on account of cash shortages or stock deficiencies from wages payable to a retail worker on any pay day cannot exceed one-tenth of the gross amount of wages payable to the worker on that day. And an employer loses his right to deduct or demand payment on account of cash shortages or stock deficiencies unless he does so within 12 months of finding the shortage (or such earlier date when he ought reasonably to have done so). However the one-tenth provisions do not apply to a 'final instalment of wages'. 'Final instalment of wages' includes a payment in lieu of notice.

Complaint in the event of breach of the provisions of the Act is made to the industrial tribunal and complaint must be made within the period of three months beginning with either the date of the payment of the wages from which the deduction was made or, in the case of a complaint relating to a payment received by an employer, the date when the payment was received (or in either case, within such further period as the tribunal considers reasonable in a case where it is satisfied that it was not reasonably practicable for the complaint to be presented within the relevant period of three months). If the complaint is well founded, the tribunal has to make a declaration to that effect and has also to order repayment of any deduction or payment contravening section 1 or in the case of breach of sections 2 or 3 the amount of any deduction or payment in excess of the one-tenth limit.

It is important to note that if there has been a breach of the Wages Act and a tribunal makes an order for repayment in a particular case, although an employer will immediately consider whether he may make a fresh attempt to recoup the sum in question, such action is in fact circumscribed. If the tribunal has made an order for repayment, the amount of the employer's claim is treated as reduced by the amount ordered to be repaid by the industrial tribunal. This means that if the employer gets it wrong and makes an improper deduction, he is prevented from pursuing the amount of that deduction again 'by whatever means' (section 5).

The aim of the Act was clearly to curtail an employer's ability arbitrarily to make stoppages from wages and to make demands for repayment of sums alleged to be due to him. Particular concern, for example, had been voiced in recent years about the plight of those suffering deductions on account of cash or stock shortages, such as cash handlers and petrol pump attendants.

It is unlikely that it was ever contemplated that the Act was designed to include a case where an employee complains of a withholding of an entire payment such as arrears of wages, holiday pay, sick pay or even a payment in lieu of notice. However, it is argued that because of the very wide definition of wages in section 7 which includes 'any sums payable to the worker by his employer in connection with his employment' not only can a 100% deduction be covered by the Act but also non-payment of notice monies.

Examples

In *Howard v Credit Default Register Limited* (industrial tribunal) an employee recovered the entire amount of arrears of wages withheld from him.

In *Maddison v A P Fielding* (industrial tribunal) an employee absented himself from work, the employer assuming this was through his own conduct, that is through a drinking bout. The employer wrongly assumed that the employee had been guilty of gross misconduct and therefore withheld both holiday pay and notice. However the industrial tribunal said there had been no gross misconduct on the facts and not only was the holiday pay ordered to be repaid to the employee, but also the payment in lieu of notice.

Other tribunals have been unwilling to allow 100% deductions as opposed to partial deductions from pay and a number have, for example, declined to order re-imbursement of a payment in lieu of notice. The reason for this is that to adopt a broad interpretation of the Wages Act as in *Maddison* (above) gives, in effect, industrial tribunals jurisdiction over contract claims by the back door, whereas at present their jurisdiction is expressly limited to statutory employment claims.

At the moment, this issue remains controversial. But as discussed elsewhere, this may become academic in the future if the Department of Employment Consultative Document on the formal conferment of jurisdiction over contract claims results in industrial tribunals being able to hear contractual claims (10.33).

Finally, an award of compensation under the EP(C)A for non-supply of an itemised pay statement is set off against any award by an industrial tribunal under the Wages Act 1986.

10.48 Sex and race discrimination in employment

Discrimination on the ground of sex or marital status (sex) may be unlawful under the Sex Discrimination Act 1975. Discrimination on racial grounds, may be unlawful under the Race Relation Act 1975.

'Racial grounds' means colour, race and nationality or ethnic or national origins.

Discrimination has been briefly discussed already in relation to recruitment (10.3). The principles are similar in relation to employment generally and the subject is given a fuller treatment under this section.

10.49 Discrimination in the employment field: definition

Although the expression 'employment field' is used here it is important to note that these Acts apply both to employed and self-employed workers.

Discrimination in the employment field can occur on recruitment or in employment (Sex Discrimination Act 1975 s 6; Race Relations Act 1976, s 4.) In recruitment it occurs:

(1) in the arrangements an employer makes for the purposes of determining who should be offered employment, or
(2) in the terms on which an employer offers that employment, or
(3) by refusing or deliberately omitting to offer employment.

It can happen in the case of persons employed:

(1) in the terms of employment which an employer affords to a person, or
(2) in the way an employer affords a person access to opportunities for promotion, transfer or training or to any other benefits, facilities or services or by refusing or deliberately omitting to afford access to them, or
(3) by dismissing a person or subjecting a person to any detriment.

10.50 Direct and indirect discrimination

There are two types of discrimination, direct and indirect.

Direct discrimination means directly treating another person less favourably on ground of sex or race. The employer's motives are not relevant. Thus, in *Greig* v *Community Industry* (1979) an employer turned down an application from a girl to be a painter and decorator. It was found that she would not have been treated this way had she been a man. This was therefore direct unlawful sex discrimination even though the employer was in good faith and thought his decision was in the interests of the girl.

Another important example of direct discrimination is sexual or racial harassment, where the employee is subjected to 'a detriment' (see above).

Example

In *Strathclyde Regional Council* v *Porcelli* (1986) Porcelli, a woman, was the victim of a campaign of sexual innuendo and harassment. She was forced to transfer to another school. She claimed she would not have been treated in this way had she been a man. The court upheld her claim and there was unlawful sex discrimination.

Indirect discrimination applies where a requirement or condition is applied which:

(1) even though it applies equally to all persons it is such that the proportion of people of one race or sex who can comply with it is considerably smaller than the proportion not in that race or sex;
(2) cannot be shown to be justifiable on non-race/sex grounds;
(3) is to the detriment of the individual because he or she cannot comply with it.

It has been suggested that since the European Court case of *Bilka Kaufhaus GmbH* v *Weber von Hartz* (1987) (an equal pay case — see 10.61) that what is justifiable for the purposes of sex discrimination under (2) means *objectively* justifiable. The court in that case said that it must be shown that 'the means chosen for achieving that objective correspond to a real need on the part of the undertaking, are appropriate with a view to achieving the objective in question, and are necessary to that end'. The objective test was approved as applying to the test of justifiability in indirect discrimination under the Sex Discrimination Act by dicta in the House of Lords in *Rainey* v *Greater Glasgow Health Board* (1987) and this approach has much to commend it.

The *Bilka Kaufhaus* case was not concerned with race discrimination but it is submitted that courts and tribunals should also construe the Race Relations Act consistently with the Sex Discrimination Act on this point. In any event, there are a number of cases in race discrimination law which stress an objective test. However not all cases are by any means in line with the 'necessity' test in the quotation from the *Bilka* case discussed above. Some legislative clarification would be desirable.

An example of what could be indirect sex discrimination can be found in the discussion on recruitment (10.3). Potentially indirectly discriminatory conditions may exist in advertisements, interview arrangements, letters of engagement, contracts, job descriptions, promotion rules, redundancy selection procedures, treatment of part time workers and so forth. Employment policies should be regularly scrutinised to ensure they do not operate unlawfully.

Examples

In *Singh v Rowntree Mackintosh Ltd* (1979) the employer imposed a rule that no beards could be worn. This effectively excluded Sikhs. Singh complained of indirect race discrimination. *Held* this was indeed indirect discrimination (but the employer was able to justify it on hygiene grounds).

In *Price v Civil Service Commission* (1978) the employer restricted job applicants to those between the ages of 17½ and 28. Mrs Price, who was 35, claimed indirect sex discrimination. It was conceded by the employer that the number of women who could in practice (because of child rearing) comply with this condition was smaller than men (and therefore the employer's requirements were indirectly discriminatory). The condition was held not to be justifiable and so the applicant's claim succeeded.

10.51 Genuine occupational qualification

There is also a defence (particularly relevant to recruitment) where the discrimination is as a result of a requirement for a *genuine occupational qualification*. The list of what may amount to a genuine occupational qualification is longer in the case of sex discrimination than in the case of race discrimination, as one would expect. Space permits only a couple of examples. Thus, in the context of sex, a 'goq' may apply because of demands of a job in terms of decency or privacy, or, because, in an artistic performance, authenticity may require members of one sex only. In the context of race, a goq may be established because, for example, again an artistic or dramatic context may require it or also because in a place where food and drink are consumed, authenticity may require members of one race only (eg Chinese waiters in a Chinese restaurant).

10.52 Discrimination by other bodies

Similar obligations apply also to:

(1) partnerships;
(2) trade unions;
(3) qualification bodies, eg professional associations;
(4) vocational training bodies, eg an industrial training board and the Manpower Services Commission;
(5) employment agencies.

10.53 Victimisation

It is also unlawful to treat someone unfavourably by way of victimisation which means victimisation against someone who brings proceedings, gives evidence or information, or alleges a contravention of, or otherwise acts under the Equal Pay Act 1970, the Sex Discrimination

Act 1975 and the Race Relations Act 1976 or intends to do any of those things.

10.54 Liabilities and remedies

Liability for discrimination attaches to both individuals and to employers. An employer is vicariously liable for an act done by his employee in the course of employment whether or not it was done with the employer's knowledge or approval. An employer has a defence to vicarious liability if he has taken such steps as were reasonably practicable to prevent the employee from doing that act or from doing in the course of his employment acts of that description. Therefore an employer cannot stand idly by without dealing, for example, with allegations of sexual harassment; he is required to take action to prevent the discrimination concerned. Employers would also be advised to implement an equal opportunities policy.

Individuals can also be liable if they give instructions to discriminate or put pressure on someone to discriminate or if they aid another person to do unlawful acts of discrimination.

A complaint alleging race or sex discrimination in the employment field can be made to an industrial tribunal. The industrial tribunal can, if the complaint is well founded, make a declaration, on order of an award of compensation and make a recommendation that the discriminator takes such action within a specified period as appears to be practicable so as to obviate or reduce the adverse effect on the complainant of the discrimination in question, or any of these, as appears to the tribunal 'just and equitable'.

The compensation maximum is now £8,925 (it is tied to the level of the unfair dismissal compensatory award, and so is liable to annual change (see 10.31)). It can include compensation for injury to feelings and this is a developing area. It cannot be assumed that compensation for injured feelings will be purely nominal. Recent figures have included: £3,000 (*Noone v North West Thames RHA* (1988)); £2,000 (*Pratt v Walsall Health Authority* (1988)) although these are rather on the high side. Tribunals have awarded aggravated or exemplary damages in extreme cases of discrimination.

10.55 Discriminatory retirement ages

Discriminatory retirement ages as between men and women were outlawed by the Sex Discrimination Act 1986 and an employer will now have to permit a woman to stay on at work until the same age as men if the woman so chooses.

10.56 Practical information

There are two codes of practice, the 'Code of Practice for the Elimination of Racial Discrimination and the Promotion of Equality of Opportunity in Employment' and the 'Code of Practice for the Elimination of Discrimination on the grounds of Sex and Marriage and the Promotion of Equality of Opportunity in Employment' which are of assistance to all those involved in employment practice. Additionally, there is a welter of information available from both the Commission for Racial Equality (Elliott House, 10–12 Allington Street, London SW1E 54EH) and the Equal Opportunities Commission (Overseas House, Quay Street, Manchester M3 3HN) by way of booklets and other materials which give practical advice on most aspects of the operation of the legislation. These materials include advice on how to formulate an equal opportunities policy.

10.57 Formal investigations and the role of the CRE and EOC

The Commission for Racial Equality (CRE) and Equal Opportunities Commission (EOC) can take action in the employment field or otherwise by way of formal investigations. If successful, investigations can result in the service of a non discrimination order on an employer. If this is not obeyed it can be enforced in the county court.

The CRE and EOC also exist to advise individuals about their rights and, in particular cases, both bodies can support individual claims against an employer. There is also a facility for individuals to prepare a race relations/sex discrimination questionnaire which can be served upon the employer in connection with an industrial tribunal complaint and if an employer declines to answer this questionnaire, or provides evasive or equivocal answers, this can be taken into account in future industrial tribunal proceedings. and adverse inferences drawn.

10.58 Equal pay

Under the Equal Pay Act 1970 a woman is entitled to be paid equal pay to a man for like work or work of a broadly similar nature or work rated as equivalent and, since the Equal Pay Act 1970 was amended by the Equal Pay (Amendment) Regulations 1983, for work of equal value.

The law applies to the self-employed as well as the employed, unlike most other employment protection rights. All complaints about sex discrimination in contractual pay and benefits have to be brought under the Equal Pay Act and not under the Sex Discrimination Act 1975.

Although this is too complex a subject to deal with here in full, European law has had a profound influence on the interpretation and application of Equal Pay Law. It may be possible directly to apply Article 119 of the Treaty of Rome or, alternatively, use Directive 75/117 as an aid to interpretation of domestic law where domestic law would otherwise fall short of European obligations.

Provisions in relation to retirement and pensions are excluded. Otherwise 'pay' can have a wide meaning encompassing a range of benefits including not only salary, etc. but also travel concessions and contractual redundancy pay. Some wide interpretations have been as the result of the application of European law.

The foundation of a claim is a comparison between a woman and a man (or vice versa). The comparator must be another person of the opposite sex in the same employment (or in the employment of an associated employer) at the same establishment, or at another establishment if common terms and conditions of employment are observed. European law in *McCarthys Ltd v Smith* (1980) allows comparison with another not only presently employed, but also a predecessor.

10.59 Equal pay for like work and equivalent work

The main provisions concern equal pay for like work or work rated as equivalent.

Work is 'like work' if it is of the same or a broadly similar nature but ignoring any differences between the things a woman does and the things a man does if they are not of practical importance in relation to terms and conditions of employment. Regard also has to be had to the frequency with which any such differences occur *in practice* as well as to the nature and extent of the differences.

Work is rated as 'equivalent' with that of any man if, broadly speaking, the job has been rated as equivalent under a job evaluation scheme. If work has been rated as equivalent, the woman is entitled to equal pay. If not, the case may fail. It is however possible to challenge a job evaluation scheme if it is discriminatory, eg not compiled or prepared under what is known as the analytical method.

10.60 Equal value claims

Even if the comparison between a woman's job and a man's job does not fall within the two categories above, a woman may still be entitled to equal pay if her job (even though different) is regarded as of *equal value*.

10.61 Establishing an equal pay claim

The procedure for a woman who alleges she is entitled to equal pay is for her to allege that she is employed on like work or work rated as equivalent. If she succeeds at this stage, it is nonetheless open to an employer to justify the difference between the man's job and the woman's job on the ground that the variation between the man's contract and the woman's contract is genuinely due to a material factor which is *not* the difference of *sex*. In like work or work rated as equivalent claims, it has been thought that, until 1986, regard could not be had to market forces in justifying the difference between a man's contract and a woman's contract, whereas in work of equal value cases, the wording of the material factor defence has always been thought to be wide enough to allow market forces to be taken into account (in like work/work rated as equivalent cases, the material factor *must* be a material difference *between the woman's case and the man's* (the so-called 'person equation'); in equal value cases it is provided that the material factor *may* be such a difference). However in *Rainey v Greater Glasgow Health Board* (1987) (a like work case) the distinction between the two wordings was blurred. In this case it was necessary to increase the number of National Health prosthetists by attracting applicants from the private sector. This was effected by offering higher wages than were enjoyed by existing employed prosthetists. A woman prosthetist already employed claimed equal pay to a newly recruited male employee who had arrived from the private sector and who was being paid more. It was held that the correct test is whether the difference between the woman's contract and the man's contract is objectively justifiable following the European Court's ruling in *Bilka-Kaufhaus GmbH v Weber von Hartz* (1987). In the case in question it was. Therefore subject to objective justifiability, market forces can apparently be brought in whatever the type of equal pay claim is being brought.

Differences that have been held to be acceptable as genuine, material and unrelated to sex are, for example, the hours of work that an employee may have to perform, if lengthy and unsocial, if the person works in a different area of the country (eg if more expensive) and also what is known as 'red circling', that is to say keeping an employee's wage rate preserved if he has to transfer to an ordinarily otherwise lower paying job, eg through health or other reasons.

Alternatively, a woman may claim that she is employed on work of equal value to a man she has chosen as a comparator. Equal value claims are notoriously expensive and long drawn out. In the first instance the tribunal has to decide whether there is a reasonable prospect of success in establishing the claim. It is presumed that there is no reasonable prospect of success if a job evaluation study has already attributed different values to the woman's job and the man's job.

But this can be overcome if there are reasonable grounds for supposing the study discriminates on the ground of sex. It will discriminate on the ground of sex where a difference, or coincidence between values set by the study on different demands under the same or different headings is not justifiable irrespective of the sex of the person on whom those demands are made. The defence of genuine material factor (see above) can also be raised by an employer at this stage in order to persuade a tribunal to dismiss the claim.

If a tribunal has not decided that there is no reasonable prospect of success in establishing the equal value claim, the equal value claim is then referred to an independent expert appointed by ACAS who then makes a report to the industrial tribunal. This report is admitted in evidence and can influence the industrial tribunal at the end of the day in deciding whether there is a well-founded equal value claim. It is also open for the employer to argue the genuine material factor defence again at the resumed hearing when the report has been received (see above).

If an equal pay/value claim is successful a woman is entitled to the insertion in her contract of an equality clause which entitles her thereafter to be paid at the same rate as the comparator she has chosen. She is also entitled to recover arrears of pay for up to two years prior to the commencement of proceedings at the new rate.

10.62 Equal Opportunities Commission

The EOC (see above) can also assist in relation to equal pay claims.

10.63 Statutory maternity pay

Statutory maternity pay was introduced by the Social Security Act 1986. An employer is responsible for administering it and may reclaim the sums he has to pay by deduction from sums he would ordinarily pay by way of employer's National Insurance contributions (chapter 9). A woman must be employed for not less than 26 weeks continuously ending with the week preceding the 14th week before the expected week of confinement before she can become eligible. A woman who thus qualifies receives a flat rate (currently £36.25 per week) for 18 weeks. A woman who has been employed for 2 years or more is entitled to payment at the rate of 90% of her earnings for six weeks and the (lower) flat rate for 12 weeks thereafter. Statutory maternity pay commences 11 weeks before the expected date of confinement. A government booklet is available from the DSS to assist employers' administration of the payments.

10.64 Statutory sick pay

This was first introduced by the Social Security and Housing Benefits Act 1982. Statutory sick pay is a payment similar to statutory maternity pay and is administered and paid by the employer and is recovered by him by deductions from the employer's National Insurance contributions that he would otherwise make (chapter 9). Subject to qualifying conditions, the payment is made for the first 28 weeks of illness after which state benefit is applicable and statutory sick pay ceases. There is no entitlement to statutory sick pay for various reasons: for example, for the first three days of absence and also, certain individuals such as pensioners, employees on short term contracts of less than three months and those not employed by reason of a trade dispute in which they are interested, amongst other cases, do not qualify.

The qualifying days of statutory sick pay are normally fixed by the employer and the employee and normally relate to the paid days of employment (eg Monday to Friday). The rates are currently (ie with effect from 10 April 1989) as follows:

Wages per week	SSP per week
0 — £42	nil
£43–£83.99	£36.25
£84 +	£52.10

An employer can require rules as to notification procedures. There are, however, controls on what an employer can require in terms of medical evidence as a pre-requisite for claiming statutory sick pay (although he can operate separate conditions for qualification for contractual sick pay (10.11)).

An employee may be entitled by virtue of his contract to full pay under his contract (10.11) not just statutory sick pay (10.11). An employer would be advised to state in his contracts with employees that an employee is only entitled to such contractual sick pay as is necessary to top wages up to the normal level after payment of statutory sick pay or any state sickness benefit received thereafter.

An employer would not be advised to tackle this complicated administrative burden without the assistance of government booklets available from the DSS.

10.65 Employees' rights on insolvency of the employer

If an employer becomes insolvent, employees may have outstanding claims. Although certain claims are treated as preferential debts in company law (Insolvency Act 1986 Schedule 6) this is not a complete solution. EP(C)A s 122 therefore allows the Secretary of State for Employment to reimburse certain debts on employer insolvency out of the redundancy fund. These are:

(1) Up to eight weeks' arrears of pay;
(2) A payment in respect of statutory notice under EP(C)A s 49;
(3) Up to six weeks' holiday pay relating to the previous twelve months;
(4) A basic award of compensation for unfair dismissal (but, anomalously, not a compensatory award);
(5) Any reasonable sum by way of reimbursement of the whole or part of any fee or premium paid by an apprentice or articled clerk.

For the purposes of (1) above the following are included in the definition of arrears of pay in addition to what one might ordinarily understand as comprising pay, ie:

(1) A guarantee payment (10.39);
(2) Remuneration on suspension on medical grounds (10.41);
(3) Any payment for time off under the statutory time off provisions (10.44);
(4) Remuneration under a protective award made under the EPA in relation to failure to inform and consult with a recognised trade union on redundancy (10.32).

The maximum amount currently payable in respect of each debt is £172 per week. The mode of claiming is via the administrator, receiver or liquidator or trustee in bankruptcy of the employer who provides the appropriate forms.

Complaint about non-payment by the Secretary of State is to an industrial tribunal within three months of the Secretary of State's decision. If an industrial tribunal decides the claim is well founded, it may make a declaration accordingly.

Application may also be made to the Secretary of State for him to adopt liability for unpaid employer's contributions to an occupational pension scheme or a personal pension scheme.

Employment law 273

It is also provided by Regulation 9C of the Statutory Sick Pay (General) Regulations 1982 and Regulation 7 of the Statutory Maternity Pay (General) Regulations 1986 that the Secretary of State takes over liability to pay statutory sick pay and statutory maternity pay respectively on an employer's insolvency.

An employee may apply to the Secretary of State for reimbursement under section 106 of the EP(C)A if he fails to receive a redundancy payment where either the employer is insolvent or has simply refused to pay.

10.66 Data protection

Under the Data Protection Act 1984 individuals who have personal details about them processed by another on computer recording equipment may have rights to request sight of this. And persons who use computer equipment for recording data have to register with the Data Protection Registrar. This will include employers who store details about their employees in this way (although processing of data relating to basic payroll and pension matters is exempted). If data is processed without registration, use by an employer of such data can be a criminal offence. And an employee's right to see such data as he is entitled under the Act is enforced by withdrawal by the Registrar of the employer's registration. This is an important employee right which all using computer equipment for recording personnel data have to observe. The Data Protection Registrar has recently prepared revised versions of eight Data Protection Guideline Booklets, which are the best introduction for employers seeking to get to grips with the subject. They can be ordered, at the time of writing, via the Registrar's Enquiry Service by telephone ((0624) 535777).

10.67 Access to medical records

Another 'freedom of information' measure applicable to employment law is the Access to Medical Reports Act 1988 which came into force on 1 January 1989. It provides a general right of access for individuals to reports supplied by medical practitioners for employment and insurance purposes (but only in relation to medical reports prepared after 1 January 1989).

In this summary we are mainly concerned with 'employment purposes' and this means purposes in relation to an individual who is employed or who is seeking to be employed by an employer.

A medical report for the purposes of the Act means a report relating to the physical or mental health of an individual prepared by a medical practitioner who is or who has been responsible for the clinical care of that individual.

However it is likely that the Act only applies to reports commissioned from the employee's own doctor. If an employer uses a company doctor or an independent medical practitioner who, in either case, has not been responsible for clinical care of the employee (as commonly happens) the Act does not apply. This is because 'care' includes examination, investigation or diagnosis for the purposes of or in connection with any form of medical treatment. Employers might well like to consider this option. If a person has consulted a company doctor in the past however, and he is a company doctor who prepares the report on behalf of the employer, there is a possibility that the Act would cover the report concerned.

If the Act applies, an employer cannot apply to a medical practitioner for a report relating to an individual for employment purposes unless he has notified the individual that he proposes to make the application and the individual has notified his consent to the making of the application. The notification by the employer to the individual has to inform the individual of his rights to see the medical report before and after it is supplied, to withhold consent to the making of the report and the right to request amendment of the report if the individual considers the content thereof inaccurate or misleading (or if the medical practitioner decides not to amend the report in the light of that complaint, to append a statement of his own to the medical report).

It can therefore be seen that the individual has a number of rights. First, an individual is entitled to decline to consent to the supply of the medical report. How meaningful this is in practice, of course, is debatable: if the report is for the purposes of deciding whether the employee should be given a job, the employer may well decline to offer the job if a medical report is not provided. And if the request is in relation to examining whether an employee's employment may be continued in the light of ill health or medical problems during employment, an employer may in many cases be considered to have acted reasonably for unfair dismissal purposes on information known to him excluding the medical report if the medical report is refused (see 10.24).

Secondly, if consent is given to the making of a report, the individual is entitled to state that he wishes to have access to the report before it is supplied and, if so, the employer has to notify the medical practitioner of that fact when contacting him and at the same time notify the individual of the making of the application. If the individual has indicated a desire to have access to the report, the medical practitioner cannot supply the report unless he has given the individual access to it or, alternatively, 21 days from the date of making the application for a report have elapsed without the medical practitioner having had any communication from the individual concerning arrangements for access. An employer's notification to the employee must advise him of these requirements. Even if an employee fails to ask to see the report when originally giving his consent, he may later do so, provided this is before the report has actually been supplied to the employer. Similar conditions about access, etc then apply. Access to the report means making the report or a copy of it available for the employee's inspection or supplying the individual with a copy of it but in the latter case the medical practitioner may charge a reasonable fee to cover the costs of supply.

Thirdly, when an individual has been given access to a report, the report cannot be supplied unless the individual has notified the medical practitioner that he consents to its being supplied. The individual can, before giving his consent, request the medical practitioner to amend any part of the report which the individual considers to be incorrect or misleading and, if so, the practitioner may accede to that request and amend the report accordingly. If he is not prepared in his medical judgment to accede to the request, he has to attach a statement of the individual's views in respect of any part of the report which is in dispute to the report itself. Any request by an employee has to be in writing.

A medical practitioner has to keep a report for at least six months and during that time has to give an employee access to it upon request.

There are some exemptions. A medical practitioner is not obliged to give an individual access to any part of the medical report, disclosure of which would, in the opinion of the practitioner, be likely to cause serious harm to the physical or mental health of the individual or others or would indicate the intentions of the practitioner in respect of the individual. Also, he is not obliged to give an individual access to any part of the medical report, the disclosure of which would be likely to reveal information about another person or to reveal the identity of another person who has supplied information to the practitioner about the individual. This does not apply if the third party has consented or the third party is a health professional who has been involved in the care of the individual and the information relates to or has been provided by the professional in that capacity. If it appears to the medical practitioner that these problems arise he has to notify the individual of that fact.

If it appears to the medical practitioner that the whole of the report cannot be disclosed because of the above exemptions, he has to notify the individual of that fact and may not supply the report unless he is notified by the individual that the individual consents to supply.

Enforcement is by application to the County Court on complaint that an employer has failed or is likely to fail to comply with any requirement of the Act. If there is a breach, the Court may order the employer to comply with the requirement and breach of that order would be contempt of court.

Any notification required under the Act has to be given in writing.

10.68 Contracting out of statutory rights

It is generally not possible to contract out of statutory rights such as under the EP(C)A, Sex Discrimination Act 1975, Race Relations Act 1976 or the rules about SSP, SMP and Data Protection. It is possible to contract out of the EP(C)A in limited circumstances, but EP(C)A, s 140 otherwise prevents this. As an exception to the rule against contracting out, certain fixed term contracts may exclude unfair dismissal and redundancy rights on non renewal (10.19, 10.32). And we have seen that it is possible to settle EP(C)A claims and also race and sex discrimination and Wages Act claims by using ACAS (10.35).

10.69 Buying or selling a business: The Transfer of Undertakings (Protection of Employment) Regulations 1981 and Other Rules

This section deals with special employment problems that arise when businesses are being sold or purchased. Although legal advice is normally obtained at this juncture it is important that you should bear in mind that, when a business is bought or sold, the purchaser may well acquire existing employees together with all rights and obligations including continuous employment and potential liability for redundancy payments and unfair dismissal compensation notwithstanding there has been a change of employer.

10.70 Buying and selling limited companies

If you acquire a firm by buying shares in a company the company you have bought continues as before. Although in reality there is a change of proprietor, in law there is no legal change in the employer. Therefore all employment rights are uninterrupted and continuous. So if you buy the shares in a company which has a workforce you automatically inherit all obligations and duties to that workforce including accrued continuous service for the purposes of unfair dismissal and redundancy and other statutory rights.

10.71 Buying and selling a business which is not a limited company

Buying and selling a business which is not a limited company involves a legal change of employer. But for protective provisions in legislation a purchaser of a business at common law would be able to take the business free of pre-existing employment obligations. But there are special statutory provisions which protect employees. Either the provisions of the EP(C)A (discussed later) or the Transfer of Undertakings (Protection of Employment) Regulations 1981 may impose on the purchaser of a business certain liabilities in relation to the workforce including, possibly, all contractual rights and obligations and accrued statutory continuity of employment. This is a fact which often goes unappreciated by purchasers of businesses who automatically assume that when they take on the workforce of a business they take that workforce with a clean break with continuity broken and who also assume that they can impose new terms and conditions on the workforce with impunity. But this may not be the case.

10.72 The Transfer of Undertakings (Protection of Employment) Regulations 1981

These regulations, the subject of much controversy ever since they were enacted, were introduced to implement the EEC Council Directive of 14 February 1977 on the approximation of the laws of member states relating to the safeguarding of employees' rights in the event of transfers of undertakings, businesses or parts of businesses (the Acquired Rights Directive).

There have been statutory provisions for some time about continuity of employment on business transfers, for example in paragraph 17(2) of Schedule 13 to the Employment Protection (Consolidation) Act 1978 but the provisions of paragraph 17(2) of Schedule 13 to the EP(C)A deal only with bridging continuity on change of employer. The Transfer Regulations go further and provide, through Regulation 5, for an automatic transfer of contracts of employment to a transferee together with all rights obligations and duties in relation thereto. This alters the common law rule in *Nokes* v *Doncaster Amalgamated Collieries* (1940) that a contract of employment cannot be novated without the consent of the employee and is therefore revolutionary in legal terms.

In addition to transferring the contract of employment from the transferor to the transferee, Regulation 5 of the Transfer Regulations can also make a transferee liable for anything done by a transferor in relation to an employee prior to a transfer. Underpinning the protection in Regulation 5 is Regulation 8. It makes transfer connected dismissals automatically unfair (Regulation 8(1)) unless for an economic technical or organisational reason entailing changes in the workforce (Regulation 8(2)) (the dismissal is not rendered automatically *fair* if Regulation 8(2) applies: the fairness then falls to be considered under general principles ie EP(C)A s 57(3) (10.22)). As will be seen below, 'economic' 'technical' and 'organisational' tend to be construed in a manner relative to the needs of the business. Therefore dismissals simply to enhance the chances of a sale or to please the purchaser may be automatically unfair.

The Transfer Regulations also provide for the transfer to a transferee of recognition of trade unions and of collective agreements (Regulations 9 and 6 respectively). And the Transfer Regulations impose on employers obligations to inform and consult with recognised trade unions prior to a transfer (Regulation 10). It is important to note that the Transfer Regulations are intended to implement a European Community Directive and the pre-amble to the Acquired Rights Directive states that: 'It is necessary to provide for the protection of the employees in the event of a change of employer, in particular, to ensure that their rights are safeguarded'. The Transfer Regulations are likely to be construed, where possible, to give effect to this aim. The *Litster* case (discussed below) is a recent example of this.

10.73 A relevant transfer

The Transfer Regulations only apply to a relevant transfer under Regulation 3. This is a transfer from one person to another of an undertaking or part of an undertaking situated immediately before the transfer in the United Kingdom or part of one which is so situated. The requirement of a transfer from one person to another means that the Transfer Regulations do not apply to a take-over by way of change in the ownership of the share capital of a limited company.

A relevant transfer is taken by industrial tribunals and the Courts as meaning a transfer of an undertaking or part 'as a going concern'. This is a case law gloss which first arose from cases on paragraph 17(2) of Schedule 13 to the EP(C)A but it was shortly confirmed as applicable also in relation to the Acquired Rights Directive (and therefore the Transfer Regulations) by the European Court in *Spijkers* v *Gebr Benedik Abattoir C V* (1986). In a nutshell, a mere assets sale without more does not amount to a transfer of an undertaking as a going concern. Something more is needed, usually the presence of goodwill or other like factors. Recently the European Court, in cases on the Acquired Rights Directive, has stressed that a 'transfer' does not necessarily require a change of *ownership*; the Directive also covers a change in the person in control of the undertaking who assumes obligations to employees. Thus, many changeovers of tenants or licencees are often covered.

Finally, under the Transfer Regulations, there is no relevant transfer when there is a transfer of something which is not in the nature of a commercial venture (Regulation 2(1)). This might exclude many educational or charitable or non-profit making organisations. Thus in *Woodcock v Committee for the Time Being of the Friends' School Wigton and Genwise* (1987) the transfer of a Quaker school of charitable status was not a relevant transfer under the Transfer Regulations.

10.74 Regulation 5 and the transfer of employment liabilities

When Regulation 5 applies, the contract of employment of a person employed in the undertaking transferred 'immediately before' the transfer will be transferred to a transferee and also, in relation to such an employee, a transferee will be liable for anything done by the transferor in relation to the employee prior to the transfer. The sort of rights and obligations that can be transferred to a transferee when the Transfer Regulations apply include:

(1) continuous employment (because the contract itself is transferred: EP(C)A sched 13 is strictly the source of rules about whether continuity is preserved (10.79));
(2) redundancy payments and unfair dismissal liability;
(3) liability for accrued wages and other benefits;
(4) contractual seniority rights;
(5) pre-transfer acts and omissions of the transferor

but excluding, for example:
(a) pension rights;
(b) liability for a criminal offence.

10.75 Pre-transfer dismissals

So as will be seen, the transfer of the contract under Regulation 5 carries with it a wide range of obligations. Much controversy has recently been generated by the question of whether a transferee could also be liable for pre-transfer dismissals effected by a transferor. But it can be seen from the above discussion that Regulation 5 only applies if an employee is employed in the undertaking immediately before the transfer. So on the face of it, if an employee's employment ended before the transfer, eg by prior dismissal, he may not be protected. What has therefore often happened in practice is that the transferor and transferee have sought to exclude employees from Regulation 5 by making sure that a pre-transfer dismissal has effectively ended their employment before the transfer. Again, on the face of it, if this is done, their contracts are not transferred to a transferee and liability for the pre-transfer dismissal rests with the transferor. An employee would therefore be expected to claim all termination payments, eg accrued wages, holiday pay, sick pay, notice payments, redundancy payments and unfair dismissal compensation from a transferor. If re-engaged by a transferee at some future date, there would be a break in continuous employment. This possibility was endorsed by the Court of Appeal in *Secretary of State for Employment v Spence* (1986) which held that for an employee to be transferred to a transferee he had to be employed in the undertaking exactly at the point of transfer. A prior dismissal would stop this.

But sometimes hardship can occur. If an employee can be re-engaged by a transferee with no transfer of statutory continuity, employment conditions can be altered with impunity as there can be no claim for unfair dismissal until two years' service with the transferee has been accrued. Also, although certain terminal payments can be claimed from a transferor in these circumstances, hardship can ensue if the transferor is insolvent because not all of the payments are reimbursable from the Department of Employment under section 122 of the EP(C)A (10.65), for example, importantly, an unfair dismissal compensatory award. So an employee who is dismissed by an insolvent transferor can be disadvantaged.

10.76 The *Litster* Case

These policy objections were tackled by a recent landmark decision of the House of Lords in *Litster v Forth Dry Dock & Engineering Co Ltd (in receivership)* (1989). The effect of this case is that a transferee may be liable for pre-transfer dismissals even if the employees are not employed immediately before the transfer. This will be in circumstances where the dismissals are held to be automatically unfair under Regulation 8, that is to say, when they are in connection with the transfer and are not for an economic, technical or organisational reason entailing changes in the workforce. Collusive dismissals, ie dismissals arranged by a vendor and a purchaser simply to avoid the effect of the Transfer Regulations, will usually fall foul of Regulation 8 and therefore will not be for an economic, technical or organisational reason *entailing* changes in the workforce. They will not be for a reason related to the needs of the business but will be a reason related to the requirements of the purchaser to relieve himself of employment obligations.

The facts of the *Litster* case were that Forth Dry Dock & Engineering Limited went into receivership in September 1983. Forth Estuary Engineering Limited was incorporated with a view to acquiring the business of Forth Dry Dock. At 3.30 pm on 6 February 1984 the entire workforce of Forth Dry Dock was dismissed with immediate effect. The transfer was executed at 4.30 pm. Within 48 hours of the dismissals, it was learned that Forth Estuary Engineering Limited was recruiting employees. A number of former employees applied for these jobs but only three were engaged. It later materialised that the new company was recruiting at lower wages and it ended up with a similar size workforce to that employed by the transferor which was now in receivership. On these facts the transfer connected dismissal was not for an economic technical or organisational reason entailing changes in the workforce as it was not related to the needs of the business: the business still needed a workforce.

The previous authority of *Secretary of State for Employment v Spence* however put an obstacle in the way of the employees' claims to be transferred to the transferee as they were not employed immediately before the transfer. But since *Spence* the European Court had, in *P. Bork International A/S v Foreningen af Arbejdsledere i Danmark* (1989), a case on the Acquired Rights Directive, held that although it was indeed mainly true that only employees employed at the time of transfer were automatically transferred, this was subject to the mandatory effect of Article 4 of the Directive (our Regulation 8) which prohibited transfer connected dismissals which were not for an economic, technical or organisational reason. Those dismissed, even before the transfer, contrary to Article 4, should have their rights transferred to the transferee. So, the House of Lords applied European law on the Acquired Rights Directive, applying a purposive interpretation of the legislation and held that these dismissed employees were 'deemed' still to be employed immediately before the transfer so as to be caught by Regulation 5 if they had been unfairly dismissed under Regulation 8. This was the case in *Litster*.

The following is a guide as to whether a transferee will be liable for a pre-transfer dismissal effected by a transferor (although it is to be stressed that you should never enter this area without legal advice):

(1) Was the time between the dismissal and the transfer of so short a duration that in effect the employee was employed immediately before the transfer, ie the dismissal and transfer are so closely connected in point of time that for practical purposes it is impossible realistically to say that they are not precisely contemporaneous? If so, the contract of employment will be transferred to the transferee under Regulation 5.
(2) If the answer to the above is 'no', that is to say there is a pre-transfer dismissal which means there is some interval between a dismissal and the transfer, the next question is to ask whether there was a dismissal which was connected with the transfer so as to invoke Regulation 8(1) which makes a dismissal prima facie automatically unfair? If not, the transferor remains liable for dismissal liabilties. If the answer is 'yes', however, and Regulation 8 is invoked, does Regulation 8(2) apply which says that the dismissal shall not be automatically unfair if there is an economic technical or organisational reason for the dismissal entailing changes in the workforce? If there is no such economic technical

or organisational reason for the dismissal, liability for the pre-transfer dismissal will pass to the transferee.
(3) If there is a transfer connected pre-transfer dismissal but it is for an economic technical or organisational reason, then provided that the employee was not employed in the business immediately before the transfer, liabilities will remain with the transferor and *Secretary of State for Employment* v *Spence* will apply.

This decision is very controversial at present and not all its ramifications are clear (for example, some commentators think it is possible that all you have to show for *Litster* to apply is that the dismissal is 'connected' and that an economic, technical or organisational reason will not prevent transfer of liabilities; and some have wondered whether only employees who have the two year qualifying period to claim unfair dismissal (10.18) can rely on *Litster* or whether all employees, irrespective or length of service, are covered). It will certainly make potential purchasers of businesses very wary of buying businesses as going concerns. It may even result in a downturn in rescues of insolvent businesses. However, one thing is clear, that is that the decision is consistent with the UK's European obligations.

10.77 Other applications of Regulation 8

It can be seen that a vital component of a liability for a pre-transfer dismissal under the *Litster* case is whether the dismissal will be automatically unfair under Regulation 8. Regulation 8 can crop up in other circumstances. Suppose a purchaser of a business who has acquired the workforce under Regulation 5 proposes to harmonise terms and conditions of the acquired workforce with those of his own and thereby unilaterally change his terms and conditions after the transfer has taken place. Regulation 8 will catch this situation too. Even if the employer does not expressly dismiss employees on grounds of re-organisational change, he may constructively dismiss them if the change that takes place is a serious breach of contract. This dismissal will be in connection with the transfer (since but for the transfer the dismissal express or constructive would not have taken place). This dimissal is, in principle, therefore automatically unfair under Regulation 8(1). The usual employer's 'defence' in Regulation 8(2) will not apply because an 'economic, technical or organisational reason' for dismissal has to be one 'entailing changes in the workforce'. In this type of situation there is often no change in the workforce initiated by the employer, but simply a change in the terms and conditions that the workforce are obliged to observe.

Example:

In *Berriman* v *Delabole Slate Ltd* (1985) the employee was employed as a quarryman. His terms included a £100 guaranteed weekly wage. The quarrying business was owned by Mr Baker who in January 1983 transferred the undertaking to Delabole Slate. The employee went over to Delabole Slate with the transferred business by virtue of Regulation 5. This was not disputed. But he was then offered fresh terms by his employer at a reduced hourly rate which made him less per week and removed his guaranteed weekly wage. This was a breach of contract. He resigned and claimed constructive dismissal. The industrial tribunal found for the employer and held that although Regulation 8 applied, there was not an automatically unfair dismissal because there was an economic technical or organisational reason for the imposed harmonisation of terms and conditions. But the Court of Appeal held that the economic, technical or organisational reason had to entail a change in the workforce. In this case no change occurred in the workforce but merely in the terms and conditions enjoyed by the workforce. The dismissal was therefore automatically unfair.

It may therefore be very risky unilaterally to harmonise terms and conditions of employment following the purchase of a business if employees object to this. If you need to reorganise or harmonise terms and conditions following a business transfer, you should seek the agreement of the employees concerned.

10.78 Consultation with unions on business transfers

If there is a recognised trade union it has the right to information and consultation about the transfer as provided for under Regulation 10.

Regulation 10 states that long enough before a relevant transfer to enable consultation to take place between an employer of any affected employees and representatives of a recognised trade union, the employer has, under Regulation 10, to inform the representatives of:

(a) the fact that the relevant transfer is to take place, when approximately it is to take place and the reasons for it; and
(b) the legal economic and social implications of the transfer for the affected employees; and
(c) the measures which he envisages he will, in connection with the transfer, take in relation to those employees or if he envisages that no measures will be so taken, that fact.

'Affected employees' means any employee of the transferor or transferee (whether or not employed in the undertaking transferred) who may be affected by the transfer or measures taken in relation to it. If measures are envisaged, consultation has to take place. Compensation for breach of the provisions is a sum not exceeding two weeks' pay for each employee in question on application by the trade union concerned as the tribunal considers just and equitable having regard to the seriousness of the failure of the employer to comply with his duty. These obligations are similar to but somewhat less extensive than the consultation and information obligations that employers have to observe on multiple redundancies.

10.79 Statutory continuity on transfers and protection under the EP(C)A

Continuity of employment is also preserved on a business transfer not only by the Transfer Regulations but also by the EP(C)A in schedule 13, paragraph 17(2). This applies where a trade business or undertaking is transferred from one person to another. This is similar, in many respects, to the concept of a transfer of an undertaking under the Transfer Regulations and is also construed to mean a transfer of a business as a going concern and not an asset sale. However, there is no apparent limitation under paragraph 17(2) to transfers of commercial ventures only as there is under the Transfer Regulations.

There are also other cases not necessarily involving business transfers where transfer of employment does not entail a break in continuity of employment, for example, where there is a change of employer by Act of Parliament (paragraph 17(3)), where on the death of the employer the employee is taken into the employment of the personal representatives or trustees of the deceased (paragraph 17(4)), where there is a change in the partners, personal representatives or trustees who employ a person (paragraph 17(5)), where there is a transfer between associated employers (paragraph 18) and, finally, where there is a transfer between a local authority and a school and vice versa (paragraph 18(A)).

10.80 Redundancy liability on business transfers

As previously mentioned (10.32) a business sale theoretically involves a redundancy: the seller has no more work for the employee. But if the Transfer Regulations apply, it is to be stressed that there is no need for the redundancy provisions of the EP(C)A because there is deemed to be no dismissal at all, as employment is simply transferred. But in the odd area where the Transfer Regulations do not apply but there is nonetheless a business transfer (perhaps where there is a transfer of a non-commercial venture) section 94 of the EP(C)A applies.

It provides that if an employee is offered employment by a purchaser of a business and that offer is accepted, then provided the offer is made prior to the ending of the old employment and is taken up within four weeks of the ending of the old employment, there is no redundancy payments liability for the transferor and the employee's redundancy seniority is stored up for the purposes of any future claim against the transferee. If the employee declines an offer with the transferee, whether a payment is due depends on whether the offer is one of suitable alternative employment and whether the offer is unreasonably refused. Unless there is a suitable offer which is unreasonably refused, redundancy payments liability falls on the transferor. But if there is suitable alternative employment and an unreasonable refusal, the redundancy payments claim fails. There is a four week trial period where the new terms differ from the old much as in the case of the ordinary redundancy rules outside the context of business transfers (see 10.32).

10.81 Getting advice on business transfers

The Transfer Regulations and the provisions about continuity are highly complex and legal advice should be sought the moment you are considering buying or selling a business with a workforce. Lawyers will usually be able to draft indemnity clauses that might be appropriate for the parties themselves to apportion liability in these complicated cases by agreement.

11 Life assurance, pensions and permanent health insurance

by Vince Jerrard, Allied Dunbar Assurance

11.1 Introduction

Although the fine print can appear daunting, life assurance, pension and permanent health insurance policies are really just evidence of a contract between the policyholder and the company issuing the policy. In exchange for payment of a contribution or premium, the company promises to make one or more specified payments in certain defined circumstances.

Depending on the type of contract entered into, the payment from the company may be, for example, a lump sum on the death of an individual, an income in retirement for a pensioner or a replacement income for a person prevented from earning by reason of disability.

Despite the technical appearance of many of these policies (which is often due to complex tax rules offering relief on payment of premiums or benefits), it is useful to bear in mind the essential simplicity of the idea: payment of premiums (usually regular payments) to the company in exchange for the guarantee or expectation of payments back on the happening of some event in the future.

With life assurance contracts, there is one particular requirement which must be met before a policy can be effected. This is the need for an 'insurable interest'. Broadly, before a person can effect a life policy he must be able to demonstrate that the death of the person whose life is being insured will cause him financial loss. In addition the amount of the assurance must not exceed the amount of that loss.

Individuals have an automatic and unlimited insurable interest in their own life and the life of their spouse. In other cases an insurable interest must be demonstrated before a person can effect a policy on someone else's life (a 'life of another' policy).

This chapter, in Part One, looks at the contracts themselves and gives an outline of the rules which apply to them. Part Two then goes on to consider some basic uses of the contracts with reference to sole traders, partners and small companies.

Part one — The basics

Life Assurance:

11.2 Types of policy

There are three basic types of life assurance policy:

(1) whole of life policies;
(2) endowment policies;
(3) term policies.

Whole of life policies are protection-orientated policies which will pay the guaranteed sum assured on the death of the life assured, whenever death occurs.

As such, they are most appropriate where long term protection is needed, for example to meet the inheritance tax liability on an individual's death or to protect the family from the consequences of the death of the 'breadwinner'. Whole of life policies may, over the years, also acquire significant cash values, although they are not primarily investment vehicles.

Endowment policies pay a guaranteed sum on the death of the life assured during the policy term, or on survival to the end of the term.

Such policies provide a valuable mixture of protection and investment and are often used in conjunction with a mortgage to provide for a lump sum which will pay off the loan at the end of the mortgage term, or on the borrower's prior death.

Term assurance policies pay a guaranteed sum assured only if death occurs before the end of the term. They are for protection purposes only and usually provide no return to the policyholder if the life assured survives the policy term. Term assurance policies are usually the cheapest form of life assurance protection.

The cover provided by term assurances can be widened by use of renewal or conversion options. A renewal option will allow the policyholder to renew the policy at the end of the original term, without further evidence of health being required. A conversion option will

Life assurance, pensions and PHI 289

allow a policyholder to turn his protection into a whole of life assurance or an endowment policy, should his needs change. A convertible term assurance is particularly useful if the need is for life assurance protection for the whole of the individual's life but it is not possible to afford a whole of life policy at the time.

Term assurance policies can also be effected under some pensions legislation (see 11.13). These policies have the advantage of tax relief on the premiums paid.

A recent development in the UK is what is commonly called 'dread disease' protection. Dread disease cover is usually written as an additional benefit to a whole life, endowment or term policy and provides for payment of the sum assured on the life assured suffering one of the several specified diseases or events. Typical dread diseases and events are heart attack, stroke, cancer, major organ transplant, certain types of heart surgery and total permanent disability.

11.3 Traditional and unit linked policies

There are two bases on which policies are offered.

Under a traditional policy the life assurance company will estimate future mortality experience, investment return and company expenses. Using these factors the actuary will determine the premium rate for a given sum assured, both of which will then be guaranteed by the company. As the assumptions made by the company would, of necessity, be conservative, the premiums may often be higher than necessary. To counter this, traditional companies developed 'with profits' policies so that those contracts could share in the extra profits being made by the life company.

Extra profits are allocated to the policy by means of bonuses, either during the term of the policy (reversionary bonuses) or on the maturity of the policy (terminal bonuses). Once a bonus has been allocated it cannot be taken away, although the level of future bonuses is not guaranteed.

Unit linked policies are a more recent innovation introduced to the UK in the 1960s. They offer fewer guarantees to the policyholder. Premiums are invested in pooled investment funds maintained by the life company and the performance of the policy is linked directly to the actual performance of the fund. Freed from having to set up the policy with long term investment guarantees, the company can adopt an investment policy which is not unduly conservative and so can provide a fairer level of cover from the outset.

The direct linking of the policy and the investment performance of the underlying fund also mean that the policyholder is not subject to the discretion of the company in deciding the level of bonuses it should declare.

As unit linked policies do not carry the same guarantees as traditional contracts they will usually incorporate the system of reviews by which the company can ensure that the policy stays 'on track'. A review will compare the original assumptions about mortality, expenses and investment return with the actual performance achieved. Unfavourable performance will usually lead to an increase in premium and favourable performance to an increase in benefits.

11.4 Qualifying and non-qualifying policies

The other main method of categorising life assurance contracts is according to whether they are 'qualifying' or 'non-qualifying'.

This categorisation arises solely for the purpose of the taxation of the policy proceeds.

The qualifying rules are detailed and complex but, very broadly speaking, a qualifying policy will be a regular premium policy where the premiums remain fairly level and the sum assured satisfies certain minimum requirements to ensure that it provides a realistic level of life cover protection.

The Inland Revenue Press Releases which accompanied the 1989 Budget announced the government's intention for the Revenue to discuss with the industry the simplification of the life policy tax regime. At the time of writing these discussions are still proceeding and, although some technical changes are likely, the timing of their implementation and their full extent is not known. It is expected that any new regime will retain the current advantages of tax-free proceeds for certain 'favoured' policies, in much the same way as applies to qualifying policies at present, see 11.5–11.8 below.

11.5 The advantages of qualifying policies

Premiums paid under qualifying policies issued before 14 March 1984 attracted Life Assurance Premium Relief (LAPR). Qualifying policies issued before that date continue to benefit from LAPR provided that neither the benefits secured are increased nor the term extended after that date.

Subject to meeting the conditions for LAPR, relief was given at approximately half of the basic rate of income tax in force at the time, on up to the greater of $\frac{1}{6}$th of the policyholder's income or

£1,500 pa. Where LAPR is still available, it applies at the rate of 12½% for the year 1989/90.

The other key advantage of qualifying policies concerns the taxation of policy proceeds. In general, the proceeds from a qualifying policy will be entirely free of tax, provided premiums are kept up for at least 10 years (or three-quarters of the term of an endowment policy, if less).

11.6 Tax treatment of policies

While a policy is in force all the tax on income and gains attributable to the policy is the responsibility of the life company which pays tax on them according to its own corporate taxation position.

The life company

The Finance Act 1989 made some important changes to the taxation of life companies. The rate of tax paid by life companies on income and gains on policyholders' funds is reduced to 25% and a new formula is introduced to determine the proportions of the company's income and gains which should be allocated to policyholders and shareholders. Expenses in acquiring new business remain deductible by the life company but must be spread forward, and will be allowed over a period of seven years, subject to transitional relief until 1994.

The individual policyholder

The taxation of the individual in connection with income tax and life assurance policies revolves around the concept of the 'chargeable event'.

For non-qualifying policies the five chargeable events are:

(1) death of the life assured;
(2) the maturity of the policy;
(3) the total surrender of the policy;
(4) the assignment of the policy for money or money's worth (eg if the policy is sold or exchanged for something of value);
(5) excesses. (The system of 'excesses' allows partial surrenders each year of up to 5% of the premiums paid, on a cumulative basis, up to a total of 100% of the premiums paid. Only if the cumulative 5% 'allowances' are exceeded does a chargeable event occur.)

Chargeable events in the case of qualifying policies are the same as those listed above but with the following amendments:

(1) death or maturity will be a chargeable event only if the policy

has previously been paid-up within the first 10 years (or three-quarters of the term of an endowment policy, if less);
(2) a surrender or an assignment for money or money's worth or an excess will be a chargeable event only if it occurs before the expiry of 10 years (or three-quarters of the term of an endowment policy, if less) or if the policy was made paid-up within that period.

Assignments between spouses or as security for debts are not chargeable events.

As far as the policyholder is concerned, in most cases life assurance policies (qualifying or not) will be free of any personal liability to CGT. Only if the policy is in the hands of someone other than the original owner who gave consideration for it (ie who bought it or gave something of value for it) will proceeds be liable to CGT.

Company-owned policies

The Finance Act 1989, schedule 9, amends the position concerning post 13 March 1989 policies owned by companies, those assigned to secure a debt owned by a company and those held on trusts created by a company. Broadly speaking, such policies are treated as non-qualifying policies and so may give rise to a tax charge on death, maturity, surrender, part withdrawal or assignment for money or money's worth.

However, policies which would otherwise be qualifying endowments receive favourable treatment in respect of calculation of the chargeable gain, in certain circumstances where the policy has, throughout its term, been issued to secure a loan to the company which was used to purchase land (or construct, extend or improve buildings) used for the purposes of the company's trade.

11.7 Gain on the happening of a chargeable event

Where a chargeable event occurs the gain arising on the event must be computed. The calculation depends on the nature of the event but, broadly speaking, it is the investment profit made under the policy, taking into account previous capital benefits enjoyed and the total premiums paid.

Any extra amount received by way of death benefit is mortality profit and would not be included in the gain for tax purposes.

The rules for calculating the gain as a result of an excess following a withdrawal or partial surrender are somewhat different and take into account the 5% allowable withdrawals.

The favourable treatment for company policies referred to in the previous section is that the amount of the loan (or the lowest amount of the loan during the policy term) is used in place of the sum of total premiums paid when calculating the chargeable gain. Thus, if the loan has remained constant during the policy term and the policy proceeds do not exceed the loan, there will be no chargeable gain.

11.8 Taxing gains on chargeable events

The circumstances under which tax is liable on a gain are as follows:

(1) Gains made on life policies do not give rise to a tax liability at the basic rate of income tax. Accordingly, if the taxpayer's income, including the gain, does not fall into the higher rate tax band there will be no income tax charge on the gain.
(2) The gain made on the life policy is liable to the higher rate of income tax, where applicable.
(3) As the gain will have accrued over the life of the policy, it would be rather harsh to treat the total gain as the taxpayer's income in the year of receipt. This could push him into the higher rate tax band in that year despite a relatively low income level. Therefore, a measure of relief is afforded by a process known as 'top-slicing'. This involves calculating the rate of tax appropriate to a part of the total gain (a 'slice') and then applying that rate of tax to the whole of the gain.
(4) The taxpayer is usually the policyholder. Exceptions to this are that if the policy is held on trust the charge falls upon the settlor (ie the person who established the trust); if the policy is owned, or held as security for a debt owed by a company, the amount of the gain is treated as part of the company's Schedule D Case VI income (and top-slicing relief does not apply).

Further details of the qualifying rules and taxation of life policies can be found in the *Allied Dunbar Tax Guide*.

Pensions

11.9 Introduction

Pensions are usually regarded as one of the most attractive investments available. Within limits, contributions are deductible at the highest rate of tax paid by the contributor; the underlying pension funds grow free of UK taxes on income and gains; and in most the pension plan can provide a tax-free cash lump sum to the planholder together with a retirement income in 'old age'.

In recent years the pensions legislation in the UK has undergone substantial reform and development. The Social Security Act 1986 created the framework for the new 'Personal Pensions' and 'Free-Standing Additional Voluntary Contribution Schemes'; reduced the benefits provided by the State Earnings Related Pensions Scheme (SERPS); increased the scope for individuals to contract out of SERPS; and removed the ability of Occupational Pension Schemes to require compulsory membership for employees.

The legislation also allowed, for the first time, banks, building societies and unit trust groups to offer pension plans.

The Finance (No 2) Act 1987 provided much of the necessary tax legislation to support these developments but the Finance Acts of 1988 and 1989 have made significant amendments to the new regime as originally introduced.

11.10 The State pension scheme

The benefit the State provides to those in retirement falls into two main parts: the basic retirement pension and the supplementary earnings related pension.

Everyone is entitled to the basic retirement pension (payable at state retirement age; 65 for males, 60 for females), subject to payment of the necessary National Insurance contributions. For a married man whose earnings have been at the national average level throughout his working life, the State will provide a basic pension of approximately one-third of his final earnings level.

Note that recent European case law, in requiring the UK to extend unfair dismissal and sex discrimination rights to women up to the age of 65, has not affected state retirement ages or pension entitlement.

SERPS was introduced in April 1978 to provide an additional state pension which is based on earnings (within certain limits) rather than the flat benefit provided by the retirement pension. SERPS also provides a widow's benefit if a husband dies after retirement and also, in certain circumstances, if he dies before retirement.

SERPS is funded by the higher rate National Insurance contributions payable by both employers and employees. The self-employed do not contribute towards, or benefit from, SERPS.

In recent years the State pension scheme has come under pressure from increases in life expectancy and large numbers of retired people in the population. These concerns have led the Government to reduce the benefits under SERPS so that only those reaching state pension

Life assurance, pensions and PHI

age (65 for males, 60 for females) in the years 1998 and 1999 will receive the original maximum benefits.

Those reaching state retirement age in or after the year 2010 will receive a pension of only 20% of their relevant earnings, instead of the 25% originally intended, and the relevant earnings to be taken into account will be the average of lifetime earnings and not the best 20 years of earnings, as was the original rule for SERPS.

A sliding scale will operate for those retiring between the years 2000 and 2010.

11.11 Contracting-in and contracting-out

Those who are participating in SERPS (ie employees earning more than the lower threshold for standard rate National Insurance contributions) are said to be 'contracted in' to SERPS. Since SERPS was introduced it has been possible to opt out of the scheme (referred to as 'contracting-out') in which case National Insurance contributions are reduced for both the employer and employee but with the loss of SERPS benefits.

The original rules only permitted contracting-out through an Occupational Pension Scheme established by an employer, and only where that scheme provided certain guaranteed pension benefits which were broadly equivalent to the SERPS entitlement the employee was giving up.

The new legislation made significant changes to these rules to encourage contracting-out. In particular:

(1) contracting-out can be achieved on a 'money purchase' basis so that contributions can be accumulated in a fund and used to buy pension benefits at retirement, without guaranteeing a minimum level for those benefits;
(2) individuals will be able to take their own decision on whether or not to contract out of SERPS, quite independently of the status of their employer's scheme, or in the total absence of such a scheme;
(3) an additional 2% (of earnings between the lower and upper National Insurance contribution limits) incentive payment is made by the DHSS where an individual contracts-out for the first time (or where he has been in a contracted out scheme for less than two years). The incentive was introduced in the tax year 1987/8 and was available for up to six years, but 'back dating' is no longer possible to obtain the incentive for previous tax years.

Contracting-out is now possible through an Occupational Scheme (as before) or through a Free-Standing Additional Voluntary Contribution Scheme (FSAVC) used by an employee in conjunction with an Occupational Scheme, or a Personal Pension Plan (PPP) used by an employee not in an Occupational Scheme or a member of a contracted-in occupational scheme.

With FSAVC Schemes and PPPs the individual and the employer will continue to make full National Insurance (NI) contributions, the NI reduction being paid by the DHSS direct to the relevant pension plan. Contracting-out through an Occupational Scheme will mean lower National Insurance contributions for employer and employee but the employer is required to make payment of the NI reduction to the Occupational Scheme.

If the individual is contracting-out on a money-purchase basis these NI reductions, plus the 2% incentive where appropriate, are known as 'protected rights contributions' and the fund built up from them must be used to purchase protected rights benefits. It is these benefits which, in effect, replace the SERPS being lost through contracting-out and they are treated more restrictively than benefits built up through the employer's or employee's additional contributions. For example, a protected rights pension cannot commence before state retirement age and cannot be commuted for cash.

Whether contracting-out of SERPS is advisable is a decision to be taken by each employee according to his or her personal circumstances. If the incentive is available contracting-out should be considered in 1989/90 by those aged up to 52 (males) and 45 (females). In other cases the cut-off ages are approximately 47 and 40 respectively.

11.12 Occupational pension schemes

These are schemes sponsored by an employer and to which the employer must make a contribution.

Schemes are established on one of two bases: either money-purchase or final salary (often called Defined Benefit Schemes).

With Defined Benefit Schemes the employee is guaranteed a level of pension benefit based on a fraction (typically 1/60th or 1/80th) of his final salary, multiplied by the number of years' pensionable service. A money-purchase scheme will not carry a guarantee of a specific level of pension but will invest the contributions and use the accumulated fund to provide whatever pension can be purchased with the fund, at retirement.

Life assurance, pensions and PHI

To be tax efficient an Occupational Pension Scheme should be approved by the Superannuation Funds Office (SFO) which is a branch of the Inland Revenue.

'Approval' will prevent contributions paid by the employer being taxed in the employee's hands but the preferable status of 'exempt approval' offers significant further benefits. An exempt approved scheme will be able to invest in a fund free of all UK income and capital taxes; the employee will be able to claim tax relief on contributions he makes to the scheme; and employers' contributions will be deductible business expenses.

Contributions

There are no specific limits on the amount of contributions which can be paid into an Occupational Scheme but monitoring is necessary to ensure that the scheme does not become 'over-funded', ie contributions may have to be limited if projected funds in the scheme are likely to exceed the amount necessary to meet its obligations.

Employees may make personal contributions (of up to 15% of remuneration) to the scheme. This may be done on a voluntary basis (by way of Additional Voluntary Contributions) but the scheme may require some personal contribution from the employee as a condition of membership.

Benefits

To be exempt approved, the scheme must be set up under irrevocable trust for the sole purpose of providing 'relevant benefits'. These are benefits such as an income in retirement, the option to commute part of that income for a lump sum, an income for the employee's widow etc. As a result of the generous tax benefits available to such schemes, there are strict limits on the benefits which may be provided. The limits were further tightened by the Finance (No 2) Act 1987. The application of the new limits is complex, but, in general, they apply to post 17 March 1987 scheme members. For example, the maximum pension which can be provided to the scheme member is usually two-thirds of final remuneration and the minimum period of service required to achieve this level of benefits is now 20 years (previously the maximum benefits could be given after only 10 years' service).

An employee's pension can be commuted for a lump sum, also based on final salary and years of service. The maximum lump sum for a post 17 March 1987 member is one and a half times final salary but is limited to £150,000. The maximum final salary that can be taken into account in the calculation is £100,000. Prior to the Finance (No 2) Act 1987, the only limit was that of one and a half times final salary.

The Finance Act 1989 has introduced new rules for members of schemes established on or after 14 March 1989 and members joining older schemes after 31 May 1989. For such members no benefits can be provided in respect of any remuneration in excess of £60,000 per annum (which figure will be indexed in future years in line with the RPI). This remuneration 'cap' restricts funding of such schemes (by the employer and by the employees' personal contributions) as well as payment of the various benefits the scheme can provide.

Schemes may also provide a lump sum of up to four times final remuneration (capped where necessary) on the death, in service, of the employee. This can be paid together with a refund of any personal contributions paid by the employer. It is usually possible to pay the death benefits free of inheritance tax.

It is possible to contract out of SERPS through an Occupational Scheme but the availability of contracting-out is largely in the hands of the employer.

The new FSAVC Schemes (see 11.13 below) can be structured to enable an Occupational Scheme member to contract out on an individual basis. A contracted-in occupational scheme member is also able to contract out through a Personal Pension Plan (providing no contributions other than the NI rebates, appropriate tax relief and incentive payments are paid to the Plan). In practice, few, if any, FSAVC schemes offer the facility to contract out, the personal pension plan route being more favourable to the majority of individuals.

Top-up occupational schemes

The Finance Act 1989 introduces the concept of unapproved top-up occupational pension schemes. These schemes will, for example, allow employers to provide highly-paid employees with pension benefits in respect of salary which exceeds the earnings cap introduced in the Act, and to provide more than the usual maximum pension benefits. However, these top-up arrangements receive few tax benefits and it is not yet clear whether they will prove popular.

11.13 Personal pensions

Prior to October 1987 the main personal plan was the Retirement Annuity Contract (also called Section 226 Plans, a reference to the legislation giving them tax effect). In October 1987 FSAVC schemes were introduced, enabling an occupational scheme member to effect his own top-up pension as an alternative to making personal voluntary contributions to the employer's scheme. In July 1988 the s 226 plans were replaced by the new Personal Pension Plans.

Life assurance, pensions and PHI

The wider scope of the PPPs and the ability of individual employees to use them to contract out of SERPS means that the individual has never before had such a wide choice of pension planning opportunities.

(1) *Retirement annuity contracts*

Although it has not been possible to effect a Retirement Annuity Contract since 30 June 1988, plans in force by that date are allowed to continue.

An individual was eligible for one of these plans if he had Relevant Earnings. These are earnings which do not carry pension rights, eg the earnings of sole traders, the self-employed, partners and employees in non-pensionable employment. Controlling directors of investment companies are excluded from eligibility.

Unlike Occupational Schemes, these 'Section 226' contracts are not controlled by reference to the maximum benefits which can be provided; rather, restrictions are applied to the amount of contributions which can be made. The contribution limit is $17\frac{1}{2}\%$ of net relevant earnings, with larger percentages applicable for those over 50. Net relevant earnings (NRE) are, broadly speaking, an individual's earnings after deduction of any business expenses. Contributions made to these plans up to the limits are fully tax-deductible and the funds in which the plans invest are free of all UK income and capital taxes.

The plans are issued on a money-purchase basis, the fund accumulated at retirement being used to provide a lifetime annuity for the planholder. The planholder need not actually retire in order to take the benefits from these plans but the benefits must be paid between the ages of 60 and 75 (earlier for some specified occupations).

The annuity paid can be in various different forms, guaranteed or not, flat rate or increasing etc. If the planholder dies before taking his annuity a lump sum can be paid, not exceeding the contributions made to the plan plus a reasonable amount of interest or bonuses. Alternatively, an annuity can be paid to the individual's widow or dependants.

Annuities can also be effected on a 'joint life basis' for the planholder and spouse, so that the annuity payments will continue until the death of the surviving spouse.

The annuity is treated as earned income when it is paid, and the planholder can elect to commute part of his annuity at retirement.

This commutation permits a maximum lump sum of three times the remaining annual annuity, but limited to a £150,000 lump sum per contract for contracts entered into on or after 17 March 1987.

In addition to pension benefits, such plans can provide life assurance protection. The maximum contribution which can be used to provide life cover is 5% of NRE (any such contribution is taken into account in determining the overall contribution limit applicable to the individual).

Death benefits payable under such plans can be assigned or put in trust so that payments of benefits on death can be arranged in a way effective for inheritance tax planning.

If, in any year, an individual pays less in contributions to a plan than would be permitted, it is possible to carry forward the shortfall in contributions for up to six years. It is also possible to 'carry back' a contribution to the previous tax year (and sometimes the year before that).

(2) *Personal pension plans*

These plans were introduced on 1 July 1988, having been postponed from the original introduction date of 4 January 1988.

In many ways PPPs are more flexible than the Section 226 contracts which they replace. For example, employers may make contributions to an employee's PPP; an 'appropriate' PPP can be used by employees to contract out of SERPS; benefits can be taken between the ages of 50 and 75 (again, earlier for some specified occupations). Employees' contributions to PPPs are payable net of basic rate income tax under the Pension Relief at Source (PRAS) rules.

PPPs are, like Section 226 contracts, money-purchase arrangements with controls on the maximum contributions which can be made. Where an employer contributes to an employee's PPP, the employer's contributions must be taken into account in determining the employee's maximum permissible contributions.

For the tax year 1989/90, and subsequently, the contribution limits for PPPs are increased for those aged over 35. However, PPPs are now subject to a similar income cap to that referred to in relation to occupational pension schemes (see 11.12) and earnings over the appropriate limit must be ignored in calculating entitlement to pay contributions.

The benefits provided by a PPP are, again, very similar to those available under a Section 226 plan but the tax-free cash which can be taken is a maximum of 25% of the fund.

FSAVC Schemes are also 'personal' pensions in that they can be effected without the consent and participation of the employer (and administrative improvements to the rules have been made in the Finance Act 1989 which should make establishing such a plan very simple for those wishing to contribute up to £200 per month). In spite of this, they also have similarities to Occupational Schemes in that they share the same source of tax legislation and the benefits from any FSAVC Scheme must be taken into account in determining the benefits payable under the Occupational Scheme, the maximum benefit rules applying to the aggregate benefits under the two schemes.

11.14 Moving between different types of pension arrangement

If a self-employed individual effects a PPP but then moves into employment, for example a sole trader incorporating his business, he can continue with his PPP. The same will be true with an employee who has a PPP and moves into self-employment.

In some cases, however, it is not possible to continue with the same pension plan, for example an employee who is a member of an Occupational Scheme cannot remain in that scheme if he becomes self-employed. Similarly, if a person with a PPP joins an employer's Occupational Scheme he cannot continue to pay contributions into the PPP if he has no continuing source of relevant earnings.

In those cases where a change of status affects pension planning it is usually possible for a transfer payment to be made from one scheme to another. Many companies offer such transfers on preferential terms, particularly where the individual is moving between the occupational and personal pension regimes.

Further details of pension plans and planning can be found in the *Allied Dunbar Pension Guide*.

Permanent Health Insurance:

11.15 Introduction

Permanent Health Insurance (PHI) policies are a means of providing a replacement income if an individual is unable to work through illness or disability.

Policies will usually be available to those aged between 16 and 60 and cover will usually end no later than the normal retirement date for the individual's occupation.

In the event of sickness or disability the policy will usually provide for a deferment period and payment of benefits will only commence at the end of this period. Deferment periods may be between one month and one year (usually selected by the policyholder at outset) and are valuable to the company offering the policy because they will reduce the number of short term claims they will have to meet. The longer the deferment period the cheaper the policy will be. In some cases, especially those occupations where short term illnesses are common (eg sportsmen) the company will select the period.

The benefits payable under the policy will usually be limited to approximately 75% of the individual's pre-claim earnings, often taking into account any benefits received from the State and any other policy during the period of claim. Limiting the maximum benefit in this way provides the incentive to the individual to return to work as soon as possible.

Benefits paid by such policies are usually taxable as unearned income in the individual's hands but the Inland Revenue allow a 'tax holiday' during which payments are not taxed. The tax holiday runs until benefits have been paid for a complete tax year, eg if payment of benefits commenced in May 1989, payments would not become taxable until April 1991; ie a tax holiday of 23 months in that case.

One of the most important things about PHI policies is the definition of 'disability' which is used in the policy. Under some policies a person will not be treated as being disabled if he can do any part of his former job. Others may not treat a person as disabled if he is capable of doing some other job for which he is reasonably suited, even if he is completely unable to do his previous job.

PHI plans are usually sold on a guaranteed basis so that premiums are fixed during the life of the plan. More recently some companies have produced unit-linked PHI policies under which premium rates can be reviewed in the light of actual performance of the underlying investments, expenses and morbidity experience (morbidity is the risk of a person becoming disabled).

The most flexible PHI policies will allow the level of benefit to be increased as salary increases and will also give the policyholder the option of paying a higher contribution in exchange for the disability income which will increase to offer protection against inflation during the period of disability.

Part two — The uses

In this second part of the chapter the uses of life assurance, pensions and permanent health insurance are considered with particular emphasis on the business needs of sole traders, partners and small companies.

The chapter does not consider more personal uses of life assurance but it is most important that they are not overlooked.

Life assurance is a unique product in the paying of a lump sum on the death of an individual at some unknown time in the future. As such it plays a vital role in protection of the family on the death of the breadwinner and loss of the family's income. The inclusion of 'dead disease' benefits can also be extremely beneficial as serious illness of a breadwinner can have just as severe an impact as his or her death.

Although most people can see the need for life assurance on the life of the family breadwinner, it should not be forgotten that many men are only able to go out and earn an income because their wives are devoting themselves to looking after children and the family home. The death or serious illness of a non-earning wife can also cause major financial difficulties such as the need for boarding school fees, a cleaner, a nanny — perhaps even the need for the surviving spouse to give up work to look after the family.

So-called 'wife assurance' should be considered in all family situations.

Life assurance is also important in inheritance tax planning, being able to provide a fund from which the liability may be met, thus preserving the deceased's estate intact.

Also not covered in this chapter is the very important use of life assurance as a means of investment, even though qualifying endowment policies and single premium savings bonds may have advantages for the individual investor and, in some cases, corporate investment.

Sole traders:

11.16 Life assurance

(1) *Keyman assurance – loss of profits*

Although the sole trader himself will usually be the driving force behind the profitability of the business, there may be cases in which an employee is also essential to the well-being of the undertaking. Where the death or disability of such a key person would weaken the profitability of the business or reduce its capital value as a going concern, the owner of the business should consider effecting a life policy (with dread disease benefit) on the life of the keyman. The status of the individual will usually satisfy the requirement for an insurable interest, providing this sum assured is reasonable in view of the keyman's value to the business.

Receipt of the policy proceeds on the death or disability of the life assured will not normally constitute a chargeable event, and so will not trigger a tax charge on the policy, if the policy is a qualifying policy, but it is important to consider whether the policy is an asset owned by the sole trader personally or is a business asset. This will determine the ultimate tax treatment of both the premiums paid and the sums received.

If the policy is a business asset contributions paid to it, in general, will be tax-deductible provided:

(a) the policy is a short-term assurance; and
(b) the insurance is intended to meet the loss of profit resulting from the employee's death; and
(c) the sole relationship between the policyholder and the life assured is that of employer and employee.

These principles were laid down in a statement in 1944 by the then Chancellor of the Exchequer Sir John Anderson. In general, the first requirement is an indication that premiums paid on a policy with a term of more than five years will not be tax-deductible.

If premiums are tax-deductible, this usually means that the policy proceeds will, in turn, be taxable as a trading receipt of the business. If the premiums do not attract tax relief, usually the proceeds will be received as a tax-free capital sum. The tax-free nature of the receipts in such cases is not guaranteed but it is normal Revenue practice. In cases of doubt it may be wise to contact the local Inspector of Taxes.

(2) *Security for loans*

If a sole trader has to borrow money for business purposes, the lender may often require assignment of a life policy on the sole trader as security. The policy should ensure that such loans are repaid on the death of the sole trader.

Life assurance, pensions and PHI

Premiums are unlikely to be tax-deductible as a business expense because the purpose of the plan will be to satisfy a capital liability so that the premiums are not an income expense at all.

(3) *Insurance for redundancy payments*

If a sole trader's business ceases on his death, his personal representatives are liable for making redundancy payments to eligible employees (see 10.25). The amount of any payment will depend on various factors, such as salary level and length of service, but for a sole trader employing several staff, such payments could be a significant burden on his estate.

11.17 Pensions

(1) *For the sole trader*

Pension provision for a sole trader must be through a Personal Pension Plan (PPP) or a Section 226 contract if effected prior to 1 July 1988.

As a sole trader is not an employee, Occupational Pension Schemes are not available and the question of contracting-out of SERPS does not arise.

It should be remembered that the individual can effect life assurance protection through a PPP. This can provide very cheap term assurance cover, because the premiums are tax-deductible, but paying for life cover in this way does lead to a reduction in the contributions which are going towards pension benefits.

(2) *For his employees*

For employees of a sole trader the choice is wider. The employer could establish an Occupational Scheme for his staff or, in the absence of an employer's scheme, the employees could effect PPPs for themselves.

Most sole traders will not want to assume the responsibility of establishing and running an Occupational Pension Scheme but may well be able to make contributions to their employees' PPPs. Some pension providers will offer a group PPP arrangement which will be particularly suitable in these circumstances. Members of staff would still own individual plans but some aspects of the administration will be centralised.

If the employer does decide to set up an Occupational Scheme for his employees, a money-purchase arrangement is likely to be preferable because of the absence of long term guarantees which have to be met by the employer.

Employees should consider whether contracting-out of SERPS will be beneficial to them. This can be effected in a variety of ways: the employer may offer contracting-out under the main Occupational Scheme; those in a contracted in Occupational Scheme may be able to contract out of SERPS by means of a FSAVC Scheme (or, more likely, a PPP in the restricted form described at 11.12); or the PPPs taken out by those not in the Occupational Scheme can be used to contract out on an individual basis.

If the sole trader's spouse is employed in the business, he or she is like any other employee as far as pension planning opportunities are concerned but, of course, may be treated more favourably by the employer.

(3) *For the sole trader's spouse*

If the spouse is not employed in the business, consideration should be given as to whether this could be done, especially if the sole trader's wife is not otherwise employed.

The salary paid by the sole trader is deductible at his top rate of tax and, if it is less than the wife's earned income relief and the lower rate for National Insurance contributions, no income tax or National Insurance contributions will have to be made by either husband or wife in respect of that salary. Of course, it must be possible to justify the employment and the salary being paid by reference to the duties undertaken by the wife.

Once the wife is employed in this way, she could contribute to a PPP, or an Occupational Scheme could be set up for her by her husband. Although the Occupational Scheme may be a little more expensive to run and, if it is an insurance company scheme, may have higher minimum contribution levels, it will usually offer the chance to provide higher pension benefits for the wife than would a PPP, where the contribution is limited to a percentage of a salary.

In order to obtain the benefit of tax relief through PPP contributions, the wife should earn more than her tax allowances but this could lead to payment of National Insurance. In such cases, it may be better for the husband, as employer, to make the PPP contributions for her.

11.18 Permanent Health Insurance

(1) *For the sole trader*

It will often be the case that if the sole trader is not able to work, the business will soon become unprofitable. Although state benefits do exist (the sickness and invalidity benefits) they are designed more to avoid poverty than to maintain an individual's standard of living. Accordingly, a PHI policy is one of the first things which the sole trader should consider.

(2) *For his employees*

Employees of a sole trader will usually be entitled to the same state benefits (with the addition of Statutory Sick Pay) but may be treated more favourably under the terms of their contract of employment.

If the employer has undertaken to maintain the full, or a proportion of, salary during periods of sickness, he should consider effecting a PHI policy on the life of the employee, so as to 're-insure' the liability for continuing salary. Benefit received from the policy by the employer would be taxable as a trading receipt but normally deductible as a trading expense when paid to the employee. There would be no 'tax holiday' on the payments in these circumstances.

Even if the employer has not agreed to maintain salary payments beyond that required by statute, he may still consider effecting a PHI policy on key employees to maintain the profitability of the business during their absence from work.

Partners:

11.19 Life assurance

The majority of the uses of life assurance applicable to sole traders also apply to partners. Perhaps the main difference with partnerships is that they are more likely to involve key people and that consideration should be given to the future of the partnership on the death of one of the partners.

Quite apart from loss of the earning potential of a deceased partner, the surviving partners may, subject to the provisions of the Partnership Deed, be faced with having to pay the beneficiaries the value of the deceased's partnership share. For a partnership which has made no provision, this burden can be acute and might necessitate expensive borrowing or even the sale of vital partnership assets.

Life assurance can help in these circumstances. The partners can set up an arrangement so that each of them has life cover which will be paid to the survivors on his death. The survivors then have the funds to pay the deceased partner's share to his heirs, without affecting other aspects of the viability of the business.

This partnership assurance arrangement may be achieved by each partner owning a life assurance policy on the life of every other partner but this can be unwieldy and expensive where there are more than three or four partners. An alternative is for each partner to effect a policy on his own life and write it in trust for the benefit of the other partners.

Both sorts of arrangement should be accompanied by a cross-option agreement by which the surviving partners can compel the personal representatives of the deceased to sell the deceased's partnership share to them and vice versa. The cross-option agreement can also contain further provisions to deal with the valuation of the partnership share, time for payment, the destination of surplus policy proceeds and payment of additional capital, should the policy proceeds be insufficient.

A policy incorporating dread disease benefits can also be particularly useful in partnership arrangements where the serious illness of a partner can have effects equally severe as his or her death.

11.20 Pensions

(1) *For the partners*

> Again, the pension planning routes available to partners are the same as those available to the sole trader, ie a PPP from 1 July 1988 or a Section 226 contract before that time.
>
> The life cover which can be provided under such pension arrangements can be extremely useful for partnership assurance planning as it provides tax relief on the life cover contributions, at the individual's top rate of income tax.
>
> However, these plans are term assurances which must end no later than the individual's 75th birthday although most life companies will give favourable consideration to a partner applying for a new life policy on the termination of life cover under a pension scheme with that same office.

(2) *For their employees*

For partnership employees the position is, again, the same as for employees of a sole trader and the comments made there also apply to spouses of the partners who are employed by the partnership.

11.21 Permanent Health Insurance

Once again, partners are in much the same position as sole traders when considering PHI policies. A partnership may be better placed to absorb the loss of profits resulting from a partner's long term absence through injury or illness but a PHI policy can secure the position still further. A policy could be taken out by each partner for his own benefit with the Partnership Deed providing for a corresponding reduction in that partner's share of profits for the period of absence. Alternatively, policies could be owned by all the partners as partnership assets so as to replace the income at the partnership level. The former method has the advantage of the availability of a tax holiday and of putting this provision into the hands of each individual.

Companies:

11.22 Life assurance

(1) *Keyman assurance*

Keyman assurance is particularly important for small companies where, for example, the Managing Director, Sales Director etc may be fundamental to the profitability and continuance of the business.

Frequently, small companies effecting keyman policies will not be able to obtain tax relief on the premiums but will not be taxed on the proceeds. This is because the keyman being insured will have a material interest in the company so that the relationship between the life assured and the policyholder will not be only that of employee and employer (11.16(1)).

In the absence of such an interest in the company on the part of the keyman, deductibility of premiums might be achieved if the policy is a short term assurance. A policy of this nature might be appropriate in the early days of the company's existence (for example, where it is expected that the company will grow sufficiently over the next five years so as to absorb the loss of the keyman after that time).

Although keyman policies are caught by the new rules described in 11.6, the high level of life cover being provided will usually mean that any investment profit under the policy will be small, so that the tax charge on a chargeable event will not cause undue difficulties.

(2) *Loan protection and repayment*

A form of keyman assurance might also be appropriate where the company is obtaining a loan and the lender requires a life policy on a key executive by way of additional security.

Even where the lender has not required a life policy as security for a loan, life assurance has a key role to play in respect of company borrowings. Although the company will usually be the borrower, it is common for lenders to require a personal guarantee from one or more directors to ensure repayment of any loan (1.3).

By having to give a personal guarantee the director is losing one of the main benefits of trading through a company — that of limited personal liability.

Bearing in mind that the death of a key person in the company organisation may well precipitate profitability difficulties and so make a calling in of the loan more likely, this is another good reason to effect life assurance on the lives of key individuals. Receipt of the policy proceeds will enable the company to repay its borrowings and so free the personal estate of the guarantor from the potential liability.

Repayment of loans should also be considered in respect of any company overdraft which could be called in on the death of a key person and in relation to directors' loan accounts where the director's estate may require repayment on the director's death.

Note that the new rules described in 11.6 will mean that policies effected after 13 March 1989 (or older policies which are varied after that date to increase their benefits or extend their term) are treated as if they were non-qualifying and may give rise to a chargeable gain unless they are qualifying endowments and have been used to secure specific types of borrowing.

(3) *Key shareholder assurance*

Another aspect of small companies which needs to be considered is that of transfer of shares on the death of one of the shareholders. In many cases small companies will not be declaring dividends on the shares, but those involved in the running of the company will be drawing benefits by way of salary and director's fees. On the death of a director, those inheriting the deceased's shares may find that they have a minority shareholding in the company. The shares may be producing no dividends and may be insufficient to enable the new shareholder to become a director. In such a case the shares may be virtually unsaleable except to the other shareholders who may be able to use their position to depress the value of the shares.

Although in exceptional cases minority shareholders may have some rights against an oppressive majority under company law (5.63), the problem can be tackled by life assurance arrangements in at least two specific ways.

The company could effect life policies on the individual shareholders so that, on the death of a shareholder, it will receive a capital sum in order to buy the shares from the deceased's heirs. It has only been possible for companies to buy their own shares since 1982. An agreement can be entered into between the shareholders and the company itself in which various questions can be addressed, for example, options can be given to both sides to require a sale or purchase of the shares and to determine the method of calculating a fair price for them.

However, the deceased's personal representatives may have difficulty in enforcing their option to require the company to buy the deceased's shares in some circumstances, eg where the purchase price is to come out of the company's capital. In addition, there are various legal procedures to be gone through before an agreement to buy a company's own shares can be set up and further clearances from the Inland Revenue need to be obtained when the purchase is made to ensure there are no adverse tax consequences.

An alternative and relatively simple method of arranging a share purchase scheme is to establish an arrangement similar to that used for partnership assurance (11.19). In this way each shareholder would effect a policy on the life of each of the others, or each would effect a policy on his own life and put it in trust for the benefit of the other shareholders. The life policies will be accompanied by a cross-option agreement which would enable both the deceased's personal representatives and the surviving shareholders to enforce the sale and purchase of the deceased's shares and would tackle such questions as valuation of the shares etc.

11.23 Pensions

(1) *For the directors and other top executives*

The directors of the company may plan for their own pension benefits through an Occupational Scheme or a PPP. In most cases the directors and key executives will join a company Occupational Scheme as this will enable them to maximise their pension benefits in a tax-efficient way.

PPPs with direct contributions from the company, will also be efficient for the purposes of income tax and National Insurance contributions, but the limit on the PPP contributions which can be made will usually favour the choice of an Occupational Scheme.

Life assurance protection can be provided under either type of scheme. Usually it is possible to provide a higher sum assured under a PPP (where the maximum life cover contribution is 5% of net relevant earnings) than under an Occupational Scheme where the maximum sum assured is four times' salary. Despite this, the Occupational Scheme will often be preferable as the provision of life assurance under the PPP will reduce the maximum amount which can be paid towards the pension benefits.

(2) *For employees*

For other employees the choices are very much the same as for the employees of sole traders and partners. If the company does not want to make pension provision for its staff through an occupational scheme, they will be able to plan for themselves by effecting PPPs (or Section 226 contracts if effected before July 1988). The company may choose to make contributions to its employees' PPPs. A group PPP arrangement could be 'sponsored' by the company if it wishes to indicate a greater commitment to the provision of pensions for its employees.

(3) *For spouses of the directors*

The comments made in 11.17 apply equally to employment of, and pensions for, spouses of directors and top executives of small companies.

11.24 Permanent Health Insurance

As with sole traders and partnerships, the smaller the company the more vulnerable it will be to the long term absence of a key individual. The company may effect PHI policies on its directors and top executives either to enable the company to maintain payment of salary or to cushion the company itself from the possible loss of income due to the absence of the key person. The question of whether premiums paid on such a policy are tax deductible for the company is not entirely clear.

Despite the long term nature of the policy it seems likely that premiums paid by a company on a PHI policy on an employee, to enable the company to maintain payment of salary to the employee during a period of disability, should be tax-deductible. Certainly it would appear that the receipt of payment by the company from the policy would be taxable (although matched by tax relief on the payment of the salary). In cases of doubt, companies should consult their local Inspector of Taxes.

12 The business and the outsider

Part A Contract law

12.1 Introduction

Contracts are concluded between individuals every day, when shopping, when borrowing money, when eating out in a restaurant or buying a car. Small wonder, then, that a business will conclude many contracts during the course of its life. As the stakes are often much higher in business contracts it can be useful to be aware of the basics of contract law. The usual reminder is made here that Scottish law may differ (in parts considerably) from the discussion here, which is based on English law.

12.2 Components of a contract

Not all agreements are binding. A legally binding contract has to contain at least three elements, viz:

(1) an intention to create legal relations
(2) a valid offer and acceptance
(3) consideration.

These are expanded on in turn below. It is important to note that if any is absent, there is no contract.

12.3 Intention to create legal relations

If A and B decide to meet in a public house one evening for a drink there may well be an agreement to do so; but the parties would be surprised if you told them that if either failed to show up, the other could sue for damages for breach of contract. In fact their agreement could not be sued upon. This is because the parties, in all likelihood, had not contemplated that there would be any legal consequences if their agreement were broken. In other words, there was no intention to create legal relations.

12.4 Presumptions about legal enforceability

There exist legal presumptions about intention to create legal relations. First, in relation to *social and domestic* arrangements, it is *presumed* an agreement is *not* legally binding. As to arrangements in a *commercial* context it is *presumed* that the agreement *is* legally binding. Most contracts concluded by businesses will, therefore, be presumed to be legally binding.

One notable exception is a collective agreement between a firm and a trade union, which is governed by a special rule. By virtue of section 18 of the Trade Union and Labour Relations Act 1974 it is provided that in relation to collective agreements entered into after 1974, and before 1971, there is a presumption that a collective agreement is not legally enforceable unless it is in writing, and it contains a provision which states that the parties intend that the agreement shall be enforceable. (The reverse applied between 1971 and 1974 when the Industrial Relations Act 1971 governed the position.)

Finally, the presumptions about intention to create legal relations are rebuttable. Even an agreement between two businesses (which would ordinarily be a binding contract) could be expressed to be 'binding in honour only' and not legally binding.

Examples

In *Rose and Frank Co v J R Crompton Brothers Ltd* (1925) the parties concluded an understanding about future purchases of paper, but declared that they would 'honourably pledge themselves' only to the arrangement and used other words stating that the arrangement was not to be regarded as a legal agreement. It was held that legal relations had been excluded and the arrangement was not legally enforceable.

In *Kleinwort Benson Ltd v Malaysia Mining Corpn. Bhd* (1989) a 'letter of comfort' from a parent of a subsidiary company to a company that had lent money to the subsidiary to the effect that the parent's policy was to ensure the subsidiary was 'at all times in a position to meet its liabilities' was, on the facts, merely a statement of present fact, and not a contractual promise.

Such expressions are rare. In business life you mostly need the certainty and security that comes from a binding contract.

On the other hand it may be important, where a formal contract is eventually to be prepared by lawyers, to state that correspondence and understandings are 'subject to contract', which in that case means there will be no contract until the formal documentation is exchanged or executed. If you are intending to transact any important business of any value, you should qualify your 'agreement' with the words 'subject to contract' until you have consulted your solicitor.

12.5 Offer and acceptance

Every contract must have both an offer and an acceptance to be binding. The rules about this are more involved than might at first sight appear.

12.6 Offers and invitations to treat distinguished

An offer must be distinguished from an 'invitation to treat'. An invitation to treat is *not* an offer but is, instead, an invitation to make an offer; and a purported acceptance by another party of an invitation to treat will be construed in itself as an offer, which, in turn, has to be accepted. Some examples of the distinction between offers and acceptances are as follows:

(1) Advertisements for sale will commonly (though not always) be construed as invitations to treat.

Example

In *Partridge* v *Crittenden* (1968) P was charged with contravening the Protection of Birds Act 1954 by offering for sale some wild birds. He had inserted an advertisement in a periodical, which read: 'Bramblefinch cocks and hens, 25s each'. It was held that no offence had been committed, as this was an invitation to treat, not an offer.

(2) The display of goods in a shop window or on shelves in a shop or supermarket will commonly, of itself, not amount to an offer, but may be, instead, an invitation to treat.

Example

In *Pharmaceutical Society of Great Britain* v *Boots Cash Chemists (Southern) Ltd* (1952), Boots ran a newly opened self-service store. Under the Pharmacy and Poisons Act 1933 a listed poison could not be sold unless under the supervision of a registered pharmacist. The company's practice was to place a pharmacist at the cash desk who had ultimate authority to prevent a customer leaving the store with any drug. The question arose as to whether this contravened the Act. In other words, had a sale taken place before the involvement of the pharmacist, ie when the customer selected the goods from a shelf? Boots successfully argued that the display of goods on shelves was merely an invitation to treat, not an offer. The customer himself, by selecting the goods and taking them to the cash desk, made the offer which the store could accept or reject. Acceptance in practice would be ringing the price into the till. At this stage the pharmacist could supervise the sale.

12.7 Termination of offers

An offer may be revoked at any time before acceptance unless an option has been granted. But withdrawal of an offer must be *communicated* to an offeree and, to be effective, notification of withdrawal must actually *reach* the offeree before he has accepted; otherwise it will not be valid. An offer can terminate through lapse of time, either because the terms of the offer expressly say so, or by implication after a reasonable time. Where the proposed contract contemplates performance personal to the offeror, death of the offeror will cause the offer to lapse; otherwise the offer can nonetheless be accepted, at least where the offeree is unaware of the offeror's death. Offerees should take the precaution of stipulating that an offeror is contracting not only for himself, but also for his heirs, assigns and personal representatives, in order to avoid doubt in borderline cases. A counter offer by an offeree may terminate an offer (12.8). If the offer is made subject to a condition, which fails, the offer will thereby lapse.

12.8 Acceptance

As stated, an offer must be accepted. An anomalous rule applies about the manner of acceptance. Normally, communications related to contract formation must be *actually received* to be effective. Thus, if you want to withdraw an offer, it is not enough simply to decide to do it, or to post a letter; communication of your decision must actually be received by the other party. But in the case of acceptance only, a special rule has grown up called the 'postal rule' whereby a posted acceptance in response to a posted offer is valid from the time of *posting, not* receipt. This can have strange results. Thus:

Example

A offers to B in writing by post to sell him his car. B receives the offer on 1 October. B ponders, but writes back, accepting the offer on 8 October. On 15 October, having heard nothing from B, A writes to B withdrawing the offer and, on the same day, concludes a sale with C. B's letter of acceptance arrives at A's house on 21 October having been delayed in the post through no fault of B. There was a binding contract between A and B and A was not in a position to sell to C.

The business and the outsider

On the other hand, the rule does not apply:

(1) where the letter of acceptance is not properly addressed or stamped;
(2) where the terms of the offer expressly or impliedly indicate actual communication is necessary;
(3) where other forms of communication are used by both parties, ie telephone, telex and facsimile equipment, where a party communicating may not be able to rely on a communication unless it has been properly received by the other.

An acceptance must be unqualified, or it may be construed as a counter offer. A counter offer terminates an offer. Thus:

Example

A offers to sell his car to B for £3,000. B says 'I accept at £2,500'. A then sells to C, who has offered to buy at £2,750. B, unaware of the sale to C, telephones A later to say, '£3,000 will be fine after all. I take it the car is now mine'. But B's earlier 'acceptance' was a counter offer. This terminated A's offer and B is not in a position later to revive A's original offer. The sale between A and C is valid.

12.9 Offers, counter offers and acceptances illustrated in business contracts

The above rules can be illustrated in the context of the use of standard written terms and conditions. Sometimes a buyer and a seller of goods each have their own terms and conditions of contracting, probably printed on invoices and orders. These may often conflict. For example, a buyer's terms might say 'the buyer shall be entitled to one month's grace in payment of his account'; a seller's terms might say 'payment must be made within seven days of delivery'. Or, a buyer's terms might say 'the price to be paid for the goods is fixed no matter what increase there may be in the price of raw materials'; and the seller's terms might say 'the seller may vary the price to be paid for the goods upon giving notice thereof due to increase in the price of raw materials.' What happens when such terms conflict?

The answer can be found using the principles in 12.5–12.8. Thus, if you order goods from a supplier under your own conditions of purchase, that will be an offer to him to contract on those conditions. If that order is not accepted unconditionally by the supplier, but, instead, upon the basis of the supplier's own conditions, there will be no contract. The introduction of the seller's conditions would be a counter offer and would be effective to reject your own conditions. No contract can be formed at this stage unless you accept that counter offer. If nothing further is said, but you take delivery, then you may have accepted that counter offer by conduct. To avoid that, you would have to respond to the counter offer before taking the goods, saying that you only want to contract on your own conditions, and so on.

This so-called battle of forms sounds intriguing, but it is usually lost by accident. Although it is important to bear in mind that each case turns on its own facts, two cases illustrate the above propositions.

In *BRS v Arthur V Crutchley Ltd* (1967) the sellers delivered some whisky to the buyers for storage. The seller's driver handed the buyer's foreman a delivery note incorporating the seller's conditions of carriage. This note was stamped by the buyer's foreman: 'Received under the [buyer's] conditions'. It was held that the buyer's action amounted to a counter offer which the sellers accepted by handing over the goods. The contract therefore incorporated the buyer's, and not the seller's conditions.

In *Butler Machine Tool Co v Ex-Cell-O Corporation (England) Ltd* (1979) the sellers offered to sell a machine tool to the buyers for £75,000. The sellers' offer was subject to their conditions which provided that they would 'prevail over any terms and conditions in the buyer's order'. The conditions of the sellers also included a price variation clause. The buyers replied by placing an order for the machine in question but their order was subject to their *own* conditions which were materially different from the sellers' conditions and which, in particular, contained no price variation clause. The sellers completed and signed an acknowledgement of receipt of the buyers' order. It was held, in the circumstances, that the buyers' conditions prevailed. The sellers had made an offer which had been responded to by the buyers not by an acceptance but by a counter offer which had, in turn, been accepted by the sellers.

12.10 Consideration

Consideration is a difficult concept, even for lawyers. It can perhaps be described as the value or price that you have to give to the other party to pay for what the other party is giving you. Any promise must be paid for in money or money's worth or, alternatively, something of value in the eyes of the promisor. Thus if A's grandmother promises him that he will receive £5 on his birthday, this will not be a promise supported by consideration because A has given nothing in return for it. It will be a gift.

On the other hand, although there must be consideration which the law regards as sufficient, the law will not inquire too closely into its adequacy (eg cases of a 'peppercorn rent').

The business and the outsider

You can pay for a promise and make it enforceable by giving money in return for it, or promising to do something for it, or transferring something to the promisor in money or money's worth, or doing something for the promisor that you are not obliged to do already, or forbearing from doing something which you are entitled to do.

Most contracts entered into by firms involve a promise to pay a price for delivery of goods or services or other commodity and, in return, a promise to provide those goods or services or commodity, and so, consideration will ordinarily be present.

Occasionally a promise made without consideration may have some effect under what is known as the doctrine of promissory estoppel. For this to apply, there must be an existing contract and a promise by one party to the other that his strict rights under that contract will not be enforced. The promisee must have relied on that promise and changed his position accordingly. If the promisor reneges and seeks to enforce his rights the courts may prevent this where it would be inequitable. On giving reasonable notice, however, the promisor may require his strict contractual rights to be resumed, at least for the future. It should be noted that the use of the doctrine is limited and it can only be used as a 'shield' and not a 'sword' ie as a defence and not a cause of action.

Finally, contracts made by deed are binding even if they would otherwise fail for lack of consideration. If there is any doubt about the sufficiency of consideration in a transaction or arrangement, it may be prudent to consider providing for the promises to be made in a deed.

12.11 Privity

Another rule that must be observed in contract law is that there must be privity of contract. This means that only those parties to a contract (or 'privy' to it) can, ordinarily, sue on it. Thus if A promises B that A will pay C £100, C cannot enforce this promise since he is not 'privy' to the contract in question. (C's action might also fail here on the ground that he has not given consideration (12.10)). The contract would, however, be enforceable by B as against A as long as B has given consideration to A.

12.12 Form

Contracts can generally be made formally or informally and can be oral or written. However, it is always wise to have a written contract, or at least written evidence of it, as it will then be easier to prove the *existence* of a contract. A few types of contract have to be in writing, ie bills of exchange, promissory notes, bills of sale and, because of the rules about content and format in the Consumer Credit Act 1974, relevant consumer credit agreements (see below).

Also, by virtue of the Statute of Frauds 1677, a contract of guarantee has to be evidenced in writing. If it is not, it is unenforceable. Under the Law of Property (Miscellaneous Provisions) Act 1989 contracts for the sale or other disposition of land must be made in writing.

12.13 Terms of the contract

Contract terms are either express or implied. Terms may be implied either because of:

(1) custom or commercial usage; or
(2) statute (eg terms implied by the Sale of Goods Act 1979 as to title, fitness for purpose and quality etc (12.32)); or
(3) by the courts.

12.14 Terms implied by the courts

These may be either:

(1) to give business efficacy to the contract; or
(2) to fill in a term omitted by the parties that would be to an 'officious bystander' perfectly obvious for insertion.

A different, perhaps more flexible, approach to the implication of terms can be found in non traditional contract areas such as employment law (10.11). Otherwise, the courts are fairly circumspect about implying terms; it is not a court's job to rewrite a bargain for the parties. Generally, an express term overrides an implied term.

12.15 Excluding terms

At common law it is permissible, within limits, to contract out of liability for breach of contract or tort (although the courts tend to construe excluding terms quite narrowly, and against the person relying on them: this is known as the *contra proferentem* rule). Obviously it is wise to try and limit your exposure to liability (especially for consequential loss) as far as you can.

However, this position is qualified by the Unfair Contract Terms Act 1977 which applies, in the main, to business liability. Under the Act:

(1) Under s 2(1) it is not possible to exclude or restrict liability in negligence for death or personal injury and, in other cases of

loss or damage due to negligence, the excluding term will only be enforceable if reasonable.
(2) Under s 3, which applies to contracts

(a) between a business and a consumer or
(b) between two businesses as long as one deals on the written standard terms of business of the other

it is not possible to exclude or restrict liability for breach of contract unless the excluding term satisfies the test of reasonableness.

Also caught by the test of reasonableness are indemnity clauses in contracts so that, under s 4, a consumer cannot be made to indemnify another for negligence or breach of contract unless the term satisfies the test of reasonableness. (Curiously though, s 4 does not apply to any contract other than one between a business and a consumer (unlike s 3 which is wider)).

What is reasonable for the purposes of the test of reasonableness will depend on the facts of each case. Factors could include the strength of bargaining position of the parties, availability of an alternative contract without the excluding term, whether any goods supplied were produced to the special order of a customer and whether there is any trade usage with regard to the term and so forth.

The controls about exclusions of contract liability in s 3 do not apply to contracts between two businesses where the standard written terms of one party are not employed. In that case, the parties are free to exclude liability for breach of contract (subject to extreme examples and subject to the rules of construction a court will apply at common law to exclusion clauses including the *contra proferentem* rule) within the framework of the common law.

Finally, the Act says that a manufacturer of goods cannot, in a guarantee of goods ordinarily supplied for private use or consumption, exclude liability for loss or damage arising from consumer use of the goods and arising from negligence of the manufacturer or distributor (12.53 (product liability of manufacturer)).

There are special applications of the Unfair Contract Terms Act 1977 to contracts for the sale of goods and these are discussed at 12.37.

Any exclusion clause, even if it survives the Unfair Contract Terms Act, must be incorporated in the contract before it is effective. Thus, if standard terms are used, it is imperative that your own terms are not superseded by those of the person you are contracting with (see 12.9). In any event (and particularly in the case of use of notices and statements on tickets) excluding terms which are not sufficiently brought to the notice of the other contracting party, may not bind the other party. And one line of authority holds that, the more onerous or unusual the term sought to be relied upon, the more steps a party should take to bring it to the other party's attention (see eg recently *Interfoto Picture Library* v *Stiletto Visual Programmes* (1988)).

12.16 Conditions, warranties and other terms

The law draws a distinction between conditions and warranties. A condition is a major term, breach of which entitles the innocent party to terminate (as well as to claim damages).

Example

> In *Bunge Corpn.* v *Tradax SA* (1981), the buyers contracted to buy some soya bean meal. They were to provide the ship to transport it and were obliged to give at least 15 days' notice of readiness. The buyers gave only 13 days' notice. The sellers therefore terminated the contract. It was held they were entitled to do so. The 'readiness' term was a condition, breach of which gave rise to the right to terminate, however slight the consequences of the breach.

A warranty is a more minor term, collateral to the main purpose of the contract, breach of which entitles an innocent party to damages only. Whether a term is a condition or warranty is a question of construction of the contract. Use of the words 'condition' or 'warranty' is not conclusive (although it will be very persuasive). For a stipulation may be a condition although called a warranty in the contract and vice versa. This is because the courts, exceptionally, have power to remove an inappropriate label that the parties placed upon a particular term.

The categorisation of terms into conditions and warranties is not exhaustive. The courts may also find that some terms cannot, in truth, be characterised as either conditions or warranties. These are so-called 'innominate' or 'intermediate' terms. A party's remedies on breach of such terms (ie whether the injured party may claim damages only, or whether he may withdraw from the contract as well) depend on how drastic the consequences of the breach are to him.

Oddly, the meaning of the terms 'condition' and 'warranty' is transposed in the case of insurance contracts. There, in general, breach of *warranty* allows the injured party (the insurance company) to repudiate the contract whereas breach of a mere condition allows the insurance company only to sue for damages (chapter 13).

12.17 Vitiating elements

Contracts may be affected by the presence of:

(1) mistake
(2) misrepresentation
(3) duress and undue influence.

Generally, it is thought mistake makes a contract *void*. Misrepresentation, duress and undue influence make a contract *voidable*. In the former the contract has no effect whatsoever and does not exist. In the case of the latter the contract remains on foot until it is avoided by the injured party. The injured party's option to avoid may be lost in certain circumstances (12.19).

12.18 Mistake

The law rarely allows a contract to be unravelled because of an alleged mistake. Thus, many people may enter into a bargain not quite appreciating the extent or nature of their obligations. In that sense, they may be mistaken. But contract law relies on certainty and only exceptionally will mistake be allowed to operate to set aside the contract. There are said to be three types of mistake.

Common mistake

This is where both parties share the same assumption, which turns out to be wrong. Generally, the courts will only set aside the contract if the parties are mistaken as to a *fundamental* aspect of the subject matter of the contract (eg both parties contract for the salvage of a sunken ship, but, unbeknown to them, it never existed).

Mutual mistake

This is where both parties are mistaken, but they are at cross purposes, ie A thinks he is contracting about X and B thinks he is contracting about Y. Often a court will determine what an objective third party might consider had been agreed judging the acts and deeds of the parties and give effect to such an apparent contract. Occasionally, however, the picture may be so confused that it is impossible to tell what the parties are contracting about and, if so, there will be no contract.

Example

In *Scriven Bros & Co v Hindley & Co* (1913) an auctioneer engaged by the plaintiff was instructed to sell lots of both hemp and tow. The catalogue did not indicate which lots were which. The defendant bid for the tow under the impression that he was bidding for hemp. The plaintiff sued to enforce a contract when the tow was knocked down to the defendant. It was held, however, that there was so much uncertainty as to the subject matter of the deal and as to the parties' intentions that there was no contract.

Unilateral mistake

Here, one party only is mistaken. Ordinarily this is unlikely to affect the contract. If you are subjectively mistaken about the terms of a contract but you nonetheless *appear* to wish to contract, the other party may assume you want to be bound and there will be a contract. The exceptions to this are where:

(1) the other party knows of your mistake and is taking advantage of it or
(2) the other party contributes to your mistake.

Example

In *Hartog* v *Colin and Shields* (1939) the offerors offered to sell hareskins at so much per pound. The offerees thought the skins were being sold for so much per piece. It was held that the offerors could not enforce the contract on the basis of a price per pound. In the light of previous negotiations and trade practice they must have known of the offerees' mistake and could not take advantage of it.

Occasionally, the courts can order rectification of a written contract that, because of a mistake in its drawing up, does not represent the actual intention of the parties.

Generally, however, a person is bound by a document he signs even if he is mistaken about its nature or contents or did not read it. The limited exception is where the doctrine of *non est factum* ('it is not my deed') is available. This applies in favour of a person who, whether permanently or temporarily, is unable to appreciate or understand the document and who is induced (usually by fraud) nonetheless to sign it. *Non est factum* then operates *provided* the document is fundamentally different from the one the signatory thought he signed *and* he was not careless. Thus in *United Dominions Trust Ltd* v *Western* (1976) a person who had left blanks in a document to be filled in by a third party was bound by the document even though the items inserted were different from the signatory's wishes. Not surprisingly, his conduct was considered careless!

12.19 Misrepresentation

A representation which induces a contract may affect a contract if it turns out to be wrong, ie is a misrepresentation. Generally, there has to be a positive representation for liability for misrepresentation to lie. Silence does not generally amount to a misrepresentation and there is in general no duty to disclose to the other party. However this has exceptions. First, there are certain contracts of the utmost good faith (*uberrimae fidei*) where full disclosure is required. Such is the case in insurance contracts (chapter 13). Second, even in general contracts, there are qualifications to the rule that silence does not amount to misrepresentation. Thus, if you begin to represent, you must paint the whole picture and not just part. Otherwise this would be misleading. And if a representation is made at the outset, this must be revised for the benefit of the other party before the contract is concluded if circumstances have changed which make the original representation misleading.

A misrepresentation can be fraudulent, negligent or innocent. All types of misrepresentation allow rescission at the instance of the injured party. But the right to rescind may be lost if a 'bar' to rescission operates, ie if:

(1) you have affirmed the contract after learning the truth
(2) too long a time has elapsed
(3) *restitutio in integrum* (ie restoring both parties to their former positions in full) is impossible
(4) third party rights would be prejudiced

Also, under the Misrepresentation Act 1967, a court has discretion to declare that the contract should continue and award damages in lieu of rescission.

Damages are available:

(1) for fraudulent misrepresentation at common law
(2) for negligent mis-statement at common law
(3) for negligent misrepresentation under the Misrepresentation Act 1967 and
(4) even for innocent misrepresentation under the Misrepresentation Act 1967, if damages are awarded at the discretion of the court in lieu of rescission (see above).

The Misrepresentation Act 1967, s 3, provides that a contract term which excludes liability for misrepresentation is of no effect unless it satisfies the requirement of reasonableness (a similar test to that which applies to terms excluding liability for breach of contract (12.15)).

328 Allied Dunbar Business Tax and Law Guide

Occasionally a representation may become a term of a contract, main or collateral, and if a representee suffers loss as a result of breach, he may sue for damages for breach of contract instead.

Example

> In *Andrews v Hopkinson* (1956), P bought a secondhand car from D, a car dealer. D's sales manager induced the sale by saying 'It's a good little bus. I would stake my life on it. You will have no trouble with it.' The car turned out to be seriously defective. Although there were difficulties in suing under the main contract because of exclusion clauses, it was held that P was entitled to sue for damages for breach of a separate warranty that the car was in good condition and safe. (He would, of course, have additional rights under the Sale of Goods Act if the claim arose today, particularly in view of the controls now existing in relation to exclusionary statements or terms).

12.20 Duress and undue influence

A contract may be avoided by reason of *duress* if illegitimate pressure is applied to a contracting party to induce him to contract. For long, the law recognised only physical duress, ie threats to the person. 'Economic duress' is now recognised too. But the test is quite strict and is only rarely satisfied. There is a distinction between economic duress and hard bargaining; only the former may affect a contract (although contrast the rules in some consumer legislation: see eg 12.49).

It may not be possible to avoid a contract for duress if you have affirmed the contract thereafter.

Examples

> In *North Ocean Shipping Co Ltd v Hyundai Construction Co Ltd* (1978) a firm of shipbuilders contracted with a firm of shipowners to build a ship. The price was fixed in US dollars, but the US dollar was then devalued. The shipbuilders threatened to pull out unless the shipowners agreed to a price increase. The shipowners had taken on commitments in relation to the vessel and had no real choice but to agree to the increase. When the contract was completed the shipowners sued to recover the increase, partly on the basis that it had been extracted under economic duress. It was held that the shipbuilder's actions could, in principle, amount to duress, but the shipowners had chosen to go ahead nonetheless and had thereby, on the facts, affirmed the contract.
>
> In *Pao On v Lau Yiu Long* (1979) the plaintiffs held shares in a private company and the defendants held shares in a public company. The plaintiffs agreed with the public company to sell their shares in the private company in return for shares in the public company. The plaintiffs agreed not to sell the consideration shares for a period. A collateral agreement provided for the repurchase of the consideration shares by the defendants at the end of this

period. The plaintiffs then refused to complete the main agreement unless they were given a guarantee by way of indemnity against losses that might arise from the transaction. To avoid adverse publicity the defendants agreed. The price of shares fell and the plaintiffs sought to enforce the guarantee. The defendants, *inter alia*, said it had been obtained under duress. It was held on these facts, though, that there had simply been commercial pressure, not coercion and this did not amount to duress.

Undue influence can set aside a contract only where there is a special relationship between the parties, often, but not necessarily a fiduciary one. This can include solicitor and client, doctor and patient, parent and child, but the list is not exhaustive. In such cases there is a *presumption* of undue influence. That is why, if such a relationship ever exists between you and the other party to a proposed contract, you should get the other party to seek independent advice.

A more unusual case is illustrated by *O'Sullivan v Management Agency and Music Ltd* (1985) where the musician Gilbert O'Sullivan entered into various management contracts with a manager. He had no business experience, trusted his manager implicitly and neither received legal advice nor was warned to obtain it. The agreements were less favourable to O'Sullivan than if they had been negotiated with the benefit of independent advice. It was held that the contracts should be set aside on the ground of undue influence.

12.21 Termination of contracts

A contract may come to an end by various means apart from performance, viz:

(1) breach of contract
(2) effluxion of time
(3) agreement
(4) frustration.

12.22 Breach of contract

A contract may come to an end through breach of contract, but only if:

(1) the breach is repudiatory in nature, ie shows that one party has shown an intention no longer to be bound by the essential terms of the contract, and
(2) that breach of contract is 'accepted' by the injured party, ie responded to by an election to terminate.

Thus, contract law applies what is known as the 'elective' theory of termination, that is to say, a contract must end by the election of the injured party who, in law, accepts the breach of the guilty party as ending the contract and treats himself as thereby discharged. For example, if A, who is an employer of B, unilaterally reduces B's salary by 50%, B is not necessarily discharged from the contract. B, however, may discharge and release himself from the contract by accepting A's breach.

Breach of contract leads to the availability of remedies on the part of the injured party such as, principally, damages for breach of contract whether or not the breach is repudiatory, and these are not prejudiced by the injured party's election to terminate the contract.

If, however, the injured party wants to seek some sort of order from the court by way of specific performance, or an order obliging the guilty party to carry out his obligations, the injured party *has* to keep the contract alive and *not* terminate it. A good example would be a conveyancing transaction. If a seller of a house refused to convey it, it might not be in the interests of the injured party (the buyer) to terminate the contract and seek to put the relationship at an end if he wants the house, rather than seeking damages alone. The injured party should, in that case, keep the contract alive and seek specific performance of the contract.

12.23 By effluxion of time

If, for example, the parties have entered into a fixed term contract expressed to expire on a specific date, when that date comes around, the contract will expire by effluxion of time. This rule is modified in employment contracts for unfair dismissal and redundancy purposes (10.18, 10.25).

12.24 By agreement

The parties to a contract can at any time, notwithstanding continuing obligations to each other, terminate their agreement by mutual consent. This arrangement will be binding because it will have consideration, as each party is giving up continuing obligations to the other. That mutual release of obligations can amount to consideration in law.

12.25 Frustration

Frustration is an occurrence which can terminate a contract *automatically* by operation of law, irrespective of the will of either party. The doctrine means that if the parties have entered into a contract upon a certain assumption about the way it will be carried out, and if that assumption is thwarted, the courts may exceptionally say that the contract is frustrated and has thereby come to an end.

Examples in decided cases have been where a contract for the sale of goods has become impossible because of the outbreak of war rendering delivery impossible or, in the case of a contract for personal services, where one party has become incapacitated through illness for a very long time, or where, in a contract to stage a concert or theatre production, the theatre has burned down (and no alternative venue is possible).

For frustration to operate, the basis of the contract must have been thwarted. It is no defence to breach of contract for a person trying to relieve himself of responsibilities under the contract to say that it has been frustrated because it is simply more difficult and onerous to perform. Thus, in cases arising from the Suez War in the 1950s, where contracts for the delivery of goods had to be diverted via a longer and more expensive route via the Cape, as opposed to going through the Suez Canal, contracts were held not to be frustrated as they *could* be completed, albeit more expensively. It simply meant that carriers were put to very much more trouble than they had anticipated.

Sometimes, if frustration has occurred, the Law Reform (Frustrated Contracts) Act 1943 can re-allocate the loss and inconvenience to the parties that has arisen thereby.

12.26 Remedies

Breach of contract leads to various remedies, namely:

(1) a declaration of breach of contract
(2) damages for breach of contract
(3) an action for an agreed sum
(4) specific performance

12.27 Declaration

A declaration is a judgment of the court declaratory of the parties' positions. It could state, for example, that a party was in breach or that a contract subsists, where there is doubt about this.

12.28 Damages

Damages in contract law

(1) are designed to put the injured party into the position he would have been in had the contract been performed;
(2) should, in the reasonable contemplation of the parties, be likely to arise from the ordinary course of things or from special circumstances that the parties were aware of or ought to have been aware of (like loss of a sub-sale for example).

These rules, as they apply to sale of goods contracts are discussed again at 12.45.

The injured party must take reasonable steps to mitigate his loss and he cannot recover avoidable loss. Thus, for example, a wrongfully dismissed employee has to take reasonable steps to get another job (see 10.33) and a disappointed buyer of goods has to take reasonable steps to find a replacement contract.

Damages calculated on the basis of speculating what would have happened had the contract been performed, ie 'loss of bargain' are sometimes referred to as 'expectation damages'. Occasionally, too, where there is no quantifiable damage for loss of bargain a court may also award what are known as 'reliance damages', ie expenses that have to be thrown away by the injured party as a result of the breach that must have been contemplated by the parties would be incurred under the contract.

Finally, sometimes parties put 'liquidated damages' or 'penalty' clauses in their contracts (12.47). You have to be very careful here. If you have provided say, that if a machine is delivered late, there shall be payable £1,000 per week until it is installed, this *may* not be enforceable. It will be enforceable if it is a genuine pre-estimate of the buyer's loss for late delivery. If so, it will fix in advance the amount of damages due; and, normally, in that case, the buyer will not be able to sue for any more even if it turns out that estimate was wrong. But if it is excessive and penal it is a penalty in the legal sense of the word and it will not be enforceable. Some perfectly enforceable liquidated damages clauses are called 'penalties' in contracts and some clauses claiming to be 'liquidated damages' clauses are really penalties in law. A court can assess what the effect of the clause really is; but it is best to avoid the use of the term 'penalty' if you are including a liquidated damages clause, as the word does have pejorative overtones.

12.29 The action for an agreed sum

Where there is a contract for the sale of goods or the provision of services for an agreed sum, transfer of the goods or completion of the services will entitle the seller or contractor to sue for the contract price. In this case no question of assessing the amount of the claim arises: the sum has already been agreed. (An additional claim for consequential loss arising out of failure to pay money due is not normally applicable. But, exceptionally, this might not be the case if it were in the contemplation of the parties that additional loss would ensue as a result of late or non-payment. A court may also award interest on judgment debts). And the injured party will, ordinarily, not have to mitigate his loss.

For example, 'A' is employed by 'B' but 'B' fails to pay the agreed wages for work already completed by 'A'. 'A' can sue 'B' for the wages in an action for an agreed sum, ie, in debt.

However, if 'A' is employed by 'B' under a contract which gives 'A' the right to three months' notice of termination of employment and 'B' purports to terminate that contract without notice, 'A' cannot sue for his wages in lieu of notice in an action for an agreed sum in debt because he has not earned the wages for those three months. In this case 'A' must sue 'B' for damages based on the loss of his opportunity to earn the wages during that notice period and the principles of mitigation of loss will apply.

12.30 Specific performance

Sometimes, instead of damages, specific performance may be obtained. Thus, if a buyer and seller contract for the sale of a house, damages may be inadequate for the buyer if the seller refuses to convey. An order for specific performance, ie compelling the seller to convey to the buyer, may be given by the court. As discussed above (12.22) for specific performance to be granted, the contract must still be alive and not terminated by the injured party. Specific performance can occasionally be granted in cases of sales of things as well as real property, such as sales of machines and other *specific* items.

Specific performance is discretionary and will not be granted in cases of hardship, or where it is impracticable or in cases where personal services are the subject of the contract. Thus, only exceptionally will a court order specific performance of a contract of employment or contract for services (chapter 10).

An injunction to restrain a breach of contract may also be available. However, where this concerns a contract for personal services, a court will not order an injunction which indirectly has the effect of an order for specific performance. This issue commonly arises where an employer wishes to restrain an employee from breaking his contract by leaving the employment before he is entitled to do so, commonly to join another employer. If there is an express negative covenant in the contract obliging the employee not to work for another during the life of the contract the court may grant an injunction in such circumstances, provided, though, that it does not have the effect of a 'work or starve' order. Thus, in the celebrated case of *Warner Bros Pictures Inc v Nelson* (1937) the actress Bette Davis had undertaken to work exclusively for the plaintiff but broke the agreement and sought to work for another film company. An injunction to prevent this was granted. It was argued on behalf of the defendant that this was a 'work or starve' order because she was an actress who starred in films. But this was rejected, the court finding that if the defendant did not really wish to work for the plaintiff there were other means by which such a well known actress might earn a living apart from appearing in films.

A more modern attitude can be found in *Page One Records Ltd v Britton* (1967). In this case the 'Troggs' pop group had contracted with their manager not to employ another manager during their contract with their present manager. The group broke this promise. The case has similarities with the *Warner Bros* case. So why not grant an injunction to the manager? However the court took notice of the position that although *in theory* the group could earn a living without a manager, in practice they could not. Similarly, very recently, in *Warren v Mendy* (1989) a boxer's manager claimed that a third party had, by taking over management of the boxer, induced a breach of contract of management between the manager and the boxer, Mr Nigel Benn. But the claim for an injunction against the third party was refused because it would *in effect* have compelled Mr Benn to work under the former manager.

Occasionally, an employer will decide not to accept a breach of contract by an employee but instead will keep the contract alive by continuing to discharge his side of the bargain ie pay salary until the end of the contract. Thus, in *Evening Standard Co Ltd v Henderson* (1987) Mr Henderson was employed as production manager of the London Evening Standard. Under his contract he was required to give one year's notice of determination and he was further bound not to work for anyone else during the contract. He then purported to join a rival concern without giving due notice. The employer exercised its rights under contract law not to terminate the contract but kept it alive (see above). The employer also performed its side of the contract by continuing to pay wages. In the circumstances the court gave an injunction to the employer to prevent the employee from working elsewhere. The circumstances under which the employer who is a victim of a breach of contract is willing to continue wages irrespective of whether he receives the employee's services must be rare, but, depending on the facts, if the issue is that important to the employer, it seems, on the authority of *Henderson*, an option available to him.

Finally injunctions are commonly issued to restrain breach of a restrictive covenant in a contract or to enforce confidentiality obligations (see chapter 10 and below).

12.31 Illegality and unenforceability

Some contracts may be unenforceable because they are *illegal*. These would include contracts to supply the enemy in wartime, to defraud the Revenue and to commit a breach of the law.

Example

In *Miller* v *Karlinski* (1945) an employer and an employee contracted that an employee should be paid a basic salary and an additional sum disguised as expenses. It was held that the contract was unenforceable as it was a contract to defraud the revenue.

Certain contracts may not be enforceable by reasons of public policy because they are in *restraint of trade*. Thus, restrictive covenants entered into by employees with their employer (10.12, 10.15), and by sellers of businesses with buyers of businesses not to compete with their former employer or with the former business as the case may be, may be unenforceable and void if contrary to this principle. They will be unenforceable if the covenants are too wide and go too far beyond what is necessary for the protection of the business interests of the party in whose favour the covenant is drawn and beyond what is reasonable in the circumstances. Firms should take specific legal advice upon the drawing up of these sorts of agreements as the issue of their enforceability can be very delicately balanced. Restrictive covenants in employment contracts are discussed in chapter 10. Restraints in business agreements, particularly business sales, are often more kindly looked on by the courts than in the case of employment contracts because the parties are more likely to be equal in bargaining power.

A contract or contract term may be void if it falls foul of the competition laws of the EEC, particularly Article 85 of the Treaty of Rome or, if falling under the Restrictive Trade Practices Act 1976, the parties fail to register the agreement with the Director General of Fair Trading (see below) if registrable under that Act.

Part B Sale of goods

12.32 Introduction

In general, the rules relating to the sale of goods can be found in the law of contract (see Part A). But there are additional rules for this type of contract that have to be observed.

The implied terms in the paragraphs which follow govern all contracts for the sale of goods save in relation to the implied terms as to merchantable quality and fitness for purpose (12.35), which apply only in relation to goods supplied in the course of a business and not otherwise.

Some of the implied terms are conditions and some warranties. The difference between conditions and warranties has been discussed generally at 12.16. (As far as other terms in the contract for the sale of goods are concerned, the Sale of Goods Act 1979 repeats that whether a stipulation in a contract is a condition or a warranty (breach of the former giving rise to a right to reject the goods (ie repudiate), the latter giving rise to damages), is a question of construction of the contract.)

12.33 Title and quiet possession

(1) Under section 12 of the Sale of Goods Act 1979 there is an implied *condition* on the part of the seller that he has a right to sell the goods.
(2) There is an implied *warranty* that the goods are free from any charge or encumbrance not disclosed to the buyer before the contract is made.
(3) There is an implied *warranty* that the buyer will enjoy quiet possession of the goods except so far as it may be disturbed by the owner or other person entitled to the benefit of any charge or encumbrance that the buyer knew about before the sale.

12.34 Conformity with description

Under section 13 of the Sale of Goods Act 1979 where there is a contract for the sale of goods by description there is an implied *condition* that the goods will correspond with the description.

If the sale is by sample as well as description (ie if you are sent a sample to inspect to see if you want to contract for the purchase of the real thing) then it is not sufficient if the bulk of the goods corresponds with the sample if the goods do not also correspond with the description.

What is a sale by description is a question of fact in each case. It will usually mean an active description by the seller, say in a letter or a catalogue or even an oral statement. A sale of goods is not prevented from being a sale by description simply because, having been displayed for sale, the goods are selected by the buyer.

12.35 Merchantable quality and fitness for purpose

(1) Under section 14 of the Sale of Goods Act 1979 there is an implied *condition* that where a seller sells goods *in the course of a business* the goods supplied under the contract are of merchantable quality. However this does not apply in the case of defects specifically drawn to the buyer's attention before the contract is made. Nor does it apply in favour of a buyer who examines the goods before the contract is made as to defects which his examination ought to reveal to him.

Goods are of merchantable quality under the Sale of Goods Act 1979 if they are as fit for the purpose or purposes for which goods of that kind are commonly bought as is reasonable to expect having regard to any description applied to them, the price and all the circumstances.

(2) Where a seller sells goods *in the course of a business* and the buyer expressly or impliedly makes known to the seller any particular purpose for which the goods are being bought, there is an implied *condition* that the goods supplied under the contract are reasonably fit for the purpose in question. This applies whether or not this is a purpose for which goods of that sort are commonly supplied. However, this does not apply where the circumstances indicate that the buyer does not rely on the skill and judgement of the seller or that it is unreasonable for him to rely on the seller's skill and judgement.

12.36 Sales by sample

Under section 15 of the Sale of Goods Act 1979, in a contract for sale of goods by sample, there is an implied *condition*

(1) that the bulk will correspond with the sample in quality
(2) that the buyer will have a reasonable opportunity of comparing the bulk with the sample
(3) that the goods will be free from any defect which renders them

unmerchantable and which would not be apparent on reasonable examination of the sample in question.

12.37 Exclusion of liability in contracts for the sale of goods

As in the general law of contract, the law governing exclusion clauses in contracts for the sale of goods is affected by the Unfair Contract Terms Act 1977.

Under the Unfair Contract Terms Act 1977, in contracts other than with consumers it is possible to exclude liability for:

(1) Liability for non-conformity with description (12.34)
(2) Non-merchantable quality of goods (12.35)
(3) Liability for goods being unfit for the particular purpose for which the purchaser requires them (12.35)
(4) Non-conformity with sample (12.36)

provided that the contract term which excludes liability satisfies the test of reasonableness.

It is not, however, possible to exclude liability for breach of those terms if you are dealing with a consumer. Any such excluding term would be void.

Also, it is not possible to exclude liability for breach of the terms relating to title and quiet possession under s 12 of the Sale of Goods Act 1979 (12.33) at all, whether you are dealing with a business or a consumer. Again, any such excluding term would be void.

The Consumer Protection (Restrictions on Statements) Order 1976 (an order made under the Fair Trading Act 1973: 12.50) makes it an offence in the course of sale to *consumers* to apply terms which are void under the above principles or to make statements about a consumer's rights under the Sale of Goods Act without at the same time stating that the consumer's statutory rights are not affected.

As discussed at 12.15, liability to a third party in negligence resulting in death or personal injury cannot be excluded and liability for other damage caused by negligence can only be excluded insofar as the term excluding liability is reasonable. When one party deals as a consumer or the other party deals on the other's standard terms of business, liability for breach of contract generally cannot be excluded by a business seller unless the term excluding liability is reasonable (12.15).

The Unfair Contract Terms Act 1977 does not cover certain contracts for the international sale of goods (12.51).

12.38 Implied terms in contracts other than sale of goods

Under the Supply of Goods (Implied Terms) Act 1973 and the Supply of Goods and Services Act 1982, similar implied terms as apply to sales of goods are imposed, for example, in relation to hire purchase contracts, contracts of hire, exchange or barter and contracts for work and materials. Exclusion of such terms is also controlled by the Unfair Contract Terms Act 1977.

In contracts for the supply of services the Supply of Goods and Services Act 1982 implies that the services will be supplied for a reasonable charge and where the supplier acts in the course of a business that the services will be supplied with reasonable care and skill and within a reasonable time. The implied terms may be modified or excluded by the parties, but subject to the operation of the Unfair Contract Terms Act 1977.

12.39 Other rules in sales of goods

The Sale of Goods Act 1979 lays down other rules governing the contract for sale of goods, many of which can be modified by express agreement between the parties. If any of the rules imposed on you by statute are found to be inconvenient, this may emphasise the need for you to draw up your own conditions of sale (12.47). However, the following rules apply unless you modify them in your own conditions.

12.40 Time

Whether a stipulation as to time is of the essence of the contract (ie is an important term, a condition proper) depends on the intention of the parties. You can specifically provide in your conditions when time is important. Otherwise, the Sale of Goods Act 1979 provides that time for payment is not of the essence unless otherwise agreed. But time for delivery in commercial transactions will often be regarded as of the essence in the absence of a contrary intent.

12.41 Passing of property

'Property' is synonymous with 'ownership' or 'title'. The single expression 'property' is used hereafter, but it can be taken to mean ownership or title as well. 'Title' is the expression used as an alternative to 'property' at 12.46. In a contract for unascertained goods the property in them does not pass unless and until they are ascertained (ie allocated to the contract (eg packeted, labelled or earmarked) with the consent of the parties).

In a contract for specific or ascertained goods, the property passes when the parties intend it to pass. *Unless the parties agree differently,* the following are the rules for determining that intention:

(1) In an unconditional contract for specific goods in a deliverable state property passes when the contract is made and it is immaterial whether the time for payment and/or delivery is postponed.
(2) In a contract for specific goods where the seller has to do something to put them into a deliverable state, property passes when he has done so and the buyer has notice that it has been done.
(3) In a contract for specific goods in a deliverable state but where the seller has to do something to ascertain the price (such as measuring or calculating weight or bulk or size), property passes when he has done so and the buyer has notice.
(4) When goods are delivered on approval or on sale or return property passes when the buyer signifies his approval or acceptance or adopts the transaction or retains the goods beyond the fixed time for return of the goods or, if no time is stipulated, beyond a reasonable time without indicating rejection.
(5) In a contract for unascertained goods or future goods by description property passes when goods of that description in a deliverable state are unconditionally appropriated to the contract by either party with the consent (express or implied) of the other.

The rules about when title to goods passes may be altered by consent. For example the parties often impliedly agree that ownership does not pass until the goods are paid for. This is what happens in relation to smaller consumer purchases in shops. A seller also often stipulates that ownership does not pass until the price has been paid in full in commercial contracts (see the discussion on reservation of title at 12.46). In short, the whole issue is subject to the intention of the parties.

12.42 Risk

Risk usually follows passing of property. So a buyer stands the risk of accidental loss to the goods as soon as property passes (12.41) even though he may not be in possession of them (although if delivery is delayed through the fault of a party the goods are at the risk of the party in default in respect of any loss arising therefrom). This may be altered by consent (12.46), so that a seller can transfer risk and possession but retain property, for example.

12.43 Delivery

It is the duty of the seller to deliver goods and of the buyer to accept and pay for them in accordance with the contract. Delivery involves passing of possession of the goods from one person to another and is distinct from the passing of property in the goods (see above).

Whether delivery is to be by collection by the buyer from the seller or physical delivery by the seller to the buyer depends on the contract. In the absence of agreement, the Sale of Goods Act 1979 assumes delivery is by collection by the buyer from the seller. This is often varied so that the seller takes on the job of delivery.

Delivery usually involves transfer direct to the seller but you can agree otherwise. For example the seller may deliver to someone having authority to receive the goods like a dyer or finisher of textiles who may be treating the goods before they reach the purchaser on the purchaser's behalf.

If there is short delivery the buyer may accept the goods at the contract rate or reject them. If there is over delivery the buyer may accept only the correct amount or accept all of the goods at the contract rate or reject all of the goods. If the goods are mixed with other (non contract) goods the buyer may accept only the right goods and reject the rest or reject all of the goods.

12.44 Acceptance

The buyer accepts the goods when he intimates this to the seller or when, after delivery, he does any act in relation to the goods which is inconsistent with the seller's ownership (like selling them to someone else), or if after a reasonable time he retains the goods without intimating to the seller he has rejected them. If goods which have not previously been examined by the buyer are delivered he has a reasonable opportunity of examining to see that they conform with the contract requirements. Until that time has elapsed he will not be deemed to have accepted them.

12.45 Remedies

A *seller's* remedy for breach of contract (ie non payment by the buyer) is an action for the price or an action for damages for non-acceptance. In the latter case, the measure of damages is the estimated loss directly and naturally resulting in the ordinary course of events from the buyer's breach under the principles at 12.28.

Where there is an available market the measure of damages is usually the difference between the contract price and the market value when the goods ought to have been accepted or if no time is fixed, when the buyer refused to accept.

'Special damages' are also recoverable where the law allows this (eg unusual loss which was, or ought to have been, in the contemplation of the parties: 12.28). The principles of mitigation of loss (12.28) apply to a claim for damages.

If the seller is still in possession of the goods he may have a lien on them (ie a right to withhold until the price is paid). Sometimes he may have the right of stopping the goods in transit if the buyer has become insolvent. Advice should always be taken in this area, though, as a mistake could lead to legal action by a buyer.

The remedies of the *buyer* include recovery of the price on a total failure of consideration, rejection of the goods for breach of condition, and damages for non-delivery. The measure of damages is the loss directly and naturally arising in the ordinary course of events from the seller's breach under the principles at 12.28. This will usually be the difference between the contract price and the market price at the date of the seller's breach. The remedy for a breach of warranty is damages measured by the estimated loss directly and naturally resulting, in the ordinary course of events, from the breach. *Prima facie* this will be the difference between the value of the goods when delivered and the value they would have had if they had fulfilled the warranty.

If delivery is delayed, the measure of damages is, *prima facie*, the difference between the value of goods when they should have been delivered and their value at the time of actual delivery.

'Special damages' may be recovered where there is consequential loss in the contemplation of the parties (see above). Again, the principles of mitigation of loss apply to damages claims by the buyer.

Specific performance is also available but only in the case of specific or ascertained goods (12.30).

As can be seen, the above is a specialised application of the rules set out in relation to contracts generally in Part A.

12.46 Reservation of title clauses

It is for the parties to agree when property and risk in the goods passes. Otherwise, risk in the goods passes when property is transferred and property is often transferred upon delivery, or even earlier (12.41).

However, those imposed rules can be altered by contract if appropriate. One problem in recent times has been the all too common insolvency of purchasing companies who, at the time of failure, have not yet paid for goods delivered to them by a selling firm. If property has passed upon delivery by the seller, the seller has no further claim to the goods. The goods become part of the buyer's property. As such they can be sold on or seized by a receiver.

Accordingly, if a buyer becomes insolvent before a seller has been paid, the seller is at considerable risk. In those circumstances, a seller will only be an unsecured creditor of the buyer and cannot reclaim the goods. If he is an unsecured creditor, he will in practice rarely be paid, or if he is paid, will only be paid a small proportion of his debt.

In *Aluminium Industries BV v Romalpa Aluminium Ltd* (1976) (the 'Romalpa' case) a seller purported to reserve property or title to goods that had been sold pending receipt in full by the seller of payment from the buyer. Until such time the goods were to be treated as the property of the seller and all proceeds of sale of the goods in the possession of the buyer would also be treated as being the property of the seller. The court gave effect to this clause.

Nowadays it is common for conditions of trading to contain a 'Romalpa' or reservation of title (property) clause which purports to reserve title in goods sold to a buyer until payment in full has been received by the seller.

Such clauses are generally regarded as valid but it is important to take advice upon the exact wording of such a clause. In particular, the following points have to be noted:

(1) Both legal and beneficial title in the goods must be reserved, not simply beneficial title.
(2) It will only be possible to reserve title to goods which maintain their original identity. Thus, if you are a supplier of glue which becomes incorporated into a chair by reason of application of the glue to various bits of wood, your product may lose its identity. Your reservation of title clause will probably not work.
(3) It should be possible to reserve title to proceeds of sale if your goods are sold on your behalf by the buyer whilst a reservation of title clause in respect of the goods is still in force. This sounds inconsistent, but can operate if the reservation of title clause is properly worded. However, in practical terms, it is very unlikely that you will be able to claim priority over such proceeds of sale, bearing in mind that the company will not usually have put these proceeds of sale into a separate bank account or have separately identified them for you.

Therefore, in practice, a reservation of title clause, assuming it is properly drafted, may operate so as to allow you to recover specific ascertained goods from your buyer that have not changed their identity in respect of which money has not been received. In practice, intense and swift negotiations with a liquidator or a receiver are necessary when your buyer becomes insolvent in order that you can rapidly take possession of the goods which you maintain are still yours and which have not been paid for. Slightly different rules may apply when an administrator is appointed under the Insolvency Act 1986 who has certain powers of sale over goods which are subject to a retention of title clause (subject to the consent of the court and to accounting to the holder of the rights under the clause for the net proceeds of sale) (chapter 5).

Finally, it is to be stressed once more that this is a complicated legal matter and your conditions of trading should really be drafted by a lawyer. The next section deals with conditions of trading generally.

12.47 Conditions of trading

Many of the rules in the Sale of Goods Act 1979 can be modified by contract and there are other reasons why you might wish to have your own conditions of trading, for example, to insert further terms into the contract in your favour (such as a *Romalpa* clause, discussed at 12.46). Common terms in conditions of trading of a *seller* can include the following. The emphasis should be changed if the terms are for use by a purchaser.

(1) confirmation that the purchaser is contracting in the course of his business
(2) that variations of conditions are not applicable unless authorised by a senior officer of the seller
(3) that certain warranties and conditions are excluded (subject to the Unfair Contract Terms Act 1977: 12.15, 12.37)
(4) that the buyer is deemed to have adequately inspected the items to be purchased after a certain time has elapsed (subject to the Unfair Contract Terms Act 1977)
(5) that title does not pass unless certain conditions are satisfied and that, until then, title is reserved (12.46)
(6) that liability for consequential loss is excluded (subject to the Unfair Contract Terms Act 1977)
(7) that payment terms are as laid down in the contract
(8) that cancellation is expressly not permissible
(9) that the seller reserves the right to correct clerical errors
(10) that risk passes to the purchaser upon departure of goods from the seller's premises

The business and the outsider 345

(11) that drawings and designs and intellectual property in relation to production of goods remain with the seller
(12) that acceptance of the goods denotes acceptance by the buyer of goods in a satisfactory condition (at least if there is time for inspection) (subject to the Unfair Contract Terms Act 1977)
(13) that an arbitration clause applies (optional)
(14) that the contract shall be governed by English Law (essential if you contract with a foreign company)
(15) possibly, that a liquidated damages clause regulates certain losses (but see 12.28).

As discussed, the above examples are slanted towards the seller. Conditions of trading can be slanted towards a seller *or* a buyer and you may wish to have two sets. Thus if you are a manufacturer and seller of goods you will want to have seller orientated conditions for the sale of your goods and buyer orientated conditions for when you are buying your raw materials or components. In the latter case you will be very concerned to seek some warranty about quality and an indemnity against product liability (see below).

Of course, other contracting parties may have thought of this too and, unfortunately there will, from time to time, be a clash between your own conditions and those of your contracting party. In that case, it is important that you win 'the battle of forms' by making sure your own conditions prevail in the interchange of orders, confirmations of orders, invoices and delivery notes that often ensues. These rules are set out at 12.9.

Alternatively you can, if there is time, negotiate a special contract with the other party, incorporating items from both sets of terms, ie a compromise. It is important to note, however, that certain provisions of the Unfair Contract Terms Act 1977 which prevent unreasonable exclusion clauses only apply to contracts between businesses and consumers or between businesses where written *standard* terms are employed (12.15, 12.37). A specifically negotiated contract may not be such a standard form contract and if between two businesses, may be outside the protection of that part of the Act.

12.48 Credit sale, conditional sale, and hire purchase agreements

Certain goods are sold on credit. The most common of these contracts are:

(1) *A Credit Sale Agreement*
This is a sale of goods by instalments. The money is not payable

forthwith but property in the goods passes to the buyer straightaway. Thus if there is default in payment of any instalments there is no automatic right for the seller to get his goods back (but this may be altered by agreement: 12.46). He can only sue and get a financial remedy.

(2) *A Conditional Sale Agreement*

This is where goods remain the seller's until they are paid for in full by the buyer. The seller can therefore regain possession if there is default in payment.

(3) *A Hire Purchase Agreement*

This is where a supplier hires out goods on payment of a number of agreed instalments but has also, coupled therewith, an option to buy at the end of the period of hire for a nominal sum.

12.49 Consumer credit

It is not within the scope of this book to discuss credit and security at length. But if you want to sell goods or give services on credit to individuals you may have to be aware of the Consumer Credit Act 1974. This Act regulates personal credit agreements (ie agreements with individuals, including partnerships, but not companies) where the credit does not exceed £15,000 (excluding interest which is called a 'charge' for credit).

If you are a seller of goods on credit who is covered by the Consumer Credit Act you *must* get a *licence* from the Director General of Fair Trading. This requirement covers not only creditors who are running a consumer credit or a consumer hire business within the meaning of the Act, but also credit brokers such as retailers who have arrangements to introduce customers requiring credit to finance companies. Activity and lending by unlicensed creditors is a criminal offence. The Director General of Fair Trading also controls advertisements by credit dealers and also statements by dealers describing the terms on which they offer credit.

Agreements controlled by the Act are subject to rules requiring certain information and copies of agreements to be given to a debtor, and requiring contracts to conform to a certain type, size and colour of print and to give details of the rights and duties of either party.

There is a statutory right of cancellation over a limited period in favour of a debtor. This applies where there have been any antecedent oral representations and where an agreement is signed otherwise than at the trade premises of a creditor owner, party to a linked transaction or negotiator. If the agreement is cancellable under the Act, the debtor must be given certain information. During the credit period there are rules inhibiting summary termination for default without notice and restraining a creditor applying for an enforcement order by the court before certain procedures are followed.

In hire purchase and conditional sale agreements covered by the Act there is an implied right for the debtor to terminate the agreement on notice, return the goods, pay off arrears and relieve himself of liability for future payments if the agreement becomes too much for him. There is control over penal (12.28) minimum payment clauses on termination.

A court has powers to reopen certain agreements which are 'extortionate', ie if they require debtors to make exorbitant payments or contravene fair dealing. This includes evaluating such an agreement against prevailing interest rates, considerations of the debtor's age, experience and financial pressures, and the basic price of the goods charged.

Finally, an interesting and sometimes useful provision for consumers is section 75 of the Act which states that in the case of certain debtor-creditor-supplier agreements regulated by the Act (a debtor-creditor-supplier agreement is one where there is a transaction between a supplier and a debtor which is financed by a creditor, where, for example, a finance company or other creditor is introduced by the supplier) both the supplier and the creditor are jointly and severally liable to the debtor for the supplier's misrepresentation or breach of contract. There are financial limits to the provision (it does not apply where the item cost less than £100 or more than £30,000) but it could be useful to a consumer where the goods are not, for example, of merchantable quality (see above) and the supplier has gone out of business.

12.50 Other examples of consumer legislation

(1) Under the *Unsolicited Goods and Services Act 1971* (as amended) it is an offence to send unsolicited goods to other parties and as a result, those persons to whom goods are sent may decline to pay for those goods and, after a certain minimum period of time, may keep the goods as if they had full title to them. There are also provisions dealing with the rife problem of unsolicited order forms for entries in telex and other directories. Unless such forms comply with the Act this may give rise to criminal liability for the sender and claims for subscriptions may be unenforceable. Although these provisions are discussed here under the heading of consumer legislation they apply equally in favour of businesses.

(2) Under the *Fair Trading Act 1973* it is possible for the Director General of Fair Trading to issue codes of practice under which bodies or trade associations are encouraged to operate their own arbitration systems in relation to consumer complaints. Several orders have been made under this Act. Further, under the Fair Trading Act 1973 it is possible for action to be taken in relation to an undesirable trade practice or other undesirable conduct prejudicial to consumers.

Under the Consumer Protection (Restriction on Statements) Order 1976, an order made under the Fair Trading Act 1973, it is an offence to supply goods to consumers by the use of notices, advertisements or statements containing void exclusion clauses under the Unfair Contract Terms Act 1977 (12.37). It is this order which also prohibits suppliers from making statements about a consumer's rights about merchantable quality and fitness for use, etc without at the same time stating that a consumer's statutory rights are not affected.

(3) Under the *Trade Descriptions Act 1968* it is an offence to:

    (a)   apply a false trade description to any goods; or
    (b)   supply or offer to supply any goods to which a false trade description is applied.

(4) Under Part III of the *Consumer Protection Act 1987* it is also an offence to make a misleading indication of the price at which goods, services, accommodation or facilities are available. This scheme, in force from 1 March 1989, replaces section 11 of the Trade Descriptions Act 1968 and the Price Marking (Bargain Offers Order) 1979. The Consumer Protection Act covers prices at which any goods, services, accommodation or facilities are available. The provisions are complex and, as they are new, if your business sells goods or provides services to consumers, legal advice should be taken on pricing policies. There is a statutory code of practice which is available from the DTI. Breach of the code does not of itself give rise to liability, but its provisions can be relied on in court when the prosecution seeks to show an offence has been committed. Conversely, it may be a defence to show compliance with the code.

12.51   International sales of goods

Special rules apply in relation to imports and exports (not all of which can be set out here).

There are particular types of contracts in relation to international sales of goods, including fob and cif contracts.

Under an fob contract, the seller's duty is to place the goods free on board a ship nominated by the seller. That is, the seller is responsible for costs up to loading but excluding freight and insurance. Property and risk usually pass on shipment.

Under a cif contract, the price includes cost, insurance and freight. The seller's duty is not only to ship the goods but also to obtain bills of lading and policies of insurance and to transfer these documents to the buyer. He usually does so against payment by the buyer.

Export and Import Licences are usually required and your local Chamber of Commerce can assist in giving you information in that area.

There is a specialised mode of securing payment applicable to international contracts for the protection of both parties where either is unsure of the creditworthiness of the other. This is through the system of banker's commercial credits.

Under this system a buyer instructs his bank to open a credit with a bank in the seller's favour which the bank then agrees to do. But the buyer says to his bank that the seller is only allowed to draw on the credit on presentation of the usual selling documents, viz the seller's invoice, bill of lading and (in cif contracts) the insurance policy or certificate.

Export credit guarantees, which may also, in effect, insure a seller against failure by a buyer to pay, may be available from the Government's Export Credits Guarantee Department.

Finally it is prudent to specify in your conditions of trading that English law will apply (12.47).

12.52 EC and domestic competition law

Distribution, patent licensing, know how, manufacturing and other agreements within the EC of an exclusive nature, are subject to EC competition law rules, particularly in Articles 85 and 86 of the Treaty of Rome, which regulate how far parties can restrict competition within the Common Market. Specific advice is necessary on your business contracts in this regard to make sure you do not infringe EC law and on whether the terms you want in your agreement are exempt from the provisions either individually, after notification to the commission, or under one of the block exemptions in force. Breach of Article 85 makes the relevant restrictions void, may attract fines and may allow third parties suffering loss to sue.

The Restrictive Trade Practices Act 1976 requires particulars of certain restrictive agreements to be registered with the Director General of Fair Trading. In appropriate cases the Director General may refer agreements to the Restrictive Practices Court in which case the parties have to justify the restrictions as being in the public interest. If an agreement is registrable and particulars are not furnished to the Director General within three months or before the restrictions come into effect, whichever is the earlier, the restrictions are void and third parties suffering loss may sue the parties to the restrictive agreement. The Act applies to agreements or arrangements between two or more persons carrying on business within the UK in the production or supply of goods or provision of services under which restrictions are accepted by two or more parties in respect of certain matters specified by the Act. Legal advice is essential here. Your lawyer will also be aware of the possibility of delivering particulars to the Director General on a 'fail safe' basis where there is doubt as to whether registration is required.

Part C Product liability

12.53 Introduction

It is important to note that a manufacturer of goods may be liable to other persons or companies for harm or damage caused by him irrespective of his obligations to a direct purchaser of those goods under a contract. However, this is generally not achieved under contract law itself.

Contractually, the framework is usually that a manufacturer manufactures goods and sells them to a retailer. A contract is concluded between the manufacturer and the retailer. When the retailer sells to a third party who is often (but not always), the ultimate consumer of the goods, a further contract is concluded between the retailer and the consumer. Contractually, if a defective product causes damage or loss this consumer will be able to sue the retailer for breach of contract. The consumer may be able to sue the retailer under the general law of contract (see Part A) or under the implied terms in a contract for the sale of goods (see Part B). If this is well founded, the retailer may be able to mount an individual separate action claiming breach of the retailer's contract with the manufacturer.

But the multiplicity of actions that results through this contractual ladder is cumbersome and expensive. It would be simpler if the consumer could sue the person responsible, ie the manufacturer, direct. To require the consumer to sue the retailer and the retailer to sue the manufacturer requires two actions where, arguably, one would do. But the consumer cannot sue the manufacturer direct in contract because of the doctrine of privity of contract (12.11). Occasionally there can be a direct link between the consumer and the manufacturer if the manufacturer issues a *guarantee*. But such guarantees are often exclusionary (subject to the Unfair Contract Terms Act 1977) (12.15) and can be of limited value.

The law of tort can, however, transcend problems of privity of contract.

12.54 Liability in tort

A tort is a civil wrong inflicted on another causing him harm which can make you liable to that party, irrespective of whether you have a contract with him. You can be liable in tort to another for accidents to your employees and visitors (and under the Occupier's Liability Act 1984), for interfering with another's goods (eg wrongful detention), for dealing wrongfully with another's goods (ie conversion), sometimes for allowing dangerous matter or things to emanate from your land (eg discharge of waste from your factory) and also for negligent misstatements or negligent advice and under the law of negligence generally (see below). In this section we look in detail at potential liability for defective products.

The law of tort opens up the possibility of a manufacturer's liability directly to third parties (even someone who has not bought, but has nonetheless used, the products) at large under the tort of *negligence*. Under the tort of negligence, a person may be liable to another where:

(1) a duty of care is owed by one person to another person
(2) that duty is broken; and
(3) harm or damage is suffered by the person to whom the duty is owed.

There have been many attempts to define the terms under which a duty may be owed to a third party. But, in short, a person will be liable in negligence to another if it is reasonably foreseeable that his actions will cause damage to another. Liability could arise not only from manufacture but also from failure to issue appropriate warnings or instructions about a potentially dangerous product.

Under the test of reasonable foreseeability, a manufacturer may be liable to an ultimate consumer of products supplied by a manufacturer if the products are defective. A duty of care may therefore be owed by the manufacturer of such products to a third party who is a purchaser of those products or whom it is contemplated may consume those products even if not a purchaser. In the seminal case of *Donaghue v Stevenson* (1932) Lord Atkin said: '. . . a manufacturer of products, which he sells in such a form as to show that he intends them to reach the ultimate consumer in the form in which they left him, with no reasonable possibility of intermediate examination and with the knowledge that the absence of reasonable care in the preparation or putting up of the products will result in an injury to the consumer's life or property, owes a duty to the consumer to take reasonable care.'

Donaghue v Stevenson concerned a lady who became ill after consuming a bottle of ginger beer which had been contaminated by a dead snail and who successfully sued the manufacturer of the product. However, the range of products to which a manufacturer's liability in negligence could apply is very wide, from mechanical things, through food, to chemicals and pharmaceuticals. The range of persons to whom the duty is owed is also potentially wide, including purchasers, other users, passengers and bystanders, depending on the facts. A manufacturer may be liable in negligence if:

(1) he has failed to exercise reasonable care in the production of the products
(2) the defect in question is unlikely to be discoverable by any reasonably foreseeable subsequent examination
(3) the defect caused the damage in question.

Loss is recoverable as long as it is not too remote, ie the extent of harm is foreseeable. Generally a court seeks to place the plaintiff in the position he would have been in had the tort not occurred (cf contract law). However, a detailed account of the extent of recovery of damages for negligence is extremely complex and beyond the scope of this book. Obviously in this sort of area, very specialised advice needs to be taken. One thing is clear, though: compensation in this area usually has to relate to loss or damage consequent on harm to the person or property. Pure economic loss is not recoverable in a typical product liability case (a House of Lords Case in 1982, *Junior Books v Veitchi*, appeared to open the door to claims for pure economic loss in negligence generally, but it has now been outflanked by recent cases which have expressed reservations and confined it to its own facts).

The question of exclusion of liability for negligence has been discussed, under the headings relating to the Unfair Contract Terms Act 1977, above.

12.55 Product liability

It is therefore most important to seek to take out insurance cover for product liability arising from these principles (chapter 13). Of course, we have seen cases in the courts (such as cases alleging liability for defective drugs) where the task of the ultimate consumer of products in making a manufacturer liable is extremely difficult. A product liability case depending on negligence can be hard to prove and can go on for many years. Nonetheless, the risk is there for a manufacturer, and insurance should be taken out (chapter 13). This is all the more important should goods be exported and even manufactured in foreign countries, such as the United States, where product liability laws may be stricter than in this country. Further and very specific advice should be taken in these circumstances.

There is also legislation governing dangerous and defective goods, the most important of which is the Consumer Protection Act 1987 which considerably widens the possibility of liability for defective products.

12.56 The Consumer Protection Act 1987

This came into force on 1 March 1988 and was intended to implement the Product Liability Directive of the EC (No 84/374).

Part I of the Act imposes civil liability for damage caused by a defective product. A product is defined as 'any goods or electricity' and includes a product which is part of another product whether by virtue of being a component part or raw material. The importance of this significant new statutory liability is that it is strict: it can impose liability *without the need for proof of negligence* (contrast the common law, discussed at 12.54).

Liability is imposed on:

(1) the producer of the product
(2) any person who by putting his name on the product or using a trademark or other distinguishing mark in relation to the product has held himself out to be the producer of the product
(3) any person who has imported the product into a member state of the EC from a place outside the EC in order in the course of any business to supply it to another.
(4) Any supplier who has been requested by a person who has suffered damage to identify one or more of the persons referred to in (1) to (3) above in relation to the product causing the damage and who fails within a reasonable period of receiving the request either to comply with it or, instead, to identify the person who supplied the product to him. (The victim's request must have been made within a reasonable period of the damage occurring and at a time when it was not reasonably practicable for him to identify those persons.) Obviously, here, the need for suppliers to keep proper records of who originally supplied them is vital.

Where two or more persons are liable for the same damage their liability is joint and several.

Any such person is directly liable to any person who suffers damage in respect of the defective product.

A defect is defined under the Act as occurring where the safety of the product is not such as persons generally are entitled to expect. In determining what persons generally are entitled to expect in relation to a product, all the circumstances have to be taken into account, including:

(1) the manner in which and purposes for which, the product has been marketed, its get up, the use of any mark in relation to the product and any instructions for, or warnings with regard to, doing or refraining from doing anything with or in relation to the product;
(2) what might reasonably be expected to be done with or in relation to the product; and
(3) the time when the product was supplied by its producer to another.

The type of damage for which liability can arise is death or personal injury or any loss of or damage to any property (including land). There is no liability for loss of or damage:

(1) to the product itself;
(2) to property which is not intended for private use and which is not intended by the person suffering the loss or damage for private use;
(3) to property below £275.

There are defences under the Act including where:

(1) The defect is attributable to compliance with any requirement imposed by or under any enactment or with any EC obligation.
(2) The person proceeded against did not at any time supply the product to another.
(3) The only supply of the product to another person by the person proceeded against was otherwise than in the course of business and the person proceeded against was not a producer or importer of the product and had not held himself out as producer of the product.
(4) The defect did not exist in the product at the time of supply.
(5) The state of scientific and technical knowledge at the time of supply was not such that a producer of products of the same sort as the product in question might be expected to have discovered the defect if it had existed in his products while they

were under his control (this is the controversial 'state of the art' defence).
(6) The defect constituted a defect in a product (the ultimate product) in which the product in question formed part and was a defect wholly attributable to the design of the ultimate product, or to compliance by the producer of the product in question with instructions given by the producer of the ultimate product.

It is not possible to contract out of liability under the Act.

12.57 Practical points arising out of the Consumer Protection Act 1987

The Act means that all potentially affected must seek to protect themselves as much as possible. Manufacturers should look at quality and safety standards in a new light. Suppliers should keep proper records of their own source of supply and also look at their terms and conditions of trading (and distribution agreements) to see whether indemnities and warranties can be obtained from manufacturers or exporters. Also, the need for product liability insurance is vital.

12.58 Consumer safety

There are provisions in Part II of the Consumer Protection Act 1987 governing consumer safety. Under these, it is an offence to supply goods if they fail to comply with the 'general safety requirement'. Goods fail to comply with the general safety requirement if they are not reasonably safe having regard to all the circumstances including:

(1) the manner in which, and purpose for which, the goods are being marketed, the get up of the goods, the use of any mark in relation to the goods, and any instructions or warnings given in relation to them
(2) any published standards of safety in relation to those sorts of goods
(3) any means by which it would have been reasonable (taking into account the cost, likelihood, and extent of any improvement) for the goods to have been made safer.

There are also, of course, a vast number of regulations and orders laying down standards and rules about various products, their packaging and otherwise. As they are encyclopaedic in scale, a specialist work should be consulted.

13 General insurance

by Gill Clark, Eagle Star Insurance

13.1 The need for insurance cover

All businesses, whether large or small, have to take risk. It is essential to recognise the uncertain nature of risk. Can you appreciate the financial loss which may be incurred as a result of, for example, an extensive factory fire, or a burglary? Adequate insurance cover is a fundamental requirement to ensure the continuation of your business in the event of a loss.

13.2 Protection

It is also important to recognise at this early stage that not all risks can be insured but, in return for a known premium, insurance provides for the uncertainty of most losses in your business environment to be transferred to the insurers who arrange cover for thousands of businesses.

You therefore stand to benefit from insuring the risks to which your business is subject since insurance can protect your business interests by allowing you to continue with your business plans and concentrate on production. There is then no need to make contingency plans or tie up capital in the form of reserves to cater for the possibility of a risk actually occurring and causing a loss which could not otherwise be withstood by your business. Finally, insurance can also free the businessman from a lot of the worries which are incurred in the running of the business.

13.3 The main compulsory insurance requirements

Although arranging insurance is primarily a voluntary move, governments have legislated to make some forms of insurance compulsory. The compulsory insurance requirements are a result of the following:

Employers' Liability (Compulsory Insurance) Act 1969

This Act makes it compulsory for an employer to insure against his legal liability for bodily injury or disease sustained by employees arising out of and in the course of their employment. Evidence of this policy has to be provided in the form of an insurance certificate which must be displayed in a prominent position on the premises.

Road Traffic Acts

The 1972 Act deals with compulsory insurance for the owner of a vehicle in respect of his legal liability for death or bodily injury to a third party.

There has recently been an EC directive, now incorporated in the Motor Vehicles (Compulsory Insurance) Regulations 1987, which requires that all motor insurance policies must now also provide an indemnity of £250,000 for damage to third party property. The third party cover provided by most insurers usually provides limits for property damage greater than that required under the directive. At present there is no legal requirement for insuring damage to your own vehicle.

Statutory examination of engineering plant

By law, many items of plant and machinery such as boilers, excavators, cranes, air and steam pressure vessels, lifts and lifting machinery must be inspected and certified by a qualified person. These examinations are largely in response to the requirements of the Factories Act, the Health and Safety at Work Act, and associated legislation.

These services provided by some of the major insurers are sometimes part of a wider policy cover or are on a fee only basis.

13.4 The insurance intermediary

It is possible to purchase insurance in two ways: direct from the insurance company or through an insurance intermediary. As a commercial buyer of insurance, it is recommended that your insurance requirements be arranged through an insurance intermediary to assist you in identifying the risks which confront your business. The variations in policy wording offered by the different insurers will further add to the complexity of arranging insurance cover.

The insurance intermediaries understand the market and know the various types of cover that can be provided, the most competitive premium rates and the best claims services available.

Insurance intermediaries can be classified as follows:

Insurance broker

A broker is a full-time intermediary and is expected to have a wide knowledge of the insurance market.

Until recently, anyone could describe themselves as an insurance broker. The Insurance Brokers (Registration) Act 1977 created The Insurance Brokers Registration Council (IBRC) in order to govern the registration and regulation of insurance brokers. To be registered as a broker, an individual must:

(i) have an approved qualification or
(ii) have been employed by an insurance broker or an agent for at least two years or
(iii) have been employed by an insurance company for five years.

The insurance broker, by definition, may be an individual or firm whose full-time occupation is the placing of insurance with companies. Only Lloyd's brokers can place insurance at Lloyd's and write 'and at Lloyd's' after their names.

From 1 December 1981 it has been illegal for any individual to describe himself as a broker without having registered under the Insurance Brokers Act.

The broker acts as an agent for the insured but sometimes has the authority from insurance companies to issue cover for certain classes of insurance. The broker's advice is mainly free since the broker receives remuneration from the insurance company and you therefore do not pay more for using the service of an intermediary than going direct to the insurance company itself.

Other intermediaries

In the past there were also insurance agents, consultants, financial advisers, or appointed representative working on either a full or part-time basis who may not have had such a wide knowledge of the general insurance market as an Insurance Broker. The agent, for example, may have been an accountant or solicitor who introduced insurance in the course of his main business activity.

However there have been some recent general insurance developments in relation to insurance agents. In future insurers will recognise two categories:

(i) An 'independent intermediary' who acts primarily for his client and is responsible for the advice and service provided.
(ii) A 'company agent' who is employed by one insurance company or who represents up to a maximum of six insurance companies which accept responsibility for his conduct and advice given.

13.5 Types of cover available

There are many areas of your business which will need some form of insurance cover from physical property to liability and indemnity insurances.

13.6 Property insurance

The physical assets of your business, that is the buildings, stock and machinery need to be protected from damage.

This can take many different forms:

(a) *Fire Policy*
A standard fire policy is used for almost all businesses and provides compensation as a result of damage to the property insured. The fire policy also covers damage caused by lightning and explosion. The latter is limited to explosion of domestic boilers only.

The protection offered by a fire policy may not be enough, so insurers provide cover for a number of additional risks for a comparatively small extra premium. These additional risks, known as 'special perils', provide an extension to the basic policy. They include any of the following: storm, flood, burst pipes, impact, riot and malicious damage and earthquake.

The policy can be taken out on an 'all risks' basis. In addition to fire and special perils, it includes accidental damage or loss not specifically excluded.

(b) *Theft Policy*
This provides compensation in the event of the loss of the property insured by theft. It also includes theft damage to buildings. A more detailed description of your stock is necessary, as it is usually this which is attractive to thieves. Commercial theft policies usually require evidence of entry to or exit from your premises by forcible and violent means.

(c) *Goods in Transit Insurance*
Every business depends upon the movement of goods and documents and as insurance is not provided for business effects

under a motor policy, goods in transit insurance is a necessary protection.

An 'all risks' policy will be issued if your business owns a small fleet of vehicles. The policy will probably specify the number of vehicles, with individual limits for each vehicle.

If your business owns a large fleet of vehicles, you would be well advised to insure it on 'a declaration basis' whereby the insurance is based on the maximum number of vehicles in operation at the inception date of the policy. There is usually a limit per vehicle. Any adjustment in the premium rate is made at each renewal when the total number of vehicles is again declared.

A problem arises, however, when your goods are sent via a contracted haulier. If the goods are lost or damaged while in the care of the carrier, compensation may not automatically be forthcoming as the carrier may be able to prove that he is not liable or, alternatively, can rely on contract conditions to avoid liability.

Various conditions of carriage exist, most notably those resulting from the Road Haulage Association's Standard Conditions of 1967 and 1982 and the Standard CMR conditions applicable in EC countries. Therefore you would be well advised to study the Conditions carefully or discuss these with your insurance adviser. This being the case, it is therefore well advisable that you insure your own goods under an 'all risks' policy as a carrier's policy ultimately protects the carrier rather than your business. If you export any goods you would normally need to effect a separate Marine Transit policy.

For goods transported by rail, the liability accepted by the rail authorities is slightly wider than that of the haulage carriers. Even so, additional insurance cover can be arranged at a low premium, thus enabling any loss or damage to be dealt with by the insurance company and not directly with the rail authorities.

The Post Office sets various limits of liability but, as with the above, independent insurance cover can be arranged.

(d) *Money Insurance*
This provides compensation to your business in the event of money being stolen either from your premises or while being carried to or from the bank. There are various limits which can be arranged. Some companies will also provide for compensation if an employee suffers serious injury while carrying money to or from the bank.

(e) *Engineering Insurance*
An engineering policy provides cover for damage to machinery and can also cover explosion of steam boilers and pressure plant. Cover for electrical and mechanical breakdown is also available for most machinery including computers.

Most engineering policies will provide cover for business interruption/loss of profits as a result of the above.

Most insurers will provide inspection services as many forms of inspection are compulsory by law. An engineering policy will usually therefore cover damage to or breakdown of specific items of plant and machinery, inspection services and legal liability for injury or damage caused by plant and machinery.

13.7 Liability insurances

The running of a business means legal responsibilities in respect of employees, the public and customers. It is therefore extremely important that all businesses have adequate insurance protection for legal liabilities which may arise. Insurance companies therefore provide employers', public and product liability insurances to provide protection against this.

(a) *Employers' Liability Insurance Policy*
This is a statutory requirement under the Employers' Liability (Compulsory Insurance) Act 1969 which came into force on 1 January 1972. All employers must take out insurance against liability for bodily injury or disease sustained by employees arising out of and in the course of their employment in the UK. An insurance certificate has to be displayed to provide evidence of the insurance being in force.

An employers' liability policy protects you, as an employer, against:

(i) your own personal negligence
(ii) failure to provide suitable and safe plant, a safe place to work and competent staff
(iii) the personal negligence of employees and their negligence in carrying out their duties
(iv) breach of statutory duty as defined in the 1969 Act for the health and safety of employees (re Health and Safety at Work Act 1974)

The Act stipulates a minimum indemnity of £2 million in respect of claims relating to employees arising out of any one occurrence. Many insurers provide an unlimited indemnity for this class of business. Solicitors' costs and opponents' costs are also covered.

Employers' liability insurance thus provides cover against damages which your business may have to pay for bodily injury or illness sustained by an employee and the costs of defending an action under the Health and Safety at Work Act 1974.

(b) *Public Liability Insurance Policy*
This insurance, unlike employers' liability insurance, is not compulsory by law, but public liability claims carry the same financial threat to your business.

Public liability insurance provides cover for legal action against you for accidental bodily injury to third parties and accidental loss of or damage to third party property arising through the negligence of yourself or your employees. Loss of or damage to any property which is being worked upon is excluded. A few insurers will consider offering this cover. However, the cost of repair or replacement of the actual work being undertaken by yourself will be excluded.

A public liability claim can arise through the negligence of you or your employees, if for example;

(i) customers or other members of the public are injured whilst visiting your premises
(ii) fire spreads to a neighbouring building.

The policy has a limit of indemnity which applies in respect of any one claim or a series of claims arising from one source. In view of the increasing awards made by the courts, you should ensure that your policy provides an adequate limit of indemnity, probably at least £1 million.

(c) *Product Liability Insurance Policy*
A public liability policy will provide protection for accidental injury, loss or damage caused by the actions of yourself or your employees. It will not, however, provide cover for injury, loss or damage caused by goods which you manufacture, supply or repair.

Product liability insurance provides for protection against your legal liability and there have been some important statutory developments:

(d) *Consumer Protection Act/EC Product Directive*
This Act was passed in 1987 and Part 1 which brought into Law the European Community Directive on Liability for Defective Products came into effect on 1st March 1988. This is likely to have a far-reaching effect on the product liability market. Basically

anyone who is injured or suffers damage to personal property can bring an action against you. The claimant no longer needs to prove that you have been negligent in manufacturing the product but only that the product is itself defective and has caused injury or damage.

Product liability cover is normally only available as an extension to a Public Liability policy.

(e) *Professional Indemnity Insurance*
This type of insurance provides cover for liability arising from professional negligence. This may apply not only to the professions such as doctors and solicitors but also to anyone working in an advisory capacity.

Professional negligence can result if you or your employees give defective advice which results in others suffering, either by acting upon your advice or misconstruing the meaning of the advice. Professional indemnity insurance can be provided to meet the cost of any award against you. Not all insurers are prepared to offer this cover.

13.8 Motor insurance policies

Any motor vehicles which you use must be insured for third party liability. As previously stated, all vehicles driven must meet the requirements of the Road Traffic Acts.

In addition to this compulsory third party cover you can also insure your vehicle itself for damage arising from fire and theft and this is known as a 'third party fire and theft' policy.

Finally, the most common form of cover is the comprehensive policy which includes accidental damage to your own vehicle.

Motor insurance is divided into: (a) commercial vehicles; (b) private cars; (c) motorcycles.

In a business, if you have a number of vehicles, these can be insured as part of a motor fleet policy.

A motor fleet policy covers all vehicles owned or operated by your business and can also include hired or loaned vehicles, whether they be private cars, goods carrying vehicles or motorcycles.

Comprehensive cover is essential for the small to medium-sized firms who do not have the facilities and resources to repair their own vehicles.

If the damage is so severe as to make the vehicle uneconomical to repair, the insurers will consider the vehicle to be a 'total loss' and settlement will be made on the current market value of the vehicle.

An excess may be applied in which case you will be liable for the first amount of any claim. This is usually in the region of £50 to £250. The excess is usually applicable to young drivers under the age of 25, or as a result of the past driving record of particular drivers.

You can agree to pay a voluntary excess in return for a reduced premium. Other factors such as the vehicle type, the location of your business and past claims experience are taken into account when assessing the premium.

13.9 Business interruption insurance

The physical assets of your business will be protected by material damage insurance but it is quite possible to go out of business following a loss where adequate insurance of physical assets exists. As a result the earning capacity of your business should also be protected in the form of a business interruption/consequential loss policy. However, for a payment to be made, a material damage policy must exist covering the same perils and liability must have been admitted under that policy.

Business interruption insurance is designed to protect your net profit and to meet continuing payments for fixed overheads if insured damage has occurred at your premises resulting from occurrences against which you are insured.

The essential features to be taken into consideration when arranging a business interruption policy are as follows:

Maximum indemnity period

You will need to assess how long it will take to get your business running normally again and also make sure that your cover will allow enough time for rebuilding or re-equipping your business premises and restoring trade to the level it was at before the loss.

This is incorporated into the Policy as the 'maximum indemnity period'.

Cover under the policy will cease at the end of the period and thus it is important that the indemnity period selected is more than adequate. Obviously, any estimation of the maximum indemnity period requires in-depth calculations and usually either your insurers or insurance intermediary will help in selecting the correct time period.

Careful consideration should also be given to the nature of your business, the machinery used and location of your staff. A serious interruption, for example, may force staff to leave, machinery may not be available and stock may not be readily replaced. The maximum indemnity period should take account of all these factors so that the possibility of inadequate cover is minimised.

Sum insured

As with all policies of insurance, the sum insured has to be correct as under-insurance may well mean that you will receive only partial payment in the event of a loss.

Gross profit for insurance purposes is not the figure shown in your trading and profit and loss accounts but is calculated according to a definition stated in your policy. Particular attention should also be paid to the future expectations of your business. Thus the sum insured should take into account real growth and inflation.

Most policies are now arranged on a 'declaration linked' basis where there is no sum insured. Instead, you must estimate the gross profit which you expect to earn during the period of insurance. As a result, the premium is calculated on this estimated gross profit and is altered at the end of each period of insurance when the actual gross profit is known. An allowance is made for future expansion.

Your business may, of course, be affected by losses outside your premises and therefore most business interruption policies are capable of being extended, the most common being:

(i) Denial of access — if neighbouring premises are damaged by an insured peril you may be prevented from entering your premises, thus resulting in a loss of earnings.
(ii) Failure of public utilities — if access or trade is prevented as a result of insured damage at the premises of the gas, water, or electricity supply authority.

Other extensions exist and vary from insurer to insurer depending on your type of business.

Loss of book debts insurance

Any business which allows credit for the payment of goods or services relies on its accounting records for the collection of monies due. If these records are destroyed, by fire for example, money owed to you may never be collected.

Cover for debts in this way is possible by book debts insurance. This does not provide insurance protection against bad debts. Cover is for fire, explosion, aircraft and riot and optional additional perils. The sum insured should represent the maximum amount of debt outstanding at any one time.

13.10 Other insurances to consider

Fidelity insurance

This type of insurance is centred around fraud or dishonesty on the part of your employees. Cover is provided in respect of loss of money or goods belonging to or held in trust by yourself, caused directly by an act of fraud or dishonesty committed by an employee.

As a condition of the policy, fraud or dishonesty has to be perpetrated and discovered during the period for which the risk is on cover, but occasionally a discovery period of one to two years after the expiry date of the time period is provided.

In considering the risk, the insurers will wish to know what precautions you have taken to deter such fraud and dishonesty, the frequency of internal and external audits, and the number of employees. Cover is then provided on an annual basis.

Obviously the financial impact of fraud from within can pose a serious threat to your business, particularly if, as is often the case, the fraud has continued and remained undiscovered for a long period of time. Fidelity insurance should thus be considered as a viable insurance option.

Credit insurance

This protects your business against bad trade debts and covers the risk that if you sell goods, the purchaser may not pay for them as a result of insolvency.

For foreign transactions, the government has set up the Export Credits Guarantee Department, primarily to assist exporting companies against the risk of not being paid.

Premiums are charged on a turnover basis or are adjustable according to the amount of debt outstanding at regular intervals.

Legal expenses insurance

The public in general are becoming more litigation conscious and thus there is an even greater likelihood that at some time or other your business may become involved in legal action.

Protection is available in the form of legal expenses insurance. For example, costs may be incurred as a result of legal actions brought about by an aggrieved employee who considers that he or she has been unfairly dismissed. The insurance cover provides financial support to defend or pursue legal rights. The cover extends to include the solicitor's fees and expenses along with any court costs and opponent's costs if appropriate.

13.11 Type of policies available

The policy of insurance issued by your insurance company will state what risks are covered by the policy, the premium cost, the name of the insured and the period of time over which the cover applies.

13.12 Single risk policies

Single policies such as a fire policy or a burglary policy, are usually more appropriate to the very large organisation. There will thus be one policy for fire, one for consequential loss and for various other single risks. The organisation which is large enough financially may opt to retain several risks through self-insurance.

The disadvantage of a single policy is: that the system of one premium and one renewal for each risk insured proves costly from the administrative point of view.

13.13 Package/combined policies

Obviously the single policy will not appeal to the smaller business such as shops and offices. For smaller manufacturing or distribution businesses, insurance companies can arrange a combined policy. This incorporates separate sections for fire, consequential loss, liability, burglary, money etc. The wordings would be the same as if separate policies were issued but the business has the advantage of one policy and one renewal premium. There are, however, usually maximum limits on the premium for this type of policy.

Package policies are also available covering a wider range of classes of business including property, loss of earnings, money and legal liability cover. The package policy is capable of covering almost all of your insurance needs. You select from all the options available the combination which you require. Various benefits therefore accrue:

(1) Simplified rating structure
(2) Only one proposal form to complete
(3) Only one premium and renewal.

The package policy is therefore flexible in accommodating your changing business needs. These package policies are ideally suited to shops, hotels and offices.

Other services

A number of insurers are adding extra services to their Commercial Insurance Contracts and these services are another way of increasing the benefits of arranging insurance. For example the provision of Helplines to assist on legal matters or to arrange for emergency repair to Buildings and the like. In addition a number of insurers provide booklets which can assist you in improving Fire and Security precautions at your premises.

14 Key rates and allowances — 1989/90

(Companies year to 31 March 1990)

Chapter

INCOME TAX 2

Taxable Income	Slice	Rate	Total Tax
£	£	%	£
20,700	20,700	25	5,175
Over 20.700		40	

Income Tax Allowances

Personal allowance — married	£4,375
single	£2,785
Wife's earnings allowance — maximum	£2,785
Life assurance relief — only on pre-14 March 1984 policies	12½%
Additional personal relief for children	£1,590
Age allowance — single	£3,400
married	£5,385
Age 75 or over — single	£3,540
married	£5,565
income limit	£11,400
Widow's bereavement allowance	£1,590

COMPANIES 4

Full corporation tax rate	35%
Small companies rate	25%
Advance corporation tax rate	25/75ths

CAPITAL GAINS TAX 6

Rate (individuals)	25%/40%
Annual exemption (individuals etc)	£5,000

INHERITANCE TAX

Band £	Death rate %
0—118,000	Nil
118,001 upwards	40

Annual exemption   £3,000

VAT

Rate   15%
Registration threshold from 18 March 1989   £23,600

15 Glossary

Tax and law glossary

The following is a selection of terms which are explained in more detail where indicated.

ACAS	Advisory Conciliation and Arbitration Service
Ad valorem duties	Duties which are charged as a percentage of the subject matter — particularly stamp duty
Administrator	An officer appointed by the court who takes charge of the company's affairs on insolvency and one of whose aims is to secure the survival of the company (5.81)
Advance corporation tax	Tax payable by companies on dividend payments, etc, which is offset against the full (mainstream) corporation tax liability (4.8)
Articles of association	The regulations of the company governing procedure of the company and its operation from day to day and the members' relationship between themselves (5.36)
Back duty	Under-assessed tax for previous years, normally due to evasion
Basic rate tax	Income tax at twenty-five per cent for 1989–90 (2.1)
Business Expansion Scheme	Government scheme for encouraging investment in smaller companies by giving tax relief on money subscribed (4.25)
Capital — authorised or nominal	The limit of capital to which the company can go to in issuing new shares without passing a resolution to increase its capital

Insurance glossary

— issued or allotted	The amount of shares actually issued by the company to its members
— paid up	The amount of issued or allotted share capital paid up by the members
Capital duty	duty formerly paid on issue of shares at the rate of £1 per £100 or part thereof (abolished by FA 1988)
Class rights	Rights attaching to different classes of shares in the Articles (5.40)
Close companies	Companies closely controlled by generally no more than five shareholders and their associates (4.21)
Close Investment Holding Company (CIC)	A close company which is neither a trading company, nor a property investment company, nor certain other companies such as a member of a trading group (4.26)
Condition	In contract law, a term of the contract of such importance that breach would entitle the injured party to repudiate (12.16)
Constructive dismissal	In employment law, an employee initiated dismissal in response to an employer's repudiatory conduct
Continuous employment	In employment law, employment continuous under a contract of employment for the purposes of the EP(C)A (10.17)
CRE	Commission for Racial Equality
Debenture	In company law, a document evidencing a loan to a company (5.22), usually containing a charge on the company's property
Domicile	The country which you regard as your natural home. If you go abroad, it is the place of abode, to which you intend to return
Earned income	Income derived from an individual's personal, mental or physical labour and some pensions
Employee	A person who works under a contract of employment, defined as a contract of service, or apprenticeship (see EP(C)A, s 153(1)) (10.8)
EOC	Equal Opportunities Commission
Ex gratia	Without liability. Often used in

Insurance glossary

Fidelity	In employment law, a duty of faithfulness or loyalty (10.12)
Fiduciary duties	Duties attaching to the office of a director analogous to those of a trustee and involving a duty not to let his own position conflict with that of the company and to be trustee of the company's assets (5.63)
Floating charge	A charge other than a fixed charge which companies may grant to lenders and which is not attached to a specific asset or assets but attaches only to a class of asset or assets (5.23)
Frustration	A doctrine in contract law which brings a contract automatically to an end by operation of law without the need for action by either party (10.19, 12.25)
General Commissioners	Lay people appointed to hear tax appeals
Higher rate tax	Income tax at the higher rate, currently forty per cent (2.4)
Indexation allowance	Capital gains tax relief for inflation (6.11)
Industrial tribunal	A body set up to hear complaints concerning statutory employment rights such as unfair dismissal, redundancy and the like (10.30)
Interest in possession	Entitlement to receive the income of a settlement (7.20)
Liquidator	An officer who presides over and administers the dissolution of a company
Mainstream corporation tax	A company's main corporation tax liability based on its accounts (4.10)
Memorandum of association	A constitutional document of a company setting out its name, office, objects clause, statement of limited liability and capital (5.9)
Ordinary residence (individual)	Residing in a country in the ordinary course of your life
Private company	A company which may not offer its shares to the public and which is not a public company (1.11 and 5.3)

settlements of, for example, employment cases (10.35) [appears at top, belongs to preceding entry]

Term	Definition
Privity	A rule in contract law that only a party to a contract may sue under it
Public company	A company which uses the suffix 'plc' and which has a minimum share capital of £50,000, a quarter of which is paid up and which has to observe certain additional requirements under the Companies Act 1985 (1.11 and 5.2)
Resolution	A decision of a company at a general meeting or of directors at a board of directors meeting
Receiver	An officer appointed by the court or by debenture holder to take charge of the company's affairs and realise its assets. Usually he will be an administrative receiver under the Insolvency Act 1986, if a receiver and manager appointed by a debenture holder
Rights issue	An issue of shares to all shareholders *pro rata* with their existing shareholdings
Romalpa Clause	A reservation of title clause in conditions of trading of a company (12.46)
SMP	Statutory maternity pay, a maternity benefit administered by the employer, similarly to SSP (below)
Specific performance	An order, in contract law, for the enforcement of the obligations of a defaulting party under a contract (10.33, 12.30)
SSP	Statutory sick pay, a payment administered by the employer replacing state sickness benefit for 28 weeks of sickness, the cost of which is deducted from an employer's national insurance contributions
Stamp duty	Duty payable at $\frac{1}{2}$% on transfers of shares and different rates on transfers of property by companies (5.26)
Table A	Table A of the Companies (A–F) Regulations 1985 (SI 1985 No 805) or Table A of an earlier Companies Act as the context requires (5.9)

Tort | A civil wrong committed against another party, eg negligence or trespass
Ultra vires | A doctrine in company law that a company must keep within its registered objects. It is tempered by certain statutory protection in favour of third parties.
Unfair dismissal | A dismissal contrary to the EP(C)A (10.18)
Unfair prejudice | In company law, the basis of a petition by a minority shareholder under s 459 of the Companies Act 1985
Warranty | In contract law, a term breach of which will entitle the injured party to sue for damages but not to repudiate (12.16) (contrast a condition and contrast also insurance law below)
Wrongful dismissal | A dismissal in breach of contract at common law

Insurance glossary

When it comes to arranging insurance or making a claim, the following may be a basic guide to explaining some of the insurance terms which may be used:

Average | If the sum insured is inadequate the insurers will only receive a premium for a proportion of the risk and not for the entire risk. If a claim is made, any claims settlement will take this under-insurance into account by applying the condition of average — the policyholder will have to share in the loss by making a contribution to the loss proportioned to the amount of under insurance.
Certificate of insurance | This is usually required when insurance cover is compulsory by law as in the case of Employers' Liability Insurance & Motor Insurance.

Insurance glossary

Claim forms	The standard forms used by insurers to collect all the information pertaining to the loss and to provide assistance in assessing claims.
Contribution	Right of an insurer to call upon others liable to the same insured, to share in the cost of an indemnity payment. For example, if the same property is insured with two different insurers.
Cover note	Provides evidence that the insurance cover is in force before the policy document has been issued. If a loss occurs during the period the cover is in force, the insurers are liable under the terms of their standard policy.
Endorsement	An alteration in the wording of a policy is made by issuing what is termed an 'endorsement slip' and should be attached to the policy concerned.
Excess	The policy wording excludes the first £ x of loss. This may be compulsory or voluntary.
Indemnity	Exact financial compensation sufficient to place the insured in the same financial position after a loss as he enjoyed immediately before it occurred.
Index-linking	The sum insured rises in line with a pre-determined index. It is designed to combat the effects of inflation producing under-insurance.
Insured Perils	Those named in the policy as insured — fire, explosion etc.
Material fact	Any fact which would influence the insurer in accepting the risk and in fixing the premium terms and conditions of the contract. This should be disclosed at the proposal stage.
Operative clause	States the conditions under which the policy operates.
Premium	Contribution to the fund or price which an insured pays for the insurance cover.

Insurance glossary 379

Proposal form	Document issued by the insurers to record the information which the underwriter requires in order to assess the nature of the risk being proposed.
Reinstatement	A means by which indemnity can be provided; referring to property insurance where an insurer undertakes to restore or rebuild property damaged by an insured peril.
Reinstatement of sum insured	Where partial losses have been paid the insurers will usually deduct the amount of the loss from the sum insured. If reinstatement applies, the sum insured is automatically reinstated free of charge. This applies to certain types of insurance only.
Schedule	Part of the policy which records the details of the particular contract.
Sum insured	Maximum liability of the insurer and the amount upon which the premium is based. It is not the amount which the insurers promise to pay in the event of loss.
Under-insurance	The sum insured is not equal to the value at risk. Under-insurance results in the insured paying too low a premium for the nature of the risk involved.
Utmost good faith (uberrimae fides)	Positive duty to voluntarily disclose, accurately and fully, all facts material to the risk being proposed, whether asked for or not.
Warranty	In insurance contracts, fundamental conditions at the root of the contract a breach of which will render the contract null and void. (Contrast the meaning of this term in general contract law.)

Index

Absenteeism—
  unfair dismissal 10.24
Access—
  medical records, to 10.67
Accounting reference date 5.12
Accounts—
  company 5.60
  value added tax 8.3
Administration—
  inheritance tax 7.13
  value added tax 8.3
Advance corporation tax, see
    Corporation tax
Agency—
  principles in relation to
    company 5.52
Agreement—
  partnership 1.6, 5.93
  termination of contract by 12.24
Agricultural property—
  capital allowances 2.32
  relief 7.15
Anti-avoidance—
  inheritance tax 7.18
Appeals—
  value added tax 8.5
Articles of association, see Company
Assessment, see Income Tax
Assets—
  capital gains tax, see Capital gains
    tax
  dissolution of partnership 5.99
  order of distribution of 5.88
  provided for employee 9.15
  security 2.39
  short-life 2.25–2.26
Associated company 4.4
Assured tenancies—
  capital allowances 2.37

Author—
  copyright sales 2.49
  royalties 2.49

Balancing allowances and
    charges 2.22
Bankruptcy—
  avoidance of 1.8
  order 1.8
  trustee in 1.8
  undischarged bankruptcy 1.8
Books—
  company 5.60
Buildings—
  agricultural 2.32
  hotel 2.33
  industrial 2.30
  value added tax 8.12
Business—
  buying 10.69–10.81
  entertainment 8.14
  expansion scheme 4.32
  income, see Income
  incorporation, see Company
  interruption insurance 13.9
  meaning 8.7
  name—
    companies and 5.106
    individuals 5.107
    partnerships 5.107
  new, loss in 2.45
  property relief 7.14
  replacement of assets 6.26
  retirement relief 6.28
  sale of—
    advice on 10.81
    business not limited
      company 10.71
    continuity of
      employment 10.79

382 Index

Business—*cont*
    limited company   10.70
    protection of
        employment   10.69–10.81
    transfer to company   6.27

Capability—
    unfair dismissal   10.24
Capital—
    company, see Company
Capital allowances—
    agricultural buildings   2.32
    assured tenancies   2.37
    balancing allowances and
        charges   2.22
    base period   2.18
    basis of   2.17
    corporation tax   4.13
    de-pooling   2.26
    dredging   2.36
    enterprise zones   2.31
    first year   2.20
    fixtures   2.24
    hire purchase   2.28
    hotel buildings   2.33
    industrial buildings   2.30
    know-how   2.35
    machinery for leasing   2.29
    mines   2.36
    motor vehicles   2.27
    oil wells   2.36
    patent rights   2.35
    plant and machinery   2.19, 2.23
    safety at sports-grounds   2.38
    scientific research   2.34
    security assets   2.39
    short-life assets   2.25–2.26
    writing down   2.21
Capital duty   5.26
Capital gains tax—
    annual exemptions for
        individuals   6.4
    assessment   6.16
    assets—
        business, replacement of   6.26
        exempt   6.6–6.7
        liable   6.6
        owned on 6 April 1965   6.17
        re-basing to 31 March 1982
        values   6.10
        wasting   6.24
    business retirement relief   6.28
    businesses and   6.2

Capital gains tax—*cont*
    capital losses   6.14–6.15
    company reorganizations   6.20
    computation of chargeable
        gains   6.9
    disposals   6.8
    indexation allowance   6.11–6.13
    leases   6.24
    liability to   6.3
    part disposals   6.22–6.23
    partnership   3.9
    payment of   6.16
    rates   6.5
    relief
        businesses   6.28
        for gifts   6.25
        rollover   6.26
    shares—
        quoted   6.19
        unquoted   6.15, 6.21
    take-overs   6.20
    transfer of business to
        company   6.27
    valuations   6.18
Capital transfer tax, see Inheritance
    tax
Car, see Motor Vehicle
Cash basis   2.41
Charities—
    value added tax   8.21
Classes of income   2.2
Close company, see Company
Closing years   2.15–2.16
Commission for Racial
    Equality   10.57
Company—
    accounts   5.60
    articles of association—
        alteration of   5.38
        as contract   5.37
        class rights   5.40
        contents   5.9
        shareholder protection
            and   5.39
    as a whole, meaning   5.69
    associated   4.4
    books   5.60
    business expansion scheme   4.32
    capacity of   5.32
    capital—
        allotted   5.20
        authorised   5.20
        issued   5.20

Company—cont
  maintenance of 5.78
  nominal 5.20
  paid up 5.20
  raising 5.22
 capital duty 5.26
 certificate of incorporation 5.15
 charge, registration of 5.24
 close—
  abatement 4.23
  apportionment of income 4.22
  cessations 4.25
  distributions 4.24
  inheritance tax 7.17
  investment holding 4.26
  liquidations 4.25
  loans 4.24
  special rules 4.21–4.25
 compared with partnership 1.13
 constructive notice 5.34, 5.51
 controlled foreign 4.29
 corporation tax, see Corporation tax
 demergers 4.30
 Department of Trade investigations 5.77
 directors—
  acting *bona fide* 5.68
  application of powers for proper purposes 5.70
  board of, relationship between general meeting and 5.59
  care 5.62
  corporate opportunities 5.66
  duties 5.61–5.71
  fair dealing by 5.71
  fiduciary duties 5.63
  first, statement of 5.10
  first meeting of 5.17, 5.18
  interest in contract with company 5.64
  misapplication of property 5.67
  names 5.103
  PAYE 9.24
  secret profits 5.65
  skill 5.62
  statutory rules governing duties 5.71
  ultra vires acts, responsibility for 5.33
 distribution of assets 5.88
 divisions of 8.6
 floating charges 5.23

Company—cont
 formalities 1.10
 groups—
  loss relief 4.19
  other reliefs 4.20
  subsidiaries 4.18
  value added tax 8.6
 incorporation—
  advantages of 1.13
  decision to incorporate 4.33
  disadvantages of 1.13
  saving tax by 4.34
 insolvency—
  administration order 5.81
  liquidation 5.82
  receivership 5.80
 law in general 5.5
 life assurance 11.22
 limited liability, see Limited liability company
 liquidator—
  choice of 5.85
  powers 5.86
 meetings—
  annual general 5.55
  complexity of law 5.54
  extraordinary general 5.56
  general, relationship with board of directors 5.59
  procedure 5.58
 memorandum—
  alteration of 5.35
  contents 5.9
  director's responsibility 5.33
  protection of third parties 5.30
  ultra vires doctrine 5.28–5.34
 minimum membership requirement 5.16
 minorities—
  collective abuse of shareholder power against 5.72
  statutory protection for 5.73
 name—
  change of 5.102
  choice of 5.7, 5.101
  use of 5.104
 non-resident 4.27
 objects clause, scope of 5.32
 officers—
  appointment 5.41
  director 5.43
  dismissal 5.44
  removal 5.41

Company—*cont*
    secretary 5.42
    tenure 5.41
    private. See Private company
    public 1.11, 5.2
    receivers appointed by debenture holders 5.25
    records 5.60
registration of charge 5.24
    reorganisations 6.20
    resolutions—
        complexity of law 5.54
        extraordinary 5.57
        special 5.57
        types of 5.57
    secretary—
        appointment of 5.42
        statement of 5.10
    shareholders, see Shareholders
    shares—
        subscribers 5.11
        transfer of 5.27
    stamp duty 5.26
    starting up
        accounting reference date 5.12
        articles of association 5.9
        documents to be delivered 5.8
        memorandum 5.9
        name 5.7
        off shelf 5.6
        registered office address 5.13
        statement of first directors and secretary 5.10
        statutory declaration of compliance 5.14
        subscribers' shares 5.11
    take-overs 6.20
    taxation, see Corporation tax
    taxed separately from owner 4.1
    third party protection—
        actual implied authority 5.53
        agency principles 5.52
        by statute 5.30
Companies Act, under 5.48, 5.50
    generally 5.45
        indoor management rule 5.46
        statutory provisions 5.47
        ultra vires doctrine 5.30
    trade marks 5.108
    trading—
        fraudulent 5.87
        loss on unquoted shares in 6.15

Companies Act—*cont*
    wrongful 5.87
    transfer of business to 6.27
    transfer of shares 5.27
    types of 5.1
    unquoted, purchasing own shares 4.31
    winding up—
        compulsory 5.84
        order of distribution of assets 5.88
        statutory petition 5.74
        under just and equitable ground 5.74-5.75
        unfair prejudice petition 5.76
        voluntary 5.83
    with overseas income 4.28
Compensation—
    loss of office 9.27
    unfair dismissal 10.31
Conditional sale agreement 12.48-12.52
Conduct—
    unfair dismissal 10.24
Consumer safety 12.58
Contract—
    acceptance—
        business contract 12.9
        manner of 12.8
    articles of association as 5.37
    components of 12.2
    consideration 12.10
    counter offer 12.9
    director's interest in 5.64
    employment, see Employment
    form 12.12
    intention to create legal relations 12.3
    law 12.1-12.31
    legal enforceability 12.4
    offer—
        business contract 12.9
        invitations to treat distinguished 12.6
        termination of 12.7
    privity 12.11
    product liability 12.53-12.58
    remedies for breach—
        action for agreed sum 12.29
        damages 12.28
        declaration 12.27
        generally 12.26
        illegality 12.31

Contract—cont
  specific performance 12.30
  unenforceability 12.31
  reservation of title clauses 12.46
  retirement annuity 11.12
  sale of goods, see Sale of Goods
  termination of—
    agreement 12.24
    breach 12.22
    effluxion of time 12.23
    frustration 12.25
    means of 12.21
  terms—
    conditions 12.16
    duress 12.20
    excluding 12.15
    implied 12.13–12.14, 12.38
    misrepresentation 12.19
    mistake 12.18
    undue influence 12.20
    vitiating elements 12.17
    warranties 12.16
Controlled foreign company 4.29
Copyright sales—
  income tax 2.49
Corporation tax—
  accounting periods 4.5
  advance—
    distributions 4.9
    dividends 4.8
    franked payments 4.9
    setting off 4.10
    surplus 4.11
  capital allowances 4.13
  capital gains and losses 4.17
  close investment holding
    companies 4.26
  computing assessable
    profits 4.12–4.14
  distributions—
    non-qualifying 4.9
    qualifying 4.9
  imputation system 4.7
  interest 4.6
  losses 4.15–4.16
  payment dates 4.5
  rates of 4.2–4.3
  repayment supplement 4.6
  small companies rate 4.3
  terminal losses 4.16
Credit—
  insurance 13.10
  sale agreement 12.48–12.52

Damages—
  breach of contract 12.28
Data protection 10.66
De-pooling 2.26
De-regulation—
  private companies 5.4
Debenture holders—
  appointment of receiver by 5.25
Debts—
  bad, value added tax 8.18
  partner's liability for 1.7
Deeds of family arrangement 7.19
Demergers 4.30
Department of Trade, see Trade,
    Department of
Directors, see Company
Disabled persons—
  recruiting employees 10.5
Discrimination—
  by other bodies 10.52
  contracting out of statutory
    rights 10.68
  data protection 10.66
  direct 10.50
  equal pay, see Equal pay
  formal investigation 10.57
  future laws 10.6
  generally 10.48
  genuine occupational
    qualification 10.51
  indirect 10.50
  meaning 10.49
  practical information 10.56
  recruiting employees 10.3
  remedies 10.54
  retirement ages 10.55
  statutory maternity pay 10.63
  statutory sick pay 10.64
  victimisation 10.53
Dismissal—
  kinds of 10.19
  pre-transfer 10.75
  redundancy 10.32
  settling claims 10.35
  unfair, see Unfair dismissal
  wrongful 10.33-10.34
Distributions—
  close company 4.24
  non-qualifying 4.9
  qualifying 4.9
Dividends—
  advance corporation tax 4.8

Index

Documents—
company, see Company
Domicile—
deemed 7.5
Dredging—
capital allowances 2.36

Earnings basis 2.7
Employee—
contract of employment, see Employment
distinguished from self-employed person 10.7–10.8
insolvency of employer 10.65
recruitment—
disabled persons 10.5
race discrimination 10.3
rehabilitation of offenders 10.4
sex discrimination 10.3
share ownership plan 9.23
See also PAYE system
Employer—
contract of employment, see Employment
insolvency of 10.65
See also PAYE system
Employment—
continuity of 10.79
contract—
contents of 10.9–10.12
duties of employee 10.12
employer's obligations 10.11
in writing 10.13–10.15
terms 10.10
written statement 10.14, 10.40
protection 10.69–10.81
sale of business, see Business
status of workforce 10.7–10.8
statutory rights—
continuity of employment 10.17
ex gratia payments 10.36
generally 10.37
guarantee payments 10.39
itemised pay statements 10.43
maternity rights 10.38
minimum periods of notice 10.45
qualifying period 10.16
redundancy 10.32
settling dismissal claims 10.35

Employment—*cont*
suspension on medical grounds 10.41
time off for trade union activities 10.44
trade union membership 10.42
unfair dismissal, see Unfair dismissal
wages 10.46–10.47
written statement 10.40
wrongful dismissal 10.33–10.34
transfer of undertakings 10.69–10.81
Enterprise zones—
capital allowances 2.31
Entertainment allowances 9.11
Equal Opportunities Commission 10.57, 10.62
Equal pay 10.58–10.62
European Economic Community—
sale of goods 12.52
Ex gratia payments 10.36
Exempt—
supplies 8.10–8.11
transfers 7.10–7.12

Fair dealing—
partner's duty of 5.96
Family—
deeds of arrangement 7.19
Farming—
income tax 2.47
First year allowance 2.20
Fixtures—
capital allowances 2.24
Floating charges 5.23
Fringe benefits 9.9–9.10

Gifts—
capital gains tax relief 6.25
lifetime 7.11
value added tax 8.17
Goods, see Sale of goods
Groups of companies see Company

Health insurance see Permanent health insurance
Hire purchase—
acquisition of plant and machinery 2.28
agreement 12.48–12.52
Hotel buildings—
capital allowances 2.33

Husband and wife—
  partnership 3.10-3.11

Ill Health—
  unfair dismissal 10.24
Imputation system 4.7
Income—
  capital allowances, see Capital allowances
  classes of 2.2
  close company, see Company
  company, see Corporation tax
  deductions from 9.26
  losses, see Losses
  national insurance contributions, see National insurance
  partnership see Partnership
  Schedule E 9.3
  taxation of 2.1
Income tax—
  assessment—
    basis of 2.12
    closing years 2.16
    mechanism 2.50
    opening years 2.14
    partnership 3.3-3.4
  author—
    copyright sales 2.49
    royalties 2.49
  cash basis 2.41
  closing years 2.15-2.16
  computing assessable profits 2.9-2.10
  deductions from income 2.6
  earnings basis 2.41
  farming 2.47
  indications of trading 2.8
  losses, see Losses
  opening years 2.13-2.14
  payment mechanism 2.50
  personal reliefs 2.5
  post-cessation receipts 2.42
  professions 2.7
  rates—
    basic 2.4
    higher 2.4
  Schedule D Cases I and II—
    closing years 2.16
    computation 2.9-2.10
    opening years 2-14
  Schedule E—
    cases of 9.2-9.3
    income 9.3

Income Tax—*cont*
  PAYE system, see PAYE system
  stock 2.11
  sub-contractors 2.48
  trades 2.7
  vocations 2.7
  work in progress 2.11
Incorporation, see Company
Indexation allowance 6.11-6.13
Industrial action—
  unfair dismissal 10.28
Industrial buildings—
  capital allowances 2.30
Inheritance tax
  administration 7.13
  agricultural property relief 7.15
  anti-avoidance 7.18
  business property relief 7.14
  close companies 7.17
  collection 7.13
  deeds of family arrangement 7.19
  deemed domicile 7.5
  exempt transfers 7.10-7.12
  lifetime gifts 7.11
  outline 7.1-7.21
  potentially exempt transfers 7.3-7.4
  property chargeable 7.2
  quick succession relief 7.20
  rate scale 7.6-7.7
  related property 7.9
  settled property 7.21
  tapering relief 7.4
  valuation 7.8-7.9
  woodlands 7.16
Insolvency—
  corporate, see Company
  employer, of 10.65
  member of partnership 1.8
  sole trader 1.8
Insurance—
  agent 13.4
  broker 13.4
  business interruption 13.9
  combined policies 13.13
  credit 13.10
  fidelity 13.10
  health, see Permanent health insurance
  intermediary 13.4
  legal expenses 13.10
  liability 13.7
  life, see Life assurance

Insurance—*cont*
 motor vehicle 13.8
 need for cover 13.1–13.3
 package policies 13.13
 property 13.6
 single risk policies 13.12
 types of cover 13.5–13.10
 types of policies available 13.11–13.13
Interest—
 corporation tax 4.6
Investigation—
 by Department of Trade 5.77
Investment—
 close investment holding companies 4.26

Know-how—
 capital allowances 2.35

Land—
 value added tax 8.12
Lease—
 capital gains tax 6.24
Leasing—
 machinery for 2.29
Legal expenses insurance 13.10
Liability insurances 13.7
Life assurance—
 chargeable events 11.7–11.8
 companies 11.22
 gains 11.7–11.8
 generally 11.1
 non-qualifying policy 11.4
 PAYE system 9.16
 partners 11.19
 qualifying policy 11.4-11.5
 sole traders 11.16
 tax treatment of policies 11.6
 traditional policy 11.3
 types of policy 11.2–11.8
 unit linked policy 11.3
Limited liability company—
 capital structure 5.21
 choice of trading vehicle 1.9
 sale of
Liquidation—
 close company 4.25
Liquidator—
 choice of 5.85
 powers of 5.86
Living accommodation 9.14

Loans—
 beneficial arrangements 9.17
 close company 4.24
Losses—
 adjustment 2.43
 corporation tax, *see* Corporation tax
 new business 2.45
 partnership 3.5
 relief 2.43-2.44
 terminal 2.46

Machinery, *see* Plant and machinery
Maternity—
 rights 10.38
 statutory pay 10.63
Medical grounds—
 payment during suspension on 10.41
Medical records—
 access to 10.67
Meetings, *see* Company
Memorandum, *see* Company
Mines—
 capital allowances 2.36
Minutes—
 first directors' meeting 5.18
Motor vehicle—
 as fringe benefit 9.12–9.13
 capital allowances 2.27
 fuel benefit scales 9.13
 insurance policies 13.8
 value added tax 8.13

Name—
 business 5.105–5.107
 company, *see* Company
 director's 5.103
National insurance—
 categories 9.28
 class I contributions 9.30–9.31
 class IV contributions 2.40-2.51
 contributions for 1987–88 9.29
 profit-related pay 9.33
 statutory sick pay 9.32
Non-resident company 4.27
Notice—
 statutory minimum periods of 10.45

Officers of company, *see* Company
Oil wells—
 capital allowances 2.36
Opening years 2.13–2.14

Overseas—
    income, UK company with   4.28
    non-resident company   4.27
    partnership   3.8

PAYE system—
    allowances   9.11
        entertainment   9.11
        travelling   9.11
    application   9.4
    beneficial loan arrangements   9.17
    code number   9.5
    compensation for loss of
        office   9.27
    deductions from income   9.26
    director's   9.24
    employee—
        assets provided for   9.15
        share ownership plans   9.23
        shareholdings   9.18
    employer—
        change of   9.8
        returns   9.7
    form P11D   9.25
    fringe benefits   9.9-9.10
    fuel benefit scales   9.13
    general operation   9.6
    life assurance arrangements   9.16
    living accommodation   9.14
    motor cars   9.12-9.13
    pension arrangements   9.16
    profit-sharing schemes   9.19
    records   9.6
    share option schemes—
        approved   9.22
        savings-related   9.21
        unapproved   9.20
Partnership—
    agreements   1.6, 5.93
    application of assets on
        dissolution   5.99
    assessment   3.3-3.4
    business name for   5.107
    capital gains   3.9
    choice of trading vehicle   1.4-1.7
    continuation election   3.7
    dissolution of   5.98
    husband and wife   3.10-3.11
    importance of express
        agreement   1.6
    incorporation compared
        with   1.13
    indicators as to existence

Partnership—*cont*
    of   5.90
    law   5.89-5.99
    limited   1.7, 5.100
    losses   3.5
    meaning   1.4, 3.2
    overseas   3.8
    partner—
        as self-employed person   10.8
        changes of   3.6
        duties of fair dealing   5.96
        liability for debts   1.7
        life assurance   11.19
        new, liabilities of   5.95
        retiring, liabilities of   5.95
        third parties and   5.94
    personal insolvency of   1.8
    property   5.97
    rules implied by Partnership Act
        1980   5.92
    size of   5.91
    special tax rules   3.1-3.11
    terms implied by Partnership Act
        1980   1.5
Passing off   5.108
Patent rights—
    capital allowances   2.35
Pay—
    equal   10.58-10.62
    guarantee payments   10.39
    itemised statements   10.43
    maternity   10.63
    profit-related   9.33
    sick   9.32, 10.64
    See also Wages
Pay As You Earn, *see* PAYE system
Payment of tax—
    capital gains tax   6.16
    corporation tax   4.5
    income tax   2.50
Penalties for VAT offences   8.4
Pensions—
    contracting-in   11.11
    contracting-out   11.11
    generally   11.1, 11.9
    moving between different types of
        arrangment   11.12
    occupational scheme   11.12
    PAYE system   9.16
    personal plans   11.12
    personal scheme   11.12-11.13
    retirement annuity
        contract   11.12-11.13

Pensions—*cont*
  state pension scheme 11.10
  uses 11.17, 11.20, 11.23
Performance—
  unfair dismissal 10.24
Permanent health insurance—
  generally 11.1
  policy 11.15
  uses 11.18, 11.21, 11.24
Personal—
  insolvency, *see* Insolvency
  reliefs 2.3, 2.5
Plant and machinery—
  acquired on hire purchase 2.28
  capital allowances 2.19, 2.23
  leasing 2.29
  sales of 2.22
Post-cessation receipts 2.39
Potentially exempt transfers 7.3–7.4
Pregnancy—
  unfair dismissal 10.26
Private company—
  choice of trading vehicle 1.11
  de-regulation of 5.4
  meaning 5.3
  procedural requirements 5.4
  written resolutions 5.4
Product liability 12.53–12.58
Professions—
  income tax 2.7
  indications of trading 2.8
Profits—
  corporation tax, *see* Corporation tax
  profit-related pay 9.33
  profit-sharing schemes 9.19
Property—
  company, misapplication of 5.67
  inheritance tax, *see* Inheritance tax
  insurance 13.6
  partnership 5.97
  settled 7.21
Protection of employment 10.69–10.81
Public company—
  choice of trading vehicle 1.11
  meaning 5.2

Quick succesion relief 7.20

Race discrimination, *see* Discrimination

Receipts—
  post-cessation 2.42
Receiver—
  appointment by debenture holders 5.25
Records—
  company 5.60
  medical 10.67
  PAYE 9.6
Redundancy 10.24, 10.32
Registered office address 5.13
Registration for VAT 8.2
Rehabilitation of offenders—
  recruiting employees 10.4
  spent convictions 10.4
Reliefs—
  losses, *see* Losses
  personal 2.3, 2.5
  quick succession 7.20
Repayment supplement—
  corporation tax 4.6
Research—
  scientific 2.34
Reservation of title clauses 12.46
Resolutions, *see* Company
Retail prices index 6.12
Retailers 8.19
Retirement—
  annuity contract 11.12
  discriminatory ages 10.55
  relief 6.28
Royalties—
  income tax 2.49

Safety—
  sports grounds 2.38
Sale of goods—
  acceptance 12.44
  by sample 12.36
  conditional sale agreement 12.48–12.52
  conditions of trading 12.47
  conformity with description 12.34
  credit sale agreement 12.48-12.52
  delivery 12.43
  EEC law 12.52
  exclusion of liability 12.37
  hire purchase agreement 12.48–12.52
  implied terms 12.38
  international 12.51
  merchantable quality 12.35
  passing of property 12.41

Sale of Goods—*cont*
  quiet possession 12.33
  remedies 12.45
  reservation of title clauses 12.46
  risk 12.42
  rules related to 12.32, 12.39
  time 12.40
  title 12.33
Schedule D Cases I and II—
  closing years 2.16
  computation 2.9–2.10
  opening years 2.14
Schedule E—
  cases of 9.2–9.3
  income 9.3
  PAYE system, see PAYE system
Scientific research—
  allowance 2.34
Second-hand goods 8.15
Secretary, see Company
Security assets—
  capital allowances 2.39
Self-employed person—
  employee distinguished from 10.7-10.8
Settled property 7.21
Sex discrimination, see Discrimination
Shareholders—
  employee 9.18
  limited liability of 1.12
Shares—
  capital gains tax, see Capital gains tax
  employee share ownership plan 9.23
  employee shareholdings 9.18
  share option schemes—
    approved 9.22
    savings-related 9.21
    unapproved 9.20
  unquoted company purchasing own 4.31
Short-life assets 2.25–2.26
Sole trader—
  as self-employed person 10.8
  choice of trading vehicle 1.3
  life assurance 11.16
  pensions 11.17
  permanent health insurance 11.18
  personal insolvency 1.8

Sports grounds—
  safety 2.38
Stamp duty 5.26
Starting up company, see Company
Statutory sick pay 9.32, 10.64
Stock—
  income tax 2.11
Strike—
  unfair dismissal 10.28
Sub-contractor—
  income tax 2.48

Taxation—
  capital allowances, see Capital allowances
  capital gains tax, see Capital gains tax
  income tax, see Income tax
  inheritance tax, see Inheritance tax
  value added tax, see Value added tax
Third party—
  liability in tort to 12.54
  partner and 5.94
  protection, see Company
Tour operators 8.20
Trade, Department of—
  investigation of company 5.77
  ultra vires rule 5.31
Trade marks 5.108
Trade union—
  consultation on business transfers 10.78
  dismissal relating to membership 10.25
  membership 10.25, 10.42
  time off for activities 10.44
Trades—
  income tax 2.7
  indications of trading 2.8
Trading—
  conditions of 12.47
  fraudulent 5.87
  wrongful 5.87
Trading company, see Company
Trading vehicle—
  choice of model 1.2
  forming companies 1.10
  incorporation compared with partnership 1.13–1.14
  limited liability company 1.9
  main considerations 1.1

Trading vehicle—*cont*
  partnership, *see* Partnership
  personal insolvency 1.8
  private company 1.11
  public company 1.11
  shareholders, limited liability
    of 1.12
  sole trader 1.3
Transfer of undertakings 10.69–10.81
Travelling allowances 9.11

Unfair dismissal—
  absenteeism 10.24
  automatic 10.27
  capability 10.24
  compensation levels 10.31
  conduct 10.24
  ill health 10.24
  industrial action 10.28
  interrelationship with wrongful
    dismissal 10.34
  performance 10.24
  pregnancy 10.26
  qualifying factors 10.18
  reasonableness—
    establishing 10.23
    statutory test of 10.22
  reasons for 10.21, 10.29
  redundancy 10.24
  remedies for 10.30
  strikes 10.28
  test of 10.20
  trade union members 10.25

Ultra vires—
  Companies Bill, position
    under 5.32
  constructive notice 5.34
  Department of Trade consultative
    document 5.31
  director's responsibility for 5.33
  doctrine of 5.29
  third parties, protection of 5.30
Unquoted company—
  purchase of own shares 4.31

Valuation—
  capital gains tax 6.18
  inheritance tax 7.8–7.9

Value added tax—
  accounts 8.3
  administration 8.3
  appeals 8.5
  bad debts 8.18
  building 8.12
  business—
    entertainment 8.14
    meaning 8.7
  charities 8.21
  divisions of companies 8.6
  exemption 8.10–8.11
  gifts 8.17
  groups of companies 8.6
  imposition in UK 8.1
  land 8.12
  motor cars 8.13
  official literature 8.22
  penalties 8.4
  personal use 8.16
  registration 8.2
  retailers 8.19
  second-hand goods 8.15
  self-supply 8.16
  tour operators 8.20
  zero-rated 8.8–8.9
Victimisation 10.53
Vocations—
  income tax 2.7
  indications of trading 2.8

Wages—
  deductions from 10.47
  payment of 10.46
  See also Pay
Wife, *see* Husband and Wife
Winding up, *see* Company
Woodlands—
  inheritance tax 7.16
Work in progress—
  income tax 2.11
Writing down allowance 2.21
Wrongful dismissal 10.33–10.34

Zero-rated supplies 8.8–8.9